An Early Modern Dialogue with Islam
Antonio de Sosa's *Topography of Algiers* (1612)

HISTORY, LANGUAGES, AND CULTURES
OF THE SPANISH AND PORTUGUESE WORLDS

This interdisciplinary series promotes scholarship in studies on Iberian cultures and contacts from the premodern and early modern periods.

Series Editor
Sabine MacCormack,
*Theodore M. Hesburgh Professor of Arts and Letters,
Departments of Classics and History, University of Notre Dame*

Series Board
J. N. Hillgarth, emeritus, *Pontifical Institute of Mediaeval Studies*
Peggy K. Liss, *Independent Scholar*
David Nirenberg, *University of Chicago*
Adeline Rucquoi, *École des Hautes Études en Sciences Sociales*

Recent Titles in the Series

The Origins of Mexican Catholicism: Nahua Rituals and the Christian Sacraments in Sixteenth-Century Mexico (2004)
Osvaldo F. Pardo

Missionary Tropics: The Catholic Frontier in India (16th–17th Centuries) (2005)
Ines G. Županov

Jews, Christian Society, and Royal Power in Medieval Barcelona (2006)
Ella Klein

How the Incas Built Their Heartland: State Formation and Innovation of Imperial Strategies in the Sacred Valley, Peru (2006)
R. Alan Covey

Pastoral Quechua: The History of Christian Translation in Colonial Peru, 1550–1650 (2007)
Alan Durston

Contested Territory: Mapping Peru in the Sixteenth and Seventeenth Centuries (2009)
Heidi V. Scott

Death and Conversion in the Andes: Lima and Cuzco, 1532–1670 (2010)
Gabriela Ramos

An Early Modern Dialogue with Islam: Antonio de Sosa's Topography of Algiers *(1612)* (2011)
Edited with an Introduction by María Antonia Garcés,
translated by Diana de Armas Wilson

An Early Modern Dialogue with Islam

Antonio de Sosa's *Topography of Algiers* (1612)

EDITED WITH AN INTRODUCTION BY

María Antonia Garcés

TRANSLATED BY

Diana de Armas Wilson

UNIVERSITY OF NOTRE DAME PRESS

NOTRE DAME, INDIANA

Copyright © 2011 by the University of Notre Dame
Notre Dame, Indiana 46556
www.undpress.nd.edu
All Rights Reserved

Published in the United States of America

Library of Congress Cataloging-in-Publication Data

Sosa, Antonio de, d. 1587.
[Topographia, e historia general de Argel. English]
An early modern dialogue with Islam : Antonio de Sosa's Topography of Algiers (1612) / edited with an introduction by María Antonia Garcés ; translated by Diana de Armas Wilson.
  p. cm. — (History, languages, and cultures of the Spanish and Portuguese worlds)
Includes bibliographical references and index.
ISBN-13: 978-0-268-02978-4 (pbk. : alk. paper)
ISBN-10: 0-268-02978-4 (pbk. : alk. paper)
 1. Algiers (Algeria)—Description and travel—Early works to 1800.
 2. Algiers (Algeria)—Social life and customs—Early works to 1800.
 3. Algiers (Algeria)—Social conditions—Early works to 1800.
 4. Sosa, Antonio de, d. 1587. I. Garcés, María Antonia.
 II. Wilson, Diana de Armas, 1934– III. Title.
DT299.A5S65   2011
965'.3—dc22

2010052717

∞ *The paper in this book meets the guidelines for permanence and durability of the Committee on Production Guidelines for Book Longevity of the Council on Library Resources.*

To our grandchildren,
who represent hope for bridging the ancient divide
between East and West

―――――――――――

Alejandro Lloreda Field
Juliana Lloreda Field
Daniel Lloreda Velásquez
Juan Antonio Lloreda Velásquez
Lukas Lloreda Ortíz
Sebastián Lloreda Gamboa
Manuel José Rodríguez Lloreda
Antonio Rodríguez Lloreda
Gabriela Rodríguez Lloreda
Amalia Phoenix Theodoredis
Emmanuel Kairos Theodoredis
Juliana Amara Ravin

CONTENTS

List of Illustrations	xi
Transliteration and Translation	xiii
Note from the Translator	xv
Acknowledgments	xix

Introduction	1

Topography of Algiers by Antonio de Sosa

Title Page from Diego de Haedo, *Topographia, e Historia general de Argel*	81
Preliminary Materials	83
Appraisal	83
The King	84
Approval by the Court's Designated Censor	86
Approval by the Superior of the Benedictine Order	87
License of the General of Saint Benedict	88
Dedicatory Letter	89
List of Errata	92

Chapter 1. The Founding of Algiers	93
Chapter 2. Why the City Is Called Algiers	99
Chapter 3. Algiers as a Muslim Kingdom	100
Chapter 4. How Algiers Came under the Turks	102
Chapter 5. The Ramparts of Algiers	104

Chapter 6.	The Gates of Algiers	106
Chapter 7.	The Fortifications of Algiers	109
Chapter 8.	The Moat of Algiers	112
Chapter 9.	The Castles and Forts outside Algiers	113
Chapter 10.	The Houses and Streets of Algiers	117
Chapter 11.	The Inhabitants and Neighbors of Algiers	119
Chapter 12.	Turks	124
Chapter 13.	Renegades	125
Chapter 14.	Ka'ids	128
Chapter 15.	Sipahi	131
Chapter 16.	Janissaries	133
Chapter 17.	Agha of the Janissaries	135
Chapter 18.	Ranks of the Janissaries	137
Chapter 19.	Customs of the Janissaries at War	141
Chapter 20.	Customs of the Janissaries in Peacetime	146
Chapter 21.	Customs of the Algerian Corsairs	151
Chapter 22.	Catalogue of Corsairs	160
Chapter 23.	Corsairs with Frigates	162
Chapter 24.	Algerian Merchants	164
Chapter 25.	Algerian Laborers and Artisans	168
Chapter 26.	Algerian Fashions	169
Chapter 27.	The Marabouts of Algiers	174
Chapter 28.	The Jews of Algiers	181

Chapter 29.	Languages and Currencies	184
Chapter 30.	Marriage Ceremonies	188
Chapter 31.	Childbirth and Child Rearing	194
Chapter 32.	Algerian Women's Fashions	198
Chapter 33.	Women's Pastimes, Home Decorating, and Cooking	203
Chapter 34.	Islamic Feast Days and Festivals in Algiers	209
Chapter 35.	A Miscellany of Muslim Customs in Algiers	216
Chapter 36.	Algerian Vices	232
Chapter 37.	Algerian Virtues	244
Chapter 38.	Death and Burial in Algiers	247
Chapter 39.	Algerian Buildings and Fountains	253
Chapter 40.	The Natural Beauty of Algiers	261
Chapter 41.	The Government of Algiers	265

List of Abbreviations	273
Glossary	274
Notes	287
Archival Sources	353
Bibliography	355
Index	381

ILLUSTRATIONS

Figure 1. Map of Algiers [*Algerii Saracenorum vrbis fortissimae*...] (1575?). Reproduced from Braun and Hogenberg, *Civitates orbis terrarum* (1575–1612). Division of Rare and Manuscript Collections, Cornell University Library.   14

Figure 2. Facsimile of title page from Diego de Haedo, *Topographia, e Historia general de Argel,* princeps edition (Valladolid, 1612).   80

For figures 3–18, see gallery following page 208.

Figure 3. Plan of the City of Algiers [Plano en perspectiva de la ciudad de Argel... El designio de Argel que dieron unos captivos que se huyeron con la galeota. Año de 1563]. Reproduced by permission of Spain, Ministerio de Cultura, Archivo General de Simancas, MPD, 7, 131.

Figure 4. The City of Algiers (ca. 1700). Reproduced from Epalza and Vilar, eds., *Planos y mapas hispánicos de Argelia,* 1:324, map 412.

Figure 5. The Gate of Babazoun. Reproduced from Dapper, *Eigentliche beschreibung der insulen in Africa* (1671), 260. Division of Rare and Manuscript Collections, Cornell University Library.

Figure 6. Henri Bonnart, *A Turkish Soldier from Algiers.* Reproduced from Esquer, *Iconographie historique de l'Algérie,* vol. 1, plate 27, no. 75.

Figure 7. Andreas Matthäus Wolffgang, *Algerian Corsair Captain.* Reproduced from Esquer, *Iconographie historique de l'Algérie,* vol. 1, plate 12, no. 33.

Figure 8. Andreas Matthäus Wolffgang, *Admiral of the Algerian Fleet.* Reproduced from Esquer, *Iconographie historique de l'Algérie,* vol. 1, plate 12, no. 73.

Figure 9. Andreas Matthäus Wolffgang, *A Jew from Algiers.* Reproduced from Esquer, *Iconographie historique de l'Algérie,* vol. 1, plate 29, no. 77.

Figure 10. Henri Bonnart, *Marabout from Algiers.* Reproduced from Esquer, *Iconographie historique de l'Algérie,* vol. 1, plate 29, no. 78.

Figure 11. Janissaries. Reproduced from *I TURCHI Codex Vindobonensis 8626,* 43. Olin Library, Cornell University.

Figure 12. Armed Sipahi. Reproduced from *I TURCHI Codex Vindobonensis 8626,* 55. Olin Library, Cornell University.

Figure 13. Solak Soldiers. Reproduced from *I TURCHI Codex Vindobonensis 8626,* 58. Olin Library, Cornell University.

Figure 14. Pilgrims to Mecca. Reproduced from *I TURCHI Codex Vindobonensis 8626,* 141. Olin Library, Cornell University.

Figure 15. Funeral March. Reproduced from *I TURCHI Codex Vindobonensis 8626,* 142. Olin Library, Cornell University.

Figure 16. Funeral Procession. Reproduced from Dapper, *Eigentliche beschreibung der insulen in Africa* (1671), 248. Division of Rare and Manuscript Collections, Cornell University Library.

Figure 17. Preparing the Body. Reproduced from Dapper, *Eigentliche beschreibung der insulen in Africa* (1671), 249. Division of Rare and Manuscript Collections, Cornell University Library.

Figure 18. An Algerian Family. Reproduced from Dapper, *Eigentliche beschreibung der insulen in Africa* (1671), 168. Division of Rare and Manuscript Collections, Cornell University Library.

TRANSLITERATION AND TRANSLATION

Imposing an entirely consistent system for titles, technical terms, and personal names in this translation has proved an insuperable challenge. We have used a modified transliteration system from the *Encyclopaedia of Islam* (*EI*), 2nd ed., for Arabic and Ottoman Turkish names and technical words, omitting diacritical marks beyond the ʿ*ayn* (e.g., al-ʿAsr) and the *hamza* (e.g., Qurʾan). For plural of words, we have added an *s*, except for the plural of *raʾis* (A), which is given as *ruʾasa,* and various Spanish plurals, such as *real* (pl. *reales*). Although the transliteration scheme adopted by the *EI* has elicited a polemic among Arabists—especially in its use of *dj* (= modern Turkish *c*) and the substitution of *k* for *q*— we have opted to follow the *EI,* which is now available online, for its accessibility to a wider English-speaking audience. The *EI* has proved invaluable not only for our understanding of Muslim cultures but also for our labors of double translation: Sosa attempted to transliterate into Spanish thousands of sixteenth-century Algerian words and phrases— Arabic, Turkish, Berber, and Lingua Franca—that we, in turn, have struggled to render into modern English.

Turkish and Arabic terms familiar to English speakers—such as Algiers, Istanbul, Muhammad, *janissary, marabout, pasha, sultan*—are offered here in their accepted Anglicized form, without diacritical marks. For familiar Spanish and Italian proper names and toponyms, we have used conventional English equivalents when available (e.g., Charles V, Philip II, Barbarossa, Moors, Rome, Naples, etc.).

Place names in North Africa have posed special difficulties, as most of them have more than one name. An instructive example is the ancient city of Hippona (Hippo Regius)—site of the episcopal seat of Saint Augustine—which reappears throughout history as Bône and, in the Algerian postcolonial era, as Annaba. For ease of recognition of North African cities, we have used modern toponyms as given by the

Oxford Atlas of the World, 15th ed. In the interests of fidelity to Sosa's text, however, we have kept the Spanish appellation for various Iberian cities in North Africa (e.g., Orán for Ouahran; Ceuta for Sabta). Cities in Spain are given in Spanish (e.g., Córdoba instead of Cordova, etc.).

Arabic, Turkish, Italian, and Spanish words without conventional English equivalents (e.g., *agha, bagnios, beylerbey, bashi, escudo, gandura, kadi, mahalla*) are italicized upon their first occurrence within each chapter and endnote.

NOTE FROM THE TRANSLATOR

Translation work on Doctor Antonio de Sosa's chronicle has been challenging on two fronts, linguistic and ideological. On the linguistic front, the frequency of Arabic and Turkish words within the original Spanish text, which Sosa transliterated to the best of his knowledge, involved the thorny problem of double translation. Sosa's translators must translate what is already a translation. *An Early Modern Dialogue with Islam* attempts to render Sosa's Spanish transliterations into the English versions adopted by the *Encyclopaedia of Islam*. Translating his views of Algerian culture has been an extraordinary learning experience. Our dialogue with Sosa has enlightened us about many facets of Muslim cultures. We trust it will do the same for our readers.

When Sosa was writing in the 1570s, Algiers was a fiefdom of the Turkish Empire, a "jewel in the Ottoman crown." Even after the Battle of Lepanto (1571), the Ottomans were still a world power, albeit a fading one, with an immense military machine. Doctor Sosa was imprisoned in a city still gripped by an imperial regime and densely populated with a diverse mix of cultures: Ottoman rulers, Moorish and Berber colonials, elite janissaries, Christian slaves, poll-taxed Jews, and pan-European renegades. The task of translating Sosa's text involved a complex negotiation between the different codes, ideologies, and worldviews of these multiple Algerian cultures and our own Anglo-American culture.

Translation problems on the ideological front have been equally daunting. In spite of Sosa's insatiable curiosity about Muslim customs—which moved him to investigate such unlikely topics as women's fashions, marriage and childbirth rites, death and burial ceremonies—his crusading moments may astonish readers unaware of the mutual demonizing between Christians and Muslims during the sixteenth century. The royal censor who endorsed the *Topography of Algiers* stressed "the great benefits that Christianity would reap from it." Sosa's chronicle was ideologically motivated in many parts. The parts that pleased the censors, however, may dismay contemporary readers who confront stereotypes they do not endorse.

This translation does not screen Sosa's "demonizing" moments: it recognizes his ethnographic reporting as subjective and trusts readers to understand the limitations of his subject position. Sosa was first and foremost a theologian—a churchman trained in Spanish Catholic doctrines. He was also a captive of Algerian Muslims for almost five years, a victim of what he called "Barbary cruelty." As such, his lapses into the dominant ideology of Christian Spain are predictable. His demonization of Islam, his disapproval of women's pastimes, and even his deafness to Algerian music reflect the attitudes of countless sixteenth-century European Christians, or *Franj*—the word used in colloquial Arabic to designate the enemy. What Sosa never mentions are the Christian cruelties visited on Hispano-Muslims, exacerbated by the creation of the Spanish Inquisition in 1478 and by the conquest of Moorish Granada in 1492. Victims of these Christian/Muslim holy wars have fallen—and continue to fall—on both sides.

Beyond the clash of monotheisms in Sosa's chronicle, this translation aims to provide a cross-cultural understanding of North African life and customs during the era anticipating both Cervantes's *Don Quijote* and Shakespeare's *Othello*. Cervantes would choose an Arabic narrator for his great novel about a would-be Christian knight, and Shakespeare would give us a vivid profile of a Moor in the service of a Christian republic. Both writers understood the horrific impact of religious wars on the life and times of their heroes.

An English translation of Sosa's reflections on sixteenth-century Barbary is not a mere academic exercise. While reading his text, we keep stumbling against ourselves, bumping into our own American history. We remember that the first overseas war the United States ever fought, at the turn of the nineteenth century, was against the Barbary States. Whatever triggered "Jefferson's War," it has become the topic of dozens of books published (or republished) since 9/11. Sosa's in-depth study of Algerian corsairs should also enlighten the twenty-first century rise of piracy off the African coasts. But Sosa's text, above all, helps us to see that Muslims—like Christians—have from the start been members of many different ethnic groups, and that Muslims—like Christians—also have "barbarians in their midst."

An abysmal gulf between East and West, not always unbridgeable, seems to have existed since Herodotus. We hope that this English translation of Sosa's intercultural "dialogue with Islam" will contribute to a more historical, *and more complex,* understanding by English-speaking readers about Muslim societies in and beyond Barbary. In response to whatever holy wars may yet threaten our world, I would echo a remark by the sixteenth-century renegade Martin Luther—hardly a model of tolerance—who once said that he would rather be ruled "by a wise Turk than a foolish Christian."

ACKNOWLEDGMENTS

In a work of this international scope, acknowledgments of support—intellectual, linguistic, editorial, and bibliographical—are, inevitably, multiple and widespread. Friends, colleagues, librarians, and archivists from Spain, Algeria, Colombia, France, Italy, and Portugal, as well as the United States, have been invaluable to this project.

The editing and translating of this book was made possible by a Collaborative Research Grant (2007–2011), for which the authors would like to thank the National Endowment of the Humanities. An earlier Fulbright Fellowship for archival research in Spain (2004), as well as a supplementary travel grant from the Program for Cultural Cooperation between Spain's Ministry of Education, Culture and Sports and the United States Universities (2007), allowed María Antonia Garcés to carry out research in several Spanish archives. She would also like to acknowledge a fellowship from the Society of the Humanities at Cornell University (2008), together with additional aid from the Mario Einaudi Center, the Society for the Humanities, and the Department of Romance Studies at Cornell.

Both the editor of this work, María Antonia Garcés, and the translator, Diana de Armas Wilson, would like to thank Professor Vincent Barletta of Stanford University for his invaluable help with textual notes and Arabic terms. This project could not have been possible without the support of Ali Houissa, the Middle East and Islamic Studies Librarian at Cornell University's Olin Library, who read the whole manuscript several times, advised us regarding Arabic and Turkish terms, and sought out difficult bibliographical references, web pages, and publications in various languages from across the world.

We also want to thank Anna Elisabeth Jessen, a journalist from Danish Radio and Television, for traveling from Copenhagen to Ithaca, New York, in order to film an interview about our work on Doctor Sosa for a documentary titled *White Slaves, Muslim Corsairs,* to be broadcast in 2011 across various European countries. We are particularly indebted to Luis Avilés and Ivette Hernández, who organized a mini-symposium on our NEH project, titled "Translating Captivity in the Early Modern Mediterranean World," which allowed us to present our work at the University of California, Irvine. More recently, the Majorcan novelist Carme Riera kindly invited us to present our project at the Universidad Autónoma of Barcelona. Last June, Robert P. Parks, director of the Centre d'Études Maghrébines en Algérie (CEMA), Université d'Oran es-Senia, and Javier Galván Guijo, director of the Instituto Cervantes de Orán, invited us to discuss our work about Doctor Sosa's *Topography of Algiers* to an interested Algerian audience.

María Antonia Garcés expresses her deepest gratitude to a series of friends, scholars, and researchers in Spain, Italy, Algeria, Colombia, and the United States. Mercedes García-Arenal has responded in detail to queries about Arabic words, Islamic rituals, and bibliographies on the early modern Maghreb. Emilio Sola generously offered valuable information about Turks, renegades, and spies in the early modern Mediterranean. Vittorio Sciuti Russi provided important data about the Spanish Inquisition in Sicily, as well as fruitful contacts for archival sources in Agrigento, Catania, Palermo, and Siracusa. María Jesus Viguera and María Esperanza Alfonso translated an important Arabic article into Spanish. Ángel Alcalá answered innumerable queries on Church history and Latin tomb inscriptions. José María Usunáriz illuminated many obscure questions about early modern Spanish Church history. Ahmed Abi-Ayad, from the University of Oran, explained Islamic religious rituals and calendars, and served as an enlightened guide during our trip to Algeria. José María Anguita transcribed and translated numerous sixteenth-century Latin documents for us with meticulous erudition. María Aguirre Landa kindly researched several archives in Madrid and transcribed various documents. Alessandro Serio and Carlo Taviani deciphered a spy's report from Algiers that was written in Genoese dialect. Chiara Agnello painstakingly helped to translate the same document into Spanish. Jean Pierre Dedieu offered suggestions regarding an erratum in Sosa's text. Virginia Aksan and Gábor Ágoston answered many queries about Turkish vocabulary, especially in regard to the complex ranks of janissaries. Leslie Peirce contributed information about Ottoman officials and government institutions. Anthony Puglisi transcribed archival documents and reviewed an earlier version of the introduction with particular care. Elena Mogollón deciphered tomb inscriptions and accompanied the editor on her first trip to Sicily. Maria Rita Savitteri examined notarial documents on Bishop Diego de Haedo in Agrigento. María Antonia Garcés recognizes her profound debt to José Menéndez and Isabel Fuentes Rebollo for their research findings on Doctor Antonio de Sosa at the Archivo General de Simancas, Valladolid.

Much of this book has come into being over food and wine. Memorable lunches or dinners in Madrid, Pamplona, Rome, Palermo, Agrigento, Denver, and Cali provided the settings for enticing discussions about Muslim culture in North Africa, Spanish and Sicilian church history, and archival resources. Anthony Sampson and María Cristina Tenorio have shared many dinners and offered continuous encouragement. The following friends and scholars enthusiastically supported our project: Ignacio Arellano, Benjamin C. Brower, the late María Soledad Carrasco-Urgoiti, José Luis Gonzalo Sánchez-Molero, José Luis Gotor, Luce López-Baralt, Ciriaco Morón-Arroyo, Fernando Rodríguez Mediano, Maria Caterina Ruta, and Edwin Williamson. José María Rodríguez-García has been a consistently generous interlocutor. Nicolás Wey-Gómez provided constant support and valuable information on Renaissance cartography. Elizabeth Wright read a draft of the introduction and offered judicious commentaries. Armando Garcés Eder and Chiara Agnello facilitated the editor's research at the Vatican Secret Archives by the loan of their Rome apartment. Diana de Armas Wilson is especially grateful to Andrea Wilson Nightingale, who illuminated several obscure questions on ancient Greek culture; to Rachel Jacoff, who read various drafts of the translators's note; to Andrés Lema-Hincapie, who translated a paper on the janissaries; and to Joseph Szyliowicz, who generously contributed to our knowledge of the Ottoman Empire. We thank all of the above for sharing in our scholarly lives.

María Antonia Garcés would like to give her special thanks to former and current chairs at the Department of Romance Studies, Cornell University: Professors Mitchell Greenberg, Debra Castillo, Walter Cohen, and Jonathan Culler, who offered indispensable support as well as special funds in different stages of this project. In the department, Colette Walls was instrumental in preparing the NEH budgets and helping in other organizational matters. Debra Kastenhuber and Brent Hollenbeck have proffered timely support in administrative issues.

For their friendship, intellectual support, and generosity, María Antonia Garcés wishes to thank various colleagues, friends, and students at Cornell University. Laurent Dubreuil engaged in many stimulating exchanges. Ross Brann deserves special gratitude for his friendship and wise advice regarding Islamic topics. The former director of the Society for the Humanities at Cornell, Brett de Barry, as well as Mary Ahl and her staff, provided a wonderful atmosphere at the A. D. White House, Cornell, in which to work on this project. Former and current students who have helped this research in innumerable ways include Loredana Comparone, Pablo García-Piñar, Luna Nájera, Martín Oyata, and Michella Scotto. Daniel Duque deserves special thanks for his kind contributions to this volume.

In the course of research for this book, the following archivists and librarians from different countries have assisted our work. José Luis Rodríguez de Diego and Isabel Aguirre from the Archivo General de Simancas, Valladolid, have offered continuous guidance and uncommonly rich material. Victoria Barcina Cuevas, from the Archivo Histórico, Universidad de Salamanca, uncovered a timely document about Antonio de Sosa. Mercedes Noviembre, director of the Biblioteca Zabálburu, Madrid, was a helpful guide to this private archive. In addition, María Antonia Garcés would like to thank the archivists and staff of the Archivo del Ministerio de Relaciones Exteriores, the Archivo Histórico Nacional, the Instituto de Valencia de Don Juan, and la Biblioteca Nacional de España, Madrid, for their tremendous kindness and aid. Concha Lois Cabello, from the Biblioteca Nacional, has been a constant source of assistance. Finally, Ana Maria Leitão Bandeira, from the Arquivo da Universidade de Coímbra, furnished valuable information on degrees granted by this university in the sixteenth century.

María Antonia Garcés extends her gratitude to the archivists and staff of the Vatican Library and the Vatican Secret Archives, in Rome, for their assistance; in Palermo, to the archivist and librarians of the Archivio di Stato and of the Biblioteca Communale; in Agrigento, to the director of the Archivio di Stato Maria Gerardi, to Don Giovanni Scordino at the Archivio Capitolare; and to Canonico Calogero Faustino Infantino, director of the Archivio Diocesano, who discovered important documents signed by Doctor Sosa. Thanks are also due to Monsignor Giuseppe Greco, vicar general of the Archdiocese of Siracusa and director of the Cathedral Archive; and Father Gaetano Zito, director of the Archivio Diocesano in Catania. The late art historian Father Biaggio Alessi, a generous interlocutor and guide, opened many doors in Palermo and Agrigento.

Librarians and reference staff at Cornell University's Olin Library have provided continuous support. David Block, Olin Library's former and outstanding Ibero-American Bibliographer, promptly ordered numerous books needed, as well as the microfilm of the princeps edition of the *Topographia, e Historia general de Argel,* edited by Diego de Haedo (Valladolid, 1612). Katherine Reagan, Assistant Director for Collections and Ernest L. Stern Curator of Rare Books and Manuscripts at Cornell University Library kindly purchased a 1575 map of Algiers to be used on our cover. Reference Librarian Virginia Cole has assisted us week by week, locating early modern rare editions and unraveling complex bibliographical problems. Maureen Morris and Bob Kibbee have similarly granted their efficient aid with obscure texts and questions of geography. Caitlin Finlay and Joy Thomas at the Olin Interlibrary Services have offered their competent help. Laurent Ferri, curator at the Division of Rare and Manuscript Collections at Olin Library, has been a vivid interlocutor who located early modern Latin, German, and Italian books and illustrations for the project. María Antonia Garcés wishes to thank all these friends, archivists, and librarians for their invaluable support.

Finally, we wish to express our warmest gratitude to Mary Katherine Lehman, assistant editor at the University of Notre Dame Press, for her meticulous, attentive, and wise editing of our text.

Introduction

An Early Modern Dialogue with Islam: Antonio de Sosa's Topography of Algiers *(1612)* is the first English translation of a riveting chronicle of European and North African cultural contacts. Written by the Portuguese cleric Doctor Antonio de Sosa while he was held prisoner in Algiers between 1577 and 1581, and published posthumously in Spain thirty years later (1612), the *Topography* is a fascinating eyewitness account of cultural life in Algiers near the end of the sixteenth century.

No other European work takes us so deeply into the quotidian life of an Islamic city during the early modern period, a time of expansion and glory for the Ottoman Empire and its territories, especially for its farthest western province, the Turkish-Algerian Regency. In 1519, at the culmination of a seven-years' war of conquest of the Barbary Coast, Khayr al-Din Barbarossa, the most formidable of all corsairs operating in the western Mediterranean, sought help from Sultan Selim I against the Spaniards, offering to place Algiers under the mantle of the Ottoman Empire.[1] Algiers soon became a *sandjak,* or province, attached to the Ottoman Porte, while Barbarossa obtained the title of governor-general, as well as two thousand Turkish janissaries and artillery, a force later expanded by four thousand other Levantine Muslims and corsairs who enlisted in the Algerian militia.

During the next fifty years, the influx of Turks, Christian converts to Islam, and corsairs from all over the world turned Algiers into the greatest of the North African seaports dedicated to privateering. The arrival of thousands of Christian slaves and booty, seized each year in attacks on the coasts of Spain and Italy or its islands and on Christian ships that ventured into the Mare Nostrum, turned Algiers into the corsair capital par excellence of the Mediterranean. Surpassing in captives and riches the powerful Christian corsair centers of Valetta (Malta) and Leghorn (Livorno) on the Tyrrhenian Sea, with their *bagnios* (slave prisons), their slave markets, and their sordid transactions, Algiers became known in Europe as the "the scourge of Christendom."[2] By the mid 1570s, when the soldier Miguel de Cervantes and the cleric Antonio de Sosa arrived in the city as captives, Algiers had become the principal naval power of the western Mediterranean.

The *Topography of Algiers,* the first book of Sosa's *Topographia, e Historia general de Argel* [Topography and General History of Algiers], paints a lively portrait of daily life in this prosperous Muslim city in the last years of the 1570s.[3] A crossroads of civilizations, Algiers was a booming urban center inhabited by a sophisticated multilingual society, consisting of Turks, Arabs, Berbers, Christian captives, Jews, exiled Hispano-Muslims (Moriscos), and converts to Islam from different parts of the world. Recreating the quotidian existence of this multicultural society, the *Topography* brings to life the colorful facets that characterized its social, cultural, religious, military, and commercial activities. Sosa's work, in effect, stands out for its complexity, its vitality, and the sharpness of the author's ethnographic vision. Anyone who peruses this text will be fascinated by the vibrancy of its descriptions, the wealth of astounding customs presented, and the amount of historical detail that frames its chapters. In the words of a French critic, no other account of captivity in this period "offers such a complete, animated, and live tableau of Algerian society at the end of the sixteenth century."[4]

Sosa's monumental *Topographia, e Historia general de Argel* is divided into five books. The first, the *Topography* proper, contains a meticulous description of the city of Algiers and of its inhabitants and their customs. The second book, *Epítome de los reyes de Argel* [History of the Kings of Algiers], chronicles in detail the history of its rulers from the foundation of the State of Algiers by the Barbarossa brothers to the last decades of the sixteenth century.[5] The third part of the *Topographia* contains two dialogues on captivity, *De la captividad* [On Captivity] and *De los mártires de Argel* [Of the Algerian Martyrs], and one on theological disquisitions, *De los morabutos* [Of the Marabouts]. Such dialogues furnish the eloquent testimony of a writer who endured the torments suffered by thousands of Christian captives in Barbary. Our present English translation focuses on the first book of Sosa's notable chronicle, the *Topography of Algiers*.

Complexities of the *Topography of Algiers*

A unique source of information on early modern Algiers, the *Topography of Algiers* offers numerous complexities to the literary historian. The first question that challenges the reader concerns the profoundly interdisciplinary scope of this work, which is at once an ethnographic, historical, and literary production. An anthology of its best pages would demonstrate a fine narrative gift, significant power of characterization, and a keen talent for ethnographic observation. Marvelous and sometimes even humorous anecdotes, distinguished by a conspicuous literary flavor, traverse the *Topography*. A noteworthy example is the story of a dwarf revered in Algiers, "who for being a dwarf was considered a marabout and a saint. They believed that anyone he cursed would be doomed by what he said and that if they prayed to him for blessings he would grant them" (chapter 35). In addition, many passages of the *Topography* stand out for their lucid eloquence. Yet no anthology could do the work justice. To appreciate the *Topography* properly, one must read it entirely, letting chapter after chapter enkindle one's imagination through the avalanche of characters, métiers, and key aspects of Algerian culture portrayed from beginning to end.

A second difficulty of the *Topography* emerges from its various and at times contradictory perspectives, which give the work a kaleidoscopic quality. Indeed, one could infer now and then that we are dealing with two authors. The first decries the religious beliefs and practices of Turks and Algerians, while the second praises the piety of good Muslims. For instance, when speaking of the Qur'an, Sosa states: "the whole text consists of an infinite number of tall stories that Muhammad dreamed up, all contrary to good doctrine and repugnant to reason and all philosophy and science" (chapter 27).[6] An ensuing passage, in turn, reveals his respect for certain admirable qualities of Muslims:

He who finally determines to live like a good Muslim is indeed a devout one, and the elders are as observant of the Law and as devout in making the salat at the proper hours, . . . fasting, and abstaining from wine and liquor. Christians, God willing, should be as devout in their holy observances of the precepts of God." (chapter 37)

The text abounds in such ambiguities. Turkish immigrants to Algiers "are the vilest of people, stupid and villainous, and for this reason the Turks call them jackals." Yet "some have turned out, and still turn out, to be men of worth and valor" (chapter 12). As a man of the Church, Sosa could not avoid prejudice, as we shall see, and his purpose was in part propagandist. As a result, his chronicle is marked by a radical cultural distance that separates the author's worldviews from the customs and religious traditions of the Algerians.

Nonetheless, the Portuguese captive produced a meticulously comprehensive and methodical work. As suggested earlier, readers will be struck by the multiplicity of customs and events described in the text and by the clarity of its images and characterizations. Sosa's views, however, fluctuate according to the topics that pique his interest. Women's lifestyles, for instance, their quotidian activities, religious rites, marriage customs, celebrations, and fashions, attracted so much attention on Sosa's part that he dedicated three long chapters to such issues. If his research about Algerian women and their mores is, indeed, exceptional, his curiosity for the minutiae of their daily life is astounding. In relation to women's hair, the author affirms:

Unlike the women in Christian lands who prize their hair and try to make it blonde and golden, here on the contrary all the women—Moors, Turks, and renegades—try to make their hair as black as possible, for which they use certain products, largely oils with a good scent that the merchants of Valencia tend to bring. (chapter 32)

Not even women's makeup escapes his keen eye:

Their makeup is different from that used by Christian women, because they use a great deal of bleaching agents and even more rouge.

And they also use a very black product made from certain materials to paint designs on their cheeks, chin, and forehead, such as marks, cloves, and rosettes. (chapter 32)

Sosa's fascination with Algerian women, with their intricate hairdos and headdresses, their jewelry and elaborate clothing, including their footwear, is extraordinary, especially for a man of the Church: "All the women, be they Moors, Turks, or renegades, ordinarily tend to walk around their homes barefoot, although sometimes they wear some slippers of gilt leather on their feet, with open toes and some fringes or tassels of silk, not very high and always very elegant and well designed" (chapter 32). Again, this outlook does not impede the author from severely criticizing Algerian women for living a leisurely life, dedicated to continuous parties and celebrations:

> The seventh activity of Algerian women is partying. They keep busy continually going to weddings and feast days that other women host throughout the year. . . . Not content to dance away the whole day, the women dance well into the night too, and a husband has to be all the time looking out that his woman returns to her home. (chapter 33)

Evaluating the author's intricate subject positions in the twenty-first century, then, is a demanding job, first because of his oscillating views on Algerian society, and second, because our perception of the cultural frontiers across the Mediterranean differ widely from that of a Portuguese theologian brought up and educated in sixteenth-century Spain.[7]

"I Know Everything that Occurs in Algiers"

Sosa's statement, repeated with variations throughout the *Topographia*, functions as a leitmotif for his fascinating account of life in a Muslim city in the last decades of the sixteenth century. A member of the Church hierarchies in Spanish Sicily and closely connected to Philip II's court in Madrid, Sosa was captured by Algerian corsairs in 1577 while traveling from Barcelona to Valetta (Malta) on his way to Sicily.[8] His own allusions to his sufferings as a Barbary slave during four and a half years suggest that his captivity was one of the hardest in Algiers. If this ordeal colored his view of the Algerians, especially of Turks and renegades, it was further darkened by his being a man of the Church, influenced by early modern apologetic treatises that argued for the religious superiority of Christianity over Islam. A long history of atavistic conflicts between the peoples of East and West colored these polemics, as much as for the Christians as for the Muslims.

On the Christian side, scholars of the period emphasized a widespread belief in the perils and evils of "Islam."[9] Not only did Muslims represent a fundamental hedonism that Christians radically condemned, but also their religion was regarded as a farce created by the devil.[10] Christian apologetic works characterized Muhammad as an impostor, a great heresiarch, and the creator of a false religion operating by diabolical inspiration. He was, moreover, accused of being sexually promiscuous, a man trapped in his preoccupation with the body.[11] Dante's placement of Muhammad and his son-in-law ʿAli in that *bolgia* in hell into which are thrown the "sowers of scandal and schism" [seminator di scandalo e di scisma] sheds light on the Christian vision of Islam (*Inferno* 28.35).[12] According to these views, Muslims were peculiarly treacherous, malicious, and characterized by their unbridled sexuality.[13] Christian authors portrayed them as inconstant and undetermined, using such arguments to explain the disorderly ways and frequent disruptions of North African governments. Other Europeans affirmed that Muslims lacked the fundamental beliefs needed for the constitution of modern societies.[14]

An erudite man, especially familiar with the Greek and Roman classics and the works of the church fathers, Sosa was determined to prove the errors of Islam and, above all, to portray the tortures inflicted by the Algerian corsairs on their white slaves. This enterprise illustrates his overt efforts to document the sufferings of Christian captives in Barbary, as confirmed by the subtitle of his five-book *Topographia*: "Which will Exhibit Strange Cases, Horrific Deaths, and Extraordinary Tortures that Christianity Needs to Understand." This subtitle, probably introduced in 1612 as a sales pitch for the whole work, should only apply to Sosa's two Dialogues on captivity in Algiers, which constitute the third part of his monumental chronicle together with a theological debate with Islam.

From an ethnographic perspective, however, Sosa was a careful observer of Algerian customs, one who worked tirelessly to gather a massive amount of information on the history and mores of the city. He reiterates throughout his work that his informers were Christian captives and galley slaves, janissaries, Turks, Jews, and Islamicized Spaniards or Italians, that is, converts to Islam. Furthermore, the writings of both Sosa and Cervantes on Algiers suggest that captivity can be viewed as a mode of continuous eyewitnessing that transforms the captive (*malgré lui*) into an intimate observer of a different culture. In this sense, Sosa often presents himself as a witness who testifies about a custom or experience he has personally observed or lived through. His statement "cuanto pasa en Argel sé, y aun lo escribo todo, día por día" [I know everything that occurs in Algiers, and I even write it all down completely, day by day],[15] not only draws attention to his insatiable curiosity about contemporary events occurring in this Muslim capital, but also to his interest in collecting all kinds of ethnographic information for the composition of his texts.

On various occasions, the *Topography* alludes to Sosa's dialogue with Muslim, Jewish, or renegade interlocutors. For instance, speaking of the Jews in Algiers, the author states: "I can attest to this, having debated with some of them not infrequently" (chapter 28). Likewise, referring to the religious beliefs of Muslims: "I could never convince them (although I argued with them about this)" (chapter 35); and in relation to the religious "obstinacy" of the Algerians: "one can hardly find somebody who wishes to listen to reason, let alone obey" (chapter 36). Evoking a sophisticated social arena that allowed encounters, conversations, and even religious discussions among Muslims, Jews, Christians, and renegades, such phrases also speak to the fluidity of relations across the Christian-Muslim divide in Barbary. Certainly, the high levels of immigration and mobility common to a bustling seaport such as Algiers were likely to encourage a wide range of cultural exchanges among the ethnic and religious groups that inhabited the city.

Circuits of Exchange

Sosa's chronicle particularly highlights these cultural exchanges. In this sense, his work implicitly questions facile distinctions between East and West: his reiterated mention of the "renegades," as Christian converts to Islam were called in Europe, speaks for itself. The fact that these "Turks by profession"—Christians who decided to "turn Turk"—constituted more than half of the population of Algiers around 1580–1581 stresses the continuous crossings of religious and political boundaries in the early modern Mediterranean. Such crossings led to the creation of a new frontier society that lived in the *in-between,* simultaneously partaking of various cultures. Bringing with them their technical proficiencies and abilities, the renegades would often attain lucrative positions and successful lives as corsairs, soldiers, artisans, translators, or secretaries to the Ottoman rulers, both in the Maghreb and in Constantinople.

Many sections of the *Topography,* moreover, corroborate the particular physical and social mobility linked to the raids launched by the Barbary corsairs for the capture of slaves in the western Mediterranean. Paradoxically, the extreme geopolitical tension produced by the privateering war between western Europe and the Muslim Mediterranean intensified the flow of persons, as well as linguistic, cultural, and commercial exchanges, in a parallel way to the conflict. In effect, the expansion of both North African and European corsair activities multiplied the circulation of men and, to a lesser degree, women, from many countries and social categories. Corsair activity, Fernand Braudel reminds us, necessarily demands a circuit of exchange; it is inseparable from commerce.[16] Algiers would not have become a great corsair center had it not been, at the same time, an active commercial center. In order to obtain provisions and victuals, as well as to resell its slaves, the city welcomed the arrival of foreign ships and caravans from all over Europe that came to ransom captives and to do business with Algerian merchants.

Some of Sosa's chapters, in fact, shed light on the multiple passages and intensive commercial activities of these merchants, who traded in various European cities and regions, such as London, Marseille, Genoa, Naples, Sicily, Valencia, and Barcelona, as well as Constantinople and several North African seaports and capitals.[17] The author highlights the momentum created by the "wheels of commerce" radiating from early modern Algiers, a city famous for its privateering, its traffic in human lives, and its reputation as a land of riches for the Ottoman Turks.[18] His chapter on the languages spoken in Algiers, especially on the lingua franca of Barbary—"a mixture of various Christian languages, largely Italian and Spanish words with some recently added Portuguese terms"—as well as his detailed discussion of the currencies used in this thriving urban center, sheds light on these issues (chapter 29).[19]

The constant presence in the North African littoral of Iberian merchants, shipmasters, and mariners negotiating the liberty of Christian slaves demonstrates that the repeated prohibitions of the Spanish Crown regarding commerce with Barbary were always revoked in response to the pressures of the cities, merchants, or viceroys who provided new licenses for these endeavors.[20] Certainly, the *Topography*'s frequent allusions to economic exchanges and relations with other countries situate both the role of privateering and commercial ventures launched by the city of Algiers in the arena of world economics.[21] In his *Diálogo de la captividad en Argel* [Dialogue of Captivity in Algiers], Sosa's spokesman and interlocutor, Antonio González de Torres, a Knight of Saint John of Malta, affirms that in Turkey, Romania, Anatolia, and Syria, "they all talk of Algiers as we [the Iberians] speak of the Indies."[22]

Along these lines, Braudel has suggested that the sixteenth-century Mediterranean functioned as a world economy stimulated by its commercial activities. Centered especially in Venice, Milan, Florence, Genoa, Valencia, Barcelona, and Cádiz, as well as in Algiers, Tunis, Tripoli, and Constantinople in the eastern Mediterranean, these enterprises ignored papal prohibitions against engaging in commerce with the "infidels."[23] Business endeavors took no notice of the limits between cultures that divided the Mediterranean at the time: the Greek civilization, controlled by the Turks; the various Muslim cultures, assembled in Constantinople and North Africa; or the Christian culture, established in Rome, Florence, and Madrid. The *Topography* confirms that Christians and Muslims confronted each other continuously across the North-South frontier that divided the Levant from the western Mediterranean—an imaginary line that extended from the Adriatic coasts to Sicily, and to the coastal zone of Tunis. Even so, although the battles between Christians and

Muslims were literally fought on the edge of these frontiers, merchant ships crossed these limits every day.[24] Many of these vessels continuously arrived in, and sailed from, Algiers, as Sosa's chronicle repeatedly demonstrates.

Urban Topographies and City Views

Sosa's description of the city of Algiers and its inhabitants in the 1570s demonstrates an obsessive concern with detail in regard to its urban topography. The very title *Topography of Algiers* highlights the urban scope of his enterprise, centered on the description of a Muslim city with its principal landmarks, walls, buildings, and streets. Certainly, the Renaissance rediscovery of Ptolemy, whose *Cosmographia,* translated into Latin in 1410 and subsequently reprinted in many editions, appears to have inspired many writers and artists as well as multiple cartographic projects promoted by European rulers, popes, and noblemen.[25] The discovery of the New World in the last years of the fifteenth century, moreover, produced a cartographic revolution represented in the lapse of time that stretches from Juan de la Cosa's *Portulano* (1500), where the Americas appear for first time, to the Atlas produced by Mercator in 1569, the projections of which facilitated the construction of spheres and even the development of the art of piloting. Fueled by early modern science, Atlantic navigation, and the enormous success of the printing press, this cartographic revolution created an extraordinary production of maps of all kinds, among which city views and topographies were mostly favored in Europe.

Yet the Europeans in the Middle Ages and the Renaissance also wrote about the cities where they lived. Renaissance architects privileged the notion of the city as *urbs*—that is, as a physical unity, with stone or brick houses—a concept, in turn, influenced by the Roman architect and engineer Vitrubius (ca. 80–70 BC–ca. 15 BC). His popular work *Ten Books of Architecture*[26] not only offered precise details on how to construct an ideal city but also inspired many Renaissance architectural treatises, especially *De Rei Aedificatoria* (ca. 1450), the most important study on the city of that period, composed by the Florentine humanist Leon Battista Alberti (1404–1472). Together with other contemporary architects, Alberti helped to transmit the idea that the nobility and greatness of a city essentially depended on the quality of the *urbs,* which was reflected in the architecture and magnificence of its edifices, in the strength of its ramparts, and in the design of its plazas and streets.[27]

Such interest in the physical aspects of the city illuminates the ongoing production of urban maps and panoramic views, which created a new genre in the Renaissance, the topographic landscape. These paintings presented the city in a bird's eye perspective that no eye had ever enjoyed. As Michel de Certeau has argued, this fiction turned the spectator into a "celestial eye. It created gods."[28] The panoramic city view included plans of antique urban centers, townscapes, perspectives, and panoramas, such as those produced by Georg Braun (1541–1622) and Franz Hogenberg (1535–1590) in their *Civitates orbis terrarum* (1572–1616), an impressive collection of 564 large and small city maps and plans from Europe, Africa, Asia, and Spanish America, which was a bestseller in Europe.[29] A celebration of European history and culture, the *Civitates orbis terrarum* was conceived as a companion to the great atlas produced by Abraham Ortelius, *Theatrum orbis terrarum,* published in Antwerp in 1570, as confirmed by their similar titles and the complementary nature of both works.

About the same time, an explosion of urban sceneries and topographical representations arrived in Spain with the reign of Philip II, who promoted massive projects for the drawing of city maps and sweeping views of Iberian cities and towns. Between 1562 and 1570, the Flemish painter Anton van den Wyngaerde, known in Spain as Antonio de las Viñas, traveled through the Iberian Peninsula, with orders from Philip II to produce a pictorial record of Spain's principal cities.[30] Distinguished by their topographical accuracy, Van den Wyngaerde's panoramic views of sixty-two cities and towns constitute a unique visual record of sixteenth-century Spain.[31] The artist also produced a series of paintings for Philip II's palaces, which included panoramic views of London, Amsterdam, Ghent, Lisbon, Genoa, Naples, Milan, Rome, and Madrid, as well as of thirteen Spanish cities and Mexico City, displayed at the Alcázar, the royal palace in Madrid.

Certainly, large-scale urban vistas and bird's-eye city views graced the palaces of kings, popes, and other statesmen in the second half of the sixteenth century.[32] But a great revolution in mapmaking occurred when the cities of the *Civitates orbis terrarum* appeared in print.[33] Both Braun and Hogenberg's *Civitates* and Ortelius's *Theatrum* arrived at a time in which printed books, adorned with lavish illustrations, were sold at prices that were accessible to the well-to-do classes. As Lucien Febvre and Henri-Jean Martin have suggested in their classic work on the impact of printing, *L'Apparition du livre,* print-capitalism not only created a new reading public in Europe but also exploited each potential vernacular market through a veritable international chain of publishing houses that crossed national frontiers in its search for new markets.[34] A new group of readers arose who were interested in learning about the material and political reality of their kingdoms, including novel discoveries and utopias. The birth of the travel book, then, went hand in hand with the emergence, among the European bourgeoisie, of the reader and collector of maps and urban topographies. As printers and artists connected to matters of the market, the creators of the *Civitates* understood the need for illustrated travel books and collections of printed maps. In Georg Braun's words, "What could be more agreeable than the reading of these books and the observation of the form of the earth from the comfort of one's own home, far away from any danger?" Braun argued that the fact that these books were "adorned with the splendor of cities and fortresses" would help readers, "through the contemplation of these figures and the reading of the accompanying texts, to acquire a knowledge that they could have only obtained, in a partial way, through the suffering caused by long and difficult journeys."[35]

Pedro García Martín claims that the plates of the *Civitates* already illustrated all the utilities that maps can present to the historian. To humanists these maps offered explicit knowledge of the world beyond their direct sphere of influence; to kings and rulers, the promise of future conquests. To merchants they represented novel commercial opportunities, to travelers, the way to explore exciting new worlds.[36] The maps often allude to political regimes, such as the views of Venice, the symbol of a model republic, or the vistas of Cuzco and Mexico City (Tenochtitlan), which evoke the exoticism of the New World. Other plates highlight economic issues or shed light on specific societies, such as the drawings that show a contingent of Spanish ships docked in Seville, the gateway to Spain's colonies in America.[37]

Most important, "mapmaking was one of the specialized intellectual weapons by which power could be gained, administered, given legitimacy and codified."[38] The use of maps ranges from strategizing wars to establishing property rights or land control. Because map production is based on a specific function or intention, maps are studied for their symbolic and rhetorical nature, including their narratives. Maps such as those depicted by the *Civitates* may elicit the military interest of their readers, illustrating city ramparts and fortifications, as shown in the plates of Palestinian cities or in the panoramic view of Algiers, discussed below. The *Civitate*'s lavish map of Constantinople (1572), the lost capital of Byzantium conquered by the Turks in 1453, demonstrates the central place occupied by the Ottomans in the political and intellectual preoccupations of the period.[39]

The *Civitates* also includes an extraordinary map of Algiers with Latin and Italian inscriptions, entitled *Algerii Saracenorum urbis fortissimae, in Numidia Africae Provincia structae, iuxta Balearicos fluctus Maediterranei aequoris Hispaniam contra Othomanorum Principum imperio redactae* [Image of Algiers, Powerful City of the Sarracens, Constructed in Numidia, African Province, Not Far from the Balearic Waves of the Mediterranean Sea, Facing Spain, under the Yoke of the Ottoman Princes] (1575; fig. 1). This map circulated widely throughout Europe and was reprinted several times. Its title emphasizes not only the impact produced by the "powerful" city of Algiers in the Mediterranean Sea but also the situation of this urban center under the yoke of the Ottoman Empire. The military relevance of this bird's-eye view for European viewers lay, as we shall see, in the meticulous portrayal of the formidable Muslim city, with its impressive fortifications and gates, its well-guarded port and harbor, and the strong fortresses that surrounded it.

Helen Hills has called attention to the fact that, rather than being objective representation of places, maps and plans are complex visual representations, which "draw on cultural codes and are enmeshed in power relationships."[40] Along these lines, Braun and Hogenberg's map of Algiers significantly reflects Christian Europe's preoccupation with the expanding geopolitical world, in particular, with the aggressive presence of the corsair capital in the western Mediterranean. More important, the specific political context in which this map of Algiers is

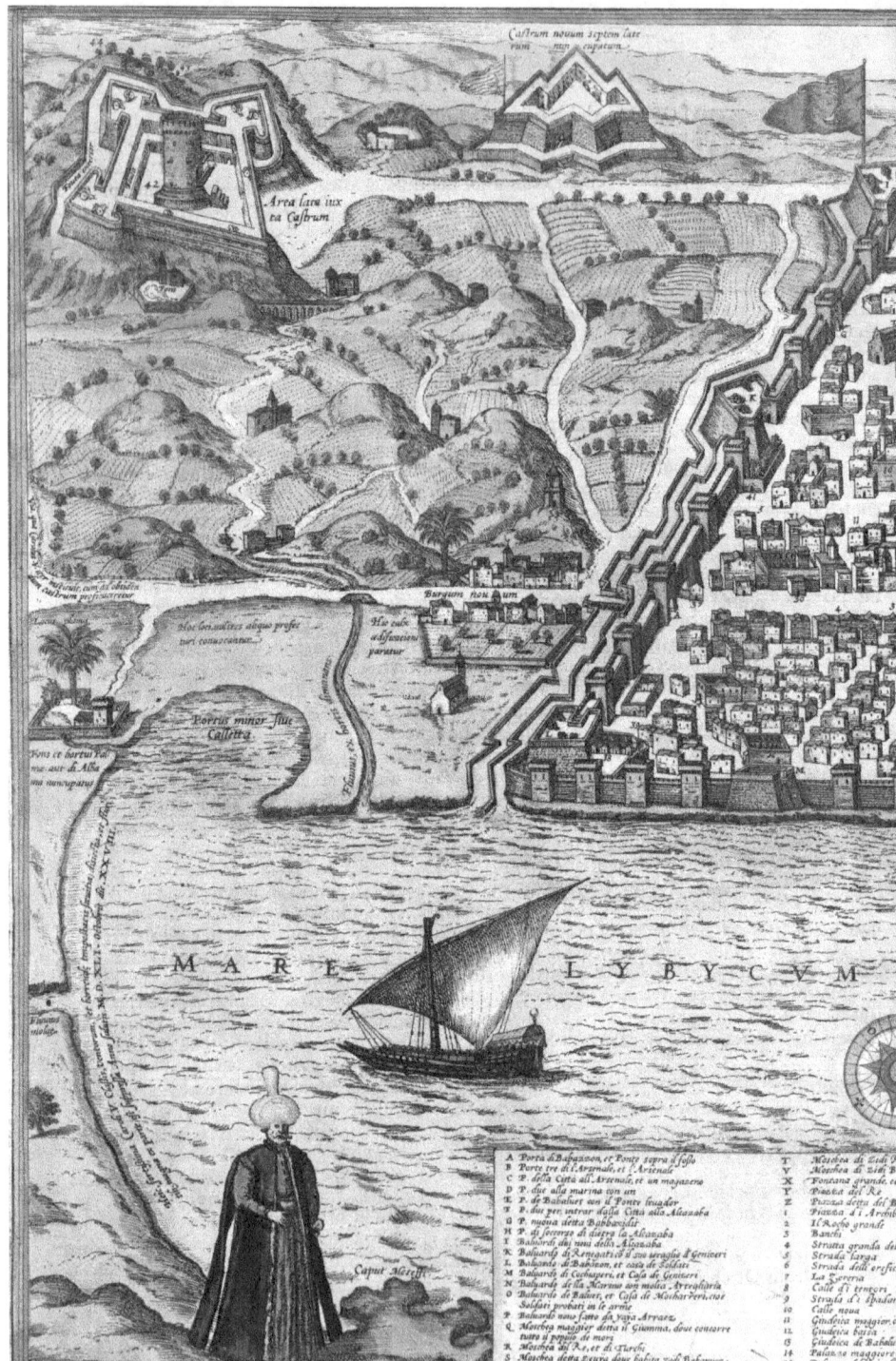

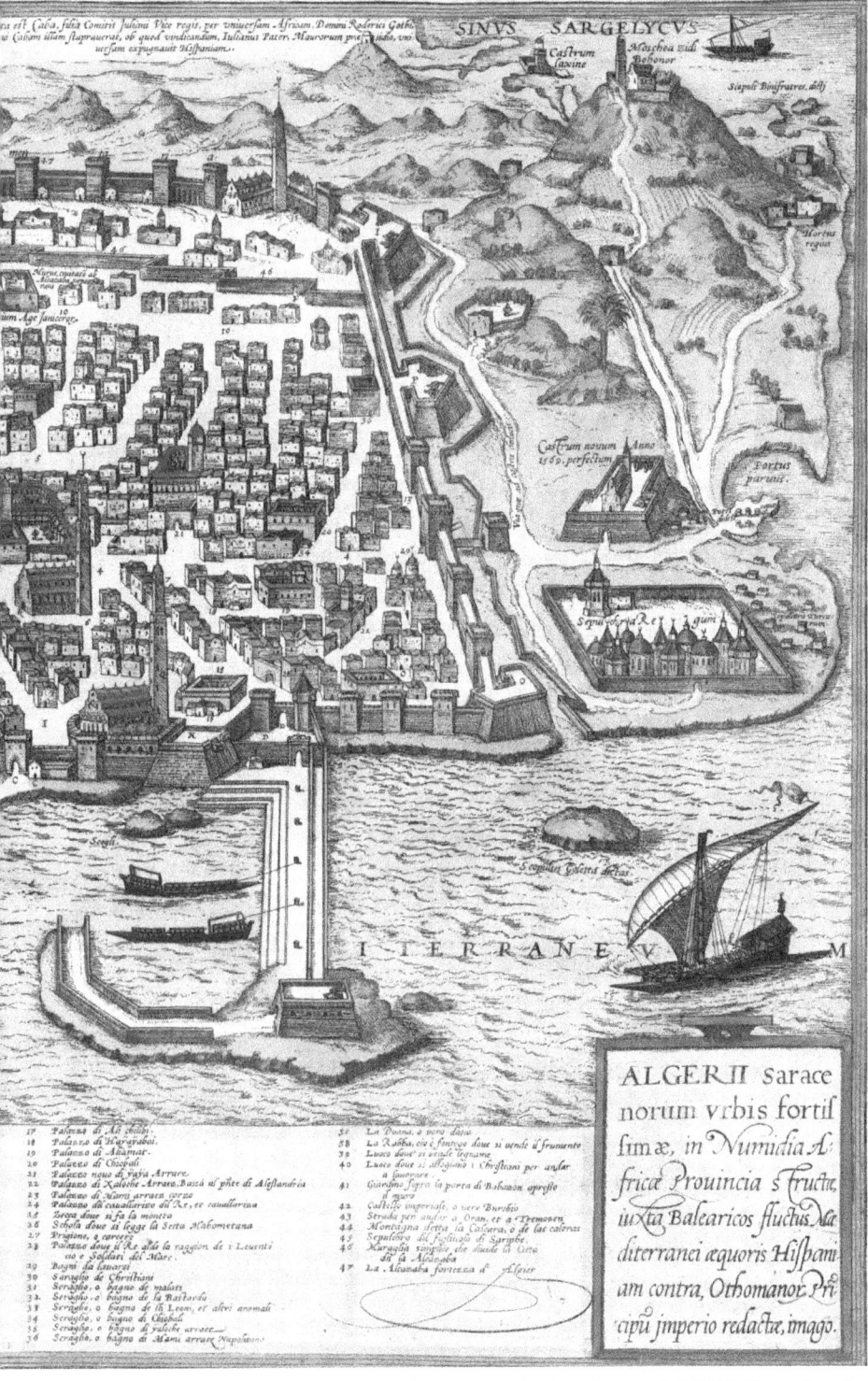

Figure 1. Map of Algiers [*Algerii Saracenorum vrbis fortissimae . . .*] (1575?). Reproduced from Braun and Hogenberg, *Civitates orbis terrarum* (1575–1612). Division of Rare and Manuscript Collections, Cornell University Library.

embedded sheds light on the way that maps are constructed around power relations. Critics have stated that, as much as cannons and warships, "maps have been the weapons of imperialism."[41] Ricardo Padrón has argued in this sense that maps helped in the planning of military operations, in the construction of ramparts, and in the exploration of trade routes, especially maritime courses.[42]

The panoramic vista of Algiers by Braun and Hogenberg ratifies the importance of large city maps for the exercise of power, both physical and symbolic. Aided by textual indications in both Latin and Italian, the map allowed the city of Algiers to be discovered, explored, and (literally) conquered. In effect, this urban vista of Algiers exhibits the city's inner secrets and its potentially vulnerable military points, such as a non-occupied fortress to the left and another to the right, clearly marked as such, several bastions and fortifications with their cannons, plainly viewed, including various sites marked by their significance for European spectators, such as the site of Charles V's disembarkation during his 1541 failed attack on Algiers. Beyond the major mosques and houses of the principal *ru'asa* (plural of *ra'is*, corsair captain) and government officials, identified with different codes and place names in Italian, this panoramic view of Algiers shows the location of various palaces, such as the "Palazzo maggiore del Ré" [Principal palace of the king], the "Palazzo del Ré alla Marina, detto il novo" [The king's palace at the harbor, called the new palace], and the "Palazzo di Luchiali, che é al presente Ré d'Algier" [The palace of 'Uludj 'Ali, who at present is king of Algiers]. This townscape depicts the janissary barracks and the bagnios, or slave-prisons, such as the Bagnio of the Christians, the Bagnio de la Bastarda, as well as the "Bagnio de Mami Arraez Napolitano" [Prison of Mami Ra'is the Neapolitan], one of five private slave prisons. Additional amenities include a public prison for criminals, the Bagnio of the Lions and Other Animals (a zoo), the Hammam, or public baths, and the "Schola dove si legge la setta Mahometana" [School where the Muslim sect is taught]. Most interesting for contemporary readers are the references and marked sites of three synagogues then existing in Algiers, to wit: the principal *giudeica*, or synagogue, called "the Tall One" [Giudeica maggior, ouero alta], the Giudeica bassa [Low synagogue], and the Giudeica of Bal al-Wad.

Yet beyond the military ambitions of the Spanish Empire, clearly readable in this map, the lovely panoramic vista of the city of Algiers also evokes the European fascination with the colorful features and exotic qualities of this sophisticated Muslim metropolis. Sosa's *Topography of Algiers,* with its detailed physical description of this urban center, can be read side by side with the contemporary map depicted in the *Civitates orbis terrarum.* Both works, composed in the same decade, reveal their attraction for the city of Algiers. Although we cannot be sure that Sosa was directly acquainted with this map, we may presume that, following his liberation and return to Madrid in 1581, or even after his return to Sicily in 1584, he could have admired the magisterial production by Braun and Hogenberg, which circulated widely throughout Europe. Be that as it may, Sosa's work falls in the realm of urban topography or chorography, as defined by Apianus and other ancient and early modern cosmographers.[43]

"Walking in the City"

Topography, in the Ptolemaic method, was close to chorography, whose task was "to describe the smallest details of places."[44] Petrus Apianus (1495–1552), a close follower of Ptolemy and one of Charles V's science teachers, gives the following definition of chorography:

> Chorography is the same thing as Topography, which one can define as the plan of a place that describes and considers its peculiarities in isolation, without consideration or comparison of its parts either among themselves or in relation to other places. But, at the same time, chorography carefully takes note of all particularities and properties, as small as they may be, that are worth noting in such places, such as ports, towns, villages, river courses, and all similar things, including buildings, houses, towers, walls, and the like. The aim of chorography is to depict a particular place, just as an artist paints an ear or an eye or other parts of a man's head.[45]

Sosa's *Topography* is constructed according to the medieval schema through which every city, no matter how important, was described.

This plan depicted diverse elements in a repetitive identical order: first, the systems of defense, ramparts and fortresses; second, aspects of the streets, monuments, and particular houses; third, the political regime of the urban center and its administration, including its judicial organization; and fourth, the customs (both praiseworthy and reprehensible) of the population and, especially, of princes and leaders who governed the country.[46] Roughly following this topographical model, Sosa departs from it in his introductory historical presentation, which relates the ancient history and the founding of Algiers, including how it came under the Turks. He also separates himself from this model by placing his illustration of the fertility and richness of the countryside at the end of his *Topography*, instead of at the beginning, as was the custom.

The canvas portrayed above thus functioned as a frame of a vision that begins in the outer region (the walls and ramparts of the city) and enters the city, approaching first the buildings, and then, the inhabitants, in order to focus on their customs. Each of the cited elements could be more or less expanded according to the circumstances. The canvas was especially developed in the case of the capital of a great kingdom, say, a seat of political power and theater of economic expansion, such as Algiers or Constantinople. Hence, among the cities described by travelers and geographers, Constantinople occupied the first place. Multiple portraits of the city confirm the validity and permanence of such a scheme. Between the early sixteenth and the end of the seventeenth centuries, and probably beyond, the descriptions of the Ottoman capital, whether from French, Spanish, or Italian writers, always obeyed an identical model.[47]

The first chapters of Sosa's *Topography*, in particular, illustrate Michel de Certeau's concepts on "pedestrian speech acts." The French philosopher posits that "the act of walking is to the urban system what the speech act is to language or to statements uttered." In effect, walking constitutes a "process of appropriation of the topographical system on the part of the pedestrian."[48] De Certeau proposes that one can conveniently transfer to manners of inhabiting and moving across a spatial order those interpretative categories applied to manners of inhabiting and traversing a linguistic order: "the courses taken by passers-by present a series of turns and detours that can be compared to 'turns of phrases' or 'stylistic figures.'" For de Certeau, there is a rhetoric of walking. The art of "turning phrases finds an equivalent in an art of 'diverting' itineraries."[49]

Sosa's literal walks about the city of Algiers, together with the steps he takes in one and another direction create the space, weave the urban sites. His steps, counted and measured in his text, accompany his detailed descriptions of the ramparts, gates, fortifications, moat, castles, and forts outside Algiers, as well as those of the houses and streets of the city. In the case of an urban context, moreover, Sosa's writings somehow function like a virtual, heuristic object that traverses prearranged routes, everyday itineraries, social divides and prohibitions, against which his detours acquire their significance and direction. Paraphrasing de Certeau, one could say that Sosa's walks about Algiers are not only indicative of his distinct appropriation of a Muslim urban space—and of his fundamental encounters with the other: Moors, Turks, and renegades—but also of a more profound unconscious process, significantly redoubled, as it were, by his writing about "walking in the city."

As de Certeau claims, the operations of walking can be traced on city maps in such a way as to set down their paths and their trajectories. Nevertheless, these thick or thin traces "only refer, like words, to the absence of what has passed by." What cannot be recovered is "the act itself of passing by."[50] In Sosa's case, however, there was a will to memorize, to recuperate his itineraries and his lost steps as he wrote about them each night after returning to his prison in Muhammad's house. Like a travel story, Sosa's itineraries throughout the city constitute both a tour and a map of early modern Algiers, which mark the military, political, architectural, and commercial figurations of his detailed geographical plan. His movements, shortcuts, and detours through the North African metropolis at once explore and transgress intimate or sacred places, even as his trajectories "speak" in various eloquent ways.

Certainly, walking about the city as a captive could not have been easy, as Sosa himself confirms when he relates his experiences with hard labor in Algiers, in 1578, when he was forced to haul rocks and sand and to mix lime, while chained, or to stagger around the city dragging his heavy chains behind. Guarded by two renegades, Sosa was sent to work in shackles and irons, burdened with fetters, not being fed until the evening.[51] He states that the French captive Juan Gasco [Gascon], a compassionate friend, helped him in these trying labors, aiding him to carry rocks and sand, while they both worked at a construction site owned by Sosa's owner Muhammad. As a high-ranking member of the Hispano-Italian Church, Sosa would normally not have been destined to hard labor. This may have been a strategy devised by his master in order to pressure his slave to write to the Spanish Crown requesting his ransom. In "The Captive's Tale," Cervantes recounts that elite captives were usually incarcerated in the "king's" bagnio:

> The king's slaves, when they're going to be ransomed, don't get sent out to work with . . . [the common slaves], unless their ransom money is late coming, in which case, to make the captives write and urge that the money be sent faster, they force them to work with the others on public jobs and gathering firewood—which is no picnic (*DQ* I, 40).[52]

Such were some of the torments to which Sosa and other captives were subjected in Algiers.

As a slave who was dispossessed of everything that had given meaning to his life, Sosa attempted to search for, or confirm, his Iberian identity by writing down, at the end of each day, his keen observations in regard to the Muslim city and the people he encountered daily. Yet there is an oneiric quality in this walking/writing that goes hand-in-hand: in spite of his vicissitudes as a captive in Algiers, Sosa's *Topography* reveals a tacit love affair with the multicultural metropolis, the real protagonist of his work. The houses of this Mediterranean capital, so "very pretty and polished," its fine mansions, "all with elegant and open patios," as well as the "very sturdy and beautiful" Bath of Hasan Pasha, among other buildings, speak to Sosa's attraction for the Muslim city that captivated him in body and soul (chapters 10; chapter 9). His text also discloses his fascination with the fertile countryside that surrounded this urban center, with its "infinite number of farms, orchards, and vineyards," irrigated by "the great freshness of the streams," so charming that "nobody could desire more" (chapter 40).

Visions of Early Modern Contacts with Islam (1983–2009)

The publication of this book at the turn of the twenty-first century comes at a vital moment in history, when both North Americans and Europeans are asking more informed questions about the relations between Muslims and non-Muslims across the globe. In the United States, the debates on ethnic minorities, already vibrant since the 1960s, have been intensified by the tragic events of September 11, 2001. The complex dimensions of the United States' political, military, economic, and cultural engagement with Muslim countries in the Middle East has had powerful consequences for both sides. The catastrophic events of September 11, as well as the wars in the Middle East, "demonstrate that Americans cannot afford to remain as uninformed as they have generally been about the histories, politics, and cultures of that region."[53] The past decades, then, have produced a great deal of criticism of, as well as polemics on, the way in which U.S. and other Western scholars have studied the peoples and cultures of the Middle East.[54] On the other hand, the increasingly multiracial and multicultural components of European societies, with their millions of immigrants from both Muslim and non-Muslim nations, have led to exacerbated conflicts in various countries of the Old World.[55] Such tensions have brought about a renewed attention to the history of the relations between Islam and the West on the part of European scholars. These vital concerns perhaps account for the proliferation of important books recently published in Europe and the United States that attempt to elucidate how the encounter between Muslims and Christians was negotiated in the past.

In Spain since the 1980s, Morisco studies have come into their prime. The plight of the Moriscos—the Hispano-Muslims who were obliged to convert to Christianity after the fall of Granada in 1492—including their history during the sixteenth century and their expulsion from Spain between 1609 and 1614, became a crucial topic in the final decades of the twentieth century, both in Spain and other European countries. Multiple publications, conferences, new academic journals, translations and re-editions of extant works on the last Moors of Iberia, as well as innovative courses, have appeared in the last twenty years. Historian Mercedes García-Arenal, a worldwide authority on

Hispano-Muslim historical studies, explained in 1983 that the revival of such topics responded to the political situation of Spain, "which has elicited a new interest for local histories, for the search and recovery of the cultural and historical patrimony of each zone, for its particular characteristics and its signs of identity."[56] García-Arenal has published more than a dozen books on the subject, as well as on the relations between Spain and North Africa in the sixteenth and seventeenth centuries.[57] Her research reflects the significance of the political, commercial, and cultural contacts between Spain and the Barbary countries Morocco, Algiers, and Tunisia in the period studied.

Yet these publications have not only been confined to Spain. Cutting-edge studies, coming out of France, Italy, England, Tunisia, Algeria, Morocco, and the United States, have similarly focused on the Moriscos and the European relations with North Africa in the early modern times.[58] Many of these works explore the poignant topic of captivity in Barbary, which affected every Mediterranean country in the sixteenth and seventeenth centuries, including England and northern European populations. Among the more relevant books on captivity in Barbary, including the subject of converts to Islam, that have appeared in the last decades we should mention Bartolomé Bennassar and Lucile Bennassar, *Les chrétiens d'Allah* (1989); Ottmar Hegyi, *Cervantes and the Turks* (1992); Lucetta Scaraffia, *Rinegatti* (1993); Emilio Sola and José F. de la Peña, *Cervantes y la Berbería* (1995, 1996); María Antonia Garcés, *Cervantes in Algiers* (2002, 2005); Linda Colley, *Captives* (2002); Robert C. Davis, *Christian Slaves, Muslim Masters* (2003, 2004); and José Antonio Martínez Torres, *Prisioneros de los infieles* (2004). Our English edition and translation of Antonio de Sosa's *Topography of Algiers* engages in a dialogue with these suggestive scholarly productions.

New trends in historiography and literary history touching on both sides of Gibraltar, moreover, have been inaugurated by critics and historians across the globe, such as Manuel Barrios Aguilera, Vincent Barletta, Luis F. Bernabé Pons, Miguel Ángel de Bunes Ibarra, Trevor J. Dadson, Benjamin Ehlers, Barbara Fuchs, Álvaro Galmés de la Fuente, L. P. Harvey, A. Katie Harris, Francisco Márquez Villanueva, María Teresa Narváez, Mary Elizabeth Perry, Bernard Vincent, and Gerard Wiegers, among others. A special mention is due to the lifework of the late Soledad Carrasco Urgoiti, whose first-rate scholarship and passion for Morisco studies illuminated many obscure facets of Golden Age Spanish literature. Among this astounding production of books, the outstanding works by Luce López-Baralt, such as *Islam in Spanish Literature, Un Kāma Sūtra español* [A Spanish Kamasutra], and, in turn, her fundamental study, *La literatura secreta de los últimos musulmanes de España* [The secret literature of the last Muslims of Spain], have opened exciting new horizons, both historical and literary. Publications on Morisco topics have continued to appear with renewed vigor, as demonstrated by García-Arenal's recent review article, "Religious Dissent and Minorities: The Morisco Age" (2009). The twelve important books appraised by García-Arenal, published in Spain, France, Italy, and the United States between 2003 and 2009, bring up questions of collective identity, particularly in regard to the multiple cultural and religious facets that fashioned Morisco character, creating either conflict or integration. Although two of these studies focus on *conversos* or converted Jews, often called Marranos, all of them speak to the vital need to rethink our approaches to the study of communal or individual identities in early modern Europe and Spanish America.

In addition, fresh studies on the Moroccan diplomat and traveler Leo Africanus have appeared in France and the USA, where Natalie Zemon Davis's biography of al-Hasan ibn Muhammad al-Wazzan al-Fasi [the man of Fès], titled *Trickster Travels* (2006), became a bestseller, translated into various languages.[59] Along these lines, it is important to underscore the work of historian Jocélyne Dakhlia, whose dazzling interdisciplinary study of the lingua franca of the Mediterranean appeared in France, in 2008. Finally, two critics in particular, Nabil Matar and Daniel Vitkus, have illuminated early modern English history and literature in their work. Matar has published an impressive trilogy about Britain and the Islamic world that focuses on the impact of Islam and the Barbary region on Elizabethan and later British culture. The period studied in these three books extends from the accession of Elizabeth I to the death of Charles II: *Islam in Britain, 1558–1685* (1998); *Turks, Moors and Englishmen in the Age of Discovery* (1999); and *Britain and Barbary, 1589–1678* (2005). A recent study, titled *Europe through Arab Eyes*, also by Matar, presents a suggestive compilation of letters and travel accounts composed by Arab travelers in Europe between 1578 and 1727. Likewise, Vitkus has edited, with an erudite introduction, *Three Turk Plays from Early Modern England* (2000) and, more recently, has put out a fine study on the manner in which Ottoman culture, especially early modern encounters between English and Turkish merchants in the Mediterranean, influenced various works by Marlowe and Shakespeare—*Turning Turk: English Theater and the Multicultural Mediterranean* (2003). All of these works speak to the prescient nature of studies that explore early modern relations between Islam and the West, including the ways in which these interactions impinged on the complex fashioning and refashioning of identities in Spain, Britain, and other countries in Europe. Our English translation of Sosa's *Topography of Algiers*, then, follows these preoccupations with the study of sixteenth-century European contacts with Muslim cultures in North Africa, especially with the Turkish Algerian Regency. Likewise, both my Introduction and many chapters of Sosa's work explore a complex set of questions in regard to the crossing of cultural, political, and religious frontiers in the early modern Mediterranean.[60]

As noted earlier, the first book of Sosa's magnum opus—the *Topography* proper—focuses initially on the geography and topography of Algiers and, secondly, on the portrayal of its inhabitants, their laws, religions, and ways of life. Yet this is also a work grounded in history, through constant reference to the rulers who governed the Turkish-Algerian Regency during the sixteenth century, men who participated in the construction of this impressive North African capital and in the formation of its civic, military, and naval institutions.

My critical aim is to situate the *Topography* within the corpus of early modern Spanish historiographic and ethnographic works. I approach this text—an overt and self-conscious attempt to "write culture," as George Marcus and James Clifford have framed it—both as a form of symbolic capital and as a transcript of intercultural dialogue in the late sixteenth-century Mediterranean.[61] As has been the case with colonial Spanish American texts such as the *Naufragios* [*Castaways*] of Alvar Núñez Cabeza de Vaca and the *Brevísima relación de la destrucción de las In-*

dias [*The Devastation of the Indies: A Brief Account*] of Bartolomé de las Casas, it is necessary to place the *Topography* within the long tradition of ethnographic texts devoted to Algeria and North Africa. Canonical anthropological studies, such as Pierre Bourdieu's analyses of Kabyle (Berber) society in Algeria and Lila Abu-Lughod's later studies of gender and poetic performance in western Egypt, depend directly upon images of North Africa authored and widely disseminated throughout Europe during the early modern period.[62] As is the case with Latin America, the very seeds of North Africa's colonization by Europeans were planted during this period of contact.[63] The fact that numerous anthropologists working on Algeria and North Africa tend to ignore Spanish—French and English being the dominant languages of their studies—makes our English translation of this work all the more important.

The *Topography* remains virtually unknown by Anglo-American scholars, even though early in U.S. history many American sailors and merchants were held hostage in the same geographical space, which led Thomas Jefferson to bombard Tripoli five times in 1804. Written over two centuries earlier, Sosa's work is essential for an understanding of how the Christian West has worked to understand, dominate, and refashion Muslim cities and peoples in North Africa. Apart from the English historian Joseph Morgan, who unabashedly "picked" entire chapters from the *Epítome de los reyes de Argel* for his *Complete History of Algiers* (1728–1729), there is no extant English edition of this work.[64] The first two books of the *Topographia,* ascribed to Diego de Haedo, were translated into French in 1870–1871 and 1881, respectively. Both works were reprinted in France in 1998.[65] Although the French translation of the *Topography* proper is generally accurate, it is, in fact, an abridged version of Sosa's work, which often summarizes entire paragraphs in order to avoid repetitions and long-winded phrases. As for the Spanish editions of these intercultural dialogues with Algiers, beyond the rare princeps edition (Valladolid, 1612),[66] the only extant Spanish version of the *Topografía* (1927–1929) is inaccessible and deficient, lacking any sort of critical apparatus.[67]

Our plan is to translate three of Sosa's works: the *Topography of Algiers,* which we now offer readers; the *Epítome de los reyes de Argel* [History of the Kings of Algiers], as well as the long second dialogue on captivity in Barbary,[68] titled *Diálogo de los mártires de Argel* [Dialogue of the Algerian Martyrs], adding to these translations all the required scholarly apparatus.[69] We hope that our first installment of these three works, the English translation of the *Topography*, will become a useful resource for scholars in the humanities, researchers of social history, Spanish history and literature, the study of the relations between Spain and the Barbary Coast, including that of the sixteenth-century Mediterranean, historical ethnography, and comparative religions (broadly framed). Our translation of Sosa's *Topography* provides all the necessary critical tools for readers of English to access this important early modern text.

"This Is Not an Enemy to Be Taken Lightly"

To situate Antonio de Sosa's life and work in the complex Mediterranean world of the sixteenth century, I will outline the main landmarks in the wars between the Ottoman Turks and the Spaniards for control of the Mare Nostrum. The capture of Constantinople in 1453 by the Ottomans was seen in Europe not only as a political and military disaster, but also as an imminent threat to the survival of Christianity. Viewed as a cultural cataclysm for humanist Europe, the fall of Constantinople was described by Aeneas Sylvius Piccolomini (later Pope Pius II) as "the second death of Homer and Plato."[70] In his speech at the Diet of Regensburg (1454), the future pope conveyed his profound personal distress at the news of the catastrophe, while insisting on the atrocities perpetrated by the Turks: "This is not an enemy to be taken lightly . . . , he is driven to persecute Christians by a kind of instinctive hatred, rising from deep-seated wickedness and an inborn thirst for blood."[71] The Turks' reputation for brutality, in effect, spread together with their further conquests in the Balkans and the Mediterranean. After the fall of Constantinople, references to Ottoman savagery and viciousness became a common motif in European literature. The capture of Constantinople was relentlessly described across fifteenth-century Europe in tales of rape, pillage, and murder of children, virgins, matrons, monks or nuns, all of whom were violated, massacred, or sold into slavery by the Turks.[72]

Further Ottoman conquests of the Balkan Peninsula and what is now known as Romania followed in the sixteenth century. Sultan Süleyman the Magnificent captured Belgrade in 1521, conquered Rhodes in 1522, destroyed the Hungarian army at Mohács in 1526, and besieged Vienna with an army of 400,000 men in 1529. On the western Mediterranean front, the Turks captured Tripoli from the Knights of Malta in 1551, destroyed the Spanish armada at the island of Djerba in 1560, and attacked Malta in 1565, where the Knights of Saint John—soldier-monks dedicated to fighting Islam on all fronts—had established themselves with the help of Charles V after the loss of Rhodes to the Ottomans. Finally, the Turks seized Cyprus, the most distant of the Venetian outposts, in 1571. The relentless advance of Islam in Eastern Europe and the Mediterranean pressured Pope Pius V to form a confederation of Christian states, which included Spain, the Holy See, the Republic of Venice, and Malta under the Knights of Saint John. The impressive armada of the Holy League, with more than three hundred vessels, defeated the Ottoman navy and its Algerian allies at the Battle of Lepanto in October 1571.

Such conflicts between Islam and Christianity over the Mediterranean frontiers were exacerbated by the rise of Algiers in the first half of the sixteenth century as both the greatest corsair city of the Mediterranean and a highly organized Ottoman sandjak (political region). The fall of the Nasrid kingdom of Granada to the Catholic Monarchs, Ferdinand and Isabella, in 1492 triggered an important chain of events in Spain and North Africa, which radically altered the state of affairs in the western Mediterranean. Concurrently, from the end of the fifteenth century until the deportation of the Grenadine Moriscos in 1571, a colonial society was created in Granada and surrounding territories, where the victorious Iberian Christians imposed their way of life on the Muslim population of the ancient Nasrid kingdom. Thousands of Hispano-Muslims (Moriscos) from Granada and Valencia, who faced increasing persecution from the Old Christians in the Peninsula, immigrated to the North African coastal towns, stimulating a guerrilla war against Spain, their most despised enemy. Joined by other Muslim corsairs from the eastern and western Mediterranean, these émigrés launched raids against Iberian ships and the coasts of the Spanish Levant, including those of Italy, pillaging towns and capturing hostages, who were turned into slaves.

At the same time that Castile was consolidating its hold on the kingdom of Granada and its inhabitants, Spanish and Portuguese soldiers crossed the Strait of Gibraltar, expanding their conquests to the North African coastal regions. The fall of Granada, then, was not, as was commonly believed, the last chapter of the so-called Reconquista: it led to the continuation of the Iberian crusade against Islam in North Africa. At the turn of the sixteenth century, thousands of Spanish soldiers and adventurers flocked to the North African littoral, conquering the ports of Mers-el-Kebir (1505), Orán (1509), and Béjaïa and Tripoli (1510).[73] Algiers surrendered in 1509 to the Spaniards, who constructed a fortress on an islet in front of the city (El Peñón de Argel).[74] Two papal bulls by Pope Alexander VI—the Spaniard Rodrigo Borgia—from 1493 and 1494, sanctioned the African crusade while offering Spain legal titles of possession.[75] With this blessing, the pope continued the extraordinary tax, the *cruzada,* which would defray the expenses of such expeditions. In her last testament (1504), Queen Isabella gave her support to the African crusade by urging her Castilian subjects to continue the war against Islam in African territories.[76] Barely six months after Isabella's death, in August 1505, Ferdinand prepared an army of seven thousand soldiers and 190 vessels to attack Mers el-Kebir "to make war on the Moors."[77] The frontier between Christian Iberia and Muslim North Africa was thus displaced at the turn of the sixteenth century to the Strait of Gibraltar and the Maghrebi coastal areas.

These conflicts across the Christian-Muslim frontiers in North Africa and the western Mediterranean were intensified by the constant migration of Morisco refugees from Granada, Valencia, and other Iberian locations throughout the sixteenth and seventeenth centuries, refugees who settled in the North African coastal towns. Such a large influx of immigrants reinforced Muslim piracy, the great resource of the Maghrebi ports, such as Tangiers, Algiers, Béjaïa, Salé, and Tunis, among others. Privateers and renegades from all over the world, moreover, found a haven in Algiers, the prosperous Muslim city that provided skilled labor and supplies as well as the pleasures of a port of call. Certainly, this great seaport exceeded all estimates on corsair activities in the western Mediterranean. As I have suggested elsewhere, when the cleric Antonio de Sosa and the soldier Miguel de Cervantes arrived in Algiers as captives, between 1575 and 1577, the city functioned as the apotheosis of privateering in the internal Mare Nostrum.[78]

Creation of a Stereotype

The overlapping events of the conquest of Granada and the invasion of the North African coastal towns by Iberian soldiers would bring a radical change in the description of Muslims on the part of Christians who for centuries had coexisted with Islam in medieval Iberia.[79] For the first time, Iberian soldiers holding a dominant political, military, and religious position were able to access the core of Muslim societies on both sides of Gibraltar. Their military triumph over the Muslim armies of Granada and of the North African towns—in addition to the technical superiority of Iberian soldiers, especially in firearms— led to the opinion that the inhabitants of North Africa had not been proficient at creating sophisticated political organizations like the ones known to Europeans. In turn, such encounters led to new descriptions of Muslims in Europe.[80]

This rediscovery of the Muslim world was generated by the processes of territorial and maritime expansion created in the Renaissance. Europe at this time had to face two great challenges: the discovery of a New World and the intrusion of the Ottoman Turks into both the territories and the history of the Old World. Paradoxically, as Iberian Christians celebrated the erasure of the last vestiges of Moorish culture in Spain, together with the capture of the African coastal towns, Europeans were also confronted with the spread of Islam in eastern Europe and the Mediterranean through the Ottoman conquests of the Balkans, Palestine, Egypt, and almost the entire North African littoral.

The conquest of North African towns by Iberian Christians would produce new types of stories and travel accounts that tried to establish the character of Muslims. Jocélyne Dakhlia has suggested, in this sense, that in early modern times the Maghreb became one of the most privileged laboratories of European observation in regard to Islam and of

Western reflections on oriental despotism. While many eyes and interests in Europe were turned toward the Ottoman Sultan and the Sublime Porte, the quotidian experience of the Muslim Orient for Europeans was frequently obtained from the Maghreb rather than from the proper Orient.[81] European texts on North Africa encompass sixteenth- and seventeenth-century travel accounts, chronicles by Spanish and Portuguese conquerors of the Maghreb, soldiers' autobiographies, reports written by ransoming priests, as well as stories composed by former captives who related their vicissitudes in Barbary or composed general histories of these territories. Such a vast compound of printed works and manuscripts also includes a great number of plays and literary texts produced in England, France, Spain, and Italy in the sixteenth and seventeenth centuries.[82] Along these lines, we can mention the Barbary plays by Cervantes, as well as some of his novellas, among other texts that reflect a concern with the experiences of Europeans captives or travelers across the Mediterranean, or with the description of the peoples of North Africa.[83] Many of these works depict not only commercial and negotiating procedures common to the Maghrebi societies, but also the inner functioning of the Barbary States, including data on their rulers and functionaries.

During the so-called Reconquista of the Iberian Peninsula, Christians had been able to meet and know Muslims as religious or military enemies over a porous frontier that permitted cultural and political interaction. Crossing the Strait of Gibraltar, however, implied meeting and describing Muslims anew and in a space that was both unfamiliar and different in terms of political structures. To be sure, the conquest of the Nasrid kingdom of Granada was viewed by Iberian Christians as the final stage of a struggle advanced since medieval times, a conviction that led to the rapid Christianization of Granada itself, as well as of the surrounding region in southern Spain. The former Muslim culture was partly assumed by the conquerors, who proceeded to appropriate palaces and Nasrid buildings without changing their design, turning mosques into Christian churches, and even introducing elements of Islamic architecture into their new constructions. Nonetheless, as Barbara Fuchs has recently argued, the fall of Granada in 1492 did not lead to a radical rupture with Spain's Moorish past: instead, this past survived throughout the sixteenth century in quotidian practices, dress codes, household décor, and architecture, among other cultural traditions.[84] Grenadine ways, in fact, were often adopted inadvertently by the local vernacular and the aristocracy, who were not even aware of the wide range of Moorish customs they had espoused. In turn, the defeated Hispano-Muslims who inhabited Granada and its adjoining territories were initially seen as mistaken or misguided individuals who had to be kept in rein through forceful campaigns of evangelization and repression.

The passage to North Africa, on the other hand, required a new set of views, including legal backing for these invasions, such as the two papal bulls of Alexander VI that authorized Spain to continue the crusade against Islam on these territories and the treaties that divided the recently discovered New World and West Africa between Spain and Portugal. Most European authors, in effect, insisted on the unlawful occupation of the North African lands by the Muslims, who had invaded regions that once belonged to the Romans, the Byzantines, and the Visigoths, including spaces that were formerly described by the great geographers of antiquity. This approach—a direct result of Spanish and Portuguese efforts to dominate the new territories that emerged on the other side of Gibraltar—also endeavored to assume the legacy of the ancient world through Christianity, while discrediting the Muslims, presumably descended from a false Prophet, for usurping territories that did not belong to them.[85] The conquest of the North African littoral was thus vindicated as a valid action that, in the words of a sixteenth-century Spaniard, tried to "recuperate what in past times, and with much damage and dishonor, they [the Muslims] stole from us."[86] This idea of a "lost land" is a leitmotif that recurs in many Western texts on North Africa. Such beliefs would explain Antonio de Sosa's continuous references to Ptolemy, Strabo, Pliny, or Antoninus in his initial chapters on the geography and early history of Algiers (chapters 1 and 2). His attempts to establish a continuum with Roman history also endeavor to deny a rupture with the classical past in this region of North Africa.

Iberian military incursions into the Maghreb, then, generated a vision of North African Muslims and, by extension, of the Ottoman

Turks, partly based on the medieval Christian ideas that denigrated Islam and its practitioners. The massive quantity of writings produced by Spanish soldiers, captives, religious men, travelers, and diplomats who visited the Maghreb or Constantinople, voluntarily or involuntarily, produced a stereotype of Muslims and Turks that found its way into Iberian literature, among others. In spite of the curiosity inspired by the new cultures and customs encountered by Western travelers, political and religious positions generally prevailed in these texts. Many Iberian writers thus condemned the ways of life and political organization of the Muslim countries they visited. Although the image of oriental despotism was actually formulated in seventeenth-century Venice, its seeds already appear in sixteenth- and seventeenth-century Spanish and Portuguese political treatises. Concomitantly, the permanent confrontation with the Maghreb, as well as the considerable volume of ransom and exchange operations, including commercial transactions, had a powerful influence on the constitution of the myth of oriental despotism in Europe. Numerous sixteenth- and seventeenth-century works describe Muslim rulers as despotic and capricious men, known for their uncontrollable lust, while other accounts depict the more remote Ottoman Sultans as tyrannical rulers, notorious for their treachery.

Such were the views of countless Europeans who represented Turks and Moors as the picture of barbaric ignorance and lust. As noted earlier, the stereotype of the devilish Moor or the vicious Turk was often employed by European writers to demonstrate the iniquities of Islam, and to portray Muslims as agents of Satan.[87] A typical example is that of the Trinitarian Pierre Dan, a ransoming friar who visited Algiers, Tunis, Fès, Tripoli, and Salé in the 1630s. His *Histoire de la Barbarie et de ses corsaires* [History of Barbary and of its corsairs] (1649), published upon his return to France, abounds in bizarre stories of cannibalism, terrible tortures, and unspeakable horrors. Significantly, the second part of this title emphasizes the cruelty, banditry, and witchcraft of the Algerians: *Ov il est traitté de levr govvernement, de leurs mœurs, de leurs cruautez, de leurs brigandages, de leurs sortileges* . . . . [Which discusses their government, their customs, their cruelty, their brigandage, their spells . . .].

Some enlightened Europeans, however, viewed Islam under different perspectives. Two examples suffice. The Habsburg Ambassador to the Sublime Porte, Ogier Ghiselin de Busbecq (1522–1592), who sojourned in Constantinople between 1554 and 1562, recounted both his personal experiences at Süleyman's court and his views of Ottoman politics. His lively *Turkish Letters* (1585), which circulated throughout Europe in Latin and in various vernacular languages, constitute an extraordinary and keen source of information on the Ottoman Empire. Worth noting are Busbecq's comments on Süleyman's court, included in his First Letter (1555), especially because they implicitly contrast Ottoman customs with contemporary European mores:

> The Sultan's head-quarters were crowded by numerous attendants, including many high officials. All the cavalry of the guard were there, the Spahis. . . . and a large number of Janissaries. In all that great assembly no single man owed his dignity to anything but his personal merits and bravery; no one is distinguished from the rest by his birth, and honor is paid to each man according to the nature of the duty and offices which he discharges. . . . The Sultan himself assigns to all their duties and offices, and in doing so, pays no attention to wealth or the empty chains of ranks.[88]

Certainly, such commentaries disclose a veiled criticism of western Europe's obsession with nobility and aristocratic lineage, as well as a clear admiration for Turkish meritocracy.

Another suggestive work on the Turks is the anonymous *Viaje de Turquía* [*Voyage to Turkey*] (ca. 1558), a sixteenth-century Spanish treatise influenced by the ideals of Erasmus. Although the author presents the Ottoman Turks as Spain's religious and political enemies, he praises their way of life and the good functioning of their society, which he contrasts with the decadence of contemporary Western mores, especially Spanish. Cervantes's fictions similarly confirm that educated Europeans who had lived in close contact with Muslims were not prone to demonizing Islam in such a coarse way. The case of Antonio de Sosa is a special one. Certainly his books were written from the point of view of religious faith and political propaganda. Yet his personal experience as a captive in Algiers, including that of his family who suffered the same fate, suggests that these events influenced his vision of Muslims and of Algerians in particular. In spite of his sufferings, let us recall that the first book Sosa may have composed in his prison, his *Epítome de los reyes de Argel,* is a balanced work of research that shows a meticulous and impartial historian at work.

Sixteenth-Century Spanish Literature on North Africa

Sosa's *Topography* should be situated among the sixteenth-century Spanish ethnographic and historiographic works on North Africa.[89] One of the best known premodern works on Africa and the Maghreb is Leo Africanus's *History and Description of Africa,* initially released in Italian in the collection of travel accounts published by Giovanni Ramusio, entitled *Delle navigationi e viaggi* (Venice, 1550). Although Leo Africanus cannot be strictly considered an Iberian author, he was also known as al-Gharnati [the Grenadine], because he was born in Granada around 1489, or by the name al-Hasan b. Muhammad al Wazzan al-Fasi [the man of Fès]. Sometime after the conquest of Granada in 1492, Leo and his family immigrated to Fès, then a center of learning.[90] Around 1510, the future geographer joined the entourage of the Sultan Muhammad al-Burtughali (1505–1524), the ruler of Fès. Many of Leo's travels across the Maghreb, and through Constantinople, Egypt, Arabia, Babylonia, and parts of Persia, were conducted while carrying out diplomatic missions for the Sultan. Sailing back to Morocco in 1518, Leo was captured by Sicilian corsairs in Djerba and presented to Pope Leo X (Giovanni de' Medici), who had him catechized and baptized with his own name. Leo's *Description of Africa,* soon translated into French and Latin, was not only the first document known in the West on the Maghreb since the times of the Greco-Latin authors, but also an instant bestseller. Leo Africanus's firsthand geographic and ethnographic descriptions of the lands visited at the beginning of the sixteenth century make him one of the most important geographers and cultural commentators of the early modern period. His work greatly influenced various texts composed by Iberian authors, especially that of Antonio de Sosa, who often cites him as a source of information on premodern Algiers. Sosa himself reveals that, in 1579, he had a copy of Leo Africanus's *Descrip-*

tion of Africa in his prison cell.⁹¹ The book had been loaned to Sosa by a Morisco émigré from Granada brought up in Fès. This may be one of the most suggestive allusions to the circulation of Leo Africanus's book in Algiers and the Maghreb among exiled Moriscos and other learned Moors.⁹²

Equally worth noting is Luis del Mármol Carvajal's work on the Maghreb. This author had an insider's view of Morocco, having spent many years in Marrakesh as a prisoner. In 1535, he traveled to Tunis with Charles V's army and sometime thereafter was taken prisoner by corsairs off the coast of Tunisia. A captive of the Saʿdi Sultan Ahmad al-Aʿraj, who brought him to Marrakesh, Mármol only stayed in this city from 1541 to 1542, although he remained in captivity for almost eight years. During that time he learned Arabic and traveled across the Maghreb. After his ransom, he chose to remain in Africa and journeyed as far as Ethiopia and Egypt, collecting material for his extensive *Descripción general de África,* which he began writing upon his return to Spain, around 1570. An ambitious treatise with bookish pretensions, Mármol's *Descripción general* juxtaposes the author's experiences and observations with material borrowed from previous authors on the region, such as Leo Africanus, the Portuguese Damião de Góis, and various Arabic writers, such as Ibn Rashiq.⁹³ The first part of Mármol's *Descripción general* was published in Granada in 1573. The second part came out in 1599, financed by the author.⁹⁴ Both works were soon translated into French (1636, 1667).

Another sixteenth-century writer who turned his attention to the Maghreb was Diego de Torres, whose *Relación del origen y suceso de los Xarifes y de los Reinos de Marruecos, Fez, y Tarudante que tienen usurpados* [*Account of the Origin and Deeds of the Sharif and of the Kingdoms of Morocco, Fès, and Taroudant, which They Have Usurped*] was published in 1586. Torres's work has been praised as a first-rate source for the study of Morocco in the sixteenth century, in particular for the origins of the Sharif dynasty of the Saʿdis. The author arrived in Marrakesh in 1546, charged with ransoming captives for the Portuguese king João III, and remained there until 1550. Like Mármol, he learned Arabic and established good relations with Sultan Muhammad al-Shaikh, who is the protagonist of his history. In 1550, Torres was imprisoned for debts and had to follow Muhammad al-Shaikh's son, Muhammad al-Haran, across the Atlas Mountains to Taroudant, where Torres remained as a captive until 1553. He then traveled to Fès, where he lingered for a year. Not a cultured man, he nevertheless had a remarkable curiosity and great talents of observation. The book based on his experience was probably written after his return to Spain, between 1554 and 1575. Originally dedicated to King Sebastian of Portugal, it provided strategic information for the upcoming African campaign that resulted in the Battle of the Three Kings (1578). Torres's book was published posthumously in 1586.[95]

The *Relación del origen y suceso de los Xarifes* is a history of the Moroccan kingdoms from 1502 to 1574. The author recounts the ascension of the Sa'dis and their relations with the Portuguese "plazas" on the West coast of Africa. Torres also describes the various regions of Morocco, with emphasis on urban centers, economic and military resources, as well as their inhabitants, religious rites, and customs. The first part of his work, which depicts events that occurred from 1502 to 1546, is virtually lifted from Mármol's *Descripción general,* although Torres added much information directly taken from captives. The valuable and interesting second part includes fine chapters, such as those dedicated to the brief government of Abu Hassun in Fès, and to the participation of the Turks in this venture.[96]

The third Iberian work on North Africa, written in the sixteenth century, is Antonio de Sosa's *Topographia, e Historia general de Argel,* a study of Algiers and of Ottoman politics and social organization, which was ascribed to Diego de Haedo since its publication in 1612. The present work, the *Topography of Algiers,* constitutes the first part of this monumental five-book ethnographic and historical treatise, which, according to historian Mercedes García-Arenal, is "the most sophisticated and by far the most original of these histories and descriptions of North Africa."[97] I will shortly explain the reasons for this fraud that attributed Sosa's work to another man. Yet the idea underlying all of these works, including Sosa's *Topography,* is that of colonization, as suggested by the title of Torres's *Relación del origen y suceso de los Xarifes y de los Reinos de Marruecos, Fez, y Tarudante que tienen usurpados.* By turning the rulers of the Moroccan kingdom into "usurpers," this title reveals the clear political agenda of Torres's work.

"Captive Territories"

García-Arenal has argued that European colonizers of the Maghreb, coming from diverse countries and in different periods, have used similar ideological arguments to justify their occupation of such areas. In effect, French colonial historiography, when referring to North Africa, frequently interpreted the history of this region as founded on the brilliant past civilizations created by the Roman and Byzantine empires. This approach viewed the Arabo-Muslim conquest as a catastrophe that plunged the North African territories into anarchy and obscurity, a situation that begged for the intervention of the Christian West, who would return these lands to their native populations, the Berbers.[98] As discussed earlier, these ideas were already being discussed by sixteenth-century Spanish writers. Torres himself begins his description of Barbary by stating that, in the time of Heraclius (ca. 575–641), the Byzantine Empire lost these territories; since then, they have "been occupied by primitive and base people without refinement in letters or arms. So, that it can be rightly said that they [the territories] have been held captive."[99]

Both Torres's and Sosa's works expose their political program by providing detailed information on the defenses of cities, the weak points in the ramparts, and the state of their artillery, among other data. Sosa, moreover, gives explicit directions for a Spanish invasion of Algiers. Describing the forts outside the city walls, he states:

> This whole fortification is dominated by and vulnerable to a mountain on its right hand, directly toward the west at some 150 paces, more or less, where an enemy with artillery could disturb all help coming from the city. There are also three other hills toward the south and east . . . , from which locations it would be easy to put up a good cannon fight. Between the fort and the mountains there are, in addition, great fissures . . . . Because these are deep, they could serve as trenches for as many soldiers as one would want, great numbers of men, who could remain hidden in them and, from there, attack the Turks in the castle (chapter 9).[100]

Mármol Carvajal also agrees with these interventionist opinions, as expressed in his prologue to his *Descripción general de África*. He reiterates throughout the first part of his work that Africa offered marvelous possibilities to the Spanish Crown for economic and commercial operations. For similar reasons, the chronicler Ambrosio de Morales, who approved the *Descripción general de África* for publication, praises the subject matter of this treatise: since Africa is "so close to Spain, and such an enemy, it is of great benefit to know her particularly well, both for peace and war, so that it can be treated with the advantages that come from knowing the land and its particularities."[101]

Andrew Hess has demonstrated that, after 1580, the Spanish and North African civilizations separated paths and responded in distinctive ways to the problems that arose within their own societies.[102] Yet the way they regarded each other continued unchanged for a long time. Moroccan travelers in Spain, such as the Wazir Muhammad ibn ʿAbd al Wahab al-Ghassani, ambassador of Mawlay Ismaʿil, who visited the Peninsula from 1690 to 1691, wrote accounts analogous to those composed by Iberians on the Maghreb. Like other reports composed by Maghrebi voyagers, al-Ghassani's *Voyage en Espagne* includes detailed descriptions of routes, bridges, and fortifications, to strategic military ends. In the same way that Christians attempted to find vestiges of Roman or Christian civilizations in North Africa or among the Berbers, Moroccan travelers in Spain constantly encountered Islamic relics and residues in the places they visited, including the descendants of the Moriscos who still felt an attraction for Islam.[103] Prejudices and outlooks, then, were not only amazingly similar in both societies in their views of each other, but also subsisted over time, conditioned by centuries of frontier life, war, and mutual mistrust. The current battles between Islam and the West suggest that the reciprocal demonizing remains unchanged.

Antonio de Sosa and Miguel de Cervantes

Antonio de Sosa's captivity in Algiers is so tightly connected with that of Cervantes that it is impossible to mention the Portuguese captive without referring to Spain's greatest writer. During the course of research for my study *Cervantes in Algiers: A Captive's Tale,* I encountered the figure of Doctor Antonio de Sosa, not only one of Cervantes's close friends in captivity but, as it turns out, also his first biographer. My interest in Sosa centered on his reading and writing day after day during his captivity, obsessively recording every bit of information obtained from Christian slaves and their captors. The fact that Sosa transformed his captivity into a scenario for writing, and his tiny prison cell into a writer's "garret"— complete with books, paper, pen, and ink—is astounding. Sosa was Cervantes's interlocutor and literary critic for almost four years, during which time the young soldier Cervantes and the erudite cleric Sosa shared numerous conversations about poetry and literature. Their relation sheds an intense light on Cervantes's life in Barbary.[104]

The story of Cervantes's second escape attempt—the episode of the cave—appears in Sosa's *Diálogo de los mártires de Argel,* included in the *Topographia,* among various reports on the martyrdom of several Christian captives and renegades. Sosa identified Cervantes as a "hidalgo" [a gentleman] from Alcalá de Henares. This information, discovered in 1752, led Agustín Montiano y Luyardo to look for Cervantes's baptismal records in the churches of this city.[105] Sosa's work, then, was crucial to the eighteenth-century discovery of Cervantes's birthplace. In turn, vital information on Antonio de Sosa emerges in the testimonies collected by Cervantes in the so-called *Información de Argel,* a notarized inquest organized by Cervantes himself after his liberation in 1580.[106] For this legal inquiry, Cervantes wrote twenty-five questions regarding his captivity and habits, answered by twelve witnesses in the presence of the head of the Trinitarian rescue mission in Algiers, Fra Juan Gil, and of the apostolic notary Pedro de Rivera.[107]

Doctor Antonio de Sosa appears in this inquest as the most respected witness among the group of captives and free men who testified on Cervantes's behalf. Sosa verifies his close friendship with Cervantes as well as their confidential conversations (*conversación estrecha*) during the time of their captivity in Algiers: "all the time that I have been a captive in Algiers, which is three years and eight months, I have known him [Cervantes] and have very often dealt and communicated with him in a familiar way."[108] Alluding to his literary exchanges with Cervantes, Sosa confirms that the former soldier wrote poetry during his captivity, such as the religious poems he composed "in praise of

Our Lord and his blessed Mother," some of which he sent to Sosa and discussed with him in private.[109]

Yet Cervantes also wrote secular poetry during his imprisonment in Algiers, such as the recently rediscovered "Epístola a Mateo Vázquez," a monumental epistle in verse written in 1577 to Philip II's secretary, during the feverish months when the Spanish captive and various friends planned a collective escape from Algiers.[110] The "Epistle to Mateo Vázquez" represents one of the few biographical testimonies written in captivity by Cervantes, a piece that, according to his earlier testimony, Sosa must have also read. Concurrently, Sosa states in his affidavit that Cervantes always discussed his escape plans with him: "I was one of those who communicated in heavy secrecy with Miguel de Cervantes about the said business [of the escape], and for this business I was invited several times and exhorted to come." In fact, nothing was done on this front without Sosa's considered opinion. While the fugitives were hiding in the cave, Cervantes visited Sosa and enticed him to join them, "begging me many times to hide with the others in the said cave; and the day he went into hiding in it, he came to say good-bye to me."[111] These declarations indicate a high level of friendship between the younger and older man and also an unconditional trust between them.

To be sure, Sosa surmounted extraordinary difficulties in order to submit his deposition on behalf of Cervantes in October 1580. Because Sosa's master generally kept him chained, in "continuous and tight confinement," the captive was not allowed to appear in person at the official inquiry organized by Cervantes in conjunction with Fra Juan Gil.[112] Instead, Sosa managed to send an affidavit composed in his own hand, in which he answered each and every one of the questions redacted by Cervantes. Sosa's testimony—one of the longest and most eloquent statements of the *Información de Argel*—arrived on 22 October 1580, after the inquest had been formally closed. This news pressured Fra Juan Gil to reopen the investigation in order to include the latest deposition, as confirmed by a postscript, in which he declares that he appends this affidavit in Doctor Sosa's handwriting and signature, which he knows quite well.[113] Fra Juan Gil's closing words in the *Información de Argel* reveal his high esteem for Sosa:

I, Fra Juan Gil, from the Order of the Holy Trinity, ransomer of captives in this Algiers on behalf of His Majesty, state that I know Doctor Antonio de Sosa, presently a captive in Algiers, because I deal with him familiarly and converse with him all the time that I have been in Algiers; and I know that he is so honorable and of such qualities, that in what he has declared above he would say nothing but the pure truth, as the truthful man he is.[114]

Antonio de Sosa's Captivity

Antonio de Sosa was captured in April 1577, along with 290 other passengers, aboard the galley *San Pablo* from the Order of Malta, as they sailed from Barcelona to Valletta (chapter 35). I referred earlier to the Christian military Order of Saint John of Jerusalem of Malta, which had been established by Charles V on this island after the conquest of Rhodes by the Ottomans. From Malta the Christian Knights sailed through the Mediterranean in pursuit of Muslim ships that they captured, together with booty and slaves that they took back to Valetta. Traveling aboard the galleys of the *Sacra Religión* [Sacred Religion], as the Order of Malta was then called, usually ensured a safe passage for Christians across the western Mediterranean. The galleys of the Order not only sailed together in well-armed squadrons, but they were also deeply feared by the Barbary corsairs. As was customary, Sosa was to cross the channel between Malta and Sicily in order to go to Agrigento, where he had recently obtained a distinguished ecclesiastical position.

Freshly constructed in Barcelona, the galley *San Pablo* set sail from this port in the last days of March 1577 accompanied by two other ships of the Order of Malta. A violent storm separated the *San Pablo* from the contingent of Christian galleys, which continued on their own toward Valletta. Several sailors who jumped overboard in the moment of the Algerian corsair's assault declared that the ship had been swept by a terrible tempest, running in such a wild course across the Mediterranean that the crew had to throw the oars, the sails, and most of the firearms into the sea.[115] Semi-destroyed by the storm and devoid of artillery, the *San Pablo* took refuge in the island of San Pedro, near Sardinia, where it was attacked on 1 April 1577 by a squadron of twelve Algerian galliots commanded by Dali Mami—the same corsair captain who had captured Cervantes in 1575. In the fierce battle that ensued, the captain of the ship, a knight of Malta surnamed Botello, as well as other Knights of St. John of Malta and numerous crew members, was killed. The surviving passengers, including Doctor Antonio de Sosa and his family, as well as several Knights of Malta, were taken as captives to Algiers.[116]

Throughout the five books of his monumental work, particularly in his *Epítome,* Sosa repeatedly mentions the capture of the *San Pablo*.[117] Cervantes also describes the capture of this galley in his play *El trato de Argel* [*Life in Algiers*] through his spokeswoman, the Algerian beauty Zahara. Significantly, Zahara's story corresponds almost literally to the testimonies of the sailors who escaped from the *San Pablo* in the middle of the fray, swimming ashore to the island of San Pedro. In the play, the corsair attack is later discussed by Zahara and Silvia, a Christian slave, who states: "The galley of which you speak, I believe, was called the *San Pablo,* and it was new, and of the Sacred Religion of Malta. I was captured in that galley" (*Trato* 2.1284–86). Having received firsthand information about this event from his friend Sosa, Cervantes later transposed it into his first drama staged in Madrid around 1583, giving Sosa's capture to the character Silvia.

Sosa's Master: Muhammad, the Jew

Like most captives, Sosa was probably sold in the busy marketplace of Algiers, while, according to tradition, the abducted vessel went to the *beylerbey* (provincial governor) of the Turkish-Algerian Regency, Ramadan Pasha, as his share of the booty. As an ecclesiastic who belonged to the highest echelons of the Hispano-Italian Church, Sosa was a prized captive who could elicit a large ransom. He ended up in the hands of the Jewish renegade Mahamed [Muhammad], together with a knight of Malta and another priest, both of whom were incarcerated with Sosa in Muhammad's quarters. In *Cervantes in Algiers,* I document Sosa's life as a slave in the house-prison of Ka'id Muhammad, a municipal official who was in charge of the mint in Algiers.[118] Listed as one of the twenty-three principal *ka'ids*[119] living in 1581, Muhammad also owned a fifteen-bench corsair galliot, which brought him additional revenues (see chapters 14 and 22 in this volume). This Jewish renegade had originally converted from Judaism to Islam, then to Christianity, only to return to Islam again after escaping from a long captivity in Genoa.[120] His shifting allegiances identify him as one of the numerous sixteenth-century converts to Islam, both Muslims and half-Muslims, who lived in the *in-between,* their lives plainly at the border.

Veiled allusions to Sosa's master Muhammad repeatedly surface in the *Topography,* especially in regard to the counterfeiting of money in the public treasury, where great quantities of copper were apparently mixed with silver to turn it into an alloy. In his *Diálogo de la captividad,* Sosa refers to Muhammad's illegal activities, including his involvement in usury: "He does nothing else but occupy his days and nights in rummaging through money, counting money, bustling about money, amassing money, melting gold and silver, practicing alchemy, and coining false money."[121] A clever and deceitful man, Muhammad inspired a common proverb in Algiers: "Malicious and astute like the ka'id Muhammad, the Jew." His oscillating loyalties led one of Sosa's interlocutors to portray him as an unbelieving "atheist" who did not uphold any religion.[122]

With his conversion to Islam, Muhammad probably sought to avoid the ill-treatment received by Jews in Algiers and other North African cities, where they were continuously abused. Sosa notes in his *Topography* that the Jews were situated at the lowest point of the social echelon, even below the Christian slaves in Algiers (chapter 28). Along the same lines, the traveler Mármol Carvajal claimed that "the Jews of Africa are extremely despised by the Moors and wherever they go they spit in their faces and beat them, and they don't permit them to wear shoes, except for some favorite or secretary of the king, or of the ka'ids; all the others wear straw espadrilles."[123] Leo Africanus also referred to the dress restrictions imposed on the Jews of Fès in the early sixteenth century, as well as to the contempt expressed for them.[124] By "turning Turk," Muhammad not only ensured for himself fair treatment from his fellow Muslims but also acceded to highly successful official positions, such as the management of the public treasury in Algiers.[125]

Converting to another religion in the sixteenth century was a kind of passport for those whose circumstances compelled them to live, literally, on the edge. Muhammad's conversion, in effect, freed him from the arbitrary actions of the ruler Hasan Pasha. Upon his arrival in Algiers in June 1577, the renegade Hasan the Venetian proceeded to govern aggressively with the sole aim of increasing his personal fortune. Raising taxes enormously, he also seized elite Christian captives being held for ransom from their Turkish or Moorish masters. Ka'id Muhammad was the only citizen in Algiers to oppose these actions, adamantly refusing to let go of his Christian slaves.[126] Muhammad's conversion to Islam, as well as his overt defiance of the ruler's orders, thwarted Hasan Pasha's efforts to take hold of these captives, one of whom was Doctor Sosa. If a Jew had become a Muslim, the beylerbey could not appropriate his slaves. As it turns out, Muhammad's rebelliousness cost Sosa four and a half years of captivity. The huge price invested in his mysterious liberation, as we shall see, suggests that Hasan Pasha increased the value of these captives, forcing Muhammad to pay him a sizeable quota of the ransom.[127]

Sosa's works, especially his two Dialogues on captivity and his ensuing debate between Christianity and Islam (*Dialogue on marabouts*), are rich sources of information about his incarceration in Muhammad's house-prison and the way that he occupied his time reading and writing. In fact, the unsung protagonist of these autobiographical Dialogues is a character named Antonio de Sosa. Amazing as it was, Sosa was able to convert a traumatic event (captivity) into an enriching experience that offered new perceptions on daily life in a Muslim city from the perspective of a European observer. His feat is even more astounding if we take into account the circumstances of his imprisonment in Muhammad's house. Through his spokesman Antonio González de Torres, his Portuguese interlocutor in the *Diálogo de la captividad*, Sosa represents the conditions of his captivity. González de Torres first remarks that even bandits and conspirators against a king were not held in such tight confinement. Next he asks whether it is possible that a man whose only guilt is to have become the slave of a barbarian could be kept "so naked, so hungry, charged with fetters, chained to a stone, locked up for such a long time, alone, . . . and interred in a remote, cold, humid, and obscure chamber. Can there be such cruelty or evil?" Sosa's interlocutor then adds a description of the damp and putrid dungeon below Sosa's cell, into which the captive was thrown three times, in chains, barely coming out alive. Sosa's persona intervenes here to give the exact measurements of the fetid dungeon, which was twenty spans deep by nine spans wide by eleven spans long—a narrow subterranean dungeon surrounded on three sides by a cistern.[128] One can imagine that this was a punishment imposed on Sosa by his master for some misconduct, perhaps for attempting to escape.

Obviously, the earlier criticisms of Muhammad's abuses, spoken through his friend's mouth, are part of the work composed by Sosa himself. I have chosen to take these declarations regarding Sosa's vicissitudes as a captive at face value, primarily because captivity itself plays a central role in substantiating the veracity of his account. As a Catholic priest, moreover, Sosa would have been mistreated by the Algerians in retaliation for the actions of the Inquisition against Muslims in the Peninsula. What is more, my findings in various Spanish and Italian archives corroborate that, during the four and a half years of his incarceration in Barbary, Sosa wrote continuously to Philip II about his ordeal. Like other captives, he begged the king for funds for his rescue. In another passage of his work, Sosa reveals that, during these years, he was locked in a dungeon, covered with chains, and shackled to a stone;[129] he also claims that he had been often forced to haul rocks and sand, and to mix lime, while chained, without being fed until the evening; and, finally, that he had gone hungry, when sick, for Muhammad withheld his ration of bread from him, thinking he was going to die.[130]

The treatment given to captives in sixteenth-century Algiers obviously depended on who their owners were. While some private owners kept their captives fettered in dungeons or in private bagnios, others regarded their slaves as part of their households. In this case, their living arrangements were determined by their status in that particular house. The fact that Sosa was an ecclesiastic with a prominent position in the Hispano-Italian Church surely influenced his treatment by Muhammad. Sosa recounts how Algerian corsairs, especially renegades, felt toward Christian priests, called *papaces* by the populace: "they have a terrible hatred and incredible loathing [for priests] and, therefore, with great gusto . . . they choose them and buy them in order to burn them."[131]

The persecution against Moriscos in Spain, Portugal, and Sicily, as well as the crimes committed against them by the Spanish Inquisition, certainly exacerbated the hatred felt by Algerians toward Iberian priests. The corsairs similarly exploited the status of churchmen who held important ecclesiastical posts in order to demand a higher ransom for them. Sosa depicts the standard handling of elite captives during the bargaining over ransoms that initiated captivity in Algiers. First treated with courtesy, the captive was then threatened and told that his true identity had been discovered—that he was a marquis or a grandee of Spain, the son of a duke, or even a cousin to the king—after which he was chained, often beaten, and thrown into solitary confinement with more irons. Sosa's concluding words surely refer to his own experiences as a captive: "And if he is an ecclesiastic and has a good appearance, to what position do they raise him? They don't say anything less of him . . . but that he is a cardinal, or at least an archbishop and patriarch."[132] Despite these denunciations, Sosa's captivity in the household of an important municipal officer of the city offered him a privileged point of observation on Algerian society at the end of the sixteenth century.

In another context, anthropologist Neil Whitehead has argued that captivity, "understood as a physical detention or a subjective intellectual fascination, is a crucial condition of possibility for ethnography, suggesting that as a literary form ethnography is coextensive with the emergence of travel writing."[133] Whitehead confirms that early cross-cultural contacts and close experience of others paved the way for the foundation of ethnography as a "professional practice" in the early twentieth century. Yet early modern travel accounts were no less productive of the types of insight and understanding which this discipline sought to regulate and control.[134] The *Topography*, in fact, is constructed like a contemporary ethnographic monograph with descriptions of the material culture, kinship, marriage, death rituals, and religious beliefs in Algiers at the end of the sixteenth century.

Sosa's exceptional experience as a captive who lived in intimate contact with the enemy forced him to engage actively in the lives of others. Let us recall Sosa's comments regarding the Jews of Algiers: "I can attest to this, having debated with some of them not infrequently" (chapter 28). His dynamic engagement with the inhabitants of Muhammad's household—Muslims, renegades, and Jews—would explain Sosa's rich vision of the customs of Algerian Jews, an insight also probably derived from his contacts with various visitors to his master's house. Other than Jews, we can identify a marabout who spoke to Sosa in the lingua franca of Algiers, as well as a renegade called Amud [Mahmud], who was Muhammad's son-in-law. Described as a "well-read man," Amud is Sosa's interlocutor in the *Diálogo de los morabutos,* a theological debate between Christianity and Islam that stands as one of the richest sources of ethnographic observations and autobiographical allusions in Sosa's work.[135]

In a revealing passage of this Dialogue, Sosa tells Amud: "the mistress, your mother-in-law, was telling me, the other day . . . ."[136] He then proceeds to recount a conversation he had with Amud's mother-in-law regarding certain festivities of Algerian women, such as the dinners and dances in which they invoked a familiar spirit (*djinn*) in order to cure sick women. This detailed information reappears in chapter 33 of the *Topography*. We shall never know how many of the anecdotes registered in Sosa's Dialogues correspond to real experiences lived by the author in Algiers. What these texts confirm, however, is that Sosa's data on Algerian women were acquired through his interaction with females either living in or passing through Muhammad's house.

According to Sosa, Muhammad's residence was one of the finest and largest in Algiers (chapter 39); this dwelling also accommodated various slaves as well as some of Muhammad's renegades. Following the model of an extended family, the household of an important ka'id or ra'is in Algiers would generally include a number of renegades who had been adopted or sponsored by the owner of the house, as well as Christian slaves, who varied in number according to the position and wealth of the ka'id or corsair captain. In regard to these customs, Sosa recounts that some Turks, Arabs, and other Algerian officials had "ten, twelve, fifteen, twenty or more of these renegades" in their household, "whom they call their sons and treat accordingly." When they converted to Islam, their owners generally provided them with letters of credit, including slaves and money (chapter 13).

Tal Shuval and other historians have shed light on these relations of patronage and affiliations to a certain "household," called *kapi bayt*,[137] which became a dominant feature in the Ottoman Empire in the middle of the sixteenth century.¹³⁸ Yet the kapis were not limited to the Ottoman Porte but also functioned in the provinces, where the governors modeled their "households" as a replica of that of the sultan, but on a smaller scale.¹³⁹ Such households functioned as "recruitment and integration centers in the military and administrative elites of the provinces" and of the Porte. From the end of the sixteenth century, then, the kapi became the principal military, political, economic and social unit in the Ottoman provinces.¹⁴⁰ This is illustrated by Sosa, who claims that the great corsair 'Uludj 'Ali Pasha, who was beylerbey of Algiers (1568–1571) and Grand Admiral of the Ottoman armada until his death in 1587, had in his household five hundred renegades that he called "sons" and treated as such.¹⁴¹

On a much reduced scale, Ka'id Muhammad's household in Algiers counted a Roman renegade named Jaffer [Djafar], who was being taught to read and write in Arabic by a marabout, or Muslim holy man; a French renegade called Mustafa, who died around 1579; a Greek renegade called Boluk-Bashi Farat; a young female captive from Corsica, whose cousin was also a slave in Algiers; an old Spanish slave called Pere Jordán, who was the porter of the compound; Doctor Sosa himself, as well as two anonymous captives who were his companions, a Knight of Malta and another priest.¹⁴²

The name of the Greek renegade Boluk-Bashi Farat identifies him as a high ranking janissary officer, a *boluk-bashi,* or captain of a division. This title was given to the commanders of the *boluks,* or infantry units of the *agha* (commander). The fact that he was a Greek renegade suggests that he had been recruited as a youth via the child levy (*devşirme* or *devshirme*) paid by Christian families living in Ottoman territories. His presence in Muhammad's quarters sheds light on Sosa's detailed knowledge of the janissary organization in Algiers, which allowed him to write five chapters on this elite Ottoman infantry corps, with detailed descriptions of its ranks, salaries, and customs during war and peace.

In spite of Sosa's reclusion, many Christian slaves visited him frequently, adding to the diversity of Muhammad's large household. In *Cervantes in Algiers,* I examine a long list of callers mentioned throughout his work who paid visits to Doctor Sosa, such as the galley slaves and other Christian captives who reported to the cleric about the happenings in Algiers.¹⁴³ These visitors included various renegades, such as the Spaniard Girón, known as El Dorador [The Gilder], who visited Sosa at the time of Cervantes's second escape attempt—the episode of the cave—swearing before the clergyman and his master Muhammad that he had not betrayed the fugitives. Recall that, on this occasion, all the escapees, including their leader Cervantes, were caught because of Girón's denunciation.¹⁴⁴ We may assume that these encounters were typical of the life of elite captives in the North African capital at the end of the sixteenth century. Sosa's multiple reunions with Christians of every social class and provenance—from various galley slaves to the Knight of Malta Antonio González de Torres, the captive Cervantes, and the Trinitarian priest Fra Juan Gil—illuminate the diverse relations among slaves in Algiers. In addition, the possibility of speaking to many renegades, such as those who lived in Muhammad's house, including the above-mentioned Amud, allowed Sosa to elaborate a meticulous tableau of the social practices and events of the city.

I discussed earlier the political constraints and religious ideology that marked sixteenth-century Iberian and other European travel accounts and historiographic works on North Africa. Such methods of knowing are no less problematic today than in Sosa's time. The ways in which personal inclinations subvert ideal "objective" reporting have been at the center of debates on ethnographic literature in the last four decades. Since the 1970s, in effect, valid ethnographic observation advocates the need to position the observer in the context of his or her own observations.¹⁴⁵ I also referred to Sosa's inflexible religious position and to his efforts to denounce the traffic in human lives sustained by the Algerians. Whitehead's anthropological analysis of Hans Staden's sixteenth-century captivity in Brazil, among the Tupinambá, illuminates these issues. The critic proposes that ethnographic reporting should not be seen as "objective" in the manner of social science but rather as "interpretative" in the manner of humanistic deliberation and discussion.¹⁴⁶ In the same way, during the course of his ethnographic observations in Algiers, Sosa interpreted a variety of local mores, in particular, Islamic rituals, according to his religious proclivities. For that reason, the question we should ask in regard to his ethnographic work is not how objective or progressive his intellectual approach was—it clearly raises criticisms from the contemporary reader and critic—but rather whether, as a captive in a Muslim city, Sosa was in a position to make any affirmations about Algerian culture in general, and whether what he asserts, given what we know of his milieu, conditions of captivity, and cultural frame of mind, reveals anything about his captors. In this respect, I propose that, beyond his religious proclivities, Sosa's ethnographic account offers a wide variety of riches for the contemporary reader interested in early modern cultural contacts with Islam.

"Reading Saintly and Good Books"

I would like to close this section on Sosa's captivity with a discussion of his relation to books and literature in general. As we know, Sosa was allowed to have books on hand and to write in his prison cell in Muhammad's house. As mentioned earlier, since his arrival in Algiers, Sosa wrote constantly, annotating each day the events that marked both his confinement and compulsory walks through the city en route to forced labor. Throughout his Dialogues, he repeatedly describes his writing habits, the revisions he was making to the texts he was composing, as well as the titles and subjects of the texts and books he was reading. We saw earlier that one of these works, Leo Africanus's *Description of Africa*, was loaned to Sosa by an exiled Morisco brought up in Fès. The second book Sosa had in his cell was a biography of Saint Paulinus, Bishop of Nola (ca. 355–431), an epistolary friend of Saint Augustine who spent all his fortune rescuing captives.[147] This book may have been given to Sosa by one of the visitors who came to the house, or he could have bought it from Algerian corsairs.[148]

An illuminating passage in the *Diálogo de los mártires de Argel* expands our view of Sosa's reading habits. Captain Jerónimo Ramírez, a historical personage who reappears in Sosa's text as the interlocutor of the protagonist, whose name is also Antonio de Sosa, greets the captive with this question: "So, every time I come, must I find you occupied with books?" Sosa's answer confirms that he spent much time reading: "In solitude such as this, and in an imprisonment so closed off from every talk and conversation . . . , what better occupation is there than reading saintly and good books?"[149] Sosa's introduction to this Dialogue, moreover, is a song to the book, an exaltation of the classic and Christian traditions that he absorbed, together with his legal and theological education. Significantly, his praise of books and reading is reiterated throughout his three Dialogues. For Sosa, "those books which teach and show us how to live in whatever way, form, style, and artful device, . . . are nothing less than rich and beautiful gardens, where Judgment, walking or strolling around attentively, goes about collecting lovely and very gentle flowers."[150] Granted, this was a Renaissance topos later echoed by Cervantes, but it is an important one to keep in mind in the context of Sosa's captivity. In the same way, Sosa refers to a "Republic of Letters" constituted by a crowd of learned captives in Algiers—ecclesiastics, priests, lawyers, jurists, doctors, teachers, and preachers from various nations and languages. Sosa, in fact, counted sixty-two erudite slaves imprisoned in Algiers in 1579: "Something never seen in Barbary!"[151] His allusions to the time he spent reading and writing emphasize the existence of this cultural network, one also highlighted by the conversations on literary matters that he presumably had with captives such as Cervantes. All these activities shed light on Sosa's keen interest in Algerian customs and history, an interest that allowed him to collect the abundant ethnographic and historical data included in his work.

A Tale of Two Authors

Since the 1970s, Antonio de Sosa has been definitively identified as the true author of the *Topographia, e Historia general de Argel* (1612), attributed for centuries to Diego de Haedo. As what follows will show, the reasons for the fraud that ascribed Sosa's work to another man were of a scandalous nature. The *Topographia* was edited and published in Valladolid, in 1612, by the Benedictine abbot Diego de Haedo, who credited the work to his uncle, the late Archbishop Diego de Haedo of Palermo, Sicily—*both* uncle and nephew had the same name. In his dedication, Fra Diego de Haedo affirms that he obtained the papers on captivity from his uncle (Haedo the elder) while he was in Palermo at his service. In effect, the younger Haedo traveled to Sicily in 1593 and remained with his uncle as his personal secretary until 1599. According to Fra Diego, Archbishop Haedo, "informed by Christian captives who were many years in Algiers, especially about what is contained in the *Diálogos* [Dialogues]," composed these materials "and delivered them, if only in a draft version" into his keeping. Fra Diego claimed that he himself polished these drafts, putting much diligent work into them, and "giving them final form and essence" (see his Dedicatory Letter in this volume).

Certainly, the mention of the Dialogues flashes here like a neon sign, calling attention to works clearly authored by Sosa. As noted earlier, the autobiographical nature of Sosa's three Dialogues is undeniable, more so, if we consider that Sosa is the protagonist of, and the common interlocutor in, his Dialogues on captivity and marabouts, where he appears as a persona with his own name: "Antonio de Sosa." Fra Diego de Haedo's dedication to his uncle, the late archbishop of Palermo, reveals other contradictions. To begin, there is no possibility that Archbishop Haedo could have composed this treatise from reports provided by former captives who arrived in Sicily. The *Topography* covers hundreds of pages with meticulous details about life in Algiers in the 1570s—including descriptions of its history, geography, principal buildings, streets, different inhabitants, customs, governmental institutions, and the ordeals of Christian captives—while its author speaks on numerous occasions as an eyewitness who offers his personal views. The elder Diego de Haedo, moreover, never set foot in Algiers: between 1577 and 1581, when Sosa was a captive in the North African city, Haedo was advancing his career as an Inquisitor in Palermo, known for his fierce defense of the Spanish Inquisition in Sicily.

Early in his career, the *licenciado* (graduate) Haedo had acted as the prosecutor in the Inquisition trial of the renowned Spanish poet Fra Luis de León (1572–1576), although only during the first six months of the process (5 May–13 November 1572). Ángel Alcalá has transcribed and published this atrocious Inquisition trial, revealing that the prosecutor Haedo even recommended the application of torture so that Fra Luis de León would declare "the entire truth."[152] Soon promoted to Inquisitor in Valencia, Haedo remained in this post until August 1573, when he was assigned to the Inquisition of Zaragoza.[153] In April 1577, he was appointed Inquisitor in Sicily, together with the licenciado Juan de Rojas—it was customary for the Spanish Inquisition to have two or three Inquisitors at the same time in one site. Both Haedo and Rojas arrived in Sicily in October 1577 and immediately entered into serious conflicts with the new viceroy, Marco Antonio Colonna, over ecclesiastical and civil jurisdictions in Palermo.[154]

To shed light on these controversies, we should note that the Spanish Inquisition, imposed in Sicily by Ferdinand the Catholic, consolidated its position with difficulty during the reign of Charles V. Around the middle of the sixteenth century, however, under Philip II, the Inquisition's political-institutional functions were transformed into a "specific element of absolutism and of the Spanish administrative model in the island." From being the protector of the Catholic faith, the Sicilian Inquisition turned into the guarantor of fidelity to the Spanish Crown and into a fastidious investigator of the political conscience of the ministry and the Spanish State's official character.[155]

In addition, the Sicilian Inquisition was entirely independent of the viceroy. Inquisitors were appointed by the Council of the Inquisition (called the Suprema) in Madrid, with the king's approval.[156] As Inquisitor Haedo claimed in reports sent to the Suprema or directly to Philip II regarding the role of the Holy Office in the Kingdom of Sicily, the Spanish Inquisition is "un muro fortísimo que lo defiende de la invasión de los heréticos y lo mantiene bajo la obediencia de la Iglesia y de Vuestra Majestad" [a very strong wall that defends the kingdom from the invasion of heretics and maintains it under the obedience of the Church and of Your Majesty].[157] Historian Vittorio Sciuti Russi explains that this "very strong wall" was constructed with an "extremely authoritative organization in the center," which became quite "diffuse in the periphery." At the apex, in the capital of the kingdom, were "three inquisitors and a prosecutor, various secretaries, all Spaniards, a recipient, many consultants, commissaries, and porters." At the periphery, "familiars," or lay officers, of the Inquisition, chosen "among the most spirited," were posted in every city of the island, even in hamlets with sixty inhabitants.[158] In a letter to Philip II, dated 13 November 1577, Viceroy Marco Antonio Colonna claimed that there were some thirty thousand "familiars" of the Inquisition in the island, chosen among "all the rich people, noblemen, and even delinquents."[159] Moreover, the criminal and civil law cases involving the lay officers of the Holy Office were tried in Inquisition courts. Since these cases did not involve suspected heresy, they were treated with great leniency by the judges of the Holy Office. Both Colonna and his predecessors complained bitterly about the impossibility of maintaining justice and governmental authority when the officers of the Inquisition evaded just punishment.

Webs of Patronage: Courtly and Ecclesiastical

Certainly, the Spanish court was a highly developed administrative powerhouse which functioned through institutions that had a stable and permanent character. Their activities and jurisdiction were, in turn, regulated by ordinances and regal instructions. Yet such administrative techniques, bylaws, and ordinances existed side by side with forms of power manipulation that were basically patrimonial. As Manuel Rivero Rodríguez and other Spanish historians have argued, early modern Spain functioned though a hierarchical administration grounded on legal principles that coexisted with a personalization of power. Philip II's ministers and officers of the law acted as filters between the king and the outside world, so that even if the monarch personally exerted an enormous influence and power in all of his territories, both the information he received and the decisions he took passed through the hands of his collaborators, who controlled the selection and appointment of positions, ecclesiastical benefices, and privileges.[160]

The system thus favored the creation of factions who fought for control of the power apparatus. In regard to the French court, Norbert Elias claims that, when private interests were mixed with official business, it was inevitable that government matters would be influenced by family rivalries, personal friendships and enmities, as well as by individual ambitions regarding the increase of patrimony and social promotion.[161] The webs of patronage, then, were transformed into "political parties," which could be easily represented through ideological portrayals. Their real function, however, was to snatch power resources and available posts from rival groups in order to secure and augment their own, even as factions competed ferociously for regal favor.[162] On the other hand, the political agitation and invested interests found at the Spanish court encountered their mirror image and continuation in Spain's European and American possessions. Sicily, of course, replicated these formulas. This meant that noblemen, viceroys, Inquisitors, and other corporations had their agents or ambassadors in Madrid working constantly for them, lobbying for their causes, and passing on information on the latest happenings and political maneuvers that could touch their interests both in Madrid and in Sicily. Similar movements simultaneously took place at the court. The Italian viceroyalties were rich fountains of employment and privileges, coveted by the king's ministers, who assigned them to their cliques and dependents. The political writer Scipio di Castro not only shed light on the complicity existing between the *local* (Sicilian) and *central* circles of power, but also claimed that the only way to sustain the government of Sicily was to maintain the connivance between the viceroy and those who held the reins of power at court.[163]

In a political territory such as the kingdom of Sicily, where the Spanish monarchy could barely offer posts to those who were not Sicilians, the role of the Inquisition became necessarily political: it exerted control over the institutional apparatus of power that was in the hands of the local inhabitants. Claiming independence from ordinary tribunals and the authority of the viceroy, and thanks to the privileges bestowed on the officers of the Inquisition, the Holy Office "destabilized the juridical order of the kingdom, segregating from it an important part of the social body of the island."[164] Under the circumstances, the conflicts between Inquisitor Haedo and Viceroy Colonna escalated continuously during Colonna's office, while Haedo wrote increasingly frantic letters to Madrid accusing the viceroy of sedition and other sins.[165] The warring parties were finally forced to come to an agreement through the Concordia of Badajoz, drawn by the Suprema and the Council of Italy, a document approved by Philip II in Badajoz, on 4 July 1580. Upholding and amplifying the privileges of the Holy Office in Sicily to the detriment of civil authority, this document confirmed the Spanish Inquisition's right of jurisdiction over all civil and criminal matters in which their lay officers were involved.

Colonna nevertheless retaliated with a series of pragmatics which attempted to reinforce the power of civil courts. He was then accused by Inquisitors Haedo and Rojas of printing writings against the Inquisition, of being a Lutheran heretic, of governing in immoral ways, even as they sent one memorandum after another to Madrid requesting Philip II to limit the viceroy's powers.[166] Haedo wrote increasingly hysterical letters to the king, claiming that the viceroy of Sicily could be a danger to royal authority, since rumors suggested that he was planning to sell the island to the French or to the Turks, or even make himself king, while the Inquisitors would always be faithful to the Suprema and to the king.[167] Colonna's mysterious death in Medinacelli, Spain, on 1 August 1584, sealed the triumph of the Inquisition in Sicily, especially of Haedo's conspicuous actions against the viceroy.[168]

During Haedo's tenure, then, the Spanish Inquisition consolidated its power in the island. With the support of Philip II, the Holy Office in Sicily, as mentioned earlier, was converted into an extraordinary instrument of political and social control. Philip II rewarded Haedo for his zeal by appointing him bishop of Agrigento, Sicily, in October 1584.[169] The former Inquisitor took formal possession of his new post in April 1585. Four years later, Haedo was elevated to the highest ecclesiastical seat in Palermo, where he remained until his death in 1608. In the above discussion, I have attempted to show the influence that Diego de Haedo had both in Sicily and in Madrid, the ramifications of which will become clear below. His intense activities as Inquisitor in Sicily during the time that Sosa was a captive in Algiers (1577–1581) also prove the impossibility of his presumed incarceration in Barbary during these years.

The suggestion that the true author of the *Topographia* was Antonio de Sosa is not new. French historians Ferdinand Denis and Henri-Delmas de Grammont were the first to detect something suspicious about the way the work was put together. Denis, who supposed that Haedo traveled to Algiers in 1605, found it questionable that this sophisticated treatise could have been put together in Sicily from accounts given by former slaves.[170] In 1902, the erudite Spanish bibliographer Cristóbal Pérez Pastor reproduced a Memorandum written to Pope Gregory XIII by various captives from Algiers. He clearly indicated in a footnote to this document that "Doctor Antonio de Sosa, a Portuguese clergyman and a great friend of Cervantes, captured in 1577 and rescued in 1581" was the author of both this Memorandum and "of the summaries that helped Archbishop Haedo write the *Historia general de Argel*."[171] Luis Astrana Marín also established in 1949 that the three Dialogues that constitute the third part of Haedo's *Topographia*—*De los mártires de Argel, De la captividad,* and *De los morabutos*—were composed by Doctor Antonio de Sosa.[172] Finally, George Camamis conclusively demonstrated in 1977 that Sosa composed this monumental work between 1577 and 1581, while he was a captive in Algiers.[173] More recently, Emilio Sola and José María Parreño, among others, have confirmed that the five books of the *Topographia* were written by Antonio de Sosa during his captivity in Algiers.[174] In *Cervantes in Algiers,* I provide additional evidence to prove that the *Topographia* was composed by Sosa while he was imprisoned in the corsair city. Indeed, multiple cross-references between the five books of the *Topographia* demonstrate the existence of a single author for these works.[175]

Antonio de Sosa's Identity

Through intensive research in various Spanish and Italian archives, including the Vatican Secret Archives and several church and state archives in Sicily, I have been able to determine Antonio de Sosa's identity as a respected member of the Hispano-Italian ecclesiastical hierarchy. In addition, I have discovered the motives for the fraud that saw his work attributed to another man. This information—presented here for the first time—is virtually unknown among contemporary scholars. One of the difficulties encountered in my research had to do with the name Antonio de Sosa, or de Sousa, a common Portuguese name that abounds in archives and encyclopedias.[176] In *Cervantes in Algiers,* I suggest that Sosa could have been related to the Order of Malta, first, because there were two Knights with the same name in this Order, and second, because Sosa was sailing aboard a galley from the Order when he was captured. Subsequent findings in various European archives revealed this hypothesis to be erroneous. Antonio de Sosa is always mentioned both in official correspondence and in his own letters as "Doctor Sosa," a title that referred to his status as *Doctor in utroque iure* [Doctor in canon and civil law], as specified in some of the documents involving his name. Sosa was also a Doctor in Theology, as confirmed by the title with which Pope Gregory XIII addressed him in a 1583 papal brief: *Sacrae Theologiae Professori* and by the fact that Sosa himself sometimes added the appellation *Teólogo* [Theologian] to his signature.[177]

As Sciuti Russi has claimed in his *Astrea in Sicilia*, in early modern Spain and its territories, those individuals who obtained doctorates *in utroque iure* belonged to a select sphere of society that often had a solid family tradition in the exercise of municipal offices, or in the practice of law and possession of local magistracies.[178] Consequently, if they were in the privileged position of those who acceded to university studies, the ones who acquired a title of doctor (a doctorate), in particular, were distinguished with important public offices, be it in the cities or in elevated ecclesiastical posts across the empire. The high level of competition for these posts, in both the ministerial and ecclesiastic domains, was astounding and contrasted with the small number of positions available in such spheres of influence. Thus the importance of maintaining relevant contacts at the court in Madrid, or in its satellite courts, such as Rome, Naples, Milan, and Palermo, including their political factions, which also comprised ecclesiastical and even papal cliques, as we shall see in Sosa's case.

Earlier I emphasized the respect with which Sosa was regarded by Spanish captives and ecclesiastics in Algiers, as confirmed by Fra Juan Gil, head of the Trinitarian ransoming mission to that city in 1580, a respect perhaps also elicited by his titles and studies and, as it turns out, by his distinguished ecclesiastical position. We may recall Fra Juan Gil's statement regarding Sosa's honorable character and qualities in the *Información de Argel*: "I know that . . . in what he has declared above he would say nothing but the pure truth, as the truthful man he is."[179]

One of the earliest published mentions of Doctor Antonio de Sosa among the Hispano-Italian ecclesiastics working in Sicily in the sixteenth century appears in Rocco Pirri's *Sicilia Sacra*, a monumental work originally published in 1644–1649, which recounts the history of the Christian Church in Sicily since medieval times. Sosa's name emerges next to that of Bishop Juan Orozco de Arce, a former Inquisitor in Palermo who was elevated to the bishopric of Siracusa in December 1562.[180] Pirri states that, as soon as he was ordained bishop, Orozco de Arce proceeded to appoint various vicars, among them, the Portuguese Doctor Antonio de Sosa.[181]

In various requests for favors directed to Philip II, Sosa states, in effect, that he served the king for many years as vicar general of the bishoprics of Siracusa and Catania in Sicily. A vicar was the cleric appointed by the bishop to perform ordinary jurisdiction in his place. The vicar was freely named by the bishop, who could also remove him when he wished. In general, there was only one vicar per diocese, unless it was a very large one. The vicar general had to be a priest of the secular clergy, as well as a doctor or licentiate in theology. In sixteenth-century Spain, when bishops were often absent from their seats, the post of vicar—and even more that of vicar general—was an important ecclesiastical position given to an individual who would represent the bishop's interests during his absences.[182] Orozco de Arce was promoted to the bishopric of Catania in August 1574, and Sosa again followed him as vicar general. With the death of Orozco de Arce on 28 March 1576,[183] Sosa lost his mentor and also probably his political support among the canons of the cathedral of Catania. He appears next in Rome, pressing Philip II for a higher ecclesiastical position.

In September 1576, Sosa wrote Philip II from Rome, referring to his past service as vicar general of the bishoprics of Siracusa and Catania, and requesting the position of dean and vicar general of the cathedral of Agrigento, Sicily. The position was vacant by the death of the previous dean. Sosa claimed that the Duke of Terranova, president of the kingdom of Sicily, had written a letter of recommendation on his behalf, stressing his studies and personal qualities. The marginal comments written by the secretary of the Council of Italy in response to Sosa's petition emphasize his prestige at court: "We have a very good report of Antonio de Sosa's person and letters (studies), and because the deanship can be offered this time to a foreigner or through the *alternativa*, we think it would be appropriate to give it to him."[184] The mention of the *alternativa* alludes to a law promulgated by Ferdinand the Catholic in 1503 for the kingdom of Sicily, which stated that any ecclesiastical benefits in the hands of a "foreigner"—that is, a Spaniard— should be given to a Sicilian when there was a vacancy. There was great pressure, however, in Madrid, from Spanish bureaucrats and churchmen to interpret this law as if it only concerned vacancies produced by the death of the incumbent.[185] Sosa, then, was presenting himself as a "foreigner," in other words, as a Spanish subject.

Portuguese by birth, Sosa was in all probability already a Spanish citizen in 1576: five years earlier, he had requested to be naturalized as a Spaniard—that is, as a citizen of Castile.[186] Stressing his poverty, he claimed in his 1576 petition to Philip II that he wished to continue his studies and obtain a Church position with an income, in accordance with any favor the king would grant him.[187] The favor was apparently conceded sometimes thereafter, because, in a letter written to Philip II in 1582, after his release from captivity, Sosa thanked him for granting him the status of Spanish citizen.

In regard to Sosa's nomination as dean of the cathedral of Agrigento, let us recall that, since 1486, Pope Innocent VIII had granted the Spanish monarchs the power to nominate bishops in Spain, a prerogative that was extended to Granada and the Canary Islands (1491), as well as to the American territories (1508). In the 1560s, the Patronato Regio [Royal Patronage] included all the major and minor Church dignities, a prerogative that turned ecclesiastical nominations into political appointments. Sosa's petition for the deanship of Agrigento was soon approved in spite of the long process attached to a high ranking ecclesiastical appointment. This process involved an examination by the papal nuncio in Spain of the qualities of the person elected, after which the papal nuncio sent a written report to the Vatican; then, the intervention of the Spanish ambassador before the Roman Curia; and finally, the acceptance by the pope or a consistory of cardinals of the person nominated for a bishopric or important post.

The position of dean of the cathedral of Agrigento was a distinguished ecclesiastical post with a hefty income received from lands attached to the deanship. The dean was the governing official of the cathedral chapter—that is, the doyen of the religious chapter—a position immediately beneath that of the bishop. On 26 October 1576, Philip II nominated Sosa for this deanship and sent his "presentation" to Rome requesting an official papal appointment.[188] A month later, Sosa wrote to the king from Rome acknowledging the favor and requesting the unearned income of his deceased predecessor in Agrigento. He claimed that he needed those funds to pay the taxes demanded by the consistory of cardinals, which would, in turn, issue the bulls for the possession of the ecclesiastical post. Sosa, moreover, confessed that he had no money to leave Rome. In reality, Sosa was asking the king to help him pay these taxes, because if an ecclesiastical seat was vacant, the monarchy received the rents of the bishopric involved. Philip II immediately approved a grant of two hundred ducats for Sosa, drawn from the unearned salaries of the previous dean of Agrigento.[189]

We discussed earlier Sosa's capture, which occurred on 1 April 1577, aboard the galley *San Pablo* from the Order of Malta, while he was on his way to Sicily to claim his ecclesiastical post. In the corsair attack, Antonio de Sosa and his family, consisting of a sister, a nephew, and three servants who belonged to Sosa's household, as well as other passengers and Knights of Malta, were taken as captives to Algiers. Sosa's captivity would last for four years and three months. A series of documents related to Sosa's incarceration in Algiers, between 1577 and 1581, reveals both his supplications to Philip II in regard to his ransom and the court's responses to these demands. Sosa's relations with his sister were to surprise both courtly and ecclesiastical circles. For the ransom of Sosa's family, the Algerians were requesting fifteen hundred ducats — three times the amount paid for Cervantes's ransom in 1580.[190] The king initially granted Sosa five hundred ducats from the unearned income of his post to help pay for his ransom.[191]

Subsequent letters from Philip II to the viceroy of Sicily, Marco Antonio Colonna, reveal the king's concern with Sosa's captivity. On 2 November 1577, Philip II ordered Colonna to implement, in Doctor Sosa's name, the appointment to the deanship of the cathedral of Agrigento. Because of his capture by Algerian corsairs, Sosa had not been able to present his official documents in person. The king included in this memo a copy of his original nomination for Sosa from 1576. Had Sosa been captured after taking possession of his post of dean in Agrigento, he could have used the moneys from his salary and additional income assigned to his ecclesiastical post to pay for his ransom. In the same letter of November 1577, Philip II requested Viceroy Colonna to pay to Sosa, or to whomever he had designed as his power of attorney, the two hundred ducats originally destined for the payment of the taxes to the Roman Curia.[192] On 20 December 1577, the king reiterated his request to Colonna and ordered him to pay both the five hundred ducats plus the two hundred ducats owed to the Roman Curia, a total of seven hundred ducats, to Sosa's brother, Fra Diego de Sosa, a Carmelite monk who was assembling the funds for his brother's ransom.[193] Because Sosa had apparently written to the king telling him that his appointment papers had been lost during his capture, Philip II wrote again to Viceroy Colonna on 26 October 1578, including in this letter another copy of Sosa's apostolic bulls confirming his appointment as dean of the cathedral of Agrigento. The king demanded that the bulls be formally registered and honored both in Palermo and in Agrigento.

Beyond his continuous letters to the king, moreover, Sosa also seemed to be a shrewd businessman. From his Algerian prison, he arranged a series of contacts in Agrigento in order to accede (long-distance) to his post and start collecting his income. Following these instructions, Sosa's procurator, the Portuguese Carmelite Giacomo di Spiritu Sancto, formally presented the papal bulls at the cathedral of Agrigento on 31 March 1579. Armed with a power of attorney redacted by Sosa, the Carmelite monk took possession of the deanship in Sosa's name. Under the circumstances, the vicar general of the bishopric of Agrigento requested the vicar of Naro, a nearby city, to advise the farmers who worked on the lands assigned to Sosa's deanship—that is, the lesees—to pay only Doctor Sosa's procurator and not to recognize "as Dean any other person but Don Antonio de Sosa."[194] Similar documents appear in the church archives of Agrigento, shedding light on the ecclesiastical and business transactions of Sosa's procurator.

Three years after his capture, Sosa was still desperately writing to Philip II, now stating that his master would not give him up for less than twelve hundred gold *escudos,* as confirmed by a memorandum sent to the king by the Council of Italy in March 1580. Philip II then approved the sum of one thousand ducats for his ransom from Sosa's salary as dean of the cathedral of Agrigento. A note on the margin says that they expected him to ransom himself with these funds.[195] Seven months later, however, Sosa was still in Algiers. Yet Philip II had not forgotten Doctor Sosa. On 29 November 1580, writing from Badajoz, the king corresponded again with Viceroy Colonna regarding Doctor Sosa's captivity in Barbary. The captive had sent a power of attorney from Algiers to his brother Fra Diego de Sosa, authorizing him to collect the moneys for his ransom from the deanship of Agrigento. Church officials in Agrigento, regrettably, had refused to validate the document because it was not drawn in parchment as was the custom. Ordering the viceroy to validate at once Sosa's power of attorney, even if it was drawn on paper, Philip II manifested his concern for the captive.[196]

Unfortunately, the messages between the concerned parties were becoming more and more fractured, as revealed by the incident of the power of attorney sent to Sicily from Algiers. Let us imagine for a moment the series of steps involved in these transactions after the refusal, in Agrigento, of the power of attorney drawn by Sosa in Algiers, an incident followed by other letters written back and forth between Sicily and Algiers, as well as between Algiers and Spain, including the new petition sent by Sosa to the king, which finally reached him in Badajoz on the eve of his conquest of Portugal.

Sosa's next move, then, was to intercede before the Spanish court for his exchange as a prisoner with a renegade corsair named Arnaut, incarcerated in Naples. He had first requested this exchange in 1577, adding that his master would agree on this arrangement. His second request for this type of exchange was probably sent in 1580 from Algiers, and perhaps even hand-carried by Cervantes, who was liberated in October 1580. In February 1581, the court wrote to the viceroy of Naples, Juan de Zúñiga, asking him to study the possibility of exchanging Doctor Antonio de Sosa, a captive in Algiers, for the Muslim corsair Arnaut, and to advise them as to the convenience of such a deal. Zuñiga responded in June 1581, with information on Arnaut, a Genoese renegade who had been imprisoned in Naples for fifteen years. In his opinion, this man should not be released, because he was a mariner with great experience around the Italian coasts.[197] Sosa's petition to the Spanish Crown was thus denied. Nevertheless, he would be freed in July 1581.

I have unearthed an exciting document that sheds light on Sosa's liberation. A report composed in Algiers by the Genoese merchant (and undercover agent) Luis Brevez Fresco, who resided in the city, states that Doctor Sosa escaped from Ka'id Muhammad's prison in July 1581. Luis Brevez Fresco is mentioned in the *Topography*. The first part of his lengthy report in Genoese dialect and in lingua franca reads in translation:

> On 13 July 1581, the ka'id Mamet [Muhammad], who was the slave-master of Doctor Sosa, created an enormous scandal because of the escape of the said Doctor Sosa. Muhammad has sent troops over land and sea, but he has not been able to ascertain where Doctor Sosa is, or whether he has safely arrived in Spain. Muhammad has proclaimed an edict offering a reward of one hundred doblas to whoever brings Doctor Sosa back to him.[198]

Paradoxically, Sosa never mentions his escape explicitly in letters or petitions directed to the Crown after his liberation, preferring instead to speak of a "ransom." Possibly, the reason for this was to prevent criticism of the king, since monarchs were supposed to help ransom public officials, officeholders, or ecclesiastics who worked for the Crown. Yet Sosa's move was ambiguous since, over a year after his liberation, he himself sent the spy's report from Madrid to Mateo Vázquez, Philip II's secretary. In the cover letter, signed jointly by "El Doctor Sosa" and Captain Juan de Bolaños, a former captive in Barbary, on 23 October 1582, the authors claim that Brevez Fresco left Algiers on 5 September 1582, where 'Uludj 'Ali remained at the time. Sosa confirms his desire to serve Philip II, as he did before from Algiers. He requests Mateo Vázquez to show the report to the king and to let Sosa know if they need any other service from him.

As the above shows, Sosa was liberated in July 1581, in a mysterious way that involved a daring escape. We learn from other documents sent to the Spanish court that he had first ransomed his sister, who left Algiers some days before he did. Notice that Sosa took it upon himself to rescue his sister first, even before attempting to escape. We can imagine that he used part of the funds granted for his ransom to rescue his sister, and the rest to bribe guards, sailors, or city officials in Algiers. In addition, we may presume that Sosa escaped on a merchant ship from Valencia, Genoa, or another city that traded with the Algerians—

perhaps even on a galley owned by the Genoese merchant Brevez Fresco, who recounts in the same report that he was threatened with incarceration and torture by Hasan the Venetian for presumably collaborating in the escape of various slaves.

A consultation sent to the king by the Council of Castile on 11 September 1581, regarding Doctor Sosa's liberation, is worth citing now. The document summarizes a petition from Sosa, who stated he had left Algiers a month and a half earlier: "where his ransom cost him 2,400 gold escudos, which he collected principally thanks to the charity Your Majesty bestowed on him, and, in spite of this, he is still owing almost 1,500 gold escudos to merchants for his own ransom and that of his sister, the interests of which are increasing day by day."[199] Sosa added in his memorandum that his nephew had died in Algiers, and that his two servants and his sister's maid had not yet been rescued. The previous information suggests that the king granted Sosa a hefty sum for his rescue, relevant facts in the light of the denouement of Sosa's case. More explicitly, in a letter written by Philip II to his ambassador in Rome in 1583, the king stated that he had paid fifteen hundred escudos for Sosa's liberation.[200]

The former captive resided in Madrid between December 1581 and February 1582. In two notarized statements Sosa appears as a "resident of Madrid," while in a third document, dated 3 February 1582, he seems to be passing though the city: "estante en Madrid."[201] During these months he probably saw his friend Cervantes, who had returned from his enigmatic trip to Orán, taken in 1581 for Philip II's secret services, and who was also living in Madrid. Several affidavits, subscribed in December 1581 and January and February 1582, show Doctor Sosa in the process of acknowledging a payment of 1,320 *reales* from María Ramírez, for the ransom of her daughter Mariana, a captive in Algiers, and obliging himself to add to this ransom over and above the sum received. María and Mariana Ramírez were related to Captain Jerónimo Ramírez from Alcalá de Henares, Sosa's interlocutor in his *Diálogo de los mártires de Argel*. Captain Ramírez was among those captured in 1577 on the galley *San Pablo,* along with his widowed sister and niece.[202] Since Pérez Pastor's findings at the turn of the twentieth century, no other news about Doctor Sosa's presence in Madrid or elsewhere after

February 1582 had been uncovered. Scholars thus concluded that he died soon after this date, as I proposed in *Cervantes in Algiers*.

Yet Sosa was still in Madrid in the summer of 1582, as corroborated by a letter he sent to Philip II on 26 August of that year. In this letter, Sosa thanks the king for the moneys granted for his ransom and confirms that he has recently been liberated. He adds that, because he has been sick, he could not travel to Lisbon to thank the king in person for the mercies received that led to his liberation. Sosa's letter is so rich in details that it merits to be cited almost in full:

> Knowing this [that I was sick], the president of Your Majesty's Royal Council made me go to his home, in order to seek out information about matters in Algiers and Barbary, which are presently so altered with the coming of the Turkish armada; and the same can be said about the President of the Royal Treasury Hernando de Vega, and the secretary, Juan Vázquez de Salazar, and the regents. Everyone is interested in knowing the reason for the coming of this armada, and the lengthy discussions of this issue in Algiers; the intention of the Turk with this armada, and the way that 'Uludj 'Ali would have to make war on the king of Fès, as I found out in Algiers some days ago . . . from janissaries and renegades of the king's house, who were present in the Councils and consultations. I have written all of this in some papers and memoranda that I brought with me from Algiers. [Your Majesty's ministers] were of the opinion that if, because of my illness—a relic of my long captivity—I could not go in person [to see the king], at least I should inform Your Majesty in writing. If they had not recommended this, I would not have dared to write to Your Majesty in this way, being a poor priest, although while I was a captive in Algiers I sometimes did this, notifying and describing events there because I understood this was in the service of Your Majesty.[203]

The letter goes on to thank Philip II for his continuous help and support, especially in granting Sosa, many years earlier, the citizenship in the kingdom of Castile, where he had been brought up and where he studied.[204]

Two features specially stand out in this missive: first, the fact that Sosa explicitly mentions that he often wrote in Algiers both spy's reports, which he sometimes sent to the court, and also "papers" and memorials about Algerian events. He confirms that he obtained such news from various janissaries and renegades who belonged to the beylerbey's council. Secondly, Sosa seemed to be very well connected with various key ministers of Philip II's government, such as the president of the Royal Council of Castile, Antonio Mauriño de Pazos, who had been an Inquisitor in Seville and later a special judge (*visitador*) assigned to review the functioning of the Spanish Inquisition in Sicily (1574–1577).[205] Sosa had met President Pazos in Sicily during his tenure there as a special judge. In addition, Sosa claims that he met with the president of the Royal Treasury, Hernando de Vega, and with the secretary, Juan Vázquez de Salazar, among other public officials. Pazos, however, would soon fall into disgrace after being identified with the papal party (the party that adhered to the pope's interests, which also included another of Philip II's secretaries, Antonio Pérez). President Pazos was removed from office and forced to accept an appointment as the bishop of Córdoba, where he died in 1586. The fall of President Pazos may have played a role in Sosa's vicissitudes during 1582 and 1583, as described below.

Scandalous News

Sosa's luck would change drastically between October and November 1582, as revealed by the following astonishing discoveries. A memorandum sent by the Council of Italy to Philip II in March 1583 reiterates most of the facts we know about Doctor Antonio de Sosa: that the Council had recommended him to the king because he was considered a modest and virtuous man; that he had been captured by Turks and mistreated; and that he had recently returned to Madrid, where he was trying to pay the debts incurred by his ransom. Then comes a bomb: Sosa was accused before the vicar of Madrid of being an ordained Augustinian friar, who had fled from his Order by taking the habit of a lay priest. At the time, an ordained friar could not leave his Order except to enter a more rigorous one, a move requiring a papal dispensation;

otherwise, he was considered an apostate. In the Council's words: "And because the vicar has proof that this is true, and that he [Sosa] has been living together for years with a woman who is always with him, passing as his sister, he was handed over to the prior of his Order in the Kingdom of Portugal (where he received his habit)."[206]

Other documents found in the Archives of the Ministry of Foreign Relations in Madrid, among the correspondence between the Spanish Crown and the Holy See, reveal that Doctor Sosa was incarcerated in the Augustinian Convent of San Felipe, where he was tried and convicted on 25 November 1582 for the crimes cited above. He was then handed over to the Superior of the Augustinian order in Portugal, Fra Agustín de Jesús, who was in Madrid at the time.[207] Sosa's worst sin, in fact, was not his cohabitation with his "widowed sister," but his leaving the Augustinian order and passing himself off as a lay priest. As we may recall, in order to be appointed to the position of vicar general in a bishopric, one had to be a lay priest. Sosa's case now turned into a saga involving many actors, such as Philip II, Pope Gregory XIII, Philip's ambassador in Rome, the Count of Olivares, and the viceroy of Sicily Marco Antonio Colonna, among others. Suffice it to say that, instead of imprisoning Sosa, as was requested by the vicar of Madrid, the provincial of the Augustinian order in Portugal sent him to Rome to ask for the pope's pardon.

As it turns out, Sosa was in Rome during the summer and fall of 1583 and probably in the first months of 1584. From Rome, he wrote innumerable letters to Philip II, Mateo Vázquez, Pope Gregory XIII, and the Count of Olivares, among others. In the meantime, Philip II removed Sosa from office and nominated Don Silvestre Mauroli, a nobleman from Messina, as dean of the cathedral of Agrigento.[208] Sosa's detractors, including Mauroli himself, who had also traveled to Rome to try to secure his new post, informed the king that Sosa was received by cardinals and influential ecclesiastics at the Vatican.[209]

The pope pardoned Sosa, as we shall see, but applied a punishment, which consisted in sending him back to Algiers for six months or more to console the Christian captives imprisoned in this city. One can imagine Sosa's terror at this dismal prospect, especially if he had escaped two years before from his Algerian prison. Yet the possibility of losing his position in Agrigento pressured him to write a report in impeccable Latin to the pope, making a diagnosis of the state of Christianity among the captives in Algiers and suggesting remedies to help those who frequently lost their faith among the infidels.[210] Fortunately for Sosa, the safe conduct needed to travel to Algiers in an official mission as a priest assigned to help Christian captives could not be obtained from Hasan Pasha the Venetian, who was back in Algiers as governor, at the time.[211]

Pope Gregory XIII, in turn, maintained Sosa in the position of dean and vicar general of the cathedral of Agrigento, Sicily, confirming his decision with a papal brief issued on 11 November 1583.[212] Addressing the brief in learned Latin to "Our dear son Antonio de Sousa, Professor of Theology," the pope begins by noting the clemency of the Apostolic See in benignly considering the situation of any persons who return to the fold. He adds that "there have arrived many humble supplications on your behalf," which reminds us of Sosa's connections with Church and civil dignitaries, in Sicily, Madrid, and Rome. Finally, Gregory XIII provides his absolution:

> Inclined to your supplications, . . . by means of the present document, we absolve you through one or another justice—including if you would be a defendant, with or without trial—and we liberate you totally of the crime of apostasy, of the pain of excommunication and other sentences, censures, and ecclesiastical and temporal penalties, in which, for the above mentioned reasons, you incurred . . . . We pardon you indulgently for all the fruits, income, and harvests unlawfully gained by you in the said deanship. We also condone all the irregularities committed . . . because being condemned by some censures, you celebrated mass and other divine offices, spurning all ecclesiastical authority, and you illicitly enmeshed yourself where you should not have been, contradicting the orders you received. We forgive you also of these faults . . . so that you may licitly, with the authority emanating from the present document, conduct the ministries of the altar, present yourself in the habit of a secular cleric, and freely remain in the deanship.[213]

Copies of the papal brief were sent to Madrid, to Philip II's ambassador in Rome, and to the viceroy of Sicily, among other dignitaries.

Philip II responded to this pardon with furious letters sent to the Count of Olivares, his ambassador in Rome, requesting him to intercede with the pope for the removal of Sosa from office. Olivares then wrote to Gregory XIII suggesting that he should pay more attention to the accusations proffered by those persons who had real knowledge of the culprit. Various copies of these letters, including those of Philip II's memoranda to ambassador Olivares in Rome and to the viceroy of Sicily, went from Madrid to Rome, and from there to Palermo, Naples, and Genoa, creating a scandal that aggravated the extant confrontation between Gregory XIII and Philip II regarding papal jurisdiction in Spain and its territories.[214] The relations between the Spanish Crown and the papacy were then passing through one of their most acrid moments due to the attempts by Gregory XIII to eliminate Philip II's prerogatives over the Catholic Church, which the king interpreted as an attack against his sovereignty, and the pope's concomitant opposition to the union of the monarchies of Portugal and Spain.[215]

On 31 January 1584, Philip II wrote again to the Count of Olivares about Sosa's case. The king confirmed that, because of Sosa's "apostasy," he had removed him from office and had nominated Don Silvestre Mauroli for the deanship in Agrigento. In addition, the king challenged Sosa's motives: "Of his trip to Algiers, we believe that these are falsehoods on his part in order to live there . . . as dissolutely as he has done here, beyond what we should fear from a man of such bad life and example, which is that he should leave our faith and turn Turk."[216] The passage underscores Philip II's anger against a priest he had continuously helped throughout his career, a support that included the substantial grants he had approved for Sosa's ransom.

In regard to Philip II's *ira regia,* his contemporary, the historian Luis Cabrera de Córdoba, claims that it was said of the king "que de su risa al cuchillo había poca distancia" [that from his smile to the dagger there was little distance].[217] In this sense, adds Cabrera de Córdoba, the person who trespassed against the king by not keeping his promise or his fidelity, or by infringing the law, could not obtain his pardon: "El faltar a la fidelidad o la legalidad no esperaba perdón; por eso se detenía examinando los despachos, porque sospechar y no creer, ni confiar el Rey, eran nervios de su prudencia" [Philip II could never forgive any want of faithfulness or lawfulness in his subjects, a trait that led him to spend ages examining royal dispatches, because to suspect, to disbelieve, and to distrust were, for him, the keys to wisdom].[218] More important, Philip II so detested lies that, knowing a minister was lying to him, he said in such a way: "¿Pues, así me mentís?" [So you thus lie to me?]. Hence, he killed the minister. Cabrera de Córdoba concludes, in regard to this incident: "Porque le mintió uno de su cámara y favorecido, murió fuera de ella y de su gracia" [Because a minister from his Chamber, one whom he had favored, lied to him, that minister died, excluded from the Chamber and from the king's grace].[219] Certainly, the gravity of Sosa's sins did not admit the king's pardon, not only because Sosa lied about his status as a lay priest and, even more, about his "sister," but also because he had broken faith with the king. The great irony here is that Doctor Sosa— that fierce enemy of renegades—would be accused by the king of both lying and of wanting to "turn Turk."

In May 1584, Philip II was still obsessively persecuting Sosa, as revealed by another letter directed to Viceroy Marco Antonio Colonna of Sicily, advising him to be on the alert in case Sosa appeared on the island and tried to take possession of his deanship.[220] Sosa, however, was soon in Agrigento. In July 1584, five years after his procurator Fra Giacomo di Spritu Santo acquired custody of the deanship on his behalf, Doctor Antonio de Sosa took official possession of his post and swore fidelity to the Church according to the tenets of the Council of Trent.[221] After Viceroy Colonna's death in August 1584, the president of the kingdom of Sicily, the Marquis of Briático, repeatedly wrote to Philip II in October, November, and December 1584, alerting him to Sosa's presence in the island. The king responded with a letter, dated 2 April 1585, in which he requests the Marquis to convince Doctor Sosa "to go to Rome, so that we can decide what to do with Don Silvestre Mauroli, lately named by me for the deanship of Agrigento, to which the said Doctor [Sosa] pretends."[222] The missive adds that perhaps Sosa could be "persuaded" to abandon his post with the promise of a future ecclesiastical position. This, of course, was a promise the king did not intend to keep. All the same, in spite of Philip II's insistent attempts to remove him from office, which extended well into 1585, Doctor Sosa remained active in his position until his death in 1587.

Recall that Diego de Haedo (the elder) was nominated bishop of Agrigento in October 1584. He was consecrated in Palermo on 31 March 1585 and took possession of his bishopric in April 1585.[223] We do not know the nature of the relations between Sosa and Haedo, whether they had known each other in previous years, or whether the Inquisitor was one of those dignitaries who sent "humble supplications" to Pope Gregory XIII on Sosa's behalf. Be that as it may, Haedo and Sosa worked together in the cathedral of Agrigento for at least two years. Various documents related to this cathedral were drawn under Haedo and Sosa's joint names and signatures: "Didacus de Haedo episcobus agrigentinus, Nos Doctor Don Antonio Sosa decanus Cathedralis ecclesie agrigentine" (1585).[224] Haedo also supported Doctor Sosa's claims in regard to his lessees. A petition on behalf of Bishop Haedo was presented on 13 July 1585 by the Vicar General and Dean "Don Antonio de Sosa" to the vicar of Naro, requesting him to admonish the farmers who refused to pay the tenth of the fruits, orzo, and wine owed to Sosa, and to establish a peremptory term for these payments. The letter reminded the vicar of Naro that, according to the Council of Trent, those who refused to pay the tithe were subject to excommunication.[225]

During his years in Agrigento, Sosa must have worked actively on the "papers" he brought back from Algiers, especially on his *Diálogo de la captividad,* which has countless references to classical Greek and Roman authors.[226] As we may recall, dialogues were a favorite Renaissance genre, precisely because they dramatized historical material and permitted the emergence, in direct discourse, of another voice that joined that of the narrator, thus lending credibility to the account presented.[227] In addition, Sosa's *Diálogo de la captividad* allows the author to flaunt his knowledge of historical, literary, and juridical discourses, even as he fills his text with citations and allusions to the scholarly authorities of his epoch. Regarding sixteenth-century encyclopedic tendencies, Anthony Grafton has proposed in his study *New World, Ancient Texts* that books at the time were supposed to contain all the knowledge necessary to understand the cosmos.[228] In effect, Sosa cites, among other Greco-Roman authorities, Aristotle, Arrianus, Cicero, Galen, Herodotus, Hesiod, Justinian, Lucan, Macrobius, Ovid, Plato, Pliny, Ptolemy, Strabo, Suetonius, Tacitus, Thucydides, and Virgil. He mentions the work of humanists such as Boccaccio, Paulo Giovio, Leo Africanus, Sebastian Münster, Pero Mexía, and Lorenzo Valla, as well as church fathers such as Saint Augustine, Saint Ambrose, Saint Bernard, and Saint Jerome. Because of the countless references cited in this work, one could infer that the *Diálogo de la captividad* was composed after Sosa's return from Algiers, perhaps even in Agrigento, where he surely had access to the episcopal palace's rich library.[229]

One can presume that, given the scandal that surrounded Sosa's name—a scandal that transcended the court in Madrid and reached Rome, Genoa, Naples, Palermo, and Agrigento—it was impossible for Antonio de Sosa to author a book with his name on it, at least until Philip II died. Official censure of books in Spain, as we may remember, had begun with the pragmatic of the Catholic Monarchs, Ferdinand and Isabella, in 1502, and escalated throughout the sixteenth century with the laws promulgated by Philip II (1556, 1558, and 1560). The so-called Law of Censorship was systematized on 7 September 1558, when Princess Juana, sister of Philip II and regent of the king, signed a decree prohibiting the importation of foreign books and ordered that all published books should in the future carry the permit of the Council of Castile. Additional regulations for the control of printing and circulation of books in the Iberian Peninsula and its territories were promulgated throughout the sixteenth century by Philip II. In 1545, moreover, the Inquisition had elaborated what was the first Spanish Index, followed by another in 1551. Eight years later (1559), Inquisitor General Valdés published a new Index, considerably enlarging that of 1551, thus dealing a hard blow to Spanish intellectual life.

Like other Spanish dependencies, the kingdom of Sicily was subjected to tight control regarding the publication of books and manuscripts, which could not be set in print without the official approval granted by the Council of Castile. This license, however, would only be conceded if the manuscript had passed through previous revision and clearance by the Spanish Inquisition in Palermo. Books were diffusers of heresy and the control that was applied to their printing, sale, or reception was justified for these reasons, especially in order to control the transmission of heresy. This is why a criminal process against a book, especially when it was a heterodox book, was very similar to that applied to a presumed heretic.[230] Cervantes makes this clear in his depiction of the Inquisition of Don Quijote's library (*DQ* I, 5). Indeed, those who did not comply with the laws regarding the censure of books were punished with banishment from the kingdom and the confiscation of their goods. More to the point, those who printed books without the due censure and corresponding license to print could incur a death sentence and the loss of all their goods.[231] Under the constant peril of denunciation, which could initiate a process by the Inquisition, books thus became a factor of anxiety and terror, even of social perturbation.

We noted earlier that, under the government of Philip II, the Inquisition in Sicily acquired great authority and prestige, even while it continued its forceful persecution across the island of heretics, viewed as enemies of the Spanish king and the Catholic Church. Such was the obsession of the Inquisitors with the control of writing that, in 1573, they advised the governor and judges of Caccamo, Sicily, that "no foreign school teacher, coming from suspected and heretical places, should be permitted to read and write, or to teach Latin, in any private or public place, without our license."[232] The Holy Office was particularly sensitive in regard to matters of its jurisdiction, especially apropos the circulation of manuscripts and the publication of uncensored books. Under the climate of censure reigning in Sicily in the sixteenth century, then, it would have been unfeasible for Sosa to publish a book without the approval of the Inquisitors, who also acted as political officers for the king.

One may draw various conclusions in regard to the publication of the *Topographia* under Haedo's name: perhaps both Sosa and Haedo agreed on this strategy and decided to wait until Philip II's death to publish Sosa's work, attributing its authorship to Haedo. With the passage of time, the scandal over the matter of Sosa's "sister"—and the even worse sin of defying the king of Spain—would have been forgotten, especially if the king had also passed away. A book authored by Bishop Haedo, who would accede to the archbishopric of Palermo in 1589, with Philip II's support, would be well received, since he was an important and respected member of the clergy in Sicily. Haedo would become even more renowned, as it turns out, after becoming archbishop of Palermo. Nonetheless, the possibility remains that nothing was arranged between Haedo and Sosa, who were collaborators in the cathedral of Agrigento. Death surprised Sosa in 1587, as recorded by Rocco Pirri in his history of the deans of the Agrigentine Church: "Antonius Sola [*sic,* Sosa] Hispanus, decessit 1587."[233] The manuscript of the *Topographia* then remained in Bishop Haedo's hands.

Let us remember that the younger Diego de Haedo came to Sicily in 1593, to become his uncle's secretary. At the time, Archbishop Haedo was still in Agrigento. In spite of his appointment as archbishop of Palermo in 1589, Haedo did not take physical possession of his archbishopric until 1595—he delegated his position to a procurator, who represented him in the cathedral of Palermo until then.[234] This means that Fra Diego served his uncle in Agrigento during two years before the archbishop moved to Palermo in 1595, and then, for some four more years in Palermo.[235] Fra Diego could have started to edit Sosa's manuscripts at that time, "putting much diligent work into them," as he states in his dedication to his uncle.

In 1599, after working for six years as a secretary to his uncle, both in Agrigento and in Palermo, the younger Haedo returned to Spain. Former captive Diego Galán, who had recently arrived in Sicily following his escape from captivity among the Turks in Constantinople, recounts in his *Relación del cautiverio y libertad de Diego Galán* [Account of Diego Galán's captivity and liberation] (ca. 1622–1625) that, upon his arrival in Palermo, he met Archbishop Haedo's nephew Don Diego de Haedo, who put him up at the archbishop's palace and gave him an assistance of sixty *reales* on his uncle's behalf. Galán traveled back to Spain with Fra Diego in June 1599, arriving in Valencia at the time of the festivities enacted for Philip III's marriage.[236] After his return to Spain, Fra Diego de Haedo became abbot of the Benedictine abbey of Frómista from 1604 to 1607, and then, of the Abbey of Zamora from 1607 to 1613. He died on 19 March 1613.[237]

While he was abbot of Frómista, in 1604, Fra Diego obtained permission to publish the *Topographia*. Hence, it is inexplicable that he would have waited until after Archbishop Haedo's death, in 1608, to submit the chronicle for publication under his uncle's name. Philip II had died in 1598, which may have cleared the way for the appearance of Sosa's book. Yet the work was not published until 1612, four years after Archbishop Haedo's death and twenty-five years after Sosa's passing. Cervantes certainly knew who the real author of the *Topographia* was, since he had seen Sosa writing and correcting his manuscripts in Muhammad's prison, during the time in which they were both held captives in Algiers. The future author of *Don Quijote* was also residing in Madrid in October 1582, when the scandal surrounding Sosa erupted.

"Como en gaceta de Venecia leo" [As in a Gazette from Venice]

Precisely next to the Augustinian Convent of San Felipe el Real, where Sosa was incarcerated and tried in 1582, was the famous *mentidero* (gossip place), or site of public reunion in Madrid, the Gradas de San Felipe el Real [Steps of the Royal Church of San Felipe]. Adjacent to the Puerta del Sol and the Plaza Mayor, in downtown Madrid, the Steps of the Church of San Felipe were a central meeting place for soldiers, vagrants, and citizens who got together to exchange gossip and hear the latest news. Cervantes describes this focal site in his *Viaje del Parnaso* [*Voyage to Parnassus*]: "de San Felipe el gran paseo, / donde si baja el turco o sube el galgo / como en gaceta de Venecia leo" [The great walk of San Felipe, where if the Turk descends or the Moor ascends, I read as in a Gazette from Venice].[238] In effect, on the steps of the Church of San Felipe, dissemination of news, rumors, idle gossip, and even apocryphal reports were hatched, constituting the greatest political critique in early modern Madrid. Enrique García Santo-Tomás has studied the spaces of oral culture in seventeenth-century Madrid, especially the plazas and crossroads where news and gossip circulated. He claims that people went to these *mentideros* on Sunday mornings, after mass, in order to learn the latest information and hearsay which later circulated all over town, in casinos, restaurants, and taverns, centers of oral popular culture. The Steps of the Church of San Felipe were, in fact, a crossroads par excellence, as suggested by Pedro Calderón de la Barca in his play *Antes que todo es mi dama,* where a character states that: "un mes en Madrid viví, / siendo estancia de mis pasos / las Gradas de San Felipe / y las Losas de Palacio" [I lived in Madrid for a month / and spent most of my time strolling / over the Steps of San Felipe / and the flagstones of the Palace].[239]

Neither the Convent and the Royal Church of San Felipe nor the famous steps from which news was disseminated in Madrid were the most convenient places to silence lurid information in the city. Sosa's case, with its shocking details, was discussed in the criminal trial that took place against the former Augustinian at the Convent of San Felipe el Real, in October 1582. Given the location of this convent, next to the church of the same name and to the famous *mentidero,* it would have been difficult to silence the scandal involving a distinguished member of the Spanish-Italian clergy, no less a figure than the appointed dean of the cathedral of Agrigento in Sicily, a priest who had recently returned from a long captivity in Barbary. As his companion of captivity in Algiers and one of Sosa's best friends, Cervantes must have been informed about this sensational judicial case.

When Sosa's work was finally published in Valladolid, in 1612, under another man's name, Cervantes remained silent, at least in public. The author certainly used parts of the *Topographia* as a source of information for his posthumous novel *Persiles* (1617).[240] In addition, Cervantes lived in Valladolid between 1604 and 1606, and he still had literary and editorial acquaintances in this city.[241] He probably had personal connections with the Fernández de Córdoba family, who owned various printing shops in Valladolid, such as the press that published the *Topographia*.[242] A new edition of Cervantes's pastoral novel, *La Galatea*, came out in 1617 in Valladolid, by Francisco Fernández de Córdoba's press. Francisco was a brother to Diego Fernández de Córdoba, who had published the *Topographia* five years before. One could even surmise that, through his connections in Valladolid, Cervantes managed to arrange for the reprinting of *La Galatea* before his own death in 1616.[243] We can thus infer that news about the publication of the *Topographia* in 1612, under Haedo's name, must have reached Cervantes in Madrid.

The ascription of Sosa's book to Archbishop Haedo, who had died in Palermo in 1608, leaving behind a saintly reputation, must have had a bearing on Cervantes's silence. Under the reigns of Philip II and Philip III, Archbishop Haedo had been a key player in the power circles of the kingdom of Sicily, taking part in relevant ways in the imposition of Philip II's religious and political policies, as well as serving as mediator in the relations between both sovereigns and their viceroys, and between the Crown and the Sicilian parliament.[244] During his tenure as archbishop of Palermo, furthermore, Haedo's political and spiritual power practically equaled that of the viceroy of Sicily.

The Sicilian poet Antonio Veneziano, a former captive himself in Algiers and one of Cervantes's companions in Hasan Pasha's bagnio, described Archbishop Diego de Haedo's triumphal entry as the patriarch of Palermo, the primary episcopal seat of the kingdom of Sicily, on 12 October 1595. In the grand style of a viceroy, the new archbishop marched through the city, adorned with triumphal arches, carrying a revered relic, the arm of Saint Gerlando, bishop of Agrigento. Haedo entered the impressive cathedral of Palermo while pageants celebrated his arrival with fanfare.[245] His death on 6 July 1608 was deeply mourned by the populace and accompanied by a massive funeral procession and a sumptuous memorial service.[246] As the major ecclesiastical figure of Palermo, Haedo had been very popular with the general population.

One last question remains. We may remember that Sosa was captured in 1577 with his "widowed sister" and nephew. Sosa himself stated in a letter to the Council of Italy in 1581 that his nephew died in Algiers during his captivity. We do not know whether the young man died of an illness, or whether he was executed or tortured to death for trying to escape. Sosa remains silent on this point. It is easy to deduce that the so-called nephew was probably Sosa's son, as they say in Spanish, *el sobrino del cura* [the priest's nephew]. The painful reality of the boy's death in Algiers may be reflected throughout Sosa's works, especially in his *Diálogo de los mártires de Argel* and his other Dialogue that deals with the horrors of captivity in Barbary, *Diálogo de la captividad*. The tragedy behind Sosa's experience as a captive sheds light on the subtitle of the *Topography*: "which will exhibit strange cases, horrific deaths, and extraordinary tortures that Christianity needs to understand." The strangest of these "cases," however, is certainly that of Doctor Antonio de Sosa himself, and even more extraordinary is the secret lying under the authorship of his *Topographia, e Historia general de Argel*.

Topography of Algiers

by

Antonio de Sosa

TOPOGRAPHIA,
EHISTO-
RIA GENERAL DE AR-
GEL, REPARTIDA EN CINCO TRA-
TADOS, DO SE VERAN CASOS ESTRA-
ños, muertes espantosas, y tormentos exquisitos,
que conuiene se entiendan en la Christian-
dad: con mucha doctrina, y ele-
gancia curiosa.

DIRIGIDA AL ILVSTISSIMO SEÑOR DON DIEGO
de Haedo Arçobispo de Palermo, Presidente, y Capitan General
del Reyno de Sicilia.

Por el Maestro fray Diego de Haedo Abad de Fromesta, de la Orden del Patriar
ca san Benito, natural del Valle de Carrança.

CON PRIVILEGIO.

En Valladolid, por *Diego Fernandez de Cordoua y Ouiedo*, Impressor
de libros. Año de M.DC.XII.

A costa de *Antonio Coello mercader de libros*.

Figure 2. Facsimile of title page from Diego de Haedo, *Topographia, e Historia general de Argel,* princeps edition (Valladolid, 1612).

TOPOGRAPHY
AND GENERAL HISTORY OF ALGIERS,
DIVIDED AMONG FIVE BOOKS, WHICH WILL
EXHIBIT STRANGE CASES, Horrific Deaths,
and Extraordinary Tortures that Christianity Needs to Understand:
With Copious Doctrine and Curious Elegance

Dedicated to the Most Illustrious Señor Don Diego de Haedo,
Archbishop of Palermo, President, and Captain General
of the Kingdom of Sicily

By the Reverend Diego de Haedo, Abbot of Frómista, of the Order
of the Patriarch Saint Benedict, Native of the Valley of Carranza

WITH THE APPROVAL OF THE KING
In Valladolid, by Diego Fernández de Córdova y Oviedo,
Printer of Books,
In the Year of Our Lord 1612

At the Expense of Antonio Coello, Book Merchant

PRELIMINARY MATERIALS

APPRAISAL

I, Miguel de Ondarza Zavala, secretary to the King and resident clerk in his Majesty's Council, certify and attest that a book entitled *Topography or Description of Algiers, Its Inhabitants, and Its Customs* has been seen by the members of the aforesaid Council. Written by the Master Fra Diego de Haedo, it was published with permission of the aforesaid Council members, who appraised each sheet of the aforesaid book at four *maravedís*,[1] unbound, and issued permission to sell it at this price and no more, and with this certificate printed at the beginning of each copy.[2] Let this be officially recorded as a petition on the part of the aforesaid Fra Diego de Haedo granted by the aforesaid gentlemen of this faith. In witness whereof, I signed this certificate in the city of Madrid, on 19 October 1612.

Miguel Ondarza Zavala

THE KING

Whereas we were informed by you, Fra Francisco de Valdivia, attorney general of the Order of Saint Benedict, that the Reverend Father and Master Fra Diego de Haedo, Abbot of Saint Benedict of Frómista and monk of the same order, had composed a book entitled *Topography and Description of the Things of Algiers, Its Events, and the Succession of Its Kings*,[3] which was very useful and beneficial and contained nothing contrary to good morals. And whereas you asked and entreated us to grant license and permission to print and sell his book for a period of twenty years, or for such a time as suited us; and whereas the requirements set forth in our most recent royal decree regarding the printing of books have been met in the aforesaid book, and the matter having been reviewed by members of our Council, it was agreed that we should grant our seal of approval to this book, and we took it as a good thing.[4]

To which end, in order to favor and benefit the said Father and Master Fra Diego de Haedo, we hereby grant license and permission to him or to the person who acts as his agent, and to none other, for a term and period of ten years running, which begin and are counted from the date of this our permit, to print and sell the aforesaid book in all these our Realms of Castile, according to the original version seen by our Council, which has been endorsed and signed on its final page by Miguel de Ondarza Zavala,[5] clerk of our Chamber and clerk resident of our Council; provided that each time he has the aforesaid book printed during the period of the aforesaid ten years, he should bring it before the collective eyes of our Council, together with the original which was examined by the Council, in order to document that the aforesaid book conforms to the original, or that he bring them an affidavit in due form showing that a reader appointed by us has examined and corrected the published version according to the original.[6] And we order the printer to publish the aforesaid book in this manner, not printing anything on the beginning or the last sheet, nor giving more than one copy with the original back to the author or to the person at whose expense it was published, and to none other, to effect the said correction and pricing, until the said book has first been corrected and priced by our Council. This done, and in no other manner, he may then print the aforesaid beginning and first sheet, and immediately afterward print this our permit and approval, appraisal, and errata on it, on pain of incurring those penalties contained in the pragmatic and laws of our Kingdoms, which stipulate concerning these things.

And we order that, during this given time, no one whosoever, without authorization, may publish or sell the aforesaid book, under penalty of having lost and losing any and all books, molds, types, and necessary equipment appertaining to this book, and in addition be fined 50,000 maravedís for each infraction, one-third of which fine shall go to our Chamber, another third to the person who denounces the culprit, and the last third to the judge who sentences him. And we command those of our Council, President and Judges of our Supreme Court, Mayors, Bailiffs of our house, Court and Chancellery, and all the Judges, Assistants, Governors, chief and ordinary Mayors, and other judges and officers of justice in all the cities, villages, and places of our kingdoms and domains, both now and in the future, to obey and comply with this our license and favor which we thus grant; and that they neither cross, nor pass, nor consent to go against the tenor and form of its contents, nor transgress in any manner, under penalty of our grace, and of 10,000 maravedís for our Chamber. Authorized in El Pardo on 18 February 1610.

    I, THE KING
    By order of the King our Lord: Jorge de Tovar[7]

APPROVAL BY THE COURT'S DESIGNATED CENSOR

By order of the members of the Royal Council, I have seen this book, entitled *Topography and Description of Algiers, Its Events, and the Succession of Its Kings,* written by Father and Master Fra Diego de Haedo, of the order of Saint Benedict, and I have not found anything in it contrary to our Holy Catholic Faith, nor anything against good morals; rather it is filled with much doctrine and a curious elegance, toward which the Author has labored considerably, and I believe he should be given license to publish it, for the great benefits that Christianity will reap from it.[8]

In Madrid on 18 October 1608
Antonio de Herrera[9]

APPROVAL BY THE SUPERIOR OF THE BENEDICTINE ORDER

By commission of our Most Reverend Father, Fra Antonio Cornejo, Abbot of the Royal Monastery of Saint Benedict of Valladolid and Governor of his Congregation:[10] I have seen this book, and *The History of the Things of Algiers*; I find nothing in it counter to our Holy Catholic faith, or to good morals. And thus it seems to me that it may be granted a license for publication, since it contains material of great subtlety and pleasure, together with great benefit for its readers. And this is my opinion.

From the Royal Monastery of Saint Benedict, Fra Juan de Valle

LICENSE OF THE GENERAL OF SAINT BENEDICT

We, the Reverend Fra Antonio Cornejo, Abbot of Saint Benedict the Royal Monastery of Valladolid and General of its congregation, etc. By means of this document, we give license to Father and Master Diego de Haedo, Abbot of our Lady of Mercy of Frómista, so that, having received the authority of the Supreme Council of the Inquisition, he may publish the *History of the Things of Algiers,* by virtue of the approval he has received to do so. And given what we expect from his great intelligence, and so that he may deserve more, we order him to pursue this printing in holy obedience. License given in Saint Benedict, the Royal Monastery of Valladolid, on 6 October 1604.

> The General of Saint Benedict
> By order of his Most Reverend Paternity
> Fra Gregorio de Lazcano[11]

DEDICATORY LETTER TO THE MOST ILLUSTRIOUS AND MOST REVEREND SIR DON DIEGO DE HAEDO, ARCHBISHOP OF PALERMO, PRESIDENT, AND CAPTAIN GENERAL OF THE KINGDOM OF SICILY FOR OUR LORD, KING PHILIP II.

THE REVEREND FRA DIEGO DE HAEDO[12]
Abbot of Frómista, of the Order of Saint Benedict,
Wishes him health and perpetual happiness.

Among many other reasons that move me (Most Illustrious Sir) to dedicate these writings to Your Most Illustrious Lordship [Y.M.I.L.], I count two as most important. The first (without any flattery) is that many praiseworthy virtues are contained in your person. But Your Lordship is so humble and modest that you disdain and flee from them as from offenses. And thus I entreat your Lordship to give me license to say something, if not all that I would say. The second reason for this dedication is that Your Lordship, informed by Christian captives who were many years in Algiers, especially about what is contained in the *Diálogos* [Dialogues], has composed these materials and delivered them, if only in a draft version, into my keeping while I was in Palermo in your service. They could not therefore be published, nor ever come to light, without the diligent work that I have put into them, giving them final form and essence.[13] And since these materials belong to Y.M.I.L., I hereby return them and trust they will be received and esteemed in keeping with the great worth of their author, through which will be known the saintly zeal that resides in Y.M.I.L., sorrowing for the immense labors which the Christian captives suffer in Algiers, and for the enormous harms to Christianity caused by these sufferings, and manifesting such things to the world in this history, so that all men who are pious may be moved to find a remedy.

In this Y.M.I.L. shows your pious and generous soul, and the noble blood of your birth derived from the most illustrious Duke of Cantabria, gentleman of Vizcaya, called Don Heduo, and of his most ancient ancestral home of Haedo, situated in the Valley of Carranza, which in his honor they called Heduo Palace, from which Alonso Tegui, true historian of the noble lineages of the Mountains, and of Vizcaya,[14] writes in his heroic verses:

> Also of the famed lineage of Haedo
> I shall say how they come from powerful Dukes,
> From him who was called Don Heduo,
> Loved and esteemed by all men.
> From this house the landed gentry would take its surname,
> And devouring time would corrupt it.
> Because it has changed from Heduo to Haedo,
> Remaining most esteemed among all peoples, etc.[15]

And although the nobility of your Lordship's blood is great (to speak without lies or flattery), even greater is that of your virtues, the true ornament of man, which in your person blaze out with great eminence, especially that of Charity, as fervent in Your Lordship as in a second Saint Martin. The better to help the poor, and to attend to the rescue of the captive Christians in Algiers with great quantities of money, and to look to the hospitality of travelers who pass through this Kingdom from all parts of the world, you—a compassionate Christian—deplete yourself and your coffers, and sacrifice the adornment of your Archbishop's palace. This makes Your Lordship a highly skilled and great ecclesiastical Prince, whom God had kept for the glory of his Church, where he is so loved that it seems excessive. In Sicily and in my very presence, I heard many people say, sometimes even shout, the following words about Your Lordship: "Most illustrious Monsignor, may God take the years from my life and give them to Your Illustrious Person instead." You are so esteemed that in this Kingdom and others they call you a saint. And it was the custom among many that whenever a line from Your Lordship fell into their hands, they kissed it and esteemed it as the relic of a saint, saying: "This is from that saint, the Archbishop of Palermo."[16]

And Y.M.I.L. is so favored by God, as all Palermo witnessed in a disaster that befell it around the year 1591, which happened when Don Diego Enríquez de Guzmán, Count of Alba de Listes and Viceroy of the Kingdom of Sicily,[17] left Palermo to visit that Kingdom. When he returned home in a fleet of galleys, the city made a more than one-hundred-foot bridge from land out to sea, so that the stern of the galley could moor itself there, where the Viceroy could arrive and disembark. And since Palermo is the Court of the Kingdom, the cream of society attended his arrival, including Your Lordship, although you could have been excused from attending. Even before the galley was moored, the weight of so many people on the bridge caused it to break down, so that more than five hundred people fell into the sea, including Your Lordship, who was over sixty-five years of age. But God freed you from that danger, in which more than thirty men drowned, while Y.M.I.L. floated on the waters without sinking, blessing them and making the sign of the cross over them until a boat arrived to deliver Y.M.I.L., leaving behind you three drowned servants.

And finally, the great valor of understanding and prudence, the rectitude, integrity, and fortitude in administering justice, with the many divine and human letters of Y.M.I.L. merited that his Majesty light his eyes on Y.M.I.L., most deservedly naming you as Archbishop of this primary Church, and as President and Captain General of this Kingdom.[18] And after these and many other increases here on earth, it is to be hoped that God will give Your Illustrious Lordship in Heaven other major gifts of glory, as this your humble Chaplain entreats, etc.

From Frómista,[19] 25 December 1605
Fra Diego de Haedo

LIST OF ERRATA[20]

[The original ends with a list of errata.]

Doctor Agustín de Vergara[21]

In Valladolid on 3 June 1612

CHAPTER I

The Founding of Algiers

The city commonly known as Algiers—infamous these days for the great and ceaseless harm its people inflict on all the coasts and provinces of the Christian world—is located in the province of Africa known by the ancients as Caesarean Mauritania, on the edge of the Mediterranean Sea, at some 37 degrees latitude.

Who first founded the city, and when, is not exactly known. The learned and curious Moorish author Leo Africanus[1] claims in his *Description of Africa* that it was constructed in ancient times by an African people called the Mesgrana, and that the city itself was named Mesgrana. He never says when this occurred, however, nor does he cite any authorities to confirm his claim. Because neither in Strabo,[2] nor Pliny,[3] nor Polybius,[4] nor in the Tables of Ptolemy,[5] nor the *Itinerarium* of the Emperor Antoninus[6] (writers who diligently and minutely describe all the provinces of Africa, and even great parts of the known world, with all its towns and cities) can there be found any nation, peoples, or city called Mesgrana.

Strabo, an author of the greatest authority, provides some knowledge from antiquity when, in a discussion of the towns and cities of Caesarean Mauritania, he writes about this city under another name: "On this seacoast there once was a city called Iol, which Ptolemy's father Juba rebuilt and changed its name to Caesarea: it has a port and a small island in front." That Strabo should mention here the city that today we call Algiers, and that it would be the same as what more than one author called Iol Caesarea, may be deduced by the latitude of Algiers, which is, as mentioned above, 37¾ degrees, where Ptolemy also more or less locates it.[7] We may conclude the same from the location and formation of today's Algiers—including its distance from and correspondence to other towns—all of which point to where Ptolemy in his Tables, Strabo in his *Geographia,* and Emperor Antoninus in his *Itinerarium* situate Iol Caesarea. And should this not suffice, Strabo gives the clearest proof when he says, in the above citation, that Iol Caesarea was a coastal city in Caesarean Mauritania, and that it had a port and a small island in front.[8] It is clear that present-day Algiers boasts every one of these features, which come together in no other city on the whole coast of Caesarean Mauritania. And from this we may infer the great antiquity of this city, built well before the times of Caesar Augustus and perhaps collapsed from age, since Strabo says that King Juba rebuilt it.[9]

To better understand why this king gave it the name of Caesarea, we must recall that Strabo does not here mean Juba I,[10] son of the great Boccho, king of Mauritania, who handed over Jugurta, king of Numidia, into the hands of Lucius Silla, the legate of Marius. This elder Juba, an ally to the Roman general Pompey, joined his wars until Julius Caesar conquered the Pompey faction, along with all the spoils of Africa. In response to this defeat, Juba I committed suicide.[11]

Strabo refers here to the dead man's son, Juba II, still a young man when his father died. This youth fell into the hands of Julius Caesar, who in the pomp of his African victory carried him off with other captives, as was the custom in a triumphal procession, chained to the front of his chariot. Juba II later came to Rome, where he was educated, and being of such rare intelligence and notable erudition, he wrote a most learned and diligent history, which Pliny and others tend to cite not infrequently.[12] Some say that Juba II evolved from a barbarous Numidian into one of the most learned writers of his day, a man remembered more for the excellence of his studies than for his kingdoms.

For this and for many other personal merits, Juba II was greatly loved by Caesar Augustus (Julius Caesar's successor), who not only granted him his freedom but also married him to Selene,[13] a daughter of Mark Antony and Cleopatra, queen of Egypt. As Suetonius tells us,[14] Augustus brought her out of Egypt along with the other children of the same couple, whom he reared in his home as if they were his own offspring. By way of a dowry, Augustus gave Selene all the kingdoms of her dead father: the whole of Mauritania, which according to the division of those times included the kingdoms of Sousse, Morocco, Taroudant, Fès, Tlemcen, Orán, Ténès, Algiers, Béjaïa, and even Bône [present-day Annaba]. This is a very large spread, in both length and width, of rich lands and excellent provinces. Which is why Plutarch[15] claimed, with some justice, that Juba had a most fortunate captivity.

After the kingdom of his fathers had been returned to Juba with great honor, he rebuilt the city of Iol and called it Caesarea. As was customary in those times, the majority of kings, princes, and other friends of the Romans would rebuild selected towns and cities in their states and kingdoms in honor of Caesar Augustus, giving them his name, as Archelaus did in Capadoccia,[16] the Roman veterans in Hispania, and others in many other places. (Suetonius writes in his Second Book that they did this either to flatter Caesar or to show gratitude for the many benefits he doled out to them.) These rulers would rebuild and restore their cities, enlarging and gracing them with the most magnificent walls, towers, theaters, aqueducts, and temples, and giving them new names of Julias, Augustas, or Caesareas, as Herod did to the Tower of Stratton, magnifying that old Phoenician trading post with the most splendidly elegant and admirable buildings, and calling it Caesarea in honor of Augustus Caesar.[17] Showing no less gratitude than all these rulers to the Caesar who had showered him with so many benefits, King Juba, according to Strabo, rebuilt the city of Iol and called it Caesarea.

We may gather that this city must have earlier been a notable town, for among so many other famous cities of his kingdoms, King Juba especially chose it to illustrate the name of so valiant and powerful an emperor, to whom he owed so much. The importance of this city must have grown considerably after so rich and powerful a king rebuilt it with such good will, and to such an important end, as to honor the name and fame of so great an emperor as Augustus. Beyond such an aim, King Juba chose, from among the many powerful cities of his kingdoms, only this city of Iol Caesarea for his own home, habitation, and royal court, as Pliny writes in his history.[18]

With King Juba dead, the Emperor Caligula foully murdered Juba and Selene's remaining son Ptolemy, a close relation of Caligula through Mark Antony's daughter Selene (because Caligula was the great-grandson of Mark Antony and grandson of his daughter Antonia the Younger, who gave birth to Caligula's father Germanicus from her union with Nero Claudius Drusus). According to Suetonius, Caligula then took for his own the entire kingdom of Mauritania and divided it into two very large provinces.[19] He called one of them Mauritania Tingitense, named after the city of Tingis, which today we call Tanger [Tangiers], a very major city built in the most ancient times by Antheus, and thus selected by the Emperor to head the whole province. And to the other city he gave the name of Iol Caesarea (of which we speak), because it remained the head and metropolis of the whole of this great province.

From all of the above, in short, we may deduce the great nobility and excellence of that city in antiquity, because were it otherwise, the Roman Emperor would never distinguish it as the head and metropolis of such a fine and noble province, as the seat and residence of the Roman magistrate and proconsul, and as a site for the Roman chancellery, in keeping with all the cities of the metropolis where the Roman governors resided. The Romans gave these the name of chancelleries, or *conventus provintiarum* in their Latin tongue, because all the cities and towns of the provinces had recourse to them and convened there to have justice administered and every grievance sorted out.

Claudius, the emperor who followed Caligula, ennobled this city even more, because, as Pliny remarks, he made it into a Roman colony, that is, he sent many Roman soldiers, by then veterans, to live there. And it should in no way be thought that they left behind a great lifestyle — all the treats and delicacies of Italy and of a Rome that had served as their birthplace and home — in order to go live in Africa, a place so remote. These veterans went to a capital site, a place of great quality, goodness, nobility, abundance, and riches. All of which, naturally, would suffice to compensate for what they were leaving behind and make them forget the absence of, and perpetual exile from, such a sweet homeland. And thus Pliny says that in his day, which was after the reign of Claudius (because Pliny flourished in the time of Nero and Vespasian, to whose son Titus he dedicated the books of his history), Iol Caesarea was a very celebrated city.[20]

For greatness, nobility, or preeminence, at least in those times, a city could do no better than to be a Roman colony. Because, as writers of the age inform us, the graces, privileges, liberties, and exemptions of the Roman colonies were manifold, and their inhabitants regarded as people of equally high quality, status, and reputation as the citizens of Rome themselves. Beyond their equality to Romans, the colonists also enjoyed, like them, suffrage, being able (as long as the custom survived) to vote in all the businesses and causes touching the Roman Republic. And along with Romans, they competed for all the government posts, in all times and places, of the city of Rome, of Italy, and of all the provinces and domains of the Romans.[21]

Finally, the inhabitants of the Roman colonies were as Roman in their laws, statutes, usages, customs, ceremonies, language, manners, buildings, games, and even in the style and size of their clothing. As Aulus Gellius writes, in all things the Roman colonies were a propagation and part of the very city of Rome; or as others put it, they were living portraits, in miniature, of the Roman people themselves.[22]

In this same good fortune, reputation, and valor, the citizens of Algiers lived during the times of Hadrian, the fifteenth Roman emperor.[23] And during the reign of the Emperor Hadrian, circa 135 AD, the geographer Ptolemy, when listing the towns and cities of Caesarean Mauritania in his Tables, recalls Algiers, or Iol Caesarea, as a Roman colony. It would have been similarly classified in the times of the Emperor Antoninus Pius, who lived around 160 AD, because in the *Itinerarium* he made of all the cities and towns of the Roman Empire, he likewise calls it a Roman colony.

Afterward, during the decline of the Roman Empire, the Vandals and Alans came over from Spain, called in by Count Boniface who governed one-third of Africa for the Emperor Valentinian.[24] Led by their kings Gunderic and Genseric,[25] these barbarians arrived in the Year of Our Lord 427, and in fire and blood devastated and destroyed all the towns and cities of the two Mauritanias and of all Africa. It is to be believed that the same fate befell Algiers as we know befell many other important places, which were sacked, destroyed, and devastated by those savage and barbarous peoples.

The same thing doubtless happened later when, in the time of the Emperor Leontius around 697 AD, the Arabs conquered and ruined all Africa.[26] Leo Africanus implies this in his *Description of Africa* when, speaking of Cape Matafuz [Temendfust][27] twelve miles east of Algiers, he notes that on that point of land there had been a major city built by the Romans. After its destruction by the Goths, almost all the city walls of Algiers were later rebuilt from its stones, because, according to him, they must have been thrown to earth when the city was devastated. He never mentions, though, when or how it was destroyed and rebuilt again.[28]

Howsoever this may have happened, what is certain is that this city, so badly treated by those two very barbarous peoples, did not cease to remain inhabited and visited, as may be demonstrated by its ancient mosques, its very old yet still erect towers, and other public buildings that today remain in this city, all of antiquated architectural modes found in other cities from ages long ago. Among the features that always drew people to live in the city with good will, and not to forsake it, was the great comfort of its sea, which pounds the walls of the city, and of the port with the island which nature created so near to it, no more distant than an arrow's fling from a crossbow. And although the ships were not so comfortable there back then as now (after Khayr al-Din Barbarossa constructed the port that we see there today), they could still be reasonably secure.[29] The same may be said about the location of this highly fortified city, excellent for an age when men fought only with lances and swords. For where could people feel more secure and without dread?

But, above all, there was the fertility of its great fields and prairies with their adjoining lands, so wide and so excellent, and the hills surrounding them on all sides, so lovely, so fruitful, so gracious and so abundant in the great number of clear and fresh waters that flow from countless fountains and sprinkle an infinite number of peaceful gardens. It is hard to believe that this land, wanting in nothing that life and human contentment may desire, would at any time lack people wishing to enjoy such great liberty and such rich bounty from nature itself.

CHAPTER 2

Why the City Is Called Algiers

Well beyond issues of religion and customs, the coming of the Arabs caused such strange and enormous upheavals in Africa, Spain[1] and its islands, and even in many other countries, that there was no kingdom or province, at least in Africa and Spain, where the Arabs[2] did not put down roots. There was no city, no town, no forest, no river, no spring, no tree, no grass that did not lose its accustomed name to be called by a new and different one.[3] And this plague of naming so ruined the liberal arts, especially those privileged by some Arabs as a profession—Philosophy, Astrology, and Medicine—that however much learned men have labored to clean up these Augean stables,[4] they have not been able to stamp out an infinite number of Arabic words and names that highly contaminate these sciences and professions.[5]

Such a frenzy for renaming is exemplified by this city, which abandoned its ancient name of Iol Caesarea with the arrival of the Arabs, who always called it, and today still call it, al-Djaza'ir, which sounds and means "like the Island."[6] And not so much, as Leo Africanus suggests, because the city faces the islands of Mallorca and Minorca located directly north of it, but because from its very beginnings it was built facing, and very close to, that small island only a crossbow's shot away from it, as we noted earlier. With the name of Algiers the Arabs wish to signify "the city of the island." And since, as is well known, the peoples of one nation cannot clearly pronounce the words and accents of another without corrupting them, we Christians corrupt the Arabic pronunciation of this word, "Algezeir." In its place we Spaniards say "Argel," and the French and Italians say "Algieri."[7]

CHAPTER 3

Algiers as a Muslim Kingdom

When, in time, the Arabs divided Hispania and Africa into diverse kingdoms and estates, Algiers ceased being the head of Caesarean Mauritania (as it had been so many times before) and became part of the kingdom of Tlemcen, whose kings it acknowledged and for a long time obeyed. This continued until a very powerful king of Tunis, called Abu al-Fehri, made himself lord of the city of Béjaïa. After forcing the king of Tlemcen to pay tribute at the hour of his death, Abu al-Fehri divided all his estates and kingdoms among his own three sons. To the youngest, called ʿAbd al-ʿAziz, he gave the city of Béjaïa, making it the head of the new kingdom, as well as many other lands and towns assigned and ordered to obey him.

After his father's death and while waging war on the said king of Tlemcen, ʿAbd al-ʿAziz experienced a continuous assault on some parts of his kingdom, including Algiers, which is no more than 120 Italian miles, or thirty leagues, from Béjaïa. The inhabitants of Algiers, seeing how badly the king of Tlemcen defended them from the king of Béjaïa, decided to subject themselves in obedience to the latter.[1] But this was done in such a way that the residents of Algiers always managed to live as free men, almost in the manner of a republic, only paying a certain tribute to the king of Béjaïa by way of recognition and subjection.

This obedience lasted as long as the kingdom of Béjaïa did, because when Count Pedro Navarro seized the cities of Orán and Béjaïa from the Moors in 1509, winning them for the king of Spain, the inhabitants of Algiers feared that the same fate would befall them.[2] Especially alarmed at how the count in his victorious march had seized and destroyed many other places along the Barbary Coast, they agreed to pledge allegiance to a powerful sheik called Salim al-Tumi, a Moorish prince of the Berbers who lived in Mitidja, the name for the great fields and prairies neighboring Algiers.³ The Algerians hoped that this sheik would defend them and take them under his wing, as he did for some years, until the Turks tyrannically seized the city and took possession of it, as what follows will show.

CHAPTER 4

How Algiers Came under the Turks

The inhabitants of Algiers have for ages been occupied with corsair activities at sea, using ships with oars for their robberies. After the Catholic King, Ferdinand, conquered the kingdom of Granada in January of the Year of Our Lord 1492,[1] the corsairs intensified this practice, causing even greater harm to Christians, because many Moors of Granada, as well as others from Valencia and Aragón, immigrated to Barbary. Being well versed in the wars across Spain, where they had been born and raised, and being familiar with surrounding islands such as Mallorca, Minorca, Ibiza and others, the corsairs had greater occasion and better equipment to rob and cause great harm in all those parts, as indeed they did.

After sending Count Pedro Navarro to capture Orán from the Moors in 1509, King Ferdinand, as mentioned earlier, dispatched a powerful Armada to Algiers and Béjaïa, intending to destroy these cities and remove all thieves and corsairs from the sea. Seeing this, the Algerians surrendered to fear and submitted to the Catholic King, making a truce with him for ten years and agreeing to pay him tribute every year. But because the main intention of the king was to have those harmful corsairs leave Algiers, either willingly or by force, he had a fort built on the island (very close, as we said, to the city of Algiers), in which he regularly kept a garrison of two hundred soldiers with their captain, well provided with ammunition, provisions, and artillery.[2]

This fort greatly restrained the Algerians: they dared not resume their privateering, much less rebel against the Catholic King. His death in January of 1516, however, gave them occasion to throw off the yoke of their subjection under the Christians. To this end, they called in 'Arudj

Barbarossa, who at this time resided in Djidjelli [present-day Jijel], a seaport 180 miles east of Algiers, begging him as a courageous and informed man of war—having shown great proof of this through his experiences—to come with his Turks and galliots to liberate them from the power of the Christians, and from the continuous vexation the Algerians suffered daily from that fort. Under great pressure to satisfy Barbarossa and his soldiers, they promised him a great enterprise.[3]

Hearing this embassy, Barbarossa was extremely flattered to be offered such a great opportunity for something he had earlier wished and later considered in depth, namely, to make himself lord of Algiers and of a great state in Barbary. And so displaying to the ambassadors his great pain at their being so badly treated by Christians, and conveying to them that he wished for nothing more than to liberate them, he quickly sent them off in a joyful and contented state.

Setting his affairs in order, within a few days he sent by sea, in eight galliots, a great number of his Turks with munitions and artillery. Then with the rest of his Turks he set out on land for Algiers where, upon arrival, he began to batter the fort of the island, showing by this act that he greatly wished to gratify the Algerians. This tactic failed, however, because his artillery, being feeble, accomplished little. But because his principal intent was to snatch up the city, within a few days he killed with his own hands the said Salim al-Tumi, a prince and sheik of the Berbers of Mitidja, and at that time lord of Algiers. Barbarossa killed the sheik—who had hosted and lodged him with much honor and courtesy—in his private bath. This deed done, and the Turks having loudly declared him throughout the city as lord of Algiers, the Moors remained greatly stricken with fright and, not daring to resist the Turks, were forced to consent and subject themselves to the yoke and lordship of Barbarossa, as explained in more detail in our *Epítome de los Reyes de Argel* [History of the Kings of Algiers].[4]

CHAPTER 5

The Ramparts of Algiers

Present-day Algiers [ca. 1577–1581], including its entire circumference and ramparts, may be envisioned in the image of a crossbow, including its string.¹ The front of this crossbow faces north-northeast, as do the city's port, borders, corridors, and the flat roofs of its houses, which, as explained below, are all windowless. The port lies in the corridor of the Gregal, or Greek north wind, which aids anyone crossing it.² The walls of the houses that form the arch of the crossbow are set close together and located on a very steep hill. Little by little this hill creeps upward to the very top, so that as the houses keep rising on an uphill slope, the higher ones jut over the lower in such a manner that, although large and tall, these lower dwellings do not impede the views of those behind them. For somebody with a frontal view of the city from the sea, the point of the right-hand arch faces north-northwest. The midpoint of the arch, the highest point of the city, looks almost toward the south, inclining slightly toward the west. And the left-hand point faces somewhere between the south and the east, or the rising sun. From this to the right-hand point of the arch, a continuous wall extends to encircle the entire city, like the arch of a crossbow and its string. This last point signals the lowest part of the city, so close to the waters of the sea that its waves continuously lap over it.

The sea wall has a defect in that — unlike the string in our crossbow simile — it does not extend continuously from one point to another in a straight line. Before reaching the right-hand point, the wall actually plunges outward for a considerable space over a tip of land made by nature, emerging and entering into the sea in the manner of a spur. The wall then keeps moving forward into the sea, making a point like an angle and a breakwater. And outside a door of the ramparts at this very juncture there begins the wharf that Khayr al-Din Barbarossa created to form the port, joining the city to the little island that faces it by means of an embankment. At this point the earth and ramparts begin to retreat again, continuing forward to join with the right-hand arch. The whole circumference of these ramparts, arch as well as string, is made of stone, and they are all filled with battlements in the ancient manner. The entire arch that encircles the city measures some 1,800 paces, and that of the string that extends over the seascape, some 1,600 paces, so that the total circumference adds up to 3,400 paces. The height of this ancient rampart—that is, of the arch that rises up the hill—is some thirty spans, although in the section founded over rocks close to the sea, the height comes to some forty spans. The width or thickness of the ramparts is some eleven or twelve spans.[3]

Beyond this wall that encircles the city on all sides, Barbarossa constructed, in 1532, another stretch of wall that goes straight over the embankment built earlier, thereby closing the distance between the city and the island in order to make the port. This wall extends in a right line from the point where earth and wall enter into the sea, continuing to the left toward the island that faces the city. With a longitude of some three hundred paces, a width of some ten spans and a height of some fifteen, this wall is lower than the other city wall. This second wall was constructed in order to impede the great impetus of the sea waves, which tend to pound furiously there under the influence of the winds, both the west and the northwest wind, or mistral,[4] and could do damage to the galliots and rowboats[5] always anchored there. The wall was also meant to protect the crowds of seamen who continually walk over the wharf.

In 1573, 'Arab Ahmad, then pasha of Algiers, continued to add to these ramparts, surrounding the whole island with them save for the southern part, because through this part the city port faces the island.[6] The wall of the island, lower than the one over the wharf between city and island, is in effect shaped more like a parapet than a rampart. 'Arab Ahmad made this wall so that in times of war the enemy could not disembark on the island, from where they could make themselves lords of the port and, as is possible, batter the earth with artillery.

CHAPTER 6

The Gates of Algiers

This city wall has nine gates that serve the people as exits and entrances in the following way. Near the point of the right-hand arch, which we noted corresponds to the north, there is a gate called Bab al-Wad,[1] situated north-northwest. Following the wall from this point and walking on its left side some eight hundred paces up the mountain to the highest part of the city—the middle of the arch—we arrive at the Kasba,[2] or ancient fortress of the city. A small door located here, called "Of the Kasba," faces almost south-southwest. Some twenty paces ahead, again along the left-hand side, another small door in the Kasba also faces south-southwest. Only the janissaries and soldiers of the fortress can use these two gates. Some four hundred paces downhill on the left-hand side of this second Kasba gate is another main and heavily frequented entry to the city, called Bab al-Djadid, or the New Gate, which faces directly southwest. And four hundred more paces downhill we find yet another main gate called Bab ʿAzzun, this one facing between south and east. This gate, with a roadway of some 1,260 paces leading out of it, corresponds in diameter to the other main gate of Bab al-Wad, where we began. The Bab ʿAzzun is heavily frequented at every hour of the day: not only do all provisions, merchandise, Moors and Arabs coming into the city enter through this gate, but also everyone traveling outside the city—to the Berber camps, to all the towns and places of the kingdom, to anywhere else in Barbary—must pass through it.[3]

The point of the arch, or the left-hand side of the city wall—as earlier noted—ends below this gate, some fifty paces toward the sea, joining there with the waves. From this point toward the north, the city wall moves some eight hundred paces close to the sea and directly to the wharf. A piece of city wall less ancient than the rest stands at three hundred paces in. Built in the form of an arch, and something more than a half moon, this wall holds back the seawaters, with all its parts encircling a plaza. With a diameter of some eighty paces, this plaza functions as the shipyards of the city, where parts of ships and galliots are made, other parts being made on the island where the port and wharf lie. Although this Arsenal has no gate of entry into the city, it does have two gates toward the sea, both in two high arches of stone and each one of a width that allows an unarmed galliot to enter and exit. The distance between these two stone gates is just enough to fit a house for the shipmasters. The first gate is always closed with a wall of tamped-down earth two *tapias*[4] in height, which can be dismantled when a ship is launched through it. The second gate has a wooden door, with locks and bolts, not reaching very high, and through this gate enter and exit all the artisans who build the ships and galliots.

Some forty paces ahead, another gate is carved into the wall. This one, which does not seem very old, was constructed as an afterthought for access from the city and its walls to the sea. And fifty paces toward the city from this small door stands yet another small gate, this one opening into yet another ancient wall, the first around the city. This second gate is secured at night by a lock and continually guarded by day. The outer gate closer to the sea is called the Customs Gate, because near it are unloaded, and through it enter into the city, all the goods that Christian merchants bring in their ships. The goods brought overseas by Turks and Moors are unloaded on the wharf. For the merchandise of Christians, there stands outside this gate and close to the sea a small building, properly known as the Customs House, where everything enters and is registered. Through this gate, as well as the one within closer to the city, all the fishermen enter with their catch to sell in the city, and many people generally exit in the mornings.

Some two hundred paces beyond this Customs Gate stands another main gate in that angle or point made, as noted earlier, by the earth and the walls of the city, entering a bit more into the sea and to where the wharf begins that will end on the facing island. This gate is called Bab al-Djazira, or Gate of the Island. Because the city's port is located there, and because it is used for the exits and entrances of all manner of people—Christians, Moors, Turks, galley slaves, rowers, artisans, corsairs, merchants, and a great infinity of others—this gate is continually frequented and there is a great bustle and much activity there all day.

CHAPTER 7

The Fortifications of Algiers

Although there are many towers or fortifications[1] all around the ramparts, because of their wretched and antiquated condition, only seven merit any attention. To these is assigned all the strength of the wall.[2] Beginning, as we did earlier, with the arch of the wall on the right-hand side — which we said faces north — at this point, very close to the sea, there is a bastion within an embankment of some twenty square feet, with nine portholes, three of which correspond to the north, three to the west, and another three between the east and the south. These portholes contain no more than five pieces of small artillery, three facing the sea and three, the land. The height of this bastion is twenty-six spans, and it was constructed by Ramadan Pasha, a Sardinian renegade, while he was king of Algiers in 1576.

Walking forward along the wall, we find, at some fifty paces down the left-hand side, the Gate of Bab al-Wad, as earlier noted, and over it a small tower or slender bastion without any embankment or kind of artillery. With only six portholes, two in front and two more on each flank, this tower faces northwest, as does the Bab al-Wad gate. Following the wall toward the south, and moving uphill some four hundred paces on the left-hand side, we encounter yet another small tower, this one in an embankment. Twenty-one spans tall and fifteen square, this tower has six portholes, all free of artillery.

Ahead and uphill some four hundred paces stands the citadel, or Kasba, the ancient fort of the city, which is nothing more than a piece of wall twenty-five spans high. Leaving the body of the city some three or four paces, no more, and continuing from north to south by one hundred paces, the wall returns along the edge to join the city again.

Similarly, there is another wall within the city, some sixty paces away from the first and very flimsy, which continues by the same distance of one hundred paces, from north to south. It ends up forming a plaza enclosed by all sides of the wall, one hundred paces long and sixty wide. Like a structure apart from the rest of the city, this plaza represents a meeting place of the city and the wall. Only the outside wall is embanked to a thickness of twenty handspans, and from it emerge two small towers, confined in a very small space and containing some eight pieces of minor artillery. Within this citadel, or enclosure between two walls, there reside in special houses up to sixty old soldiers, janissaries who are almost all married and who guard the fort day and night with great vigilance.

Walking downhill from here and always keeping the wall to one's left, at four hundred paces and to the left of the abovementioned New Gate, we find another bastion or small tower with no embankment. Twenty-three handspans high, this bastion contains six portholes, two in front that face south and two others on either side, with absolutely no artillery.

Move farther down some 450 paces and, after passing the Gate of Bab ʿAzzun, the arch of the wall ends up in the sea, as we said earlier. At this point stands another square bastion, twenty-five handspans high, all embanked and twenty feet in diameter, with nine portholes, three facing southwest, three southeast, and three northeast. This bastion has only three small pieces of artillery, all badly aligned. It was constructed by ʿArab Ahmad, when he was king of Algiers in the Year of Our Lord 1573.

Continuing from here along the wall lapped by sea waves—which we earlier compared to the string of a crossbow's arch—until reaching the wharf and port of the city, one finds no fortifications whatsoever, whether of towers or bastions. But over the Gate of Bab al-Djazira, from which the wharf emerges, is a magnificent bastion, the best and largest of all the ones in Algiers. It is thirty feet long and forty wide, not altogether a square since it has more width than length. Its main section has an embankment and a casemate. It has no porthole, but rather a parapet facing south, east, and northeast, looking toward the front of the port.

Along all the north side there are twenty-three pieces of genuine bronze artillery, the best in Algiers, of which only seven or eight are mounted. There is one among these with seven openings, which Ramadan Pasha brought from Fès in 1576, the year he made Muley Maluch ['Abd al-Malik] head of that kingdom. This bastion also has its normal guard of artillerymen, each with other sentinels who assist and guard them continuously. This bastion was constructed by Ka'id Saffa,[3] a Turk by origin, when in the Year of Our Lord 1551 and part of 1552 he governed Algiers and its kingdom as *caliph*,[4] or viceroy of the governor in the absence of Hasan Pasha, son of Barbarossa, as we shall elaborate in what follows.[5]

On the island closest to the port there are, in addition, two small towers. One was constructed as a lantern or lighthouse to show seafarers the port, although it is never lit. And another was built to serve as a watchtower for the port and the galleys moored there, so that enemies would not arrive by night to burn the ships, as sometimes happened.[6] But these two towers are of small importance, having absolutely no force of artillery. They were constructed by 'Arab Ahmad in 1573, when he fortified that island with a wall or parapet, as we said earlier.

CHAPTER 8

The Moat of Algiers

Apart from these towers and bastions, an ancient moat surrounds the city, following the arch of its wall. This moat is up to sixteen paces wide, and for the most part it is shallow, and very blocked up with dirt, trash, and infinite filth. But in all the area taken up by the wall of the citadel—or Kasba—which is one hundred paces long, twenty paces wide and the depth of a pike—everything is very clean. And similarly, in that whole distance between the New Gate, which faces south, and the bastion that ʿArab Ahmad constructed at the point where the arch or wall descends into the sea—a distance, as we said, of some 450 paces— the entire moat is open. It has the same depth and width of the moat closest to the citadel. In these two places the moat was cleaned by order of ʿArab Ahmad, pasha of Algiers in the Year of Our Lord 1573. And had his government lasted longer, he would have cleaned all the other parts of the wall and moat, as was his intention. Within the city itself there is no moat whatsoever, nor space to build one, because the houses are so close to the wall, that in case the Turks would wish to construct a moat or ditch within the city, it would be necessary to first take down all the houses closest to the wall, making space where they have been demolished.

CHAPTER 9

The Castles and Forts outside Algiers

A stone's throw from the city wall, three castles or forts serve as the main defense and fortification of Algiers. These castles, called *burdj*[1] by the Moors, were built by the Turks in recent times. The first of these castles, to begin again from the Gate of Bab al-Wad on the right hand of the city, is the one commonly called the Burdj or Fort of ʿUludj ʿAli.[2]

This fort, located some 370 paces west of the above gate and constructed over a small rock that nature created there, is in the form of a quadrangle with four points. The point corresponding to the city (which stands at its back) has neither casemates[3] nor portholes, but only a parapet. In each of the other three corners there is a casemate, and all have portholes. The corner that faces north has only one porthole, but in the other two, facing south and west, there are two portholes below for each, and in the parapets above there are three portholes on all three corners. The patio or central plaza of this castle measures up to thirty feet in diameter; it is all embanked, with a well-made cistern in the middle. The castle has some eight pieces of middling artillery and no ditch whatsoever, neither outdoors nor in.

ʿUludj ʿAli constructed this castle when he was king of Algiers, in the Year of Our Lord 1569. His aim was to defend a small beach, some 360 paces northwest of the castle, where warring parties could moor their rowboats and disembark. This castle has a great defect, however, like all the other fortifications in Algiers, since there are many dominant heights south of it. From two hills some 100 to 150 paces away, the castle could easily be battered, with its enemies receiving no harm. From these very heights, moreover, the entire road from the city to the castle is visible; and so the same people who would attack the castle from on high could also cut off and disturb any aid the city might bring to it.

Some one thousand paces south of this Fort of 'Uludj 'Ali, high on the mountain some six hundred paces from the Kasba, or citadel, stands the second castle, facing south-southwest. Built in the figure of a pentagon, it has a crossing inside of fifty paces, with twenty-five reserved for a patio. The castle is embanked from top to bottom some thirty spans, which constitute its entire height. Its parapets boast a thickness of twenty spans; in each of the five corners there are four portholes, two on each side. It has in the middle a round cistern that takes up the twenty-five paces of the patio. It also has eight habitable huts that serve as chambers for the soldiers. This castle has no moat, neither inside nor out, but there is a tunnel all around it, so high and wide that a man could easily walk through it, from its foundations to its casemates. This castle, which contains eight pieces of minor artillery, none of them mounted, is also very exposed to some mountains 100 to 120 paces to the southwest, from where it could easily be attacked, again cutting off all aid which might come to it from the city and the citadel.

Between the castle and the mountains, there are many gullies and ravines in the earth caused by the great currents of water that, with the rains across time, have come down from the nearby mountains. Many enemies can hide in these ravines, and even move from them stealthily to the foot of the castle itself without being attacked or discovered.

Muhammad Pasha built this castle in the Year of Our Lord 1568, when he was king of Algiers, which is why it is called the Burdj or Fort of Muhammad Pasha. Its engineer was Mustafa the Sicilian, also an engineer on the Goleta. While being taken to Sicily in a frigate as a prisoner of the Holy Office, he and all his companions were captured by the Turks, and a few days after being brought to Algiers, he turned renegade.

The third castle stands in front of this one by Muhammad Pasha, if one walks south some 1,100 paces and, from the Kasba and the city, some 1,700 paces. The first to begin its construction was the son of Barbarossa, Hasan Pasha, when he was king of Algiers for the first time in 1545. He began it in the very place where Emperor Charles V, of glorious memory, planted his flag when he laid siege to Algiers in the Year of Our Lord 1541, on October 27, the eve of Saints Simon and Judas. At the time Hasan Pasha built nothing more than an empty tower with no embankment, twenty-five feet across, with a vault over which he placed three small pieces of artillery. Later on, in 1579 and 1580, when Hasan Pasha the Venetian, the renegade of 'Uludj 'Ali, was king of Algiers, he continued the construction out of great fear of King Philip's very powerful armada, which his Majesty was pulling together with many men and arms in the Bay of Cádiz and other parts of the Straight of Gibraltar toward Portugal. And because the Turks of Algiers were convinced that the armada was heading toward them, the said Hasan Pasha decided to fortify this castle in great haste. Or put another way, because the castle's mountain site was very important, around that old tower he built four bastions that remain in a quadrangle figure in a space ninety paces long, and others of similar width, with the old castle in the middle.

One of these bastions faces west, the other south, another east, and the fourth, north: a total of four, with a high stretch of wall of some twenty-eight spans, and all embanked with their portholes above and below. In each point there are three portholes per side. The body or width of each of these four towers is of twenty paces, and the parapets, a width of ten spans. The plaza of arms that remains in the midst of all four towers or bastions might be some forty-four paces across. In the middle of the plaza, as we said, stands the old castle that the son of Barbarossa constructed, but they have newly embanked it, and being taller by a dozen spans than the four bastions, it lords it over them all.

Also worth knowing is that virtually in the middle of this whole plaza of arms, itself located in the middle of the four bastions, the king constructed a defensive ditch that crosses from west to east and cuts the plaza into two uneven parts. Because of this ditch, the two front bastions, the southern and eastern ones, remain separated, as if in a body to themselves, from the two rear ones, the western and the northern ones, as if they were two distinct forts, separated from each other, with that ditch in the middle separating them by no more than its own width. This division was created so that if the enemy would first gain the two front bastions, it would be possible to pull together and bring the Turks to the other second part of the rear bastions, and the ditch would retard and detain the impetus of the enemy, keeping them from moving forward. For their own retreat the Turks constructed a false door with an underground pathway in the manner of a tunnel, which runs from the plaza of the two rear bastions down below into the ditch.

For additional defense they constructed, in this same part with the two rear bastions and over the ditch, a parapet that, in the manner of a wall, runs from one bastion to the other, with some portholes in the middle. From there they could attack any enemies who may have already entered and become lords of the two first bastions, and also keep them from leaping over the ditch or climbing the rear bastions. This ditch is no deeper than twelve spans, wide by some twenty, and there is no other, neither around the fort nor in any other part. In all four bastions there are no more than twelve pieces of small and middling artillery, and another three more in the decrepit castle.

This whole fortification is dominated by and vulnerable to a mountain on its right hand, directly west at some 150 paces, more or less, where an enemy with artillery could disturb all help coming from the city. There are also three other hills toward the south and east at a distance of 150, 200, and 250 paces, from which locations it would be easy to put up a good cannon fight. Between the fort and the mountains there are, in addition, great fissures that the force of mountain water makes when it rains. Because these are deep, they could serve as trenches for as many soldiers as one would want, great numbers of men, who could remain hidden in them and from there attack the Turks in the castle.[4]

In the very site where this fortification is located, the Emperor Charles V (as we said earlier) placed his flag, and as a result, it is commonly called the Burdj, or Fort of the Emperor. Others call it the Fort of Hasan Pasha, in respect to the two kings of Algiers, the one who began construction of the fort and the one who finished it, both of whom have the same name of Hasan. The chief engineer of this fortification was a Greek renegade called Ka'id Hasan. Apart from the fact that all three of these castles can be easily assaulted, with all help from the city cut off, it also bears noting that the earth, in mountains, plains, and other parts, is quite humid here, although without too much water and dampness. And because the rocks are all so soft, tender, and easy to dig up and break, there is no land more perfectly fit for constructing some fine, secure tunnels, and this with great ease and little work, as may be seen in the multiple huge caves that exist in some of the many farms located in the hills surrounding Algiers.[5]

CHAPTER 10

The Houses and Streets of Algiers

To return to the city, the number of houses included within the circuit of its walls comes to some 12,200, large and small.[1] Because even though the urban circuit is not very large—and one cannot find a house in the whole city that does not have a bit, even a small bit, of a corral—all the streets of Algiers are narrow, even more so than the narrowest streets of Granada, Toledo, or Lisbon. Neither a horseman nor two people walking side by side could pass through them easily. The exception is the great street of the Souk, which we said crosses in a straight line from the bridge of Bab ʿAzzun up to what they call the Bab al-Wad, because this last is the marketplace, with a plaza containing an infinite number of shops on every side and all sorts of merchants. Even though the Souk is no wider than forty handspans, if that, and in places much less, it is still the main street, and the widest, in Algiers.[2] In short, the entire city is so dense, and the houses so close to each other, that it all seems like a very tight pine cone. The result is that all the streets, which have the great fault of being poorly cobbled, become very dirty whenever any rain falls. They have yet another defect: barring the great street of the Souk, or market, no other street can be found that is straight or well ordered, and even this one cannot be described as such. Rather, as is the custom and general use in Moorish towns, all the streets lack order and harmony and need repairs.

This is not the same for the style and architecture of the houses, because many if not most of them are very pretty and polished. They are all generally made of stone, with flat roofs where the washing is hung up to dry. And because the houses are so close and the streets so narrow, one could almost walk the whole city via the rooftops. Many women visit their neighbors by passing from one house to another across the rooftops. For this very reason the houses are subject to robbery, which happens if there is little vigilance and thieves enter the houses and exit through their rooftops. There are very few houses without hallways and patios and spacious centers. But there is no house, finally, with much light or clarity inside. Because the men do not want their wives and daughters to see or be seen by others, their houses have no windows into the streets as in Christian lands.

Many of these houses also have their patios and hallways beautifully worked with bricks and colored tiles, as well as their corridors and handrails, ordinarily a part of their patios in the manner of monastery cloisters. The Algerians always try to keep these patios very clean, washing and scrubbing them almost every week. And for all the water continually needed for this and other things, they often tend to have a well in each house, and many also have a cistern. These wells contain gross and salty water, not good to drink, but this lack is made up by many very pretty fountains in and outside of the city, as we shall discuss later.

Outside of the circuit of the city wall there are now no slums, as there are in other towns, unless one counts some twenty-five houses in a street fronting the Gate of Bab 'Azzun toward the south. These are partly very shabby inns with corrals for poor people, as well as for Berbers and their beasts of burden when they come to the city, and partly the dwelling of some Moors who make lime in ovens located there. And these few houses are left over from a very beautiful area of over fifteen hundred homes that this city had a few years ago. When 'Arab Ahmad was king of Algiers in 1573, he dismantled these homes, cast them down to earth, and began there to fortify the city with a moat and walls, in response to the great fear that Don Juan of Austria was coming to attack Algiers, as he did the city of Tunis, which he conquered in the summer of that same year.[3]

CHAPTER 11

The Inhabitants and Neighbors of Algiers

The inhabitants of this city are generally divided into three kinds: Moors, Turks, and Jews. We do not speak of Christians, although there is an infinite number of them of every stripe and nation, because they ordinarily arrive here as captives and slaves, including the more than 25,000 who row in the galleys or who remain on land.[1] Christians, therefore, count as neither inhabitants nor neighbors of Algiers. Nor do we include Christian merchants as inhabitants, since very few are based here: their business done and their merchandise sold, each man returns to his own land.

The Moors themselves are of four kinds: some are natives of the city itself, commonly called in their language *baldi,* which means something like "citizen."[2] They might occupy some 2,500 houses. These Moors are partly white and partly tan, tilting a bit toward brown, and none of them badly proportioned. Their women, in general, are all white and many of them of good figure and beauty.[3] The bulk of these Moors are merchants of every kind, and many of them have shops in which they sell diverse products, principally all kinds of foodstuffs. Others are laborers and artisans, and many others (the most prosperous) live off their lands or tenant farms, where they reap much wheat, barley, and legumes; produce silk; or raise many cattle and livestock. None of these citizens pays taxes, a privilege conceded them by 'Arudj Barbarossa (when he deceitfully took over the city). He did this in order to pacify and flatter them, so that they would accept and obey him as their lord with better spirit and will, as all tyrants tend to do at the beginning of their tyrannies and occupations. The Turks later confirmed this privilege, and until now these Moors have held on to it.

The dress of all these people is primarily a shirt and wide breeches of linen.[4] When the weather turns cold, they wear a tunic of colored cloth called a *gonela* or *goleila,* which falls below the knee like a short cassock.[5] But in summer they forgo this and, in its place, many will wear another shirt of fine linen, long and wide and very white, which they call a *gandura*.[6] And as a cape over everything, many wear a white *burnus,*[7] although the more solemn types will sport a black or blue one, and in cold weather, a woolen tunic of one of the same colors.

On their heads they tend to wear an impeccably white linen circlet over a cap of fine wool or quilted cloth. This head covering also covers the neck and, wrapping around under the beard, comes to fall over the chest. If it is cold, they wear colored walking boots, because few have black ones.[8] If it is summer, they walk bare-legged, and always with their shoes in the Turkish manner. Some will sport charming colored slippers, open in front and slightly high, like women's shoes, in which they show a few fringes or tassels of white or blue silk, a kind of footwear they call *medasa.*[9]

The second kind of Moors, called Kabyles,[10] come from beyond the mountains to live within Algiers. These people are actually the ancient and natural Africans, born and reared from the start in these parts of Africa. Although they are generally of a brown color, some of these Kabyles—who come from the highest mountains of the Kuko or from Labbès,[11] where there is snow the whole year—are white and not badly proportioned. They are all very poor, and necessity brings them to live in Algiers, in rented rooms or huts. They earn a living by serving Turks or rich Moors, often digging gardens and vineyards. Those Kabyles who row in galleys and brigantines, hired and paid by the job, are called Bagarinos.[12] Some of these Kabyles sell herbs, fruits, charcoal, oil, lard, eggs, and other similar things.

Among these Kabyles may also be counted some Moors called by another name, the Zwawa.[13] These are natives of both the kingdom of Kuko, some fifty miles southeast of Algiers, and the kingdom of Labbès (Banu 'Abbas), 130 miles east of Algiers and bordering Béjaïa.[14] These Zwawa, along with their wives and children, tend to have a cross carved on their flesh, on the right cheek of their faces, which friends and relatives kiss when they meet. This custom has been with them since the time of the Goths and Vandals, who as lords of these African provinces wanted to distinguish the Africans who were Christians from the idolaters. And so they ordered that all of the Christians be marked on the cheek with a cross, and along with this privilege gave them freedom from paying taxes, unlike those who did not wear the cross, later known as idolatrous Gentiles. This facial mark, originally a sign of gentility and nobility, survives to this day among the Zwawa, although they hardly know the cause of it. But they pride themselves highly on having this cross, which they claim to bear because they are sons and descendants of ancient Christians.

The Turks avail themselves greatly of these same Zwawa in war, because they are not bad soldiers. And so in all the garrisons of the kingdom—in Tlemcen, Mostaganem, Biskra, Constantine, Annaba, and other parts, and even in Algiers itself—one-third of the soldiers, and sometimes more, are Zwawa. The Turks similarly use them in the *mahallas* and camps or as squads of soldiers during their frequent trips across the year to collect tribute from the Arabs and Moors.[15] Like the Turks, these Zwawa also have their own officers, corporals for their squadrons, and an *agha,* or colonel who heads them all, although he himself is subject to the agha of the janissaries.[16]

Many women among the Kabyles and Zwawa are whiter than their men. Those who are married to soldiers live with their husbands in rented quarters and maintain themselves from their husbands' salaries. But the majority of Berber women live from the work of their hands: weaving, knitting, and providing services of all kinds in the homes of wealthier Moorish women and renegades. Many Berber women habitually paint their breasts, necks, arms and legs, making diverse designs with the tips of needles, or with knives that puncture the skin, and inserting into their wounds certain materials that leave them painted like snakes, with marks they can never again remove.[17]

Those Zwawa who are soldiers dress in the same style as the Turks, as will be discussed later. Other Zwawa, together with the Kabyles, ordinarily wear nothing more than a shirt and breeches, and many wear neither of these. But they all cover themselves with a Moorish cape called an *al-ksa*[18] or they wrap themselves up in a *barrakan,* a bolt of coarse impermeable wool.[19] On their heads many wear a piece of fabric wrapped willy-nilly over some kind of headpiece, and some wear nothing at all on their heads. A few wear whatever shoes they can find, either Turkish or Christian footgear, but the majority of them walk barefoot.

There are some one hundred houses of married Zwawa in Algiers, because the rest, as bachelors and similar to the janissaries, have rooms and public lodgings allotted to them, where, as comrades and housemates, two hundred or three hundred men and more live together. For the other Kabyles, there might be six hundred houses, more or less.

The third kind of Moors are Bedouins, who continually come to Algiers from their dwellings in fields and in tents. Ordinarily they come for no other reason than to beg for alms, because they are all such vile rabble that they would rather die of hunger than earn their bread working or serving a master. And thus an infinite number of men, women, and children roam the streets begging the whole year, and their houses are the portals of homes, or wherever they find a bit of shelter. Some Bedouins gather themselves outside the city gate of Bab 'Azzun in certain straw huts they have constructed along the city walls or the walls of houses of that poor quarter that, as we mentioned, 'Arab Ahmad, king of Algiers, leveled in the year 1573.

All these Bedouins and their women are ugly, ill-featured, of skin and bones, tan or very dark brown in color, and, above all, extremely dirty pigs. Their dress is a piece of coarse wool, old and torn, with no shirts nor breeches nor anything else to cover their bodies, and this woolen garb serves them at night as both blanket and mattress for sleeping. The same can be said about their women, save that they miraculously wear something on their heads, any old rag of linen out of the rubbish dump. And these lovely and refined gallants are the same people who conquered Africa and even almost all of Spain, and who, with God's grace, won so many victories over Christians.[20]

The fourth type of Moors[21] are those who came over to these parts, and still come over, from the kingdoms of Granada, Aragón, Valencia, and Catalonia. They come with their wives and children via Marseille and other ports of France, from where they embark at will, the French taking them in their ships. All these Moors divide themselves into two castes, coming from different parts: those who call themselves Mudéjares are Moors from only Granada and Andalucía, whereas the Moors known as Tagarinos hail from Aragón, Valencia, and Catalonia.[22] All these Moors are white and well proportioned, like people either born in or coming from Spain.

And because they all know some type of craft, they practice many diverse occupations. Some make harquebuses, gunpowder, or saltpeter; others are blacksmiths, carpenters, or builders; still others are tailors, shoemakers, potters, and similar craftsmen. Many of these Moors make silk, and some manage shops where they sell notions of every kind. But all these Moriscos are generally the foremost and cruelest enemies of us Christians in Barbary, because they can never get enough Christian blood, nor do they ever lose the great hunger and thirst in their vitals for it. These Moors all dress in the mode and manner of Turks, as we shall discuss later. There might be as many as one thousand houses of all these people in Algiers.[23]

CHAPTER 12

Turks

The Turks are also of two kinds: Turks by nature or by profession. Turks by nature are those who have come, or whose parents have come, from Turkey. Every day many Turks arrive in galleys and other ships, spurred on by the fame of the riches of Algiers as well as the great and continuous robberies made on Christian ships and lands.

These immigrants are the vilest of people, stupid and villainous, and for this reason the Turks call them jackals.[1] But some have turned out, and still turn out, to be men of worth and valor. The Turks all have robust bodies, because since childhood they are reared with neither fear nor good manners. Like brute animals, they are given free rein in all manner of vice that materializes or appeals to the flesh. And because Turkey is divided into two parts—Anatolia, which includes the kingdoms of Asia, and Romania, which includes the states held in Europe by the Turk[2]—this means that Turks differ among themselves, in both condition and color.[3] The people of Romania, although jackals and villains, are more lively and talented as well as whiter and more well proportioned. The people of Anatolia, on the other hand, are grosser and more simple-minded, somewhat more dark-skinned, and of a less attractive figure and proportion.[4]

Of all the above Turks, including every class and quality, those who live on their own, not counting the unmarried janissaries, account for some 1,600 dwellings in Algiers.

CHAPTER 13

Renegades

"Turks by profession" are all those renegades of Christian blood and parentage who have turned Turk of their own free will, impiously renouncing and spurning their God and Creator. These renegades and their children outnumber all their neighbors in Algiers—Muslims, Turks, and Jews—because there is no Christian nation on earth that has not produced renegades in this city.[1] Beginning with the remote provinces of Europe, the following renegades may be found in Algiers: Muscovites, Russians, Ukrainians, Valacos, Bulgarians, Poles, Hungarians, Bohemians, Germans, Danish and Norwegians, Scotsmen, Englishmen, Irishmen, Flemish, Burgundians, Frenchmen, Navarrese, Basques, Castilians, Galicians, Portuguese, Andalusians, Valencians, Aragonese, Catalonians, Majorcans, Sardinians, Corsicans, Sicilians, Calabrese, Neapolitans, Romans, Tuscans, Genoese, Savoyans, Piedmontese, Lombards, Venetians, Slavs, Bosnians, Albanians, Greeks, Cretans, Cypriots, Syrians, Egyptians, and even Abyssinians of Prester John, as well as Indians from the Portuguese Indies [India], from Brazil, and from New Spain [Mexico].[2]

What moves some of these men to forsake the true path of God, at such great peril to their souls, is nothing more than the fainthearted refusal to take on the work of slavery. Others are attracted by pleasure, by the good life of fleshly vice in which the Turks live. Still others are addicted since childhood to the wickedness of sodomy imposed on them by their masters. And together with all the fuss the Turks make over them—more even than over their own women—these men turn Turk in their youthful ignorance, understanding neither what they are disowning nor what they are adopting.[3] And the Turks willfully turn them into renegades, persuading themselves that, as good Turks, they do this to serve both God and Muhammad. Those who have already adopted that way of life or profession naturally want others to follow and approve of their deceits, from which, in general, they all profit.

Because it is the custom among the Turks that if a renegade dies childless, without heirs, his possessions return to his master, to whoever had formerly enslaved him, even if he had been liberated. And if his master is already dead, then his son or grandson inherit, in the same manner, the goods belonging to either his father's or grandfather's renegade. This practice—that the master or his sons come to inherit the assets of an emancipated slave who dies intestate[4]—is the same as what common law dictates among Christians. There are Turks and renegades who have ten, twelve, fifteen, twenty or more of these renegades, whom they call their sons and treat accordingly. As soon as they convert them into Muslims, moreover, the Turks also offer them letters of credit, give them slaves and money, and support them later when necessary. If the Turks die without heirs, they divide their possessions and estates among the renegades as if they were their children. And before the Turks die, they generally give their freedom to all those who are still in bondage.[5]

The ceremony and procedure they use when converting men into Turks or renegades is the following. On a chosen day, they set up an ornately decorated bed in a chamber, and when night falls (because these events are never held during the day), they host a banquet called a *sosfia*[6] for all invited friends and relatives of the would-be renegade, as many as they wish. The dinner over, either they seat him on a chair or he remains on foot and two men hold him by the arms. If he is a young boy, they place him over the knees of a seated man, who has grabbed the boy's arms behind him and propped them under a fork pole. And placing at his feet either an animal skin or a vessel full of sand to catch the blood, the master of ceremonies, usually a Jew skilled in this trade, approaches him, and with some kind of iron clamp specifically made for the job, cuts around the foreskin and circumcises him, slicing all around the prepuce of his member without leaving any skin. And because this cannot be done without causing great pain, when the master is about to cut into the flesh, all the invited guests burst into loud cries, calling for Muhammad and saying to him: "Ila, Ila Ala Mahamet hera, curra Ala, etc.," which means, "God is, God will be, and Muhammad is his prophet."[7] At the same time, other guests throw down pots or cups of water, strategically placed along corridors and balconies, so that all the noise and din will distract the newly circumcised man from feeling so much pain.

This done, and the new Turk or Muslim all bandaged up, they either lay him on a bed especially prepared for him or whisk him off to another bedroom, as they sometimes do with less favored boys whose circumcisions are less solemnized. Then each guest at the fiesta presents the new Muslim with a gift—such as shoes, laced boots, caps and toques, knives, ribbons that they call *cuzacas*,[8] shirts, handkerchiefs, or any gift they want. Some guests give the circumcised man green candles, and some give him nothing. And then they all go home.[9] When some Christian voluntarily turns Turk, whether in flight from Spain, France, Italy, or anywhere, or if he is a somewhat distinguished person—such as a soldier from Orán; or a master of arts or crafts; or the officer of a ship—he is dressed up as a Turk and placed on horseback with an arrow in hand. The janissaries publicly parade such men throughout the city the morning of the night they are to be circumcised. Some fifty or sixty or more janissaries will generally follow the renegade horseman on foot with bared scimitars in their hands, carrying the customary banner of the horse's tail, playing their usual flutes, and giving forth shrieks of pleasure.[10] The new Muslims are outfitted by the king, who also supplies the costs of their food. And if the new Turk wants to join the janissaries, he is received into their corps and given a soldier's pay, four *doblas*[11] per month.

The ceremony used in the case of a Christian female who converts to Islam is different, and much simpler. After they make her wash herself and recite prayers in a room or bedroom, they cut off a hank of her hair from the front of her head, and shave off all the scruff of her neck so that not a single hair remains on it. After that they give her a Moorish or Turkish name and nothing more.

These renegades then become the principal enemies of the Christian religion. Almost all the power and dominion, government and riches of Algiers and the entire kingdom resides in them. There are some six thousand or more residences belonging to these renegades and their offspring in Algiers.[12]

CHAPTER 14

Ka'ids

Along with their children, Turks by nature or profession generally make a living in one of six ways: as *ka'ids*,[1] or government officials; as *sipahis*, or unsalaried soldiers;[2] as janissaries, or ordinary soldiers; as corsairs; as merchants; and as masterbuilders or craftsmen. Ka'ids are those men who govern the lands and towns subject to the dominion of Algiers, with its districts such as Tlemcen, Mostaganem, Ténès, Cherchell, Miliana, Biskra, Béjaïa, Djidjelli, Bône (Annaba), Constantine, and others. Men who have governed these places at any time in the past keep the name of ka'id all their lives.

    Custom also dictates that anyone with some type of public post or jurisdiction over others, or holding a position at the house of the pashas, is also called ka'id. And so the title of ka'id is even given to the man posted at the gates of the city in charge of collecting the entry tax and tribute for items brought into Algiers. And the man who rents out all the wax or hides, keeping others from either buying them from the Moors or selling them to Christian merchants, is also called ka'id. Even the man in charge of all the king's wheat, cows and livestock, as well as others like him, is also given this title. Men like these who have held or now hold the title are all generally very rich. These offices are given neither for merit nor for services rendered, but often to a person whom the Grand Turk favors, granting him the government of a territory for several years or for life.

    More commonly the most open-handed men can buy any of these government offices in something akin to an auction. They are sold according to the profit that can be made from the land, which is from the tribute that the subject Moors and Berbers tend to pay their governments. This is principally done through extortion, coercion, violence, vexation, and the great tyrannies that the Turks foist on their poor Moorish subjects, because with or without cause, left and right, they rob and despoil them of whatever they have. And this is so general and so ordinary a practice that not only does it go unpunished, but it is even regarded among the Turks of Algiers and all other parts as both courageous and meritorious.

To top such abuses, these ka'ids and governors very commonly tend to get the kings of Algiers to give them a squad of janissaries and soldiers (whom they call *mahalla*) of 400, 500, or 600 hundred soldiers and more, by contract and based on the money they give the pasha. Using these soldiers, the ka'ids can make incursions, raids, and cavalcades throughout the lands of other Moors and Berbers who do not pay tribute to the Turk. These Berbers are dwellers in the Sahara and lands that border those of the Blacks, or other Berbers who come from remote parts with great quantities of cattle and livestock to graze and waste the lands of other Moors and vassals of the Turks. With their expeditions to sack and plunder, with the multitude of camels and livestock, which they often take from the above Moors and Berbers, and with various agreements made with these and other men, the ka'ids tend to gain great amounts of money. Out of these funds they first pay off the pasha; then they satisfy the Boluk-Bashi[3] and military officials; they give the janissaries a little something; and they pocket the rest, making themselves very rich in a short time, perhaps a few years.

The following ka'ids, the richest of the lot, lived in Algiers in the year 1581:

1. Hadjdji Murad, a renegade Slav, father-in-law of Muley Maluch ['Abd al-Malik], king of Fès who died in the battle against Don Sebastian, king of Portugal, also killed in that battle.[4]
2. Daut of Turkish origin.
3. Muhammad Çelebi, a renegade from Calabria.[5]
4. Motafer, a Turk.
5. Bendeli 'Ali, son of a Turk and a Moorish woman.
6. Dja'far Agha, a Corsican renegade.
7. Dja'far, an English renegade.

8. Resuan, a Turk.
9. Hader, son of a Turk and a female renegade.
10. Djaʿfar, a Hungarian renegade.
11. Ali Pichinino, a Corsican renegade.
12. Manes, a Spanish renegade.
13. Djaʿfar, a Neapolitan renegade.
14. Murabit Sain, a Turk.
15. Hasan, a Greek renegade.
16. Hamida Cajes, an Algerian Moor.
17. Muhammad from Biskra, a Moor from Tlemcen.
18. Liali, a Turk.
19. Murad Çelebi, son of a Sardinian renegade.
20. Murad, a renegade from Ibiza.
21. Djaʿfar, a Mallorcan renegade.
22. Muhammad, of the Jewish nation.
23. Mahamut Bey, a Turk.

There are other ka'ids of lesser substance and standing, and all told they add up to some one hundred houses.[6]

CHAPTER 15

Sipahi

The *sipahi,* as we said, are men paid for their services by means of land grants.[1] They are obliged to go to war as cavalry when the king goes on important missions in person, and they are expected to serve as deputies for the defense of the city of Algiers. The majority of these sipahi, of which there must be up to five hundred in Algiers, are obliged to keep a horse at all times. Most sipahi are elderly, and almost all are renegades who were formerly waiters or servants of former pashas. Some among them are Turks by birth, and others, as former *aghas* for the janissaries, hang on to these land grants all their lives, as will be shown in our forthcoming discussion of the janissaries. Some sipahi get twenty-five *doblas* monthly for pay, an ordinary salary, which amounts to ten *escudos*[2] of gold. But others, as favorites of former or present pashas, earn thirty, forty, and more doblas per month. Beyond this pay, many of these sipahi receive certain rents per year, which they call *pare.*[3] These are pensions constituted over certain lands, villages of Moors or dwellings of Berbers, who pay them each year in wheat, barley, rams, cows, lard, and cash. Some of these pensions are worth two thousand and three thousand ducats[4] per year and more, given to them for life by former pashas who favored them. Other sipahi have lands that they till, where they have their estates or farm houses, and fields where they raise many cows and sheep. As well as producing silk, the sipahi also produce many victuals, such as raisins, figs, or lard, serving themselves in all this bounty from the Christian captives they keep. Some lands are occasionally given them by pashas, others by the sultan through his particular charter. The sipahi can also buy lands that become vacant through the death of their owners, thereby enriching the pasha.

Nobody can own these lands for more than a lifetime, unless he bought them with his own money, in which case he can leave them to his children and heirs. All these sipahi, whose population adds up to some five hundred dwellings, are free and exempt from paying taxes on their goods and possessions.

CHAPTER 16

Janissaries

Janissaries are the body of warriors in Turkey founded by Sultan Murad I, inventor of the institution and ancestor of the present-day Grand Turk Murad III.[1] The institution of janissaries is open only to the sons of Christians, whom the Grand Turk orders to be collected every three years as tribute from the provinces of Europe, which the Turks call Romania.[2] Whoever would like to know more about janissaries—when and how the institution began, the manner in which these young men are collected throughout the provinces, how the Grand Turk later distributes them to be reared among the most illustrious Turks, how they are made into warriors and raised to other positions—should read Gesnerio, *De rebus Turcicis*,[3] Münster in his *Geografia,* and the various authors of *De origine Turcarum*.[4]

Wishing to preserve the state and dominion of Algiers that his brother ʿArudj Barbarossa had won before his death, Khayr al-Din Barbarossa wrote to the Grand Turk that by keeping Algiers in the power of his Turkish vassals, the door was open for his subjection of the whole of Africa and the destruction of all the provinces of Christianity. To this end, Barbarossa easily obtained permission from the Grand Turk that any of his countrymen willing to relocate could pass freely from Turkey into Barbary and Algiers. Not only were these Turks allowed free passage but, also, after settling in Algiers and its lands, they could even become and call themselves janissaries, even though they were not the sons of Christians, as was the custom in Turkey. They would then be granted all the exemptions and liberties that the janissaries enjoy in Turkey, which are great and even excessive.

But for many years it was also an observance in Algiers that only those corsairs and renegades who were of Turkish origin could become janissaries. This is also why corsairs never wished to have any janissaries accompany them on their raids across the sea, which the janissaries very much wanted because of the great profit in robbery. All this changed in 1568, when Muhammad Pasha, son of Salah Ra'is,[5] king of Algiers, reconciled the janissaries with the corsairs, who on this score had been great enemies. It was ordered that janissaries could go on the corsair ships as soldiers, and that every corsair or renegade, whenever he wished, could enter into the number and pay of the janissaries. This boon was, in turn, conceded to any Jews who became Turks. In December of 1580, however, soon after the arrival from Constantinople of Dja'far Pasha,[6] king of Algiers, this allowance for Jews was removed. In response to a petition from the janissaries themselves, it was ordered that no Jew turned Turk could enter their ranks, and over one hundred Jews were struck from their payrolls. The reason for this change was the discovery that Jews would turn Turk for no other reason than because, under the name of janissaries, they could give aid and comfort to their Jewish brothers and relatives, who are persecuted by everyone in Algiers. It is also the custom and usage that all children and grandchildren of janissaries and renegades could, if they wish, become janissaries, as many do.

CHAPTER 17

Agha of the Janissaries

Similar to the Turks, the janissaries of Algiers also have an *agha*,[1] who is like their colonel, the head and master of their corps. The respect and obedience they tender him is admirable, in stark contrast to Christian military usage. Only this agha and no other man, not even the king himself, can arrest, punish, deduct payment, or bring any form of justice against a janissary. What is more, the agha will punish anyone who goes to the king to complain about the janissaries. And even the king himself, when he complains about or wants something from a janissary, must have recourse to and inform the agha. Justice, or whatever the king demands, will be done only if it suits the agha. If, on the contrary, someone offended by the king asks the agha to make amends for what the king did to him, the agha can and will do so on a daily basis, in spite of the king himself and with no further reply nor appeal.[2] The same applies to those who feel offended by a *kadi*,[3] a judge or justice of these lands — one for the Turks and another for the Moors. Because if the aggrieved appeals to the agha, he can do and undo, command and order whatever he wishes without allowing any other appeal for the affront.

This office or preeminence of the agha is granted by orderly succession of age, because any janissary who lives long enough arrives at the rank of agha. For the slightest reason, however, the janissaries are given to changing their agha frequently and periodically, putting the next in line in his place; and they do this with such facility that it seems like a whim. In such a case, he who leaves the post of agha also stops being a janissary. No longer mixing with the janissaries nor attaching himself to their reunions or businesses, he remains, instead, totally separated from their corps. Such a man is then enlisted among the *sipahi*, with a monthly salary of twenty-five *doblas,* the equivalent of ten *escudos* of gold. It happens that there might be three or four aghas per year. When a new agha rises to power, the others also rise a notch ahead.

Sometimes, in truth, if the janissary who is ready to become an agha does not please the rest or is not fit for office, he is assigned his twenty-five doblas, and renouncing his desire or, better said, desisting from it, he is forced to resign without protest and is relegated, as if he had been an agha, to the ranks of the sipahi, as we said. As an example of what little reason suffices for the janissaries to do such a thing, in the month of August, 1579, when they were changing their agha, they did not wish the top four and the eldest of the line to be candidates, because they claimed that their wives, before marriage, did not have good reputations. In the same way and in the earlier year of 1578, the janissaries kept a man from becoming an agha because he was slightly tongue-tied and had a stutter, even though he was an excellent soldier. On top of this, they felt that he did not know how to salute well.

CHAPTER 18

Ranks of the Janissaries

The first rank of janissaries, starting from the bottom, is called Yol-dash[1] and is something like an ordinary soldier. A man of this rank has a starting salary of three or even four *doblas* of pay, which is little more than an *escudo* and a half, until on some journey or progress through the kingdom he achieves a notable deed, such as killing a Christian or Moor in battle, because for each severed head he presents to the captain, his monthly pay is increased by half a dobla. This means that pay increases hang on notable deeds. And what I say here also applies to the rest of the janissaries and soldiers, because they increase their pay by half a dobla per month. Newly arrived kings, out of usage or custom and to earn the good will of the janissaries, tend to increase each soldier's salary by half a dobla per month. And under the rank of Yol-dash is included every janissary, no matter how old, who does not yet hold a posting related to war.

Four of these Yol-dash are chosen at the whim of the *agha*, and these men, carrying their harquebuses, accompany the king whenever he goes hunting, or to the mosque, or for a stroll. The Yol-dash wear a headdress of white felt lined in green wool, and over that a horn of wood also covered in green wool. From this horn hang some very long feathers that descend down their backs and reach almost to their heel bones. These Yol-dash dine every day at the table of the king.

The second rank of janissaries, the Odabashi,[2] are soldiers who serve as commanders. This is an honored appointment and similar to the corporal of a squadron. Among janissaries, however, a squadron has no fixed and determined number, because sometimes it is made up of six soldiers, sometimes ten, fifteen, twenty, or more, in keeping with the agha's fancy. These soldiers ordinarily earn six doblas per month, which is less than two and a half escudos, until they receive a raise in pay for some notable deed, as mentioned above.

The third rank is the Otrak, the retired elders of the corps.[3] Only sixteen Odabashi, or squadron corporals, hold this rank, elected by vote of the janissaries and counselors of the agha. Without the permission of these men the agha is powerless to command or give orders for anything, or to punish any janissary, Moor, Christian, or Jew. These Otrak have the same ordinary pay as the Odabashi: six doblas per month.

The fourth rank, known as Bash-oda,[4] includes no more than four janissaries, the four oldest soldiers, or Otrak, from the council of the agha. Two of these continually assist the agha, and the other two, with help from the Solak soldiers (about which, more below), assist the king. Whenever the agha, either in meetings of the janissaries or in their council known as the Divan,[5] wishes to bring up something for discussion that would be ordered or determined by vote, the two Bash-oda who always assist him propose it to the sixteen Otrak and to all the Odabashi present. These ranks then propose it to all the rest of the janissaries, who resolve it on the spot, at the top of their voices and in few words. Whatever proposal receives a majority of votes is later carried out. These Bash-oda have the same salary as the Odabashi, six doblas per month.

The fifth rank, known as the Solak,[6] are four soldiers whose job and obligation is to accompany the king everywhere, within his home at the royal palace as well as outside of it, and always to eat with him at table. These men are distinguished from the other janissaries by two items: a golden horn worn on their heads and a silver sword at their waists. When the king goes out, either on foot or horseback, these four Solak soldiers, along with two Bash-oda, accompany him carrying their harquebuses. On their heads they wear certain white plumes of egrets, which to onlookers resemble brushes. Beyond drawing the same ordinary salary of six doblas, with hikes in pay like the others, these men are granted a daily ration from the king's house for their wives and children, should they have any, and if not, for their servants. The ration is a quarter of a ram each and four loaves of bread—two white ones from the king's table and another two of coarser quality.

The sixth rank is the Boluk-Bashi.[7] This is similar to a captain, since during wartime these men are in charge of various squadrons of obedient soldiers. The number of these warriors is never a fixed quantity, because at times they add up to more than four hundred. Neither is the number of squadrons that they govern in war a fixed quantity, because among three hundred soldiers who might come together in squads or in a campaign they call *mahalla,* there might be twenty, twenty-five, and thirty Boluk-Bashi, and sometimes even more, as the agha who distributes them might order. Their normal monthly pay is ten doblas.

Only one man represents the seventh rank, the Mir Boluk-Bashi.[8] Along with the Solak, his job is always to help with the king. Not only does he eat with him at table but, in addition, a man of this rank will secure for his wife, children, and extended family the same ration as the Solak, as we noted earlier. And if the king does not wish to permit interviews with those who come to negotiate with him, this Mir Boluk-Bashi will tell him what the petitioners seek or need. And in the same manner, he returns the answer of the king to them, telling them how he responded and what he said. This rank of soldier is also obliged to tell the agha of the janissaries everything that happened or was spoken of that day, so that he would know all the details. The salary for this rank is ten doblas per month.

The eighth rank, or Yayabashi,[9] guards and escorts the king on Djumʿa,[10] that is, on Friday, when he goes to the mosque to pray. These soldiers sport some tall white plumes on their heads. The oldest of these men is also in charge of securing provisions for the janissaries, speaking to the king on their behalf, and making sure that they are paid. For without pay, they would have no bread, meat, or other staples necessary for life. This rank of janissaries makes sure that the king gives the soldiers their provisions, so that they will want for nothing, even if the rest of the city does. In the same way, when some squad or mahalla goes out to plunder and pillage, or to collect taxes or make war, the men of this rank make sure that the king provides the janissaries and soldiers (as per custom and usage) with beasts of burden, carriages, tents to pitch camp, and victuals for all the days that, as we shall explain, the king is obliged to provide them. Men of this rank receive the same pay of ten doblas per month.

The ninth and most senior rank is the Bash-Boluk-Bashi, given to only one janissary, the oldest of all the Boluk-Bashi and something like their head man. As such he is most respected and holds the highest office and the leading voice and vote among them. This is because he is closer to the lieutenant of the agha, and next in line for the post. His salary is fifteen doblas a month prior to pay raises.

The tenth rank is the Kahya, or steward[11] of the agha, his deputy or right-hand man, because if the agha becomes ill, or is absent or out of office for some days (given that the janissaries often try to suspend him when he does something they disagree with or take amiss), this Kahya assumes the agha's duties. He also steps in if the agha dies, remaining in office until another agha is elected. The Kahya has much authority and is greatly respected. His normal pay is fifteen doblas per month, on top of his earlier pay-raises, in the way we said that all other janissaries or soldiers earn their pay.[12]

CHAPTER 19

Customs of the Janissaries at War

All these janissaries, of which there must be up to six thousand in Algiers and its kingdom, operate on two fronts: one in Algiers and the other on the aforementioned frontiers of the kingdom dealing with the Zwawa according to the needs of the land. Soldiers are required in places like Tlemcen and Mostaganem, which are on the frontiers of Fès and Orán; in Biskra, which borders with the Berbers of the Sahara (the ancient Numidians and Nomads);[1] and in Constantine, also on the frontiers where certain Berbers constantly wage war against the Turks, or at least disobey them. There are fewer warriors than are needed in all these areas: as things stand, relatively few men are asked to control virtually the whole of Barbary. In Algiers there are ordinarily 3,500 to 4,000 soldiers, who by no means spend all their time in the city, because across the whole year, winter and summer, they take off for all parts of the kingdom in squads of 400, 500, 600, and more, as is needed and pleasing to the king and ordered by the *agha*. They go to collect tributes at gunpoint from the Moors and Berbers, who would not pay up in any other manner save by force, as we said earlier.

The janissaries ordinarily ride out on these robberies for some four or even five months, alternating with other squads in order to rest. Some pay taxes to the agha, giving him two, three, or four *escudos* for the privilege of remaining in Algiers with their wives and children, or for any urgent necessity. Others prefer to go robbing in ships and galliots, as they do ordinarily; in such a case, if a group of janissaries sails off on one or more ships, the agha informs them that they must obey the oldest man among them, whom they then call their agha. But the majority of janissaries prefer to go out on campaigns known as *mahallas* to rob, enriching themselves by a kind of landed privateering.[2] Apart from the fact they always eat off the land what they can steal from the Moors and Berbers, they also strip them of all their goods, taking by force their wives and children, whom they beat mercilessly. And so at the end of their journey, the majority of these janissaries return with camels and beasts laden with much wheat, honey, lard, figs, dates and raisins, which can earn them a profit apart from what they bring back in their moneybags to fete their friends, wives, and children.

And when the janissaries are sent off in this way to rob, or when they leave for a war or cavalcade, in keeping either with the number of their squads or the whim of the agha, he also sends forth a number of Boluk-Bashi, who are like captains of the *boluks* of the agha in the Ottoman military organization, and whom the janissaries must obey. And all of them obey the eldest of the Boluk-Bashi, if the *beylerbey*,[3] who functions like a general in a war—about whom, more later—does not go on this journey.

Some ten or twelve days before they leave Algiers, a Turk whom the kings put in charge sets up and furnishes a certain number of pavilions, according to the number of janissaries, about two miles south of the city, where little by little they collect themselves until the day the agha signals for them to get ready to leave, and from there they take to the road. The whole lot of them then takes off divided into eight, ten, twelve or more squads, each having an Odabashi as its head and commander. And for each squad the king furnishes a pavilion of thick canvas for lodging, horses or mules in which to carry it, and clothing and some treats for them to eat. Twenty-five days after leaving Algiers, the king is obliged to give them cake to eat, lard, and *bulgur*,[4] a kind of cooked and badly ground wheat that they boil like rice. And each week the janissaries must also be given meat according to the quantity and abundance in the camp. The man in charge of providing all this is the *ka'id* who bought the mahalla from the king for a given sum, promising them, as we said, permission to make a cavalcade. And if they ride out to collect tributes, the Turk whom the king sends as their treasurer is in charge of all these provisions. But as we said earlier, these soldiers rob and despoil the Moors and Berbers to such a degree that they have an excess of rams, hens, lard, eggs, raisins, dates, and couscous[5] that they take by force, consume, and waste.

Before leaving Algiers the squadron chooses from among themselves a keeper of the larder, whom they call *wekili khardj,* or paymaster general, to carry their food.[6] His job is to take charge of all the provisions the king gives them, or that they buy or rob, and to give these to the cook, set the table, buy what appeals to or is needed for the janissaries, set up the pavilion, fold it and, along with all the clothing of the comrades, cart it on carriages pulled by beasts of burden. And after electing this man, they choose another of their fold as cook, whom they call *ashdji.*[7] This man prepares all the food for the entire squad, takes charge of the kitchen, and helps the paymaster general carry and distribute the clothing. The custom here is to choose the least experienced Janissary among them. And if he does not please them, then they choose, as I said, another from their midst.

The king gives each of the Boluk-Bashi—from the rank, as we said, of captains who govern the squadrons—two horses for the journey: one for his person, for riding and fighting whenever necessary, and another to carry his clothing and provisions. Each of these men also receives half a ram per week, plus a provision of cake, lard, and bulgur, just like the janissaries. No matter on what journey, no soldier—be he a Yol-dash or Odjak-eri (a simple janissary) or an Odabashi (a man in charge) or a Boluk-Bashi (a captain)—takes to war more than two or three shirts, a pair of breeches, and the garment worn over them. He also takes a small mat and a blanket for sleeping, as well as a cloak or robe for the rain, if it be winter, and his armaments. These last are harquebuses: they do not use arrows except at sea, nor do they use pikes or halberds under any conditions. They all fight on foot, except for the Boluk-Bashis, who fight on horse with a harquebus when they see fit. All this occurs only on ordinary mahallas, because when the occasion requires it, they take horses for fighting, and especially when the king parades in person and goes on a journey, because all the *sipahis* of Algiers, whom we discussed earlier, go with him, and almost all are obliged to keep and fight with a horse.

They also make use of a cavalry of subject Moors, as many as they wish, or of confederates and friends, which the king of Algiers takes on his journeys. They do not fight with any special method, as is the use among Christians, nor do they form squadrons or set up detachments outside of their harquebusiers. The most order they keep is to fight together in two or three files, and in this same manner they march when they go into war.

Their flags are square and much smaller than ours, with no emblem, symbol, or figure on them. At most they are made of two or three colors, and large as the squad may be, even of one thousand janissaries, they never carry more than three flags: one in front in the vanguard, another in the middle, where the captain belongs, and another in the rearguard. This last belongs to the ka'id who purchased the mahalla and takes it with him. In all the journeys and wars, no matter how many soldiers there might be in a camp, they have fewer flags than the Christians. Only when the king goes in person on a journey, or when he enters or leaves the city, or goes to a camp or on a mahalla with joy and feasting, as is the custom, they carry a flag of a horse's tail on a flagpole. The reason the Turks give for using a horse's tail as their chief and honorable flag is that once upon a time, when the Grand Turk was defeated in battle and all his flags were taken, a squadron who survived to reunite and reconfigure themselves for battle, not having any flag, cut the tail off a horse and placed it on a flagpole. Fighting in this manner, they reclaimed the victory that they had earlier lost. And in memory of this deed, the Grand Turk and his warriors always carry a horse's tail as their chief insignia on their most important journeys.

The post of standard-bearer (which in Turkish is called *sanjakdar*)[8] is also considered honorable and of special preeminence, just as it is among Christians, which is how it should be, although the flag is entrusted to any janissary, as the agha fancies. The spoils the soldiers take—such as jewels, gold, silver, captives, wheat, oil, lard, cattle, or beasts of burden—all belong to the king, or to whoever purchased the cavalcade, as we said. The exception is money and any type of clothing, which belong to the janissaries on a first-come, first-serve basis. But they also take however much they can of other things, which is neither heavily punished nor the subject of any investigations.

Home from a robbing expedition or another journey, for two or three days before entering the city they stop on the same place in the field from where they departed, where they lodge in their pavilions, and after all janissaries left behind arrive, they make their entrance into the city in double file, with the flag on the head horse and firing all their weapons. For greater solemnity, the other janissaries who remained behind in the city come forward with their shotguns to receive them. And to inflate their figures, they mix in with the arriving soldiers, and they all continue in procession up to the house of the king, always walking along a straight street known as the Souk, where the royal palace is situated. Arriving at the home of the king, on a small plaza in front of his home, they gather together as a squadron and fire off their harquebuses. And the Boluk-Bashi enter to do reverence to the king, who receives them with joy. After that they return to their homes or lodgings to rest.

CHAPTER 20

Customs of the Janissaries in Peacetime

Their journey over, with war and military affairs behind them, married janissaries live in their own homes until their next posting. Those of the council, elected by votes, as we said, are obliged to congregate in the bureau known as the Divan, for a meeting they tend to call every two or three days, where they discuss what is needed in war and peace, as we shall explain later. As for the rest of the janissaries, although almost all generally tend to remain in the Divan, they are under no obligation to do so. Of these married janissaries, of every rank there must be about eight hundred homes in Algiers. Some janissaries are like the renegades: they return to the homes of the masters they serve and accompany, where they are almost always welcomed, well received, and provided for.

Other janissaries, those who wish to live a freer life, join together in groups of three, four, five, six, or more comrades and rent a dwelling where they give themselves over to the good life. But the rest of the janissaries (the greater part) lodge in five large houses constructed in the old days by the pashas especially for this purpose. Here the janissaries live in groups of eight, ten, twelve, or more in high and low chambers, almost in the manner of religious cells. And some of these houses (at least three) are large enough to hold 400, 500, 600, and more janissaries. Because each man has no more clothing and equipment than what he can carry with him—two or three shirts and breeches kept in small chests, a few hand spans wide; armaments such as a harquebus and scimitar; some horn containers for gunpowder; and a small mat and blanket with a cape for sleeping and covering themselves—some twelve, fifteen, or more men can easily fit into a small space, where they mainly live, eat, and sleep all together, often stretched out across the floor.

These dwellings represent what the Emperor Tiberius Caesar constructed in Rome outside the Milvian gate, close to the city wall, for the soldiers known as praetors [*milites pretorii*], a cohort or company invented by Augustus Caesar to guard him and successive emperors. The janissary buildings resemble the dwelling known as Castra Praetoria, which lasted until the times of the Emperor Constantine the Great. Out of anger against the Praetorian Guard for having risen against him in favor of the tyrant Maxentius, Constantine disbanded them and destroyed the above dwelling, an excellent work of architecture.[1]

But to return to the janissaries, their mode of living is as follows: when they go out on their *mahallas* or cavalcades, they choose a paymaster general among them, whom they call, as we said earlier, *wekili khardj*, and who is in charge of buying food for everybody. Ordinarily this is nothing more than rice cooked with lard, which they call pilaf or cooked wheat, and which is afterward dried in the sun and half ground—or better said, cut with the teeth of the grinder—which they then boil up with lard, like the food they call *bulgur*. The janissaries also eat small amounts of bread, fruit in season, and water. They rarely eat meat, usually on the night before the Djumʿa, which is what they call their Friday, the same as our Sunday for us. And with this kind of parsimony, they live healthy lives: well-fed, robust, and happy. As for the expense of food, firewood, coal, and other kitchen necessities, each man contributes the same amount at the beginning of the month—or as they figure it, at the start of each new moon.

Apart from this paymaster general, they also choose from among themselves another man as cook, whom they call *ashdji,* although, as we said, the latest arrival to the company tends to hold this job until another newcomer arrives. This cook is not obliged to contribute to his expenses like the others, since for his labors he eats for free. For this reason, and to save the expense, some other janissaries, even old men, take on this job of cooking for everybody with good will.

The janissaries never lack for this basic food for two reasons. The first is because even though the whole world may fall asunder, they are well paid every two moons. And, secondly, if famine should strike and everyone, including the pasha himself, should die of hunger, the janissaries would not lack for wheat and provisions, because they would not only sack any home (as they did the winter of 1579 when there was great hunger in Algiers and they sacked the homes of the wealthiest ka'ids),[2] but they would break into the house of the pasha himself, smash the doors of his warehouses, take whatever provisions they find, and then sack the rest of his home. And after this, they would either kill him if they so wished, or send him off in chains to the Grand Turk, as they did to various men, and as they wanted to do to Hasan the Venetian, the renegade 'Uludj 'Ali, who was then king of Algiers.

Neither the janissaries nor the Moors conduct any military exercises: they do not joust, nor tourney, nor throw the javelin, nor fence, nor jump, nor run, nor play ball, nor hunt—this last despite there being an infinity of partridges, pigeons, doves, rabbits and other small game in the woods and fields. They only hold fights during their two holidays of the year, in the field where they congregate on Fridays, and this without any art or skill whatever, because everything depends on the use of force. And only during these two holidays do they run horses in pairs, and play at jousting, but also with little art, skill, or grace, save only when they toss reeds at one another.

Most commonly used is a challenge, from one man to another, as to who can throw an arrow from a bow with the greatest force, the most distance, and the most certainty, for which game two sandy areas are set aside, one outside the Gate of Bab 'Azzun and another outside Bab al-Wad. A few other men go into the wilderness with their harquebuses to kill some type of bird to eat, and still others push forward into the mountains some three or four leagues from Algiers, where they kill a pig to sell to the Christians without ever touching it. Some Algerians, although few, make buttons and braid, or they are tailors, barbers, shoemakers, or work in similar trades.

The rest of the Algerians live a bestial life of swine, constantly giving themselves over to licentiousness and lechery, and particularly to the heinous and revolting act of sodomy, abusing young boys, captive Christians whom they buy for this vice and later dress in the Turkish mode. Or from in and outside the territory, they take the sons of Jews and Moors, despite the pain of their parents, and spend days and nights with them while drunk on wine and brandy.

Some men, albeit few, play a form of guitar that is like a halved pumpkin with a long neck and split entirely down the middle, so that the echo is round where it booms and causes the sound, as hollow as the half of the head of a split gourd.[3] They pluck up to three strings of this instrument, played very discordantly and with little grace or skill. The same applies to their singing, which seems more the howling of wolves than the human voice of men.[4]

Despite all this, they have three good customs: the first is that they neither apostatize nor blaspheme, and it is certainly worth noting that neither the Turkish nor Moorish tongues include words from which any meaning can be wrung to signify some mode of blasphemy or apostasy.[5] The second is that they play neither card games nor dice, which they claim are for rogues and scoundrels (although many renegades pay no attention to this). They do play chess and backgammon, however, in the same way as Christians. The third good thing is that they rarely fight among themselves, and if this happens, it never goes beyond fistfights: they never reach for their swords, because they only carry them in war; nor for any knives they might have on their persons, because if any man does so, all the onlookers are obliged to turn against him. And for all the injuries the fighting men may inflict on one another, and no matter how much their punches may scratch and bloody their faces, the moment they are pacified they embrace and kiss each other in the French manner.

If someone who is not a janissary gives a blow, or even a push, to a janissary, though it be nothing more than putting a hand on his chest, or on an arm, the penalty is to cut off the transgressor's hand. And if someone kills a janissary, the penalty is to burn him alive, or impale him, or hook him, or break his bones with a mace, as we have seen done to many—unless the delinquent, being a Christian, turns Turk or Moor, because in that case he is pardoned. In October of 1579, for example, a drunken janissary entered a Venetian ship docked in the port and tried to steal some glass objects that the ship's owner had in his chest. For picking up a stick and giving the janissary a blow, all in self-defense, the owner was condemned to be burned alive. The wretched man, although almost sixty years old, chose first to turn Turk, losing his God rather than his miserable life.

Because the janissaries are so greatly feared and respected, they are all the more proud, arrogant, and daring. Their cooks are especially overweening: there is no stopping them from robbing the stores of bread, meat, eggs, hens, lard, honey, fruit, cabbages, and everything they might want, without ever being forced to pay or return. And there is no challenging these janissary cooks—whether on the streets, the fields where they walk, the stores where provisions are bought and sold, or the beds where they rest—because they will reach for some hatchets they always carry with them, a badge of identity some two hand spans long, and they will break heads or the teeth or arms of whoever displeases or annoys them.

It is not our intention to discuss here the customs of their Islamic Law, which they have in common with the Moors, as we shall do so in a later section. The janissaries also have a custom that each of their sons, be he Turk or renegade, receives a salary from childhood on, two or three Turkish coins, called *aspers*,[6] each valued at less than one-fourth of a *piaster*.[7] These children receive more if the king should wish it and if the parents are in favor.

CHAPTER 21

Customs of the Algerian Corsairs

Corsairs are those men who live by privateering or full-time robbery at sea. Some of these are Turks by birth and others are Moors, but the vast majority consists of renegades from all nations, men very adept on the shores, riverbanks, and coasts of the whole Christian world.

The vessels they use for their privateering are light galliots or brigantines, which they call frigates. The brigantine has eight to thirteen benches or oars per side, and the galliot, from fourteen to twenty-four.[1] These vessels are constantly being constructed in Algiers, partly in an arsenal or navy yard set aside for this work (which we earlier discussed), and partly on the island within the port, the one connected to the city through an embanked wharf.

To build and carve out these ships they use certain Christian workers who are slaves of the commonwealth or, as the Turks say, of the State.[2] Their bosses are none other than the janissaries themselves, whom the workers obey in everything and willingly serve without any salary or reward. The head bosses or foremen each receive, from king or commonwealth, six, eight, or ten *doblas* per month. As for other workers such as shipwrights, carpenters, and caulkers—because the arsenal includes men of every skill—their ration is three loaves of bread daily, which the *agha* and janissaries dole out to them. The king is obliged to provide for all these master craftsmen.

Some kings,[3] at the end of their governance, leave their captives to the arsenal for service in the commonwealth. It is true that certain corsairs sometimes have their own particular captives, masters of shipbuilding, and they use them at sea to arrange certain things. But once they are back in Algiers, these captives serve for nothing more than to help the foremen of the commonwealth, and they are charged with building and provisioning all the ships.

On the day they install a mast on some vessel either in the arsenal or on the island, the corsairs—the owner of the ship as well as the other corsairs in Algiers—tend to give the master builders various gifts: money or knickknacks or a Turkish dress that they can sell. Some corsairs give the builders various yards of cloth—some of fine wool or damask, others of satin or velvet—and similar items that they publicly drape over the rigging. These presents are sometimes worth as much as two hundred and three hundred *escudos,* of which the foremen take the greater part for themselves, using the rest to try to gratify all the other shipbuilders and dockyard workers. Until the ship pushes out to sea, the corsairs give nothing else save for some dinner they might send in for the dockyard workers and for the slaves of other captains[4] of galliots, on loan to work there.

Few are the corsairs who do not have at home the slaves needed for these and all the jobs necessary to put together a corsair ship—carpenters, caulkers, ironmongers, coopers, oar builders, and others—because these are the men that corsairs try to get for themselves, and to buy at a high price, whenever they capture a Christian ship.[5] So that if Christian workers were lacking to the Turks, there would not be perhaps one ship among them.

Whoever wishes to construct a ship sends his Christians or other slaves some twenty leagues west of Algiers into the mountains of Cherchell[6] to cut down the trees for their shipbuilding project. Great quantities of quality wood—oak, pine, and ilex—may be found there. After felling the trees, the same Christians, partly on beasts of burden or camels and partly on human shoulders, carry everything back to the port, a walk of some six leagues. And these same Christians are the ones to unload the wood in Algiers, to bring it on land, handsaw, cut, plane, and work it into perfection. The ship is ultimately constructed without the hand of a Turk or Moor, save for some oar builder or caulker hired from the exiled Moriscos of Spain.

On the day that a ship is beached and sent out to sea, its owner again gives something to the foremen. He also hosts a dinner for all the master builders and for many Christians whose owners have sent them there for heavy-duty work or to put the vessel out to sea. And when the beak of the galley first touches water, they use this ceremony: either a Turk or renegade enters the ship and, beheading over the beak one, two, or three rams (however many they wish), while the blood is running fresh and hot, they push the vessel with great force from the land into the sea. At that point the man who beheaded the rams flings them into the sea, bloodying the water. And at that very moment some artillery is fired from the bastions of the city, and everyone is festive and joyful.

They account for this sacrifice by a correspondence: in the same way that they kill these rams and spill blood on the galliots and into the sea, they will also kill Christians at sea and dye the waters with their blood. They also consider it a good omen for a prosperous voyage if some holy man or marabout[7] comes on board just as they are about to go down to the sea in ships. And given that the Qur'an of Muhammad defends their claim that no one should go privateering unless he intends, in effect, to defend or increase their sect, they have no scruples about doing evil to Christians, because they believe that robbing them and diminishing their goods and riches is a gain for their Law.

The captain who does not own a quantity of Christians, enough to arm the vessel—because almost all of them need three men per oar, and some four (at least in the quarters of the stern)—can rent Christians from merchants who have them especially for hire. And from one merchant, he may rent two, four, six, and eight Christians, and from another ten, twelve, twenty, thirty, or however many he wants from among those who most please him and seem to be the most robust. And for each oar man, he pays twelve escudos of gold per voyage. They give the same salary to Moors of the land, natives called Bagarinos, who earn their living rowing as *bonevoglie*, or "men of good will," as we said earlier.[8]

Those who have no chance of arming an entire vessel can band together with other Turkish corsairs or merchants and divide the costs: one man arms a quarter of the vessel, another a third, one may arm half, or whatever deal a company strikes up, each party contributing his ratio of the expenses and provisions for the trip.[9] And later, in the same manner, they divide among themselves a percentage of the gain and booty. And to keep tabs on all of this, the expenses as well as the profits, they choose a scrivener called a Hodja,[10] who goes on the trip to write all this down.

The number of soldiers and men of arms they carry depends on the vessel, and this is the rule: close to each bank, over the portholes for crossbows, is a wooden bench, on which are seated two soldiers. A galliot that carries two oars or benches per row, therefore, will carry the same number of rowers' benches, and in these will fit forty soldiers, two, as we said, per bench. And multiplying the benches and rowers' benches, the number of soldiers also increases.

All these soldiers of the sea—whether renegades, janissaries who go privateering under license of their agha, or Turks who live only from this work—are commonly called *lewends*.[11] None of these men earn any salary except what they can rob. They calculate their expenses in order to make a profit, and for this they join up with ten, twelve, or more comrades. The captain and the ship owners are still obliged to give them biscuits, oil and vinegar, just what they give as an ordinary ration to every Christian who rows.

The provisions that each ship carries include biscuits, rice, *bulgur* wheat, oil, vinegar, cheese, lard, olives, some raisins, and nothing else. But the ration given each day to the galley slaves, and to all the lewends and workmen on the galliot is nothing more than some biscuits, a bit of watered-down vinegar, and a few tablespoons of olive oil. The Christian galley slaves are given only biscuits.

They depart from the port of Algiers on one of two days: either on a Friday, which is their holy day, or on the Sunday of Christians, and they only sail off well into the night. Before leaving the port, every ship, whether of corsairs or merchants, salutes the sepulcher of a dead marabout or holy man. They believe that he lies outside the Gate of Bab ʿAzzun, in a cave like a buried chapel called Sidi Batqa;[12] and all turning toward it, they recite in a loud voice, and order Christians to do so also, "Bismillah, Bismillah," by which they mean "in the name of God, in the name of God."[13]

Although all the vessels preparing to leave have been cleaned and caulked with great care and diligence, before leaving Barbary to cross into the lands and islands of the Christians, they are cleaned and caulked once again. Those privateering galliots headed for Mallorca,

Minorca, Spain, or the West, are cleaned and caulked in Cherchell, twenty leagues west of Algiers. And those which head east—to such places as Corsica, Sardinia, Sicily, Calabria, Naples, the Roman coast, Tuscany, or the Genoese territories—are similarly treated in some of the following places or ports: Béjaïa, Annaba, Bizerte, Porto Farina, Kelibia, Sousse, or Djerba.[14]

Wherever and whenever corsairs head for Christian lands, before making any move they first consult their Book of Omens, searching for clues as to where they should go, and under no conditions do they do other than what their book and predictions tell them.[15] They give such credit to these predictions—and are so persuaded by the Devil—that not only to sail off but also to scale any ship, disembark, battle some Christian vessel or sack some region, and, in fact, to do anything during the time of their corsair activities, they first cast lots and consult the Book of Omens. If before their very eyes there should appear a clear and manifest occasion of great gain or booty, should the Book of Omens and its predictions not reveal the same, under no conditions will they attempt the enterprise or move one step in its direction. On the contrary, there is no adventure so arduous or difficult, no danger so manifest into which they will not plunge if their Book of Omens foretells their success. But an infinite number of times they find themselves deceived, and yet they still believe in that Book of Omens, no less than in their Qur'an.[16]

Sailing out both summer and winter, and fearlessly covering all the seas between East and West, they scoff at and attack Christian galleys even while their sailors are eating, playing games, or proclaiming news in Christian ports, killing people here and there as if they were hunting rabbits. The galliots of the corsairs are very prepared for these attacks, being orderly and swift. The Christian galleys, on the other hand, are very heavy and prone to so much confusion and mortification that there is no point in their chasing the corsairs, or in thinking that they could stop their flight to wherever they wish to go robbing at pleasure.[17] When the Christian galleys do decide to chase them, the corsairs make fun of them, displaying the ship's greasy rear in flight, as if they were showing them their posteriors. Because these corsairs are so adept and practiced in the art of privateering—and for our sins, they are so venturesome and lucky—a few days after leaving Algiers they return laden with infinite riches and captives. If they so wish, they can make three or four and even more voyages each year.

Those corsairs who head west, sell their slaves and booty in Tétouan or Larache, in the kingdom of Fès. Those who head east, take their captives to Tunis, Bizerte, Djerba, or Tripoli. And after loading themselves at these sites with provisions, they return to their privateering, and to their cargo of Christians and their goods. If sometimes by accident, usually in winter, the corsairs do not quickly find some vessel to rob, or they are victims of bad weather and tempests, they take refuge in one of seven locations. Those who go west, head for Larache, Salé, or Tétouan; those who go to Spain, head for the island of Formentera; those who go east, huddle in the island of San Pietro, close to Sardinia, or on the islands of Lipari and Stromboli, close to Sicily and Calabria. In the comfort and shelter of these ports and with an abundance of streams of water and firewood—thanks to the great negligence and carelessness of the Christians who will not deign to search for them—the corsairs can relax and await the passage of Christian galleys who sail by and slip into their hands.

Just like the Christians, Muslim corsairs take into account certain stars and times of the year. They especially take great notice of a star they call Asom,[18] which reigns over the skies on the day of Saint Matthias the Apostle, the twenty-fifth of February, and shines for seven days. And they affirm with great certainty that there will be fortunes or tempests either before or after that period. To this they add that a ship of bronze (something to laugh at) sails under all the seas during those seven days, and that if it is the first to spy other vessels, the people on them will be lost and all shall perish. But any vessels that spy this bronze ship first will be rescued, and the people in it will perish. And because of this belief, none of the corsairs wishes to sail during those fifteen days.

The corsairs are remarkable about the cleanliness, order, and concord of their ships. They think of little else, and are especially concerned that the ship's weight be evenly distributed, allowing it to run well and adapt to circumstances. Because of this, they do not have wales on the ship, nor do they permit a sword or harquebus to hang anywhere, nor to rest atop any covering: rather it must remain below with the cargo. And in the same way, the barrels and bottles of oil, vinegar, lard, and all other provisions go on a level and are packed absolutely straight, without anything moving a nail's breadth out of place. What closer attention to weight distributions could these corsairs give, when even the iron of the galliot might make some people move below to the loading zone, because if they remain above, the ship may not weigh as much in one part as in another? Finally, and for the same reason, no matter how the sea may behave, it is not permitted for any janissary—whether Levantine, Turk, or Christian—to move from the spot he finds himself on, even though he be the son of the king himself.

The beatings with sticks or fists, the slappings, kickings, whippings, hunger, thirst, and the infinity of continuous and ruthless cruelties that the corsairs use with the poor Christians who row, without letting them rest for half an hour, are inhuman. They cruelly whip open their backs, draw blood, tear out eyes, break arms, crush bones, slash ears, cut off noses, and even brutally slit throats. They cut off heads and throw bodies into the sea, so they can snatch the oars and make the ship fly faster. No human tongue can describe, nor pen declare, the things they do! We shall treat this topic at great length in its own place.[19]

The prey of captives and seizure of material booty, which they call *ghanima*,[20] all belong to the official captain of the vessel, together with those who helped him to arm it. The same goes for the money and jewels that they sack. But they do not proceed with too much rigor in these things, unless there be a tremendous ghanima of famously great wealth. Apart from this, the lewends keep all the money they rob and, ordinarily, that they can hide. All the clothing taken belongs to the lewends and soldiers, which they put to good use, the corsairs doling out equally among themselves whatever booty they have won or robbed.

If they battle against some resistant ship, the first Turk to board her and make her surrender can choose from among all the Christians on board the one most pleasing to him, as long as he is not of high quality and open to ransom. If the Turks sack some town, for each Christian that a corsair takes on board, the boss and ship owners give him ten escudos. But if the galley surrenders without a fight, they get none of the captives: only their clothing and whatever else they can grab is theirs. The hulls of ships of any kind that the corsairs seize belong to the king. A seventh part of all the captives, and even of the clothing, money, or any merchandise whatsoever that the corsairs rob, is understood to belong to the king in whose port they first secured their provision of bread and armed themselves for the voyage. Because if they arm somewhere else for a second voyage, the tribute will belong to the king of that region. And such is the custom among the kings of Algiers, Tunis, and Tripoli.

The corsairs also have a captain, who is like their head man and whom they obey wherever they run into him. Only the Grand Turk can name someone to this post, and there is one in Algiers, another in Tripoli, and another in Tunis.[21] When this captain goes privateering, however many corsairs he wants are obliged to accompany him: they follow him under orders and none can leave him without his permission. One-fifteenth of whatever the corsairs rob—whether Christians, clothing, money, or merchandise—is owed to this captain. But ordinarily he contents himself with whatever the corsairs wish to give him, without forcing them to give more, nor using the full rigor of the law.

When the corsairs return from their privateering voyage, at the moment when they anchor their galliot in the port and cease to row, all the Christian galley slaves throw their oars into the sea, remaining tied together only by a thin rope. And when their leg irons are removed, in whole or in part, the first thing they do is to carry the oars to a community warehouse very close to the port, where they are very well guarded. This is done so that, while the Turks are disembarking and carrying their goods on shore, the Christians do not revolt and take off with the vessel.

Later that same day each corsair takes home his Christian slaves, and then the captains and lewends all begin to spend heavily, each hosting a great banquet, which they call a *sosfia*,[22] with wine and a form of brandy called *raki*.[23] Indulging in every kind of lechery and gluttony, they spend whatever they robbed on the trip. All of Algiers is happy then, because some merchants buy many of the slaves and goods that the corsairs bring with them, and other merchants sell clothing and provisions to those who come home from the sea, because many of them buy new clothes. And all is eating and drinking and triumphing.

The captains tend to take to their homes some of the lewends and soldiers, keeping them fit and happy in order to go privateering with them again. To this end, the captains give them their daily bread and make much fuss over their dinners. Both the captains and lewends are given to richly dressing up their *garzones*[24] (who are actually bearded women) with clothes of damask, satin, and velvet. These young men, who sport pretty damascene knives richly trimmed with gold and silver chains, wear elegant boots or shoes on their feet and circlets on their heads. They are more pampered than the most refined and beautiful women. A point of honor and rivalry among the Turks is who has the larger number of garzones, the most handsome, and the best dressed. To this end, the Turks send them in droves to stroll about the city on Fridays and other days, as well as down to the seashore and out to the country. They regard this as a great way to have fun and a very particular form of glory. And of all the practices in the world which could be seen or imagined, this one is enough to make one weep (that such a thing should occur among men, in public and with such great shamelessness).

CHAPTER 22

Catalogue of Corsairs

The following is a list of Algerian corsairs with galliots in 1581. When some of these men do not sail, they send others in their place and with their vessels:

1. Beylerbey Djaʿfar, Hungarian renegade, one galliot of twenty-four benches.
2. Mami Arnaut,[1] Captain of the sea and renegade, one of twenty-two benches.
3. Murad the Frenchman, renegade of the above Captain, one of twenty-two benches.
4. Dali Mami, Greek renegade, one of twenty-two benches.[2]
5. Murad Ra'is the Great, Albanian renegade, two of twenty-four benches.
6. Feru Ra'is, Genoese renegade, one of eighteen benches.
7. Murad Ra'is, Maltrapillo, Spanish renegade, one of twenty-two benches.
8. ʿIsa Ra'is, native Turk, one of eighteen benches.
9. Arapsa Ra'is, native Turk, one of eighteen benches.
10. Amiza Ra'is, native Turk, one of twenty benches.
11. Murad Ra'is the Small, Greek renegade, one of twenty-two benches.
12. Sinan Ra'is, Turk, one of twenty-two benches.
13. Yusuf Ra'is, Spanish renegade, one of twenty-two benches.
14. Hadjdji Bali, Turk, one of eighteen benches.
15. Hasan the Genoese, renegade of the Marabout, one of eighteen benches.
16. The Ka'id Dawud, Turk, one of twenty benches.

17. The Ka'id Khader, son of a renegade, one of twenty-tree benches.
18. The Ka'id Giger, Turk, one of twenty-two benches.
19. Marja Mami, Genoese renegade, one of eighteen benches.
20. Mamija [Mamiya], Turk, one of eighteen benches.
21. The Ka'id Muhammad, Jew by birth,[3] one of fifteen benches.
22. Mamija [Mamiya], Genoese renegade, one of eighteen benches.
23. Mami Ka'id, Venetian renegade, one of twenty-two benches.
24. Mami Gancho, Venetian renegade, one of twenty benches.
25. Mami the Corsican, renegade, one of twenty benches.
26. Mami the Calabrian, renegade, one of twenty benches.
27. Paduan Ra'is, son of a renegade, one of twenty-two benches.
28. Kadi Ra'is, Turk, one of twenty-two benches.
29. Donardi, Greek renegade, one of nineteen benches.
30. Dja'far Montez, Sicilian renegade from the hills of Trapani, one of twenty-two benches.
31. Hasan the Genoese Fornaro (the baker), renegade, one of fifteen benches.
32. Kari Ra'is, Turk, one of eighteen benches.
33. Kaur 'Ali, son of a renegade, one of twenty benches.
34. Yusuf Remolar (oar maker), Neapolitan renegade, one of twenty benches.
35. Dja'far, Genoese renegade, one of twenty benches.[4]

CHAPTER 23

Corsairs with Frigates

Other corsairs have frigates that are brigantines, with eight to thirteen benches. These vessels are generally made in Cherchell, which is located, as we said earlier, twenty leagues or sixty miles west of Algiers, and where there is a great quantity of wood for production. The masters of these frigates are all Moors from Granada, Valencia, and Aragón, who make up a dense population in Cherchell. The men who are captains (for the most part) were all born in Spain and are familiar with its ports, coastlines, and seashores. There are also many Turks and renegades who are captains of these frigates, because as soon as a *lewend* or seaman finds himself with 150 or 200 *escudos,* he immediately joins with others in a common investment to make a brigantine and arm it with all things necessary. And with this vessel they sail everywhere doing the greatest damage.

This is especially true of the Moriscos of Cherchell, since they are well versed regarding the coasts of Spain, where they all have relatives, brothers and friends. The moment they arrive on land, they hide the brigantine with all its gear under the sands, in a ditch or great hole. Entering into the land dressed in Christian gear, speaking very good Spanish, and being very well received where there are other Moriscos, they easily find their way around, largely at night. Then after shackling all the Christians they encounter, they bring them to the marina and, unearthing the brigantine, they return home with them, much to their satisfaction.[1]

Another thing: because these ships are small, they are easily hidden in some cove or site where they are not seen. Fooling the guards in the towers of the marinas, these corsairs then emerge at midday on the roads in Christian dress, and they rob and continually kidnap many peoples. These vessels, without a doubt, cause the greatest harm in the Christian world, because they sail all the time during the summer and winter, neither ceasing nor resting. Since the robberies they make are so great, the captains of these ships quickly rise to become captains of galliots. In general, they all have their beginnings this way. Those who row these ships are ordinarily renegades, Turks, or Moors, all of whom share in the cost as well as the gain of privateering. And they all carry arms—harquebuses or strong bows and arrows with which to fight the moment their hands leave the oars. They also tend to hire some Bagarinos, or Moors, as we said earlier, who earn their living by voluntarily rowing for others.[2]

The number of these brigantines or frigates made in Algiers is not certain, although in Cherchell there may be some twenty or twenty-five. The uses and customs of these corsairs are the same as those of the galliots.

CHAPTER 24

Algerian Merchants

The merchants, as we said, are the fifth type of Turk. Also numerous, they are either Turks by birth and by profession or renegades and their sons, among whom may be counted some Jews by birth who voluntarily turned Turk or Moor, as happens every day.[1] Many of these merchants were first janissaries and *lewends,* and then finding the life of a merchant more peaceful and secure, and far less dangerous, they changed careers. Others were placed as youths into this art and practice by their masters or patrons.

These merchants deal with the kind of goods available in Barbary, in the parts corresponding to Algiers, such as wheat, barley, rice, cows, oxen, camels, sheep, oil, lard, honey, raisins, figs, dates, and silk. Trafficking in hides and beeswax is reserved for those merchants who rent the business from the king, in order to buy these two items from the Moors and sell them to the Christians. These merchants also traffic in every kind of merchandise that the corsairs rob and bring to sell in Algiers, especially the buying and selling of slaves—of Christians of every stripe and age, in which they make a great profit.

These Christians are sold by proclamation and auction in the Souk, a street that contains the most important shops of merchandise. The sale is not rounded off until the Christian has been proclaimed in the Souk for three days, at the end of which he or she is taken to the king, who is given first refusal on the auction price to take the slave for his own.

All the merchants also tend to trade in the merchandise that the Christian galleys bring into Algiers via safe conduct. The merchants buy these goods in bulk and, placing them in their shops and warehouses, often sell them not only to their neighbors in Algiers but also to the

Moors and Berbers in all the lands of the kingdom and even to people outside of it, because more Christian merchant ships come to the city of Algiers than to any other part of Barbary.

The galleys that come from England bring much iron, lead, tin, copper, pewter, gunpowder, and cloth of every kind. Those that arrive from Spain, especially from Valencia or Catalonia, bring seed pearls, scents, distilled waters, oils for marinades, sherry, cochineal dye, red caps, cochineal-dyed blankets, salt, wine, and many gold *escudos* and Spanish coins worth a quarter and an eighth of a *peseta*,[2] which is the chief merchandise and that of greatest gain.

From Marseille and other places in France come all kinds of notions, such as cotton for candlewicks, iron, steel, nails, saltpeter, gunpowder, alum, sulfur, fish, oil (if Barbary lacks it), razors, knives, paper made from gall, ferrous sulfate, rubber, good needles, pins, many hazelnuts and chestnuts, salt, wine, and other merchandise that Frenchmen ordinarily tend to carry, smuggled and forbidden, which they take on board in Spain on the pretext that they are bound for France. Once they are on the high seas, however, they take a direct course to Algiers.[3]

From Genoa, Naples, and Sicily merchants bring to Algiers much threaded silk of every color, masses of velvet, damask, satin and taffetas of all kinds. From Venice, they bring kettles, caldrons, tablecloths, damasks, boxes, chests, glassware, cakes of white soap and other items.

These merchants also contract with other Turkish and Moorish merchants who go to Algiers with their wares. From Constantinople they tend to carry many rough-hewed oars; gummed-up fabrics to make shirts and fabrics from India for turbans worn on their heads; *cuzacas*, or elaborate girdles of silk that support highly ornamented damascene daggers; rugs; smocks of taffeta and capes of camel hair; capes of diverse silks and colors, many of these lined with quilting or with various furs, such as sable; and also highly ornate spoons painted in every color, much porcelain, earthenware plates and bowls, and other highly polished and nicely worked vessels from Alexandria and Tripoli.

From Barbary, some drugs; spices of clove, pepper, vanilla, and ginger; Indian fabrics for shirts and turbans.

From Djerba, some very fine shawls worn by women, as well as oil and dates.

From Tunis, quantities of very fine oil and white soap.

From Tabarka, and the Bastion de France,[4] lots of coral, which after being worked into beads of every kind sells very well across all of Barbary.

From Bône [present-day Annaba], much lard and cured meat from cows and rams, which they call *kheli'a*.[5]

From Constantine and Kollo, cordovans tanned in every color, and many coarse shawls with which the Berbers and poor people cover themselves.

From Cherchell, honey, straw, and wheat.

From Orán, cloth from Spain and red caps.

From Tlemcen, many nicely woven caftans, in black, white, and blue.

From Fès, much gold coin and *reales* from Spain, as well as sugar and honey.

From Sousse, a certain kind of earth for washing,[6] as good as soap, and used in their baths.

And in exchange for this, they give to Christian merchants—those allowed to sell—wax and hides, which they have rented, as well as wool, dates, caps, and a certain cochineal picked in the mountains of Algiers, which if not as fine as the Spanish variety is still very good. And they also give Christian merchants goods bought from the corsairs, which the merchants then sell back to other Christians, such as clothing, stockings, doublets, shoes, hats, trimmings, swords and daggers, cakes of soap, and tuna fish. Using the coin of the realm, Christian merchants can then ransom slaves.

To Fès, Algerian merchants send fabrics from Spain, as well as many scimitars, knives, fabrics from India and Constantinople. They use rowboats and generally row to Tétouan all the time. To all parts of Barbary they send fabrics and red dye from Spain, red caps, and seed pearls. To Constantinople they send pearls, some fine jewels, coral, preserves from Valencia, and largely reales from Spain, which bring them great profit. They also send a great number of Christian boys there as presents.

To accompany this merchandise they send their sons or relatives, renegades or trusted persons, who sell the goods and charge the correct price, men whom they can re-employ. Unlike Christians, these merchants are not accustomed to form a company with merchants from other parts, because they scarcely trust even the sons of their own loins. Nor are they given to keeping books or notebooks where they write up their business dealings, unless it is one item and on one piece of paper. They do not use exchanges, nor give insurance policies or orders of payment to merchants from other parts, for the same reason that there is no trust among them.

Although their law prohibits usury, they are great usurers, because before lending one escudo, they will demand one or two coins of gain each day, and few are the men who do not do this. In the same way, although there are some who speak and act the truth—largely Turks by birth—they are very rare, like a white raven, because in general they are great liars, crooks, and unreliable people.

On this point, you may agree on something with them, and even with witnesses present they will instantly deny it, or say they do not wish to rehearse the matter; and later they respond that if they would tell the truth and keep their word, they might as well be Christians. And so it is necessary to remember, deal, and pay upfront at the very moment of the exchange. The same thing occurs in the business of weighing: they take no coin that they do not first weigh, which they do very carefully and with deceit, and they pay with coins that are faulty, diminished, and, if possible, false. In all things they work to deceive you.

These merchants have many shops, in public streets and places where they always install a son, or at least a renegade, whom they trust. The merchants themselves are always seated in their shops, squatting there like women. And in the two *souks,* the old and the new (where most of them keep their shops), there must be some two thousand shops. As for the houses where these merchants dwell across the city (because they are not accustomed to living in their shops), there must be around three thousand.

CHAPTER 25

Algerian Laborers and Artisans

The sixth kind of Turk, or rather, their sixth profession, is that of laborers and artisans. A great number of these are coral workers; tailors; silversmiths; shoemakers; tanners; shoelace-makers; basket weavers; barbers; chair makers; saddle makers; quarry workers; construction workers; makers of shotguns, bows, arrows, scimitars, gunpowder, and those who produce artillery, together with all the other jobs necessary to run a city. But the greatest numbers of these men are renegades. And beyond these and other laborers, there is an infinite number of Christians who work alongside all the above Turks in the same trades, side by side in the same stores and shops. Some Christians work for other masters who allow them to exercise their job skills, paying them by the day at an agreed-upon rate, some more, some less. Many of these Turkish artisans are also janissaries or soldiers, as we said, who serve at war when either called upon or obliged to fight, and others are *lewends* and corsairs, sailing privateering ships however and whenever they please. Consequently, among all these men one finds neither sense nor points of honor.[1] Missing also are those high spirits felt by Christian soldiers who justly equate the military with nobility, as in effect it is, and feel insulted at being a soldier and a laborer at once.

CHAPTER 26

Algerian Fashions

The general dress of everyone here is long. To begin with, they dress with a long cloth shirt, wide in both sleeves and torso. Under the shirt, they wear wide pleated breeches, so that from the waist down, the shirt does not touch the flesh but rather covers the trousers, and they go about with their shirts hanging out. If the weather is cold, the Algerians dress in a colored woolen vest that they call a *yelek*.[1] It has elbow-length sleeves because, in keeping with the commandment of Muhammad, Turks tend to wash themselves very often. To that end, they design the sleeves of all their clothing so that they can wash their arms up to the elbows without undressing.

Over this vest they ordinarily wear something called a *caftan*,[2] which is like a priest's cassock, open in front and with buttons down the chest and elbow-length sleeves. Similarly long, this caftan falls to the middle of the shins, or at least past the knees, and it is also of colored fabric. Rich men wear caftans of satin, damask, velvet, and silks, and both the vest and the caftan are low-cut and lacking any collar, so that Turks always walk abroad with their necks on view.

And since both this vest and caftan have sleeves that reach no farther than the elbows, the Algerians are accustomed to add some little sleeves to their outfits, long enough to cover their arms from the elbow to the hand, and worn in a wrinkled fashion right up to the wrists. These separate sleeves are made of satin, damask, or velvet. Over the caftan the Algerians tie some ribbons of silk, made in a woven pattern, or some very fine and colorful *sendals*,[3] which they call *hazuqah*.[4] And almost everyone hangs some beautifully ornate damascene knives from them, however possible on the left-hand side, the same way our Spanish Galicians carry their swords on their waists.

During winter the Algerians wear woolen breeches, with leather half-boots that they call *tmaks*,[5] which are all yellow, orange, or red. Rare are the Algerians who sport black or white boots. In summer, they are content with linen trousers falling to mid-calf, save for important men like ka'ids and merchants, some *ru'asa*,[6] and other older men, who in all seasons wear tmaks. With or without these half-boots, they all wear either red leather shoes or yellow pointed shoes.[7] They wear these to avoid the necessity of stooping to put their footgear on by hand or with a shoe horn (a real nuisance), and, even more, because every time they enter their homes they remove them so as not to dirty the floors with mud, and they put them on again to go out.

They generally make these shoes very stiff and hard in the heel, where they purposefully insert some splints, arched like the human heel, and in the interior of the shoe they add a thick lining and some very hard soles. In order to have these shoes last a long time, since they are expensive, all the Turks—tall and small, nobles and plebeians, even the king himself—tend to add iron taps to the heels and an iron half-moon to the soles. On the tip of the shoes, and on both sides, they hammer in some nails that remain nicely inserted and incorporated into the sole, over which the foot rests, allowing the shoe to touch the ground with these nails when they walk. So that Turks and Moors, peoples not accustomed to shoeing their horses, pride themselves on having their own feet shod with iron, so that they make a great noise when they walk with these shoes through cobblestoned streets.

Instead of a cape, Algerians generally wear a kind of coat of colored wool, and more commonly of a very fine woolen cloth, either from Courtrai[8] or from London, made in the Venetian style, of floor length, wide and open in front and without a collar, which they call a *ferdja*.[9] The sleeves of these coats tend to be wide, and longer than those of the vest and caftan, because they cover the entire arm. Men of reputation wear this over the caftan at all times, and all the rest wear it when the weather is cold. In hot or seasonable weather they carry it generally folded into four sections and thrown over the left arm, as do travelers with their capes. And in this way they walk about the city.

They all sport very shaven heads, and they shave every eight days. Important men grow a beard, or at least they do not shave it off. Many others wear only moustaches, especially the janissaries and *lewends,* and all other men who presume to be dashing.

They are all accustomed to wear either turbans or fine, very white cloths on their heads, be they Turks by birth, renegades, corsairs, merchants, or artisans. All the higher orders of janissaries, from the Boluk-Bashi (captains of the squadron) on up, wear turbans. They are not worn, however, by the lower orders of janissaries—by the Yol-dash (soldiers), Odabashi (commanders of the *agha bolukleri*), Otraks or Oturaks (retired elders from the janissary corps), and Solak soldiers (bodyguards, charged with protecting the pasha). Instead, over a skullcap of quilted cloth (which generally all of them use),[10] they wear something like a bag, half stocking, or sleeve of red woolen material or of other fine wool that the Turks call a *tartura.*[11] It is wide in the part that fits the head, and as long as two handspans or less, so that it is much larger than the caps of red wool that they wear in Genoa at sea or to sleep. And folding that tartura toward the back, and hanging over the scruff of the neck whatever does not fit on the head, the janissaries tie over this a white headdress, which with three or four turns circles the entire head over the forehead. And he who wears the tartura with a small cap or piece of cloth that covers the head is identifiable as a janissary soldier.

Some of the first rank of janissaries, which we called Yol-dash and who are of less importance and gravitas, tend to always walk about wearing only a caftan, and not carrying a ferdja on their shoulders, as do the others. The janissaries who cook, whom we have earlier discussed, have their heads and bodies very differently attired, because besides the fact that they all ordinarily walk about without an outer dress or coat and with very short (and not very clean) caftans, on their heads they wear nothing more than some caps of fine wool or colored cloth. Some caps are made of bits and pieces of cloth, and are so small that they barely cover their heads. And on these caps they place a large feather—of turkey or rooster or some other bird—so that the beret always seems fantastically dressed up. They also carry a small ax with a handle (which many of them decorate with silver), as long as two handspans, through which they are all recognized by everybody, both janissaries and non-janissaries.

But it is common to all who are janissaries that, whatever grade they might be—from cook all the way to agha—they must all wear, without any difference among them, the collars of their vests and caftans garnished with an edging of some chosen color. Neither Moor nor Turk nor renegade (at least those who are not janissaries) can wear this edging on his clothing, under penalty of a life sentence without remission, because this is properly the device through which janissaries are identified to the public.

There are also some Turks and renegades and sons of these last who, because they are neither so rich nor of such importance, wear no turbans on their heads but content themselves by wearing the tartura, or large cap (which we said are worn by janissaries who do not reach the rank of Boluk-Bashi). This cap has no head covering over it, because this is the proper gear for those janissaries, and nobody but them can wear a tartura of that kind with a cap, as we said.

Children and youths who are the sons of renegade Turks and janissaries wear vests and caftans and ferdjas as do their fathers, as well as the same kind of iron-soled shoes and colored tmak, or half-boots. And as long as these children are young, they wear on their heads small red caps, or those made from some fine wool, damascene, taffeta, velvet, and brocade, whatever their parents can afford, because they tend to dress them very elegantly.

Some Turks and new janissaries, after arriving from Constantinople with no money as yet to dress in the style of Algiers, walk about in garments worn in Turkey. These differ considerably from Algerian fashions, especially those garments from Romania and Constantinople, where they wear breeches that are all white, black, or red, all of them without a fly. They also wear short smocks and long clothes Hungarian style, with their sleeves dragging on the floor, and narrow like the clothing of university students. In addition, they sport a certain kind of colored woolen berets with great horns, as wide as those of the Germans. Moreover, they wear iron-soled shoes with four points of iron, long and high enough that they cannot reach the ground, as are worn in regions of much snow in order to walk over the ice without slipping.

And those who boast of being valiant and dashing will put feathers in their caps—the white feathers of egrets, herons, cranes, and other birds. Many men wear these feathers embedded in some holes they make on their foreheads, in the very flesh over their temples and pulses. And if these men have killed some Christians, they carry as many plumes as the number of men they have beheaded. There are men like these in Algiers who walk about very self-regarding, and they are called *deli*, which means the valiant ones.[12]

CHAPTER 27

The Marabouts of Algiers

Beyond all the manner of peoples living in and around Algiers thus far discussed, there is another kind called marabouts,[1] who are like ecclesiastical persons, because the word in Arabic means something like "saint," and they are all held in great veneration. As such, it seemed best to give them special mention here, separating them from the other inhabitants as if from laypersons.

These men, generally, are either Moors or Turks by birth. Some are renegades, among whom are men who live in one of five ways, and who are addressed by the other name of *cacizes*.[2] Their job is to discharge three duties at the mosques. The first is to light the lamps there at prayer times and keep them clean. The second duty is to call the faithful to come make the *salat*,[3] although marabouts with some authority have a Muslim servant or sacristan who performs these duties as follows. He climbs to a tower generally found in mosques—and if they do not have one, he goes to the door of the mosque—and from there he lifts his voice, as forcibly as possible, saying: "Laa ilaaha illa Allah wa-Muhammad Rasuul Allah . . . ," which means "There is no God but God and Muhammad is his prophet."[4] He says this three times, repeating the same words, and calling the faithful to prayer five times between day and night: an hour before dawn, which they call *salat al-subh*;[5] at midday, which they call *salat al-zhur*;[6] at Compline, which they call *salat al-ʿasr*;[7] at sunset, which they call *salat al-maghrib*;[8] and two hours into the night (when we Christians usually commend our souls to God), which they call *salat al-ʿisha*.[9] And at all these hours some people always go to the mosque to pray.

The third duty of the marabout is to show the faithful, after their arrival, how to pray. Facing them in their rows inside the mosque, he begins, and they all follow him, saying the same words and making the same gestures, movements, and bodily dips that he makes, so that he is like a dancing master.

The marabout of the main mosque is the first to raise his voice in the tower, and until he begins no other marabout can do the same. If it is midday, he is also the first to raise a flag, which all others can then display in their towers, so that those who cannot hear may at least see from afar the flag and understand the call to prayer. And then the rest follow him and all together raise their voices in a sound worse than the howling of wolves and dogs.

Some of the marabouts also tend to preach during their "Lent," reading some chapter of the Qur'an, creating a kind of discourse on it, and exhorting people to the virtuous life. Many men ordinarily have the custom of being seated in the mosques with the Qur'an in hand, and whoever wishes to hear some chapter goes to them, and after they have heard it they give him alms, just for the work of reading. All of these men count on this income, small or large, from the mosques, which pays for their food. And some seven or eight men who have charge of as many other mosques, greater and more important ones, are paid by the king some ten, twelve, fifteen, twenty, and more *doblas* per month. They also tend to make a living by accompanying the dead, as will be explained in what follows.

Other marabouts are schoolmasters, teaching the boys to read and write in Arabic or Turkish—because there are separate schools for each of these. And the marabouts also teach the boys to count on the abacus, and the figures of their numbers are the same as in the Christian world. Some marabouts also teach the months of the year, which they count by moons, as well as the way to track their feast days: but this is all very grossly done and of little importance.

The book used for teaching the boys, after they have learned their letters and how to combine them, is the same Qur'an. These teachers generally follow no guidelines of months or years, but when a boy reaches certain parts or sections of the Qur'an, he pays the schoolmaster some two or three doblas. And having finished going through the Qur'an (which is done in three years, at most), those who study Turkish tend to extend an invitation to their teacher and all their schoolmates. And for the teacher to dress up, they give him so many *picos* (a measure of three palms)¹⁰ of very fine wool or of some coarser wool or silk; or else they give him fifteen or twenty doblas or more, as much as they can afford, to buy the fabric. Others give the teacher a ready-made garment, a *ferdja*. All those who study Arabic, above and beyond their assignments, will on that celebration day accompany on horseback the student who has finished the Qur'an (much as among us, on the day of Saint Nicolas, the boys accompany the "Little Bishop"),¹¹ and the Algerian students all run ahead playing some flutes. And having taken a turn around the city, they accompany the boy to his home. This done, the little Muslim graduates into a Master or Doctor.

Few are the teachers and marabouts who may understand the Qur'an, although they read it constantly and conduct all their studies through it, because it is written in an ancient Arabic language, although the words themselves are in Turkish or another language.¹² It is obscure to them, even more obscure than the Latin language is to us. And if some of them understand it, they are taken for ancient scholars, and those are rare, excellent, and brilliant doctors, who can interpret and explain the text, and interpret dreams through it. Because the whole text consists of an infinite number of tall stories that Muhammad dreamed up, all contrary to good doctrine and repugnant to reason and to all philosophy and science.¹³

There was a marabout in Algiers who prided himself on being very learned in the ancient Arabic language and the whole of the Qur'an. In truth an ignorant fellow with no knowledge of any discipline or liberal arts, he went by the name of Sidi Boutayeb.¹⁴ Everyone held him in extreme veneration, and he was the caciz or marabout of the main mosque. Some of the other marabouts, as well as other men, joined him at his home or in the main mosque, where he sometimes read them the Qur'an.

These two kinds of marabouts are no different in dress from the others, who are laypersons, because those who are Turks dress like the other Turks, and those who are Moors, like the other Moors. Only in this is there some difference: that some of the Moors dress in white, both in their robes and smocks, and generally wear bulky shirts with wide sleeves and of a length almost to their feet.

The way they punish the boys in school is to tie both their feet together with a rope or cord attached to a stick, and lifting them high, with their heels toward the sky and their heads and bodies on the ground, the schoolmaster flogs the soles of their feet as many strokes as he wishes with an oxhide whip. They claim that to whip schoolboys on the buttocks is a very great sin.

Other marabouts are professed hermits, living a solitary life in small mosques, much like chapels for Christians, of which there must be some two hundred around Algiers, in the mountains that are more or less half a league away. These hermits are commonly all Moors, though a few have been renegades. All of these hermits tend to be heavily visited by the Moors and Turks of the city, and especially by the women, who always tend to be the most devout. They commend themselves to these hermits in their prayers in order to conceive children, be loved by their husbands, marry off their daughters, and other similar desires. Sometimes these hermits serve the women as studs,[15] which their husbands do not begrudge them. Rather they take it as great joy and fortune to have their wives be impregnated by these hermits.

There was a renegade from Córdoba, called Sidi Bournous,[16] lately deceased, who lived some years in the highest mountains toward the west, half a league from Algiers, and who had a great hand for the above business (as was well known). These days his tomb is visited (in the chapel where he lived) as if that of a great and excellent man.

These marabouts have the custom of praying with beads of gall, and with other things they string together, and their prayers are some of the names of God, which they repeat many times as they run their hands over the beads, and some say nothing more than "Allah, Allah, Allah," which means "God," or "astaghfiru, astaghfiru," which means "help me, God."[17] They repeat this so many times and with such great speed, that they drool all over their chests. And in the end, their brains are fried, and they fall to the ground like dead men. And these same men are taken for the greatest of saints.

All of these marabouts are highly ignorant and, being illiterate, they live from alms that they come to beg for in the city. Many marabouts have their alms sent or taken to them by devoted women who visit their hermitages. In sum, they are all so highly venerated, and tend to display such an admirable gravity of mien, that people kiss their clothing and even their feet. They generally walk about barefoot, naked, covered with an old and torn overcoat, with a bared head and a staff in hand, so that nothing is missing that is required for a seemly exterior and show of sanctity.

There are other marabouts—poor, broken, dirty, barefoot, and bareheaded—who walk about the city and beyond it. They tend to wear some large beads of gall around their necks, or diagonally across their chests. Some of them dedicate themselves to bringing water into the city in summer, and for the love of God giving it to all—Moors, Turks, and Christians—without discriminating. And they particularly regard as holy the Djumʿa (which is our Friday, when more people go to the mosques for prayer), but during midday or Compline on all other days they enter the mosques with glasses of water, and walking between the rows in which the worshippers are lined up, they give water to all who want it, so that they will pray to God for them. Other marabouts carry about water from the fountains and pour it into certain large earthenware jars found in some streets in the city, leaning against the walls of some houses whose owners, out of devotion, leave them there covered, as fixtures, without moving them the whole year. During the summer these same marabouts settle down close to the jars, and with small juglike glasses (called *bardacas*),[18] out of grace and the love of God, they give water to passersby, be they Moors, Turks, or Christians, as we said. And if they are given money, they do not refuse it.

Other marabouts out of devotion (as they put it) burn their heads with hot irons and brand themselves with knobs of fire; others slice into their chests and arms with razors, giving themselves great wounds; or they put cotton rags drenched in oil over their arms, which they set on fire and let their flesh burn until the oil and cloth are consumed. But the truth is that they do this out of love for young boys (to whom they are very addicted) when the devil makes them burn with desire and further inflames in them that dirty and filthy lust. And in this way, every man who kisses the head and wounds of these dirty rogues is a holy man.

There are still other marabouts who are crazy and witless, either born that way out of their mother's wombs or become so through illness or accident. And these above all are taken for saintly, so much so that it is a grave sin to deny them whatever they want, or disturb them when they take something from any shop where it is sold. Some of these marabouts are more scoundrels than madmen, as is often seen: on sighting a pretty and comely young woman in the street, they will throw themselves on her like studs and sexually accost her right there in public view.[19] And the madness of the Moors and Turks is so general that this behavior does not seem abnormal to them, since they instantly kiss the hand, head, and garments of so shameless a rogue as if he had performed a great and saintly work or some notable deed of virtue.

After these marabouts die, their followers do even more for them: they convert their mosques into great chapels and design beautiful sepulchers for them; they place lit lamps in front of their corpses; and they visit their bones and honor them as if they were the most notable saints in heaven. And thus, outside of the Gate of Bab 'Azzun there are three sepulchers for these madmen: one of them, to the right as you leave the gate, is that of a marabout called Sidi 'Ali Ezzouaoui, who died in 1576.[20] Another marabout lies in a chapel on the left, with a dove on a plaque that says Sidi 'Abd al-'Aziz, who died in 1577;[21] and with him, in the same chapel, rests another crazy Moor called Sidi Bou Noua; and a little farther is another chapel with the remains of another so-called marabout named Sidi Batqa, who died in 1540;[22] and outside the Gate of Bab al-Wad, before reaching the Castle of 'Uludj 'Ali[23] is another chapel and sepulcher dedicated to a highly revered marabout called Sidi 'Abd al-Rahman Tha'alibi, who died in 1530;[24] in another chapel, still higher up on the left, lies another marabout called Sidi Ahmed Tidjani, who died in 1556;[25] and walking farther on toward a hill by the beach is yet another chapel of a marabout called Sidi Yacoub el Andalusi (the Andalusian),[26] whom some people say was also crazy. Women visit this chapel every Wednesday with great devotion, commending themselves to his powers. So that among Turks and Moors the great gain and highest grade of good fortune is to be a madman with neither brains nor judgment, and from this one can also understand how little they know and understand the things of God and His goodness.

All those who take on the profession of marabouts, in general, are also sorcerers, on which their knowledge and reputation chiefly rest. You can ask none of them for a cure for something that he will not cast lots or spells, use necromancy or hydromancy,[27] with all other species of magic. Finally, all of them profess to divine and foretell good fortune, and even to bless with words, names, charms and toys, with bits of paper on which they, or someone else, write mysterious words and characters or the names of Satan and demons. These items the marabouts throw on the necks of sick children, postnatal mothers, badly married or rejected women, along with an infinity of aromatic substances that they make from frogs, teeth of dogs, eyes of cats, nails of wolves, excrement of monkeys, teeth of swine and other filthy things. The marabouts persuade all Moors and Turks, and particularly those women who adore them, to take such substances for divine things. More than not, these men also profess themselves as spiritualists, affirming that they have familiar spirits lodged in their heads called *djinns*,[28] who reveal to them all manner of things, as we shall discuss elsewhere at length.

In sum, however saintly these marabouts appear to be, they are tremendous sodomites. They pride themselves on it and commit this bestial sin publicly, in the middle of the Souk or the main street and in the eyes of the entire city. And the blindness of Moors and Turks is so engrained that they praise and endorse these acts. I choose to refrain from citing some cases here because they are so gross, dirty, and filthy. Given that these men profess so bestial a life, similarly outrageous are the tall stories, dreams, fictions, errors, and blindness that they teach, preach, and use to persuade their followers—well beyond what Muhammad left written in the Qur'an, which we shall discuss in its proper place.

CHAPTER 28

The Jews of Algiers

The third kind of inhabitants or neighbors of Algiers are Jews, who have three origins: some come from Spain,[1] others from the island of Mallorca or from the Balearic Islands, and others are natives of the lands of Africa.

They all make a living in trade (as is their custom everywhere). Many keep shops of haberdashery in which they sell notions of every kind. Some are peddlers, selling the same goods in the streets from baskets and boxes hung from their arms, and loudly advertising their wares to possible buyers. There are Jews who are tailors, workers of coral, or venders of oil and soaps. Many Jews buy clothing and other items that the corsairs have robbed, and they sell them back to Christian merchants, making a good profit. And other Jews come and go with merchandise from Djerba, Tunis, Annaba, Constantine, Orán, Tlemcen, Tétouan, Fès, Marrakech, and also from Constantinople.

Jews make up the majority of the silversmiths of Algiers, because very few are renegades and none are Moors. In the same way, Jews alone mint the coins of gold, silver, and bronze, since they are in charge of the Treasury, where they engage in great deceits and falsehoods, counterfeiting money or mixing quantities of copper to coin it into an alloy.[2] And because no investigations are made into this, an infinite number of false coins of every kind may be found in Algiers, all of its kingdoms and provinces, and those of its neighbors.

Some Jews teach their children to read Hebrew and write in Arabic, but none is truly learned or experienced in writing. As for their Jewish dreams and ceremonies, all are very ignorant and greatly obstinate. I can attest to this, having debated with some of them not infrequently.[3]

The Jews are dispersed across two neighborhoods that contain some 150 houses. Both neighborhoods feature a synagogue where Jews congregate on Saturdays and celebrate their holy days with great observance. Every day many of them go there to pray, and they intone many of their Psalms aloud in Hebrew.

Each year the Jews pay a tribute of fifteen hundred *doblas* to the king, which equals six hundred *escudos* of gold, but this is nothing compared to what the rulers extort from them every day, because for the slightest complaint or on a slender occasion, they skin them alive and fleece them of whatever they have by making them pay fines. To collect the tribute that they pay yearly to the king—which expense is shared by all according to what they have—and to speak for all and compose agreements for their whole nation, the Jews tend to elect certain leading figures, who are like counselors. They also elect another Jew to head them all, whom the king confirms and whom they call a *caciz*.

The Jews are so ill-treated by all Turks, Moors, and Christians, that it is something incredible to see. When coming upon a Jew, even a prominent one, a small Moorish boy will make him remove his skullcap from his head and take off his slippers, which the boy will use to slap his face a thousand times, and the Jew will not dare to move or defend himself, having no remedy but to flee. In the same way, if a Christian encounters a Jew on a street, he will give him a thousand slaps on the neck, and if the Jew tries to hit the Christian back and is seen by some Moor or Turk, they will favor the Christian, even though he be a vile slave. And they will scream at him to kill that "dog" of a Jew—regarding this as his just deserts and unremitting penance for the great sin and obstinacy of his tribe.[4]

And for this very reason, many Jews turn Turk every day, and among them there are some very wealthy men. But none can remain Moor or Turk for many years, since they cannot envision being good Muslims or believing in the law of Muhammad. They are as much Jewish in one manner as another.

The dress of the Jews is always the same, since they all wear wide linen trousers and shirts; a long black smock, resembling a cassock, that falls below the knee; and a kind of black or sometimes white *burnus* over all this. Those Jews who come from Spanish lands wear round berets of

Toledo needlework. Those of Mallorcan, French, or Italian extraction wear something like half-sleeves of black wool, a part of which fits over the head and the other part hangs beneath the back of the head. And those Jews from Africa and Soria[5] wear a white linen circlet wrapped around their heads over a red or quilted cap, covering their entire necks not unlike the style of Moors, except that they must exhibit the front of their heads, with hair falling to almost the middle of their foreheads, which identifies them as Jews. Those who come from Constantinople and Turkey wear turbans on their heads, as is the custom there, of some very fine fabrics marked with the color yellow. Some Jews wear *tmak*, or boots, but they must be black ones, as no Jew is allowed to wear shoes of any kind or color, although they all wear slippers.

Although some Jews are wealthy, they largely live in great poverty, and they always smell of goat, the same as their houses. They maintain their slaughter houses apart from the rest because, in keeping with their Jewish ceremonies and superstitions, they will not eat the meat of an animal killed by a Moor or Christian, as do other Algerians.

The Jews take much advantage of Christian captives that they buy. Generally, they treat their Christian slaves well, although not those who have become renegades, because these men are worse than the Moors and Turks themselves. The reason is because the Jew, as a Jew, fears that his Christian captive will complain to the king about some mistreatment, for which the Jew would be punished. But a renegade would never fear this, because the king cannot confiscate his slaves.[6] Thus the hatred that the Jew has toward Christians is doubled—hating them both as a Jew and as a Muslim. And this hatred can be more freely exercised upon his becoming a Muslim, when the Jew can vent his hatred through the bad treatment he inflicts.

CHAPTER 29

Languages and Currencies

The languages typically spoken in Algiers are three. The first is Turkish, which the Turks speak among themselves, as well as with those renegades who live in their houses or have dealings with them. There are also Moors and many Christian captives who know how to speak Turkish very well, having learned it in conversation with Turks. The second language is Arabic, generally used among all: Moors, Turks living in Algiers for some time, and Christians who must often or occasionally deal with Moors all speak Arabic. Although we generally call everyone native to Barbary a Moor, there is no one common language among them, and certainly no mode of speaking that they share. It is true that moving eastward, all the way from the Sousse[1] or most western part of Barbary to inner Arabia, all the generations and populations of Moors conform to each other, both in many of their words and modes of speaking. But because the Arabs of Arabia (who conquered these great provinces) greatly corrupted their own tongue through their communication and mixture with so many conquered nations, the language of the Arabs used today in Barbary is not properly Arabic. The same may be said for native Africans, inhabitants of those lands from antiquity, according to the custom and general uses of the word.

Each province originally had its particular language and distinct pronunciation. But after their languages were corrupted by that of the Arabs, these provinces were left with no uniform language but, rather, with something very different in diction and pronunciation — with such a degree of difference that many speakers do not understand each other. In the same way that a pure Spanish speaker does not understand a pure Italian or French speaker, one finds that, even four leagues from Algiers, those who are Kabyles[2] speak very differently from the Arabs and the Baldis; the Arabs speak very differently from the Baldis and Kabyles; and the Baldis speak very differently from the rest.

The third language used in Algiers is what the Moors and Turks call the *lingua franca*. They use this term to name both the language and mode of Christian speech, not because they themselves speak in the language and use the speech patterns of Christians, nor because this manner of speech (which they call "language of the Franks")[3] belongs to any particular Christian nation, but rather because they use this mode of speech to communicate with the Christians. It is a mixture of various Christian languages, largely Italian and Spanish words with some recently added Portuguese terms, since a great number of Portuguese captives were brought to Algiers from Tétouan and Fès after the king of Portugal, Don Sebastian, lost the battle in Morocco.[4]

When this confused mixture of so many diverse words and speech acts of different Christian kingdoms, provinces, and nations is linked to the bad pronunciation of the Moors and Turks (who do not know how to vary modes, tenses, and cases as do the Christians, to whom these belong), the result is the lingua franca of Algiers — a veritable mumbo-jumbo or, at least, a speech of the muzzled Black slave, brought to Spain anew.[5]

This lingua franca is so general that there is no home where it is not used, perhaps because there is no home that does not have one or more Christian captives. In many houses of Moors or Turks, there is always someone — big or small, man or woman, and even little children — able to speak lingua franca very well to Christians, who adapt themselves to this type of language. There are also many Turks and Moors who have been captives in Spain, Italy, and France; an infinite multitude of renegades from those and other Christian provinces; another great number of Jews who speak Spanish, Italian, and French very prettily because they have been here;[6] and even all the children of male and female renegades, who learned the natural Christian speech of their parents while suckling at their mothers' breasts, and who speak it as if they had been born in Spain or Italy.

And what may be said about Christian languages is also pertinent to the Christian monetary system, because the *escudos* of Italy, France, and especially Spain are all used, as is the *mithkal*[7] of Fès and the *sikka*[8] of Turkey. But the foreign money that they most treasure, brag about, and benefit from are the *reales* of Spain, silver coins of four and eight,[9] because they send and carry them even to Turkey and the great Cairo, and from there they move eastward to the great Oriental India, and even up to Cathay, China, and Tartary, always bringing a profit to those who carry them. And thus no merchandise is more precious, nor can anything of more worth be taken to Algiers, Barbary, or Turkey, than the reales of Spain.

Currencies particular to Algiers are made of three materials: bronze, silver, and gold. From bronze they make the smaller and more worthless coinage that they call *bourbe*,[10] which is round and the size of a Spanish *blanca*[11] or a Portuguese *cetil*[12] but twice as thick and heavy. This coinage is minted only in Algiers.

Six bourbes make up one *asper*.[13] This coin is made of silver, sized like the fourth part of a blanca or more, and shaped as a square. Ten of these add up to one Spanish real, although during a scarcity of reales, which are very prized and sought after by all, the rate of exchange is eleven and twelve aspers for a real. These aspers are minted in Algiers and no other place.

After the asper, comes the *rubia*,[14] a gold coin with much copper alloy, which cheapens its worth to twenty-five aspers; it is round in figure and the size of a very small and simple Spanish real. After the rubia, comes the *half diana*, which is also of gold, of the same alloy as the rubias, weighing and worth two rubias and fifty aspers, which come to one *dobla*.[15] The *diana* is round and like a Spanish real in size, although not as thick. There is also a *zyan*,[16] of the same alloy and make as a *half zyan*, but much greater in weight, length, width, and thickness, and it is worth one hundred aspers, or two doblas.

These kind of coins—the rubia, zyan, and half zyan—are minted only in Tlemcen, and they are engraved with certain Moorish letters that spell out the name of the king who ordered the coinage. From Tlemcen these coins are distributed throughout all the provinces, all the way to Biskra and the Sahara, the land close to the Blacks; eastward toward Tunis; and also throughout the kingdoms of Kuko and Labbès, where all this money has worth.

We should also note the *sultani* of fine gold, each worth 140 aspers, and these are coined only in Algiers.[17] The Spanish escudo was ordinarily worth 125 aspers, and Djaʿfar Pasha, king of Algiers in 1580,[18] raised the exchange to 130 aspers. And when the Spanish escudos are bought from merchants and others, they are worth more, according to the abundance of the coin or its lack. The escudos of France [of the Sun King] and Italy are worth the same, although people value most the ones from Spain, which have a better currency.

The sultani of Constantinople is worth 150 aspers, and the mithkal of Fès, 175. But in 1580, Djaʿfar Pasha raised the sultani to 175 aspers, and the mithkal to 225; and the reason for this was the scarcity of these monies. In conclusion, all the coinage of the realm—whether a real, escudo, sultani, or mithkal—has an uncertain value, because it generally rises and falls in keeping with the desire of the kings of Algiers, or as abundance, necessity, or lack of coinage demands and requires.

CHAPTER 30

Marriage Ceremonies

Although many men, Turks as well as renegades and Moors, are content with one wife, the majority of them (as per general usage and in accordance with the carnal liberty that Muhammad allows them) have two, three, four, and more wives. It is true that some marabouts are of the opinion that the number of wives should not go beyond four, and others say seven. They claim that multitudes of women are like walls, where all carnal desires are contained so that men will not stray abroad to sin with other women.

Turks, Moors, and renegades all marry indifferently, either with some Turkish women newly arrived from Constantinople (although these are few and rare), or with native Moorish women, renegades, or daughters of Jews who become Muslims. As long as the woman pleases or benefits her suitor, nobody (no matter how high in social status) cares too much about her lineage or nobility. Nor do these Algerians care about kinship, as long as she is not a sister. Their literati and marabouts have persuaded them that one may consider someone who nursed from the same breast in the same degree and grade as a sister. But they also say that if one of them also ate bread or some other nourishment while nursing, in that case they are not siblings, nor is it a sin to marry, because they are not of the same blood, since they were not reared from the same nourishment.

Ordinarily these men take the greatest pride in marrying renegades: and this is because these women are all more perfect and diligent in the service of their husbands and management of their homes. They are also better looking than Moorish or Turkish women. And if a man buys a Christian woman and makes her turn Muslim and renegade, she is always his slave unless he decides to free her. As a result, she is more obedient and does everything not to be sold, which he can do unless he has produced children with her. These men also take sexual advantage of their Christian slaves, which is not forbidden them, but if by chance they produce children, they cannot sell these women.

The Algerians have two customs in their mode of marrying, very contrary to those in the Christian world. The first is that a man will marry a Moor or renegade, or her daughter, sight unseen, because all their marriages are set up by go-betweens, particularly by procurers who go from house to house checking out the daughters of this or that man. According to the account that one of these go-betweens may give, a man may decide to marry. The second custom goes contrary to that of Christian women, as well as women from many nations of the world, who bring a dowry to their husbands when they marry to help with the burden and sorrows of marriage. Algerian men, on the other hand, are the ones who endow their women before marriage: in effect, they buy them. It is true that if the father or mother of the fiancée is dead, she brings to her new home whatever goods belong to her, and then both partners live off the woman. The husband, however, can neither sell her goods nor her belongings; rather he is obliged to keep the same amounts she brought into the marriage.

The dowry that they promise their women is settled by the prospective bridegroom with the father of the bride-to-be, if she has one, and if not, with her closest relatives. Everything is done legally, in front of the *kadi,* or judge of the city. When this is done and settled, the bridegroom then sends his fiancée a gift of things to eat, such as fritters, which they call *sfendj,*[1] and other honeyed sweetmeats. Wealthier men send a basket or two filled with oils, or with skin bleaching agents, rouge, henna, and other mixtures, as a sign that the woman is chosen and accepted as their own.

Some four, five, six, or more days (as many as they wish) before the woman is given over to her husband and the wedding is celebrated, her friends and relatives tend to have great dances and fiestas in her home, inviting all her female friends, neighbors, and women of status in the city. These dances are accompanied by the sounds of rattles and tambourines played by Moorish women, who make a living doing this and are paid by all the partygoers. The custom is that the dancer, when finished, goes among all the women asking for money with an open hand. And whatever they give her, she then gives to the Moorish women who are playing their instruments. In this manner, they pull together a great quantity of money, because many women attend these fiestas and dance for a great part of the day and night, and all of them offer money, not once but many times.

During these and many other days before the wedding, the women spend their time washing, scrubbing, bathing, soaping, applying makeup, and painting the bride-to-be, so that no matter how plain she may be, they make her look good. And all this is done by certain Moorish women who do nothing else for a living.

When the day arrives that the bride is to be given over to her intended, huge evening dinners are celebrated. The bridegroom hosts one in his home for his friends and relatives, and the parents or relatives of the bride, in her home for theirs—separating the men from the women in diverse parts and rooms of the house, so that they cannot see each other. After dinner, when they have once again decorated the bride with many jewels and seed-pearls, and painted her arms up to the elbows in black and her face in red and white—so that she seems nothing other than a mask—then the men go out into the street before the women, where others are waiting, and they arrange themselves into an orderly procession of two lines. The men go on ahead, taking with them two or three Moors playing kettledrums, tabors, and flutes. The women bring up the rear, their faces all veiled, and behind them at the very end they bring the bride, thoroughly covered up. In this procession (the men and women carrying lit white candles in their hands), they accompany the bride through the streets of the city, while the bridegroom remains at home with the rest of the people.[2] Before the procession with the bride returns, he enters the bedroom that was decorated (as best as possible) for both partners, and he sits on the pillows there, because they do not use any other kind of chair.

When the bride arrives accompanied by the designated people, her kinswoman and friends remain and take her to a special room where, removing her cloak, they roll up her sleeves to the elbows—which are painted and dyed black, as we said—and having her put both hands on her two sides (as we said, like wings), they throw over her face a very fine and subtle white veil. Then, with the Moorish women still playing their tambourines and rattles, they arrive at the door of the bedroom where the bridegroom awaits. He then comes forward to receive the bride and, taking her by the hands and closing the bedroom door, he guides her to sit on the pillows where he was first seated.

In this entry or delivery of the bride to her groom, the custom is that one of the two manages to put his or her foot over the foot of the other, because they say that whoever does this will be the rooster of the house, always dominating and giving orders to the other.

The bride being seated, the groom then removes the veil that covers her face, and then the two see each other for the first time in their lives. And no matter what the husband says, the wife will not respond a word to him if he first does not give her a gift, such as a ring, earrings, bracelets, or coins of gold.

The marriage consummated, the custom is that the new husband take his wife's undergarments (all of them made of cotton or linen) and, opening the door of the bedroom in which he was locked up with his bride, tosses it to the women outside of the bedroom awaiting this item, or else he gives it into the hands of his mother-in-law or other relative close to his wife, who is always there. They all receive this news with great rejoicing, loud voices, and howling, while playing the tambourines and rattles. And in order to testify to the virtue and chastity of the bride to date, the mother or some relative shows the underwear to the rest.

The following morning the household makes a great quantity of fritters to send as presents to all the homes of friends and relatives. On that same morning the new husband then goes to the baths, where he washes his entire body, as all men tend to do as many times as they have sexual intercourse. But the bride for seven days in a row does not go to the baths to wash, because the learned men say that in those days she is in Paradise and without sin, although after that period she is obliged to wash. And they give no reason why the one is more sinful that the other, or less lawful.

All these ceremonies of dancing, get-togethers, and strolling abroad with the bride are forgone when these men marry with some Christian whom they buy and turn into a renegade. Such a woman is not given a dowry, unless it be to buy her freedom. In such a case the man is obliged to make a written statement in front of the kadi, or justice of the land, and to declare in it the amount of the dowry he promises and is compelled to give. Because afterward, if he were to leave her, he is obliged to first pay her the dowry, just as when he leaves or divorces other Moorish women, as we will note in what follows.

Some of those who are married with many women tend to keep them in different towns, such as one in Madrid, another in Toledo, another in Alcalá, another in Salamanca, and another in Lisbon. But the men are obliged to provide for all of them, which is why the marabouts claim that it is a great sin for any man to marry more women than he can support. Many other men, however, keep them all in one house, although in different rooms, and are obliged to sleep with all of them, doling out their sexual favors by days, weeks, or months. And under peril of the gravest sin, all men are obliged (unless they are sick or have some legitimate excuse) to sleep with one of the women on Thursday nights, which they call Khamis,[3] which means something like the vigil of Djumʿa, or Friday, their holy day. And those children who are engendered in that night are *sharifs*,[4] as though consecrated to or relatives of Muhammad. So that just as no one, under pain of being burnt alive, can show the least discourtesy to those who descend from the blood of Muhammad and are their natural kinsmen (whom they properly call sharifs), anyone who mistreats those persons engendered on the vigil of Fridays would incur the same penalty because, as we said, they are considered as relatives of Muhammad.

And because this use of polygamy is so engrained, the women behave as well as possible within the home so that their husbands do not leave them. They do not generally like nor love each other, however, nor do they eat together: rather each wife guards herself from the others, fearing to be given a poison. Among these wives there are always hatreds, envy, and jealousies, and the same among their children, who never really care for each other. This clearly argues that for most women such an arrangement is contrary to natural reason and very contrary to the intent of matrimony and the ends for which God ordered it, which is love, peace, and concord among married people and their children.

Husbands are also extremely jealous of their wives, not consenting to have them seen even by their own blood brothers, which is why no windows in Algerian houses face the street. Nor might a Moor or Turk or renegade enter a house before the occupants begin shouting: "Watch out, watch out, make way, make way!" and the women instantly run to hide in their bedrooms, like rabbits to their burrows when they sense a goshawk flying near. On top of this, Turks and men in high places are in the habit of guarding their women with Black eunuchs, whom they call *aghas,* and only these men enter the women's quarters to give and take messages. But the women do not guard themselves from Christian men, whether slaves or not, except for women of high social rank and the wives of important men and *ka'ids,* who do this to maintain their reputations.

CHAPTER 31

Childbirth and Child Rearing

When a woman goes into labor, she is often visited by friends and relatives who cheer, encourage, and serve her with special diligence. During such a time, they invoke many of their marabouts, whom they consider saints, and make vows to them. These women use an infinite number of aromatic substances during labor, and there is no telling where they discover them. And if all this still does not help the birthing, they call boys out of the school to carry through the streets a sheet—held by its ends with a hen's egg in the middle—and to sing certain prayers responsively, like a chorus. The moment that Turkish and Moorish women hear these prayers, moved by pity, they run to their doors with jars of water to toss over the egg in one splash, believing that if they break the egg with this action, the woman will give birth.

If the woman delivers a boy, all the women present, and whoever else is with them, howl very loudly two or three times. At the birth of a girl they howl only once. On the night after delivery of first-born children, the families stage great dances with their tambourines and rattles, to which they invite friends and relatives. These dinners include fritters, meats, rice, couscous, and other favored edibles. By way of offering congratulations for the delivery, wealthy relatives send the new mother joints of lamb, special post-childbirth fritters called *sfendj,* and some molasses candies. Newly delivered mothers are visited only by other women friends and relatives.

Seven days after childbirth, the friends and relatives of the new mother host a dinner, after which they all take her to the baths, and her baby with her (if a girl), with a great parade of tambourines and rattles preceding them. The new infant is very richly dressed and carried in the arms of some black or Christian male or female slave, who marches in the middle of the procession. And after the mother and baby have bathed, they return to the house where another fiesta of food, music, and dance awaits them. Should there be another newly delivered mother in the same house, the two are not to see each other for a space of forty days.

The Algerians rear their children with much loving care: during the first year, and even for some time after, they give the baby no other nourishment than breast milk. They regularly take babies to be blessed by their marabouts: the living, to whose homes and hermitages they carry them, as well as the dead, whose tombs they visit. Some women, out of devotion, tend to bury their infants in the sand by the seashore, leaving them there for an hour or more, convincing themselves that he who escapes and lives will have a long and healthy life, with all kinds of prosperity.

The mothers hang about their necks countless written documents given them by the same marabouts, in which are figured many characters in Arabic or Turkish letters, and in other scripts, some with unknown names of demons[1] and some with words of the Qur'an. Also hung on their babies are an infinite number of devices and charms related to witchcraft, like the back of a sea urchin, the head of a chameleon, some bones of a turtle, the nails of a lion, some hide from the forehead of the same lion, the tusk of a pig. Because these are all considered chief among relics for children, the parents often plate them in gold or silver. They might also hang on babies' necks the beak of an eagle, a few links from coats or smocks of chain mail, tiny sea shells, a tablet or plate of silver or iron with some written words from the Qur'an, a hand made of five silver or other metallic fingers,[2] and an infinite number of other things which they worship and consider good omens. And sometimes a single infant will carry all of the above on his body.

The Algerians are fond of having their children nursed by Christian slaves who have milk, yet they give little reward to such wet nurses. It is true that a few Algerians tend to promise these Christian women from the start that they will give them their liberty when they are done nursing the child for some years.

After the child is weaned, the parents take little care to show him good manners and rearing, nor do they take him by the hand to warn or punish him. They behave as if they were no more than parents of an animal, which they let follow its own good or bad inclinations. Some parents enroll their children in school when they are nine or ten years old, to learn to read and write in Arabic or Turkish, and others (although very few) to learn both. In the same way, mothers teach their daughters to sew and do handiwork, if they themselves know how (which few do), or they send them to the house of a sewing teacher for girls, which is what the poor do.

The time for circumcising their sons is neither clear nor determined, because some are circumcised when they are small and others at twelve or fourteen years. And their way of doing this we mentioned earlier, when speaking of the circumcision of renegades.[3] Only men are obliged to undergo this ceremony, although in the Great Cairo and other parts they also circumcise young women, cutting from their members certain superfluous flesh, and there are women who make a living with this art.[4] But this is not done in Algiers (and we speak here only about the customs of its inhabitants). When the daughter has grown and is ready for marriage, they wash her very well, and, having shaved the hair from the back of her neck and having cut a few tufts from the front of her head, they make her perform the *salat* (as we said earlier about female renegades) in a bedroom. The women do not go to the mosques to pray because, according to the marabouts, this is considered *haram,* something forbidden to the profane,[5] an act that calls for interdiction or excommunication. In the view of these marabouts, women cause men to sin, and would do the same if they were seen in the mosques.

When the sons are grown, each follows the lifestyle that most agrees with him, although, ordinarily, the son of a corsair becomes a corsair; that of a merchant, a merchant; that of a janissary, a janissary and soldier; and that of a mechanic, a mechanic. All of them, in general, when they reach fourteen years of age, or even earlier, are contaminated with every kind of vice, especially that of licentiousness, continuous eating and drinking of wine or stronger alcohol, and every manner of lechery and sodomy.

To speak comprehensively here of all Algerians, let us discuss the Jews. They only marry with Jewesses, and some have two or three wives. These husbands do not give their wives dowries, nor do they buy them in the manner of Moors and Turks. Rather each woman arrives at the home of her husband with a dowry from her parents and relatives. These women are also in the habit of using cosmetics, especially Jewish brides, although they do not paint their arms black, as do Moorish women and renegades, but rather use much color and a white paste. Jewish brides also wear many seed pearls, rings, earrings, and gold bracelets.

The Jews also make a public fiesta on the wedding day, seating themselves on a patio, which they nicely decorate with many coverings of silk (or what they have). The Jewish bride is richly dressed and seated on a scaffold of netting. All the Jewesses come together to dance, sing, and strum their strings, and any onlookers—Moors, Turks, and Christians—are allowed to enter to see the fiesta. The same is not permitted at the fiestas of Moorish, Turkish, and renegade women, who can be seen only by Christians, from whom they do not hide or cover themselves, as we said earlier. Because the bride and the other Jewesses are so richly dressed and adorned with gold, jewels, and pearls in these dances and gatherings, the Jews tend to rent two or three janissaries, handpicked by the *agha,* and pay them handsomely to guard the entrance to the wedding so that no thieves (Turks, Moors, or other janissaries) might enter and rob the women.

Given that the Jews were always, and are today still, the most devoted to their children of any peoples in the past and present of the world, the love and care with which they rear their offspring is also incredible. When a boy can barely walk, the father will take him by the hand to the synagogue (on Saturdays and holy days). Later he will have the boy learn to read and write in Hebrew, and some also in Arabic. And because of the way these Jewish children are reared, no father will dare to punish them or make them angry, because at that moment many of them, for this reason, will turn Turk in spite of their parents, who cannot stop them. In the same way, many of these children, as youngsters, are very prone to vice, gambling, and drink. Some also take up friendships with Turks or renegades, whom they serve as sexual partners and to whose vice of sodomy they then attach themselves.

CHAPTER 32

Algerian Women's Fashions

The dress of women in Algiers is not entirely uniform, because Moorish (not to speak of the Kabyles) and Berber women (of whom we spoke earlier when discussing their husbands) tend to dress primarily in very thin white linen tunics, with no collar whatsoever,[1] a characteristic of every type of dress. These have plunging necklines, are floor-length and as wide as two shirts for men.

Over these tunics they wear one of three things: either a very large and wide shirt, of fine white fabric, as we said earlier, similar to what their husbands the Baldis, or citizens, wear, which they call a *durra'a*.[2] Or the women will wear a *milhafa*, or *mlahfa*,[3] which is a kind of sheet, save that it is square and some three or three-and-a-half elbows wide and eight or nine long, which they wrap around the body on top of the tunic. Or over the cloth shirt many wear another of silk, *sendal* (sheer silk or linen fabric), or very fine colored taffeta, which reaches to their feet.

If it is very cold, the women wear a smock of wool or quilting, as do their husbands, which they call *gonela* and others call *goneyla*.[4] Women who are Turks or renegades tend to wear smocks over their tunics (which come down to their feet, are very wide, and are embroidered with colored silk on the throat, cuffs, and chest openings). These smocks—either of some fine woolen cloth from Valencia or of colored satin, velvet, or damask—fall to the shins in length. The neck is very plunging, leaving it very open up to the bosom. The Moorish women call this smock—which has some large and nicely worked gold or silver buttons—a gonela.

Algerian women are not accustomed to wearing doublets of silk, or of Holland or other filmy linen. But this smock, or gonela, serves them for one and the other, and also as a skirt or shirttails. And if they feel great cold (which rarely happens since Algiers is a temperate climate), either they put on two of these smocks, or under one they wear a cloth vest, which is almost like a doublet. They cinch this smock in the same manner as do their men, with a belt, or *kursiyya,* made of veils, or sendals, of some fine colored silk.

And because the sleeves of the said smock or *ghlila* reach only to the elbows (as we said of the taffetas and clothing of the Turks and Moors)—in order that women could also wash up to their elbows whenever necessity or the ceremonies or washings of the Qur'an dictate, as when they make the *salat*—they also tend, in the style of their husbands, to wear some sleeves of silk, velvet, or satin, which cover their arms from the wrist to the elbow. Because these sleeves are as long as the entire arm, they fit over the lower arm with many pleats and wrinkles.

During the summer (in order to avoid clothing of heavy silk or wool) some women tend, for fashion's sake, to wear over their smock or camisole a kind of cape, large and wide and very white, either of cloth or colored silk,[5] of the kind used by non-Moorish women when they are sometimes pleased to dress *a la morisca.*

All these women (Moors, Turks, and renegades) tend to wear something over their heads: primarily something like a cap into which they gather their hair, called in Arabic *lartia* or *banika*.[6] This is made either of cloth embroidered in colored silk, or of thin green or yellow or red silk over which, all around the head, they wear one of three things: a Turkish plait of very fine material (like a shawl, four or more fingers wide, and eight or ten handspans long), on which ends are fixed some gold fringes, which they call *ʿasaba* or *qaffali*.[7] And tying this braid over and around the head with a knot at the base of the skull, they allow the points to fall beneath the waist. Or they wear another Moorish braid of very subtle thin silk in colors, which they tie (like the braid) around the head, and its points hang behind their backs to their waists. They call this headdress a *nkab*.[8] For their fiestas or weddings, the wealthier women tend to wear on their heads a round biretta of brocade or of satin or damask richly embroidered with gold thread, which they call *shashiyya* or *shash*.[9] Many women fashion these, as best they can, with countless seed pearls and gemstones, and they put a lining inside to make the birettas stiff.

All the women, be they Moors, Turks, or renegades, ordinarily tend to walk around their homes barefoot, although sometimes they wear some slippers of gilt leather on their feet, with open toes and some fringes or tassels of silk, not very high and always very elegant and well designed. Other women, the poorer sort, wear some well-made Turkish shoes in different colors,[10] and some of them (largely Moorish women) wear some light shoes with thin soles *a la morisca,* of some highly polished colored leather that they call *sherbil* or *serbil.*[11]

All of them generally tend to shave with a razor everything beneath the nape of the neck where the *albanega,*[12] or hairnet, does not reach, and to cut off some part of the hair from the forehead, so that to one and the other side will hang some tufts of hair, very well combed, which fall over their temples. They call these tufts *soualef.*[13]

Unlike the women in Christian lands who prize their hair and try to make it blonde and golden, here on the contrary all the women—Moors, Turks, and renegades—try to make their hair as black as possible, for which they use certain products, largely oils with a good scent that the merchants of Valencia tend to bring.

Their makeup is different from that used by Christian women, because they use a great deal of bleaching agents and even more rouge. And they also use a very black product made from certain materials to paint designs on their cheeks, chin, and forehead, such as marks, cloves, and rosettes. And these women make their brows very arched, in such a way that they reach even the hanks of hair that hang over their temples. And beyond this, they very much enjoy having the palms of their hands and their nails blackened, and their feet up to the insteps the same way, so that it would appear to whoever looks their way that they are wearing black slippers. They like to blacken their arms even up to their elbows, as we said new brides do. And they consider all of this to be high fashion and gentility. In truth, this habit turns those who are beautiful quite ugly, and the ugly women, to a great degree, even uglier.

Their principal jewels and ornaments are great quantities of pearls and seed-pearls, in chokers and earrings, which they favor in huge sizes, almost touching the shoulders, and so heavy that they stretch the ears low, because they weigh about a pound or more. They also wear earrings with dangling geegaws, gold earrings (like Christian women, although not of icons), and many rings on their fingers. On their arms they wear bracelets of silver and fine gold, although these are generally made of low-grade gold with alloy, the same materials with which they work their *cianis*,[14] the coin of the realm about which we spoke earlier. Many women wear gold chains, and on them amber knobs that hang down to their breasts. And generally they are all great friends of scents and of orange blossom, rose, or other waters, which the merchants of Valencia bring to sell in Algiers.

Many women (largely Moors, Turks, or daughters of renegades) tend to wear something like well-worked gold or silver ankle bracelets on their legs, close to their ankles, although these are not entirely round, but half round and the other half squared, tall and four or five fingers wide, something also used by the prettiest and richest Jewish women. When these women step outside their houses, they all wear very clean and white linen bloomers that reach down to their ankles. And instead of any slippers, they wear shoes of black leather with soles.

So as not to be seen when they leave their houses, they tend to cover their faces with a thin white veil, tied with a knot at the nape of the neck, leaving their eyes and forehead exposed. They also wear white capes of very thin fine wool, or of woven wool and silk, which they whiten with much soap, aromatic smoke of sulfur, and other things: and they call these capes *ha'ik*.[15] These wraps are like the milhafa we mentioned earlier, or like a piece of cloth some thirty handspans long and some fourteen or fifteen wide. They are square, so that they can be wrapped about the body. After tying one point on the breast with certain large clasps or pins of gilded silver, they can then throw the body of the wrap over their shoulders and head and take the other endpoint under the right arm. In this way, the women remain so well wrapped that nothing is left save a small space to look out of, in the manner of the Burgundian helmet of an armed man.

When the leading Algerian ladies go out, they take their slaves with them, Black ones (of whom they have many, buying them for twenty, twenty-five, or thirty *escudos* each) as well as white Christian ones, who are also very available. The number of slaves they take with them is not fixed, but every woman, depending on her status and wealth, goes accompanied. Some take eight or ten, others two, four, or six. But ordinarily they take no more than one or two slaves, who wear the same mantles (although not as pretty as those of their mistresses) or a piece of a sheet or cloth with blue stripes on the head, which cover them up to their waists.

All the other slaves walk about uncovered, unless there be one who presumes to higher status. The rest of the women who own no slaves, and even some who do, walk about the city alone and at their pleasure.

Jewish women dress in the same manner, save that instead of shoes they wear slippers of black leather. They go about neither covered with wraps nor accompanied by Christian slaves. Black women who are Muslims cannot become the slaves of Jewish women.

CHAPTER 33

Women's Pastimes, Home Decorating, and Cooking

The household activities of Algerian women are very few, because besides rearing their children, laundering shirts and some other clothing once a week, preparing meals, and kneading some bread (if by chance they do not have slaves who will do this for them, a rare occurrence), all their business is to be seated or stretched out on their mats or rugs, being lazy the whole day without doing a thing save for constantly eating and chewing. There are some women who weave now and again, but they soon tire of it; others sew or mend the odd shirt (when necessity forces them and they have no slave who can or knows how to do it). Few women know how to work on silk, unless it be some renegade or Morisca from Spain who learned it in her homeland, or daughters born of these women, whose mothers have taught them the skill. In all, there is no lack of public teachers for Moorish women, but the subjects taught are very limited and rudimentary. The women have small will to learn and their mothers even less will to pressure them to learn. This is why female Christian captives are so prized, especially those who work with their hands. For this reason, too, Algerian women keep very few furnishings in their homes, as we shall note in what follows.

Ordinarily these women spend their time on seven activities, primarily in washing themselves and applying makeup. Although many have baths in their homes, very rare are the women (even those from leading families) who do not attend the public baths two or three days a week. They tend to go in the afternoon, because the men use the baths until then. All the women take, at the very least, one slave with a basket or bundle of linen or silk, in which they carry a laundered shirt and change of bloomers, a headdress, some soap to scrub themselves with, and ordinarily a bit of very glutinous earth from Fès (like a dark brown or almost black mud, the blacker the better) that almost duplicates soap and is marvelous to whiten and soften the skin.[1] Many women also carry some scented water with which to spray the face and bosom, as well as towels to wipe themselves. When they wash at home, they use hot water boiled with roses, salvia, rosemary, orange-tree leaves, and other similar scented things.

Secondly, the women keep busy by going to the homes of their friends and visiting each other continually. They spend whole days at other people's homes, because they never lack for invitations from friends and neighbors. Their husbands have no power to stop this, as many of them would like. Almost all women tend to commit the most evil deeds during these visits, coming and going where they wish. But if the men took this custom away from them, the women would then undo the marriage.

As for the third activity, many a day is taken up by going out to farms or country houses, at all times of the year but especially in summer, when the women can pick fruits. For such outings they invite each other on given days. Since there are few married people who do not have country houses (even though small ones), travels to these places are very common. After the women get together, everyone is strumming instruments, dancing in groups, eating lots of couscous with lard, roasting and stewing much meat, and, above all, eating *sfendj,* or crullers. The women take care not to be seen there by the men. Whole days are spent in this manner, and at sunset the women return home again.

The fourth activity is visiting the chapels and the sepulchers of the marabouts, where the women bring their children. These trips resemble a pilgrimage, because on Mondays they visit the tomb of the marabout Sidi Yacoub,[2] which is on a rock close to the sea, beyond the Gate of Bab al-Wad, near the Fiumara.[3] Or they visit the tomb of Sidi Bournous, a renegade from Córdoba,[4] which is at the top of the mountain, in a chapel where he once lived. On Thursdays, they visit the tombs of Sidi Betka,[5] Sidi ʿAbd al-ʿAziz,[6] Sidi ʿAli Zouaoui,[7] and Sidi Abdilabes,[8] all located outside the Gate of Bab ʿAzzun.[9] And on Fridays, they visit the tombs of Sidi ʿAbd al-Rahman[10] and Sidi Jumʿa,[11] outside the Gate of

Bab al-Wad. The women make one of three offerings over these tombs: candles, oil for the lamps, or money. All of this is for the hermits who act as caretakers of these tombs.

The women are also accustomed to placing on these tombs some bread, raisins, and fruit, and after their prayers, they give part of that food to the poor who tend to gather there on those days. Then the women and their friends eat and, afterward, they sit outdoors and talk.

A fifth activity for these women, who are very devout, is to ritually visit the tombs of their own dead family members, especially on Monday mornings, Thursday afternoons, and Friday mornings, as will be explained later. A woman who does not make these visits is not considered a good Muslim.

Practicing witchcraft, a thing they have greatly mastered, is their sixth activity. To this end they invite into their homes other women, proficient in sorcery. Or they go out to consult with them or with the marabouts, who ordinarily profess nothing else. And so these women never cease drawing lots and casting spells, removing teeth, grinding bones, flaying bugs, stringing together frogs, making aromatic smoke, burning papers, hammering nails, creating mixtures, and calling up devils. They do all this either to be loved, have good fortunes, marry off their daughters, disclose the unknown, divine the future, cure wounds, heal sicknesses, and other such things.

Many women pride themselves on having a familiar spirit, who they claim enters into their heads and reveals whatever they and others want to know. So many make this into a profession that their number is infinite: they constitute something like a college or company or sisterhood, into which many of the most distinguished women enter. And they have this custom: after they congregate in someone's house, or in the home of a sick woman or any woman who calls them with a great need, they remove their ordinary clothing and dress in other garments reserved especially for this, of silk or wool, according to what they can afford, very clean, very perfumed and scented. And they host a *sosfia,* or dinner, for the invited women.[12] This done, they order out of the room all Christians, because they claim that the *djinn* will not respond in any way, nor enter into their heads, if any Christian man or woman observes this. After this, they all make a coterie, and one woman, chosen over the rest, steps out to dance to the sound of tambourines and rattles. She dances hunched over and with a twisted face, looking somewhat upward and with her left hand behind her back. And after she dances like this for a while, she falls to the floor senseless, frothing at the mouth, rolling her eyes, twisting her head, and making all the gestures and retching that a possessed person tends to make. And then they ask her what they want to know.

The possessed woman responds with a deformed speech, very different than her own, and when she returns to herself after a short time, she can neither remember nor explain how she fell to the ground in a deadly swoon, nor what has emerged from her mouth—no doubt something from the devil. And if this does not suffice, or the response of only one woman does not please them, they urge yet another one, or two or three, to come out to dance. Dancing in the same manner, the devil enters them in the same way, and they give the same kind of responses. Worth noting here is that there are some aged Black women among them who say wonderful things (according to others who have been present and can vouch for it).[13] And these women are held in the highest reverence by all the others.[14] These activities are not confined to women, because there is also a college of men who have the djinn (although they do not get together for dances). These are chiefly marabouts, as we will explain at greater length in another section.

The seventh activity of Algerian women is partying. They keep busy continually going to weddings and feast days that other women host throughout the year. Eight days before a woman marries, it is the custom to host continuous dances and reunions in the houses of the women (as we said earlier). And a few days prior to this, the mother, sister, and relatives of the bride, with a great crowd of women—sometimes over fifty or sixty—enter into the houses of the city and invite many women, either known to them or not, so that the feasts and dances have great multitudes, because the larger the crowd of people who come to their homes, the more formal and honorable these fiestas become. Not content to dance away the whole day, the women dance well into the night too, and a husband has to be all the time looking out that his woman returns to her home. That is why every day and every hour some highly shameful events occur: the husbands put up with everything and all is silenced and concealed. There is no trying to change these customs, because it is impossible.

Jewish women are more careful and more industrious in household activities, in knowing how to work, sew, weave, knit, make thread of all kinds. And with these activities they live and support themselves. They do not attend the public baths, nor would they be admitted in any case, and so, although they generally wash themselves at home, they remain unclean, never losing their goatish smell.

Because of this great and general laziness and sloth of the Moorish and Turkish women of Algiers, the furnishings in their homes are few, because they do not manage to augment their clothing and household items with their work and diligence as do Christian women. Even though they have large homes, with many well decorated rooms, scarcely one of these is well put together and adorned. It is true that much of the blame for this goes to their stingy husbands, poor and timid in spirit, who would not spend a *real* for home decorating nor for personal care, no matter how much money they have.

Even wealthy and leading households generally contain only the following furnishings or possessions: a bed, and not with many mattresses because, at the most, they may have two, and generally just one; two sets of sheets; one or two blankets; a pair of cushions or bolsters; two or three shirts per person and the same number of britches; a pair of towels to dry their hands; three or four handkerchiefs; a rug or two, and as many other mats in which they all sit, eat, and sleep. A pair of turbans for the husband, and another pair of headdresses for the women; some panels of curtains (when they are very wealthy) made with pieces of colored taffeta, with which they cover the walls of the room in which they live and spend most of their time; and a pair of cushions of some low-grade silk. These cushions affirm those who presume to be rich and of high class, because the rest sit down either on mats or rugs and ordinarily do not have curtains on their beds.

As for the beds themselves, they secure, at the end of a room and from one wall to another, a pair of logs some five or six hand spans up from the floor, and over these they place some planks, and atop this the mattress in which they sleep—although they generally tend to sleep on the floor over mats or rugs. In the same way, the more respectable people place a sheet in front of the bed, hanging from some cords so that they will not be seen by the family.

They have no boxes, desks, or bureaus. A chest of some four or five hand spans serves them for storing a woman's headdress, and another, smaller in size, to put in some clothing. They call these chests *sanduks*.[15] But many women tend to hang all their clothing and dresses from a rope.

Nor do they have dining tables, because the wealthiest among them eat on the ground, over the skin of an ox, which they buy and cure from skins brought over from Turkey, some of which are highly painted with colors and designs. Others eat over a plank, raised from the ground by a palm's length;[16] and the rest eat on mats or the floor. In the same way, they use no tablecloths or napkins at table. They place their food over an oxhide, a table, mats, or the earth, and they circulate among all the diners one or two narrow towels to wipe themselves.

They use no kind of tapestries, either of wool or of tanned leather, and if they rob some from Christians on the high seas, they turn around and sell them to Christian merchants. Nor do they use vessels of silver or gold: apart from the fact that they consider this a sin and their Qur'an prohibits it, they simply cannot approach this degree of elegance. Nor do they use pewter or tin in their dinnerware, but rather everything of earthenware. The wealthy use dinnerware brought from Turkey, beautifully worked with various elegant colors. They also use cups of tin-plated copper, because these do not break and last for years.

This same deficiency is found in their food preparation (and in this also their women have little to do). They rarely eat fowl, although they know how to make many diverse kinds of dishes and stews in their mode and taste. The staple food, general and ordinary for all Algerians, rich or poor, is couscous, with some fruit or meat half cooked in marinade, which they preserve in large earthenware jars between grease and oil; or a dinner of cooked meat with chickpeas and pumpkin; or a bit of rice or wheat partly ground with lard, which they tend to call bulgur. So that for the most part, the poorest shoemaker or tailor in Christendom treats himself better than the richest Moor or Turk in Algiers. Although such Christians have (as we said) very few riches, they still have more clothes, adornments, and possessions than the Algerians.

CHAPTER 34

Islamic Feast Days and Festivals in Algiers

They tend to begin the year with the birth of their Muhammad, and by 1580 from the year of the birth of our Lord Jesus Christ, they count 988 years, so that we Christians count 592 more years that they do. And whereas we divide the year into months, they divide it into moons: with twelve moons adding up to one year, their year comes to 355 days, whereas ours is 366.[1] According to this count, their year comes to eleven days less than ours, so that their present year ends eleven days before their last year ended; for the same reason their solemn feast days that correspond to the moons are also anticipated by eleven days per year.[2] Thus, with the passage of time, their feast days come to fall on, and be celebrated at, all times and months of the year. Their marabouts give an amusing reason for this, saying that Allah wished and ordained this so that the months and dates would not complain that some were more celebratory, and thus more honored, than others.

The months are counted in this order and under these Arabic names:

1. Muharram
2. Safar
3. Rabiʿ al-Awwal
4. Rabiʿ al-Akhir (or al-Thani)
5. Djumada al-Ula
6. Djumada al-Akhira
7. Radjab

8. Sha'ban
9. Ramadan
10. Shawwal
11. Dhu al-Ka'da
12. Dhu al-Hidjdja

The holy days are: first, their "Lenten" season, which lasts thirty days and is called Ramadan, during which they all fast continually and in droves.³ In the Year of Our Lord 1580, Ramadan began on the eleventh of October and ended on the ninth of November.⁴ The reason they keep this fast is because they claim that Muhammad fasted as many days to make the law.

Their mode of fasting is as follows: under no circumstances do they eat or drink during the entire day, under penalty of being burned alive if the law were to be executed with rigor. And upon the appearance of the first star, they begin to eat, and they can eat any food, flesh or fish, as much as they want and the whole night long until two hours before sunrise, when someone plays the kettle drums. And although they can (if they wish) divide the night into two meals, some prefer to eat everything in one sitting. When midnight approaches, some Muslims, out of devotion, walk the streets sounding certain drums, whose sound awakens sleepers so that they can then return to their food; and when only two hours remain until daylight, the drums are played once again so that no one might break the fast, and everyone is warned not to eat another bite.

The people who are most devout then wash themselves thoroughly and go to the mosques to make their *salat,* and to listen to the sermon and to those marabouts who sometimes tend to deliver orations, as we said earlier. This superstition of observing the fast is so deeply engrained among them, that neither pregnant women nor sick people are freed from it.⁵ But renegades, both male and female, who are ordinarily not legitimate Muslims, do not generally observe Ramadan, and they eat at pleasure whenever and however they please, although in hiding, so as not to be seen.

Some Muslims, and chiefly the marabouts, are so devout that even though they are traveling on the road or at sea, under no circumstances will they break the fast. But Muslims at sea or on the road are ordinarily not obliged to fast. In the same way, those who claim to be devout will fast three months of the year, during Radjab, Shaʿban, and Ramadan, and very rationally. The marabouts persuade them that those who keep the fast during these three months are sure to go to Paradise and cannot be damned, and that beyond this they will prosper in all their affairs. But those who believe the marabouts end up greatly duped and complain bitterly.

Halfway through Ramadan some thirty or forty or more men, all Turks and renegades, get together by custom, and using certain tied-up bundles of sticks, they design a body like that of a camel, with its hump. After putting a head on it (which they have constructed earlier) and covering the timber body, it looks like a real camel. Led by some flute players, the men all go dancing with their masks. When they arrive at the doors of the wealthiest citizens, they play until the doors open and they are given gifts of money, as much as each wants: one, two, or three *doblas* and more, which they then share equally among themselves.

And on the eve of the twenty-sixth day of Ramadan, they make a great feast and give alms to the poor, and some of them throw food in all parts and corners of the house in order to feed the evil spirits, saying that they will pacify them with this. And they call this night Laylat al-Kadr or *axerim*.[6] This is the night of the twenty-seventh.

On the last day of Ramadan falls their version of our Easter, the "small festival" known as Seker in Arabic.[7] On the morning of this day, they all exit out of the Gate of Bab al-Wad and congregate there in a closed field, and with their *caciz*, or chief marabout, before them and the king somewhere else, they all make the salat together. This done, the marabout tends to exhort them with some talk, so as to give thanks to Allah and to the observance of their law, promising them great gifts in this world and the next. Then they all return home.

After eating for some eight days, or at least for the following three, the young men and others, dressed in their finest clothing, prance around on horseback and exit from the Gate of Bab al-Wad, and on the beach they play *juegos de cañas,* or jousting games, and, afterward, run races two by two. The children get together in small groups to dance, separated by race, just as in Seville and Lisbon they separate the Blacks of Guinea, because the Kabyles stay in one part, the Moors of the Sahara in another, and the Blacks in yet another. And the Black women also come together, and each nation dances and plays its drums and flutes according to its own custom. The Bedouins do not tend to join in these dances, because they are in all things vile and weak-spirited people. Neither do Turks or renegades dance in public, because they presume to show more gravity.

Some Turks wrestle with each other, but with little skill or art. Everything depends on brute force with them, and they do not consider somebody beaten until they roll him around on the ground face-up, seated on top of him with his back to the earth. Other Turks tend to swing themselves on certain very high and fixed gallows of three sticks, and on some long ropes that hang from them, on the ends of which they tie up some planks, over which whoever wants to rock or swing will seat himself. Others make some round instruments of wood—much like the cranes that in the Christian world they raise in order to give lime and bricks and other necessary materials to those who work on some tower or high wall, and which we call a pulley, still bar, or crane. With men riding on each point of the sticks that pierce through this instrument, they are made to toss and turn all around from top to bottom. This done, each man pays an *asper* to the one who planted the sticks and played the game. And with no further games nor fiestas, they celebrate their festival.

During these days, some Christians celebrate and enjoy the good times in order to gain some *blancas,* forgetting that God did not lead them to Algiers for feasting and dancing but rather for tears and weeping in order to confront God's wrath. They dress up with masks of diverse personages, dance in the Christian mode, and play at throwing arrows at apples or oranges, a game in which the winner gains a pigeon and the loser pays an asper. Others play at puppets or the prestidigitator's game of *pasapasa,*[8] showing a great agility of hands, at which the Moors and Turks stare with great wonder as if stupefied.

Four days before Ramadan, on the night called *caba* or *axerim,*[9] Moors and Turks tend to light many of the lamps in the mosques, and some men walk throughout the night visiting all the mosques of the city, where they enter and make their prayer, as we Christians do on Holy

Thursday. But their women do not do this because they are not allowed into the mosques.

In the same way, in all the vessels in port, whether those of corsairs or others, they light many candles or lanterns. Everyone agrees that on this night all the waters shall not flow, but they shall be quiet and dormant for half an hour. And he who is venturesome, who finds the water quietly sleeping without running, will be given all he wants by God. They all agree that because ʿUludj ʿAli, the Calabrian renegade and General of the Sea for the Turks, found the sea for the third time in this way, he rose to the greatness he held.[10]

Two moons and ten days after this festival, they celebrate another, which they call the Great Festival, or in Arabic al-ʿId al-Kabir, which only lasts three days.[11] They celebrate it in the same way and with the same games, which they claim to do in memory of the sacrifice of the patriarch Abraham. And every head of a house is obliged (if he can) to kill a ram on that day, and others who are wealthy kill as many rams as there are members of their family.

The way in which they kill or, as they put it, sacrifice these rams is thus: two hours or slightly more after sunrise they come to make their salat in the fields outside the city (where they all congregate with the king, as we said they do in the other small festival). And all the rams being already prepared at home, each one takes his own, and turning to the south, first washes the ram's face and snout with water, and then smokes him with incense or some other good scent, and then beheads him with his own hand. Even the king himself does this, because they place great merit in this. The women catch the blood and guard it (or at least some of the blood that emerges first), saying that it is holy and blessed by God and good to use against curses. Some men consider it a blessing to dye their foreheads with the same fresh blood, and if they ask them when or how God blessed that ram, they respond in a serious way that God sends an invisible angel for each ram that blesses it when they behead it. They also hold that it is necessary that the ram have an ear large enough to cover its eye; if not, it is not ready for sacrifice, and for the same reason it must be at least a year old.

This ceremony done and the ram skinned, they paint it all over with saffron and they let it hang until the third day. After giving a small portion to the poor, they eat the rest at home or salt and cure it in the sun, like a blessed and holy thing.

Three moons and thirteen days after this festival, they celebrate a third one in memory of the birth of Muhammad, and they call this one *mawlid*.[12] On this holiday, unlike the others, they do not go into the country to make the salat in public; rather that night, as well as the three that follow, they light lamps in the mosques where they do their salat and they visit all the other mosques in the city. On this day, they generally wash all the toilets and latrines in the house, and they light many candles, saying that they do this for the memory that Muhammad, given his humility, was born in a privy whereas he could have been born in a wealthy palace. And together with this they make great quantities of couscous, which they cook with chickpeas and meat, and they place some dishes or bowls of this in the privy of their homes, or in the hallways, corners, patios, and even in the bedrooms. They also strew around some couscous, strands of meat, and pieces of bread, believing that Muhammad will come that night to the house of those who please him most, and to whom he wishes to grant favor and boon, and that he will eat whatever they place for their honor in the privies or latrines and what they scatter of food about the house.

Many Muslims are accustomed to reach for this boon of Muhammad's coming to eat in their homes, joining with others that night in small groups, in the middle of the patios of their houses. Swirling a large platter of couscous and meat, which they place in the middle of their patio, with great shrieks and howls they call for Muhammad (as the prophets of Baal called for their god).[13] And they beg Muhammad to come, saying that because they are poor he should not spurn them and go eat that night in the homes and privies of the wealthy. Although this is an amusing thing to witness and even to make fun of, it is also, on the other hand, worthy of the greatest compassion, given that the devil can so cruelly fool men with rational souls and judgment.

Schoolboys in particular tend to gather together both on the eve and the whole day of this festival in their schools (which the teachers make sure to decorate with bouquets, silk cloths, many rugs, and lamps), and each student brings a beautiful wax candle to present to the teacher that day, because the candle-makers tend to make highly polished candles for that occasion, with many branches and flowers and colors, just as they do in Christian lands for the Candelaria.[14] And because each student aims to bring the best and the most elegant candle, the gains on this day for the teachers are greater than during the entire year. The schoolboys spend all this day singing songs in praise of Muhammad that their teachers across the year have taught them, with one voice opening the song and the others responding in chorus.

Ordinarily their holy day is on Friday of each week (which they call Djumʿa),[15] the equivalent of Sunday for us Christians, and Saturday for the Jews. But Muslims do not observe their holy day as we do our Sundays, because they never stop working during the whole day, and the same for all their festivals and fiestas, except for those three days of the first two festivals. And many of them observe only one day of this festival.

On these solemn days they tend to put janissaries as guards in all the castles and bastions while they go to the salat, because when they worship out in the countryside, they fear that the Christian slaves on their lands might rise up in arms. And during these festival days, the king gives all the janissaries meals to eat in the patios of his house, and sometimes more than four thousand men dine at once, some sitting down to eat as others get up.

On Friday or the day of the Djumʿa, at midday, when the flag is raised over the mosques and the faithful are summoned by the marabout, they are obliged, more than on any other day of the week, to go make the salat in the mosque. Given this obligation, on that day and that hour the king himself goes in person to the mosque, accompanied by a guard of janissaries and by all the Turks and renegades of his house, although these last may not be as scrupulous about their attendance. Apart from those Fridays and their festivals, they have no other fiestas, nor do they regard as holy the days of their marabouts, whom they consider saints, just as we Christians observe our saints' days.

CHAPTER 35

A Miscellany of Muslim Customs in Algiers

To discuss all the opinions and ceremonies of their Law, which are many, would take too long. Such a discussion is also not necessary, since they are very well known to the whole world, and there are many books that deal with them. I shall jot down here only a fraction of the many opinions, customs, and usages that most Algerians follow, believe, and observe, beyond what Muhammad commands.

First of all, in their mosques they have nothing more than mats on the floor and around the walls, as well as lamps that they light during the hours of the *salat*. If a Christian enters within, either he must turn Turk or they burn or hook him alive. The marabouts give two reasons why they do not permit women to enter the mosques (even to perform the salat): the first, so that they will not incite men to sin, and the second, so that their menstrual blood will not dirty the mosque, which would be a very big sin. And for this same reason, no one is allowed to enter wearing shoes, nor to spit in a mosque except into a handkerchief.

They believe among themselves that it is of great worth to make the salat when the heart is moved to do so, and of even greater worth when not done at the accustomed hours and by obligation. If someone comes to kill a man who is occupied in prayer, wherever this may be, under no circumstances should he move to defend himself, under pain of the heaviest sin. Such a response occurred in the year 1577, when Muley ʿAbd al-Muʾmin, brother of ʿAbd al-Malik, king of Fès,[1] fled into exile in Tlemcen because Muley ʿAbdallah, king of Fès — his half brother on his father's side — wished to kill him. Within a large mosque, while making the salat at the *subh*,[2] which is two hours before sunrise, a Moor wounded him unto death with an arrow from a crossbow. Muley ʿAbd al-Muʾmin did not move nor wished to speak until his prayer was done, and he died afterward. Meanwhile, the Moor escaped, which he would not have done had his victim spoken.

The same concern for prayer leads them to claim that the salat is not beneficial if the worshipper accidentally breaks wind through an unclean orifice. On the topic of urine, they say there is no sin comparable to having a drop of it touch their pants, and for this reason they always tend to piss while squatting, like women: it would be a great sin for them to piss standing up like a Christian. Along the same lines, after they have urinated, they thoroughly scrub and re-scrub their member, cleaning it either with water, or with earth, or with some stone, or against the wall. The salat is also not valid if the worshipper has a bloody nose or loses blood from some kind of sore, even if hidden. Being obliged to wash themselves both before the salat and after they have access to their women, they claim that washing with cold rather than hot water has great benefits. As such, when the marabouts commit the sin of sodomy, by way of a great penance they go to wash themselves in the sea instead of in the baths.

The Algerians have an incredible respect and the greatest reverence for their marabouts, of whatever character they may be, so much so that, throughout all Barbary, whoever wishes a safe passage while travelling, takes with him a marabout, who will keep thieves or enemies away from the travelers by a hundred paces. And so anyone who must cross the mountains of Djidjelli (located 180 miles east of Algiers, where there is a great density of cruel thieves known as Alabesi)[3] will be able to travel fearlessly and with pleasure by providing himself the company of a marabout.

They consider it a grave sin to eat an animal or bird that has not first had its throat cut by a Moor, Turk, or renegade rather than by a Christian or Jew. And the same sin—Jewish style—comes from eating or drinking the blood of any animal that does not ruminate.

They claim as their saints some of the same ones that we Christians have and honor, and especially the apostles, whom they call marabouts and argue that they were Muslims. They also claim that the Apostle James was called ʿAli. I could never convince them (although I argued with many of them about this) that our Lord Christ lived 621 years before Muhammad, and that his saintly disciples had very different lives from the Muslims.

There was a dwarf who walked about Algiers, who for being a dwarf was considered a marabout and a saint. They believed that anyone he cursed would be doomed by what he said and that if they prayed to him for blessings he would grant them. They affirm this also of all the marabouts and, to that end, hold them in great veneration.

They also consider storks and snails to be marabouts, and it would be a grave sin to touch them or do them harm, let alone kill them. When I inquired why, they said it is not because the stork kills and rids the earth of insects, but rather because, when it awakens each morning and other times during the day, it praises Allah by raising and lowering its neck while making quacking noises. As for the snail, they say it is also a marabout because it does no harm, and therefore scrupulous Muslims hold it a sin to eat them.

They also hold as marabouts and saints all those who go to Mecca, where their Muhammad is buried, not in a steel ark, as many Christians vulgarly claim and proclaim, but rather within the earth, as the Turks and Moors themselves affirm. After they return from Mecca, they are all called *hadjdji,* which means "pilgrim."[4] Major figures such as Hadjdji Murad,[5] Hadjdji Mustafa, and Hadjdji Bali, are thus named and hold it as a great honor. And dealing with a hadjdji is like dealing with a saint, and all the people run up to kiss his hand and garments.[6] After they have seen the tomb of Muhammad, many of these hadjdji tend to enucleate themselves, removing one and, sometimes, both eyes, saying that someone who has seen this should look upon nothing else, that it is not proper for such fortunate eyes to look upon other things.[7]

Many Moors, Turks, and renegades, as long as they are not married and sometimes even after marriage, wear a braid or bristle of hair in the middle of their heads that they never shave but allow to grow very long. When asked the cause of this, they respond that the angels will carry them to Heaven through these locks of hair when they die. When asked why they wear long robes, they respond that when they enter into Paradise, those who were not worthy of admittance there (such as Christians and others), could enter with them by hanging on to their skirts without being repelled back.

Although convinced that it is not a sin to eat pork because it is a creature of God created for man and, eaten in correct quantities and in its time and place, is so excellent and medicinal a meat, they claim that they are not allowed to eat it not because the pig itself is bad, but rather because they cannot tell which of its four quarters touched their Muhammad when he brushed against it and it sullied his new garment, for which he cursed it. If they could identify the cursed quarter, they would discard it and eat the other three.

In the same way, they say that wine is good, that Muhammad permitted and praised it in the beginnings. While passing by a red-faced and merry company of drinking youths one day, he blessed them and told them to drink their fill and with God's blessing. But upon returning to the scene later, he found that they had vomited and, because of the wine, had fought one another, and some were killed. And because of this, he then cursed the wine and those who drank it, under pain of not entering into Heaven. But I have not seen greater drunks, not even among the Germans, than almost all the Turks and renegades and many of the Moors of Algiers.

Many of them do not shave their beards but let them grow long. The reason they give is that shaving a beard is something that mere brutes and rogues do, and they say the same about men who do not wear the turban.

They believe mightily in dreams, making a great thing about anything they dream and persuading themselves that dreams are prophetic. It has many times happened that they dreamed that they were killed by a captive, at which point they took him out and sold him, not to Turks or Moors, but just so that he would be free. And to someone who had no way of being ransomed, they declared him free and sent him from the house, not daring to have him around any longer. It would be good for captives if many Algerians had such dreams on a frequent basis and responded to them, as some have done.

There are some men who presume themselves courageous, known as *deli,* which means "crazy brave." They always go about naked, with no more than a pair of pants and an animal skin tossed over their backs in diverse ways, however it pleases them. And they brag that they have killed that animal with their bare hands. To demonstrate their great spirit, they tend many times to wound themselves on the chest and arms with a razor—great wounds. And some burn themselves with cotton wads dipped in oil, as we said about the janissaries, who put these over their arms and do not remove them until the cotton and oil are consumed and mixed with the blood of the burnt flesh.[8] And they say that he who burns himself this way in this world will not burn in the other. When the Turks feel pain in one of their members, they often tend to burn it with a branding iron.

They will begin no important business, nor go on a long trip, nor christen a new ship, nor build or rehabilitate a home, even though this means making only a new seat or door, without first sacrificing a ram in the manner we earlier mentioned.

In things of great importance, when they do not trust in someone's judgment, they make him swear in a particular mosque in Algiers called el-Merabta,[9] because they commonly believe that any people who falsely swear in this mosque will be impoverished within a short time and lose all their worldly goods.

Nobody is so daring that he would insult the descendants of Muhammad, who are known by the green toga that they wear on their heads and are called *sharifs*[10] by everyone; the female sharifs of the same caste tend to wear this same green headdress.

All Muslims are obliged to give the *ashor*[11] to the poor: that is, 2.5 percent of all they possess, by way of recompense of all they have earned that year; but they have reduced this figure to be understood as that sum of money with which they do business; and there are some marabouts who presume to be such saints that they hold it a sin to accept this money as alms. By the same token, because Muhammad ordered that the rent of the kings be one-tenth of what the earth produces and men reap, and the Moorish and Turkish kings have added other tributes and charges, many marabouts and learned men feel it a heavy burden not only to accept these payments or presents, but even to talk or treat with these men, considering them sinners and excommunicates.

Many are the marabouts who feel and say that neither the Law of Muhammad, nor any other worldly law, is necessary for salvation. What is needed is simply to harm no one and do good to all they can in this world. When sick unto death, a man need only remember God and call strongly upon Muhammad, and with this he will enter Heaven. Some

Muslims also hold it as a truth that women go neither to Paradise nor to Hell, but to some place where they will neither suffer nor enjoy any blessings.

They say that the dead marabouts, who are their saints, come at night to eat what the devoted offer them over their tombs, like Muhammad on the day of his birth, as we earlier noted. When I tell them that this is not possible because their bodies cannot eat, being ashes and dust in their tombs, nor their spirits either, since they are not nourished by bread, nor fruit, nor other foods, they respond that God knows that, and that in such cases the "how" or the "why" is not relevant. This is the answer of brutish people, without judgment.

In the summer of the Year of Our Lord Jesus Christ 1579, a marabout from Fès came to Algiers, a man who affirmed that with certain words he could conjure an angel from Heaven to talk into his ear. Sometimes, in the presence of many people, he pretended that the angel did not come soon enough, and he displayed great anger and rage over this. And after a little while, he let it be known that the angel had finally come, but that the marabout, still indignant and discontented, pretended he did not want to hear him. But later, after some applause and at the begging of the same angel, he would retire to a mosque, followed by many people who would ask him for answers to their concerns, and after showing that he had a consultation with the angel, the marabout gave each of them a reply, sending some of them off happy and others unsatisfied.

This business in no time came to such a pitch that not only were all those who had managed to talk to him and even kiss his hand were themselves taken for holy men, but the women (who do not appear in front of men, nor dare in any case to speak with them) forced their husbands to let them go to the marabout's house to see, talk with, and consult him. And the gathering of these women from the highest and most distinguished ranks was so large and so continuous throughout the day, that neither the temple of Apollo at Delphi,[12] nor the oak trees and urns of Dodona,[13] nor Mount Parnassus, nor as many oracles venerated and consulted by the ancients were as frequented as the house of this good man. But the marabout did not remain popular for too long, as it was discovered that, under color of giving an answer to some of these women, he had made them undress and even enjoyed himself for a while with them. And when some Moors arrived from Fès, they informed everyone how this man had done the same thing over there to many important ladies, for which the king—the Venetian renegade Hasan, at that time in Algiers—ordered that, under pain of being impaled alive, the marabout leave Algiers and all the kingdom within three days. And so he embarked in a galley headed for Tunis.

Some men who come from Christian lands where they were once captives tend to put manacles on their arms, thus advertising that they were once enchained. And they do not enter the first time through street doors into the homes of their parents, relatives, or friends, but rather they come in over the roofs, wishing to signify that their freedom came from Heaven.

Since the year 1541, they hold here in great veneration a certain marabout, who is buried outside the Gate of Bab 'Azzun and is called Sidi Betca or Sidi Batqa (whom all the corsairs and sailors leaving port salute and commend themselves to him, as we said).[14] They venerate him because they say that he made the Emperor Charles V, of glorious memory, lose his Armada on the day of Saints Simon and Judas, 28 October 1541, when he pitched camp outside Algiers. And they claim that the said Sidi Batqa (having died some years earlier) emerged from his tomb on the night before the battle and fell on his knees in prayer, begging God for that boon. And they deduce this because the lamp in his tomb had never been lit, neither night nor day, but that night it was discovered to be lit.

I responded to one Muslim (who was telling me the above and who presumed to be a great marabout) that if Sidi Batqa was, as they say, in Heaven with God, why was it necessary for him to pray to God for men on earth and for the body to resuscitate in order to light the lamp and make the prayer? It would have been enough for the soul to intercede with God in Heaven. And if Sidi Batqa's soul had to leave his body and he had to die once again, that would be small friendship that God would show him in making him pass through the cruel and terrible pains of death once again. The marabout responded both to my first and second queries in the same way: that God was powerful enough to do everything.

All the lettered men and marabouts are generally like this, greatly ignorant. And in neither what they say, nor what they believe, nor what they profess or teach the Turks, renegades, and Moors (which in effect are all fantastic dreams and pointless imaginings) do they allow anyone to ask either why or how such things could be. Instead with closed eyes and despite all arguments, they must be believed. Nor can their disciples know how to give any other answer, nor to say more than the disciples of Pythagoras would say and respond: *ipse dixit*. This is how many teachers and marabouts respond to questioning.

None of them knows logic, nor philosophy, metaphysics, geometry, astrology, or any liberal art. Nor can there be found at present in all of Barbary—nor all of Turkey, Asia, Arabia, and Persia (where the Law of Muhammad is observed and flourishes)—a school in which some or all these sciences are taught and professed. Neither can there be found a Turk nor Moor in all Algiers who can cure a sore or perform a bloodletting. All the surgeons are Christians; there is only one Muslim surgeon, a Genoese renegade called Djaban[15] and a Morisco from Valencia, both highly ignorant.

Not only do they hold it a very great sin to adore and venerate images, but they are not allowed to see them, look at them, or consent to own any. As such, in May of the year 1579, when there was a great famine and all Turks and Moors made processions to the tombs of the marabouts to ask for rain, the marabouts counseled the king to forbid Christians to say Mass, and not to permit three Christian images—which the Turks had taken from certain galleys and hung there by their feet, along with some coats of arms and round shields—to remain in the port of the marina, since that was a very public and much frequented place by all the people. The marabouts claimed that these Christian images were causing at the time a great drought from Heaven and that they made Allah indignant. In response to this, Hasan the Venetian, 'Uludj 'Ali's renegade, who was then king of Algiers, ordered on the twentieth of that month that no Masses be said in the city, a prohibition that lasted a few days. He also ordered that they carry to his door the three abovementioned images. And in a small square in front of his house, by order of the marabouts, they hacked these images to pieces and burned them in a great fire.

One of these was the image of Saint John the Baptist, which 'Uludj 'Ali had taken from one of the galleys of Malta in 1570, close to Licata, a city on the southern coast of Sicily also called by the name of St. John. Another image was that of the Apostle St. Paul that they took from the galley *San Pablo* of Malta on the first day of April in 1577, close to Sardinia.[16] And the third was of the saintly angel, which they took from the galley *Santángel,* on April 27, 1578, close to the Isle of Capri, when the Duke of Terranova was sailing from Sicily to Naples and Spain.[17] Being as barbaric as they are, the Muslims did not notice what they were asking for, nor the favor they were doing to us Christians by removing and destroying those trophies of our ill fortune: whereas for us they were like a mote in the eye, for them it would have been no small honor and glory to save them for long memories of their deeds and accomplishments.

And being asked if it is a sin to draw a figure with ink or charcoal or something else, they answer in the same way, that it is a great sin. And being asked the reason for this, they respond gracefully, saying that on the Day of Judgment, he who made the image or figure will be obliged and constrained by God to give it a soul that will be resurrected and stand in judgment, like all other men; and if one cannot give the figure a soul, God will be indignant and condemn the maker to lose his own.

They are fond of gift-giving, usually to someone from whom they think they will receive double. Or, as we like to say: "give them an inch and they'll take a yard." And if they do not receive something in exchange and remuneration for the gift they have given, or they are not paid for it, they complain to the Justices, and it is customary usage for the Justices to order them to be paid. This happened to Luís Brevez Fresco, a Genoese merchant,[18] in the year 1579. Having been given a small lion by a Moor, and not wishing to give him four meters of fine wool, which were worth much more by comparison, the merchant was condemned by the Justices to pay fifteen *doblas,* which are six *escudos,* for the lion.

If a Christian voluntarily gives or presents anything to a Muslim, they say they are not obliged to remunerate, pay back, nor even show gratitude for it, for it is owed them: God ordered and put into the heart of that Christian to give that gift and, as such, Muslims need only thank God for it. In keeping with this, there befell many amusing cases, which happened outside of Algiers in Barbary (where this opinion is generally held among Muslims). And since I have heard of these cases from people worthy of credit, I shall not refrain from setting them down here.

At the time that the Master of Montesa[19] was the captain general of Orán, a Moor from Tlemcen came to that city, as they tend to do every day in *kafilas,* or caravans with merchandise,[20] and he presented to the captain general some reasonable stirrups, of the kind well made in Tlemcen. The Master received him benignly and humanely, and showing gratitude for his gift and good will, ordered him to be given fifty escudos of gold and some fine cloth, worth another twenty, to make a garment. Although very pleased when he saw the liberality of the Master, when the Moor was urged to give thanks and to go to the palace and kiss his hands for the boon, he responded very airily that the Master was obliged not only to give him those things but also to be grateful, in no small way, that he had accepted them, since it was not the Master who sent him these items but God who ordered it. When the Master learned of this, he returned the stirrups and ordered, very justly, that they take back the cloth and the money and tell the Moor that now God had also inspired and ordered this action since he was so ungrateful that he did not acknowledge the good done to him.

In the same way, in recent years there was in Tangier[21] a citizen, Portuguese by birth, who had a Moorish friend, a neighbor living six miles from Tangier, in a place they call al Ferrobo. And when this Moor came with his caravans to sell his provisions in Tangier, the honorable Portuguese man hosted him in his home and showed him a thousand courtesies, because the Portuguese tend to be very humane in such things. When in time there was peace and a truce, the Portuguese man with some other friends went to al Ferrobo and, counting on his old friendship, directed himself to the home of his Moorish friend, who was called Mahamet. This Mahamet, when he saw him, pretended not to know him, and did not even ask him to come into his home to sit down. Seeing this, the Portuguese said to him: "Mahamet, are these the kind of courtesies that you so often received from me in my home?" To this, the Moor responded: "Look, my Christian friend, Allah (which means God) orders the Christian to behave nicely to the Moor, but not viceversa." Understanding this, the Portuguese man left in an unhappy manner. And in a few days, when the same Moor Mahamet returned to Tangier as was his custom, he stopped at the door of the same Portuguese as if he were going into his own home. Seeing this, the latter had the Moor enter his home, showing him a very good reception. But as soon as he closed the door, he grabbed a stick and thrashing him for a good while, he said that now God commanded him to behave in this way.

The Moor was very affronted that the Portuguese man would treat him in such a way, and the moment he returned home from Tangier, he complained to the *ka'id,* saying that, despite all the peace treaties and truces, he had been beaten and mistreated by a Christian in Tangier, never mentioning the cause and occasion. The ka'id, considering this a bad thing, soon informed the Captain General of Tangier about it, loudly complaining that such a thing should be done during a time of peace, and more so to a Moor who was carrying provisions to Christians. When the Captain General learned this, he instantly had the Portuguese man brought into his presence, wishing to order him to be hanged for violating the peace and security. The Portuguese told him the whole story and the reasons that moved him to act in such a manner. Not satisfied with this, the Captain General sent for the Moorish ka'id, who was to give him satisfaction. The ka'id, seeing the Christian, wished to know everything that happened, and after he heard what the Moor had done to the Portuguese man, and the great ingratitude and response that he used to one who had done him so much good, the ka'id (being a sane and prudent man) later ordered the Moor to receive another heavy beating. And for being a man of good will and having done what he did, he ordered that the Christian be given a horse and money to return to Tangier, which he did very happily. This notion that a Christian must behave well to a Moor and not vice-versa they call *gotomía*.[22]

A relative of Muhammad did something even worse, as they themselves say. Being very thirsty and having been given a cold jug of water that slaked his thirst, he instantly cut off the head of the giver, saying that he could not better repay so great a deed than by sending him directly to Paradise.

Repudiation is much practiced among them, because the law permits it. The causes are ordinarily as follows: on the part of the woman, for being unchaste; on the part of the husband, for treating his wife badly, being impotent, not doing the salat, being a drunk or even drinking wine, not supporting his wife, and other similar things. In Algiers, on the day of the blessed Saint John the Baptist in the year 1578, sixty Moors and Turks dissolved their marriages, the majority of them because wheat was very dear at the time.

Another reason for undoing a marriage is when a man sodomizes his wife, as many do. In such a case, when the woman demands justice from the kadi or judge, without talking or saying a word she arrives in front of the judge, takes off her shoe, and places it in front of him with the sole upwards, signifying that her husband knows her from the rear. And this is admitted as proof.

When Muslims die, their children, if they have any, inherit their goods in the following manner: if a Turk or renegade has daughters or a male child, the patrimony is divided equally among them; but if he is a Moor, the Grand Turk, or the king of Algiers, is substituted in place of a child. If the deceased was a Moor and only had daughters, all of his worldly goods go to the Grand Turk, and his daughters are disinherited. And if he is a Turk or renegade, the estate is divided in half, so that the Grand Turk, or king of Algiers, takes half, and the deceased man's daughter or daughters take the other half, unless during his lifetime he has procured from the Grand Turk the grace and license to have his daughters inherit all his goods, as not a few Turks manage to do at considerable cost. If the deceased has no children, everything goes to the Grand Turk. But if the deceased adopted some renegade youth for his soul, as they like to say, in such a case he can leave him a third part of his estate.

They do not make a last will and testament, nor any bequests at the time of death, and if they wish to donate or bequeath something, it must be done forty days before death, and even before becoming sick. And it must be done in the presence of a kadi or justice of the land, and by a public act of a scribe; a donation bequeathed in any other way is worth nothing and has no substance. If he who dies is a renegade and has no children, all his worldly goods tend to remain with his masters, whose renegade he was, or with their children if the masters are dead. But (as we said earlier) Djaʿfar Pasha,[23] king of Algiers (when he came from Constantinople in September of 1580), brought the following new order from the Grand Turk: that it be understood that the renegade *before* becoming sick would have made the donation, which they call a charter, to the master or his children. And in the same way that the Grand Turk inherits from the Moors, he inherits from the Jews, out of which comes a good part of the rent that the king of Algiers has each year, because this is not observed merely in Algiers but in all of the kingdom and provinces subject to him, from which he derives great benefit annually.

In the opinion of some marabouts, a renegade who has become a Muslim as an adult does not benefit from his conversion as do those who convert as children, because the latter became Muslims through ignorance and the others through malice. Conversion benefits neither one nor the other. In truth, moreover, few are the renegades who are truly Moors or Turks because they do not convert save through pure roguishness and wishing to live as they please, sunk in depravity in every kind of lust, sodomy, and gluttony. Such renegades are, in effect, neither Muslims nor Christians.

Many are the renegades, perhaps the greater part of them, who inwardly sigh to return to their lands and be Christians again, but some are kept from this by the freedom of their vices, others by the sweetness of thievery at every turn and the money they have amassed; and others, because they do not deserve to be favored by our Lord Jesus Christ, whom they so unworthily negated and despised. And with these good desires, although not very efficacious, they entertain themselves until they die and go straight to Hell.

Almost all tend to deceive themselves with a false opinion very common among them, and very persuasive, that it is enough to have a good heart and to be Christians within; and for this they frequently have the saying: "the habit and the chapel do not make a friar." They do not understand what is so manifest and clear to all judgment, that a man is obliged to serve God and his creator with all he has received, body and soul, and to profess publicly in front of all, so that they see and know this. And that our Lord Jesus Christ said very plainly that He himself would recognize and confess in front of the Eternal Father that man who was ashamed of confessing His name in front of men.

But these desires and aims of the renegades only last until they become rich, and have power and a position, and, especially, until they marry, because when they obtain this success, they turn about and rather choose what they possess in the present. And with the pleasure and contentment of the long lives they live, being happy with their wives and children (who are the most loved and sweetest treasures of the world), they no longer remember their countries of origin and the name of Christian. Instead, they then turn into even more savage and cruel enemies of the faith of Jesus Christ than even the Moors and Turks themselves.

And the same can be said of the majority of female renegades, although there are some who (even though wealthy and pampered and married with children) very truly and continuously commend themselves to our Lord Jesus Christ and his Blessed Mother, and give in His name many alms, and underwrite many Masses, and send oil for the lamps and candles for the altars of Christian chapels, and perform many good deeds as Christian women. And, finally, with great longing and farsightedness, they await that day in which the Christian armada will arrive in Algiers.

Some marabouts are scrupulous about not keeping a Christian slave for more than seven years. They say that, according to their law, they are obliged at the end of these years to give them back their freedom graciously, and even to also give them always the same things to eat that they have always eaten.[24] But this is said by those who do not keep slaves, because all the others, even marabouts who presume to be saints, do not practice what they preach.

And because of the scorn of the very name of Christian, which they suck in their mother's milk, a great and vivid hatred that grows along with them, many Algerians have reserves about acting kindly to Christians. And if we speak generally of all the neighbors of Algiers, there is no poverty in the world, no hunger, no thirst, no nakedness, no beatings, no whippings, no chains, no prisons, no insults, no injuries, no cruelties nor labors and terrible tortures that they do not inflict on the poor Christians. Moreover, there is no one among the Algerians, who, in seeing and causing the Christians to suffer these things, does not enjoy the greatest content in the world. And they even believe that with this cruelty they save their souls, making the most agreeable sacrifice and the most notable service to Allah possible, as we shall demonstrate at length in our *Diálogo de la captividad en Argel* [Dialogue of Captivity in Algiers].[25]

The method of punishing adultery is as follows: when the man is caught (if he is a Moor, Turk, or renegade, and even if he has been many times arrested), he suffers no more punishment than the payment of a fine, to which he is condemned by the kadi if he has been caught *in flagrante* and does not afterward please the *mizwar*,[26] a kind of bailiff, and all the henchmen who were present at the arrest, as they generally do without presenting themselves to the kadi. If the adulterer is a Christian, however, they either burn him alive or force him to turn Muslim without remission. And if the woman is a Moor, Turk, or renegade, for the first or second time she is caught with a Moor, Turk, or renegade, she pays a fine, but if caught many times and in the habit of adultery, they throw her into the sea with a stone around her neck. And if they find her with a Christian, the first time they whip her publically and parade her through the land shamefully; the second time, however, they also throw her into the sea with a stone around her neck.

It is also a custom among them that witnesses in all criminal and civil cases, if they do not come to testify through their own free will and without being asked, are not allowed to testify; moreover, the kadi and the judge must send for them. The legal exceptions that they use in order to reject and condemn them are, chiefly, that they drink wine or neglect the salat. Also rejected are those who are street peddlers of clothing and other items sold by auction or public proclamation, and those who earn a living in the public baths, washing and scrubbing people there, because they say that these two kinds of people, no matter how they earn their money, would give false testimony.

In the year 1580, a man was rejected as a witness (even though he was a marabout) because he crossed over the tombs of the dead without his breeches. They claimed that because he was exhibiting his shameful parts to the dead he showed himself to be neither a man of good will nor a credible person.

Among them honor is not given preeminence, nor does anyone regard himself as better than another for being the son of a Turk, renegade, Moor, Jew, or Christian; nor because his parents were kai'ds, caliphs, or kings. Peter is as good as his master, and nobody is worth more than what he has, because if a Jew who turned Turk becomes richer, he is the more honored, and the king would give him his daughter. Only being a janissary carries some kind of honor, because nobody dares to touch him, and he can beat up anybody, including the richest and most important person. From this it may be concluded that not having honor among them, what virtue can there be?[27] The result is that they very easily tolerate any affronts, and even the richest and most powerful ka'id is liable to insults or beatings, as has happened many times.

If the king or *agha* becomes angry enough with somebody, he orders him to be given two thousand blows in his presence (while stretched on the ground as if he were a Black slave). Or he can order his beard to be shaved and send him into the chain gang of a galley, as many have been seen to do, and particularly the Neapolitan Ka'id Yusuf.

They walk about alone and without any company of servants. At most, somebody may take along one or two renegades, or some very important captain may be accompanied by one or two of his *lewends,* who walk alongside him, although not very often.

Although some men may own horses, nobody goes about the city on horseback, unless it be some great ka'id, the king himself, or someone who has been a king, such as Ramadan Pasha,[28] who had his home, wife, and children in Algiers. When the king goes on horseback, the renegades who own horses, although they may have earlier been great men and distinguished soldiers in the Christian world (some even lieutenants and sergeants), now go about on foot, surrounding the king and accompanied by lackeys.

CHAPTER 36

Algerian Vices

Now that we have begun to describe the customs of all the inhabitants and neighbors of Algiers, we are obliged—not only by the enterprise of our chronicle but also by the multitude and enormity of their vices—to write about these things, more (by my faith) for the above reasons than because we would wish to speak ill of anyone. In truth, when I consider what the Apostle Saint John wrote in his Revelations, that he saw a beast with seven heads and ten horns, all of them decked with crowns, this represents to me Muhammad and his Law.[1] But I see this beast publicly adored in Algiers, with the seven capital or mortal sins being a fraction of what the Turks, Moors, and renegades of that city, and even of other parts, commit. Unlike other men who, if they sin out of fleshly weakness, still consider a vice as a vice and a sin as a sin, acknowledging that they have fallen and feeling ashamed about it. Yet these Algerians have arrived at such a degree of evil and blindness that they adore and have even crowned the vices, seeing in them honor, glory, and the greatest good.

Beginning with Superbia, or Pride, the mother of all sins, the pride and presumption shown by all the Turks of Algiers is incredible, a vain presumption well beyond barbaric behavior against Christians, because you hear nothing from them save laughter and ridicule against every Christian nation. And since, for our sins, they have gained many victories, and every day their affairs against Christian kingdoms succeed so prosperously—robbing, capturing, destroying so many Christian vessels and towns—when they discuss a Christian among themselves, they talk of a coward, a chicken, someone less than a man, which is what they call us. I will not mention the manner in which they treat their vassals the Moors, because we have already noted this, nor of the strange and incomparable pride with which they flay and destroy them, so much so that, even as Muslims these Moors sigh repeatedly for the Christian armada that will liberate them from such an evil and perverse people, as all the world knows.

The Turks have yet another thing: if after some adversity, loss, or disaster, or if they know that an armada is being prepared in Christian lands, then all of Algiers runs amok, and they all tremble with fear that Christians will descend upon them, as happened on 5 October 1571, after Don Juan of Austria defeated the armada of the Turks in Lepanto,[2] and later in 1573, when he descended on Tunis and overtook it.[3] And in the years 1579 and 1580, upon learning that His Majesty the King of Spain, our lord Don Philip, was constructing a great armada to the West, because we could see this with our own eyes, the Algerians fled to the mountains, and there was not one man among them in all the city who could look a Christian in the eye or say a bad word to him.[4]

In the same way, whenever it befalls that some Christian galley encounters a vessel or galliot at sea, there are no viler rabbits. It makes one laugh to see the fuss they make over the Christian galley slaves: how with their turbans and headdresses they wipe away their sweat so that they can row better; how they make promises and commend themselves to the Christians; and even how they take out their bags of money and place them in front of the rowers, performing the most demeaning acts that any vile, cowardly, and spiritless man could do or say. After this, if they manage to escape, they return like lions, and there is no affront nor injury that they will not attempt on those whom they were recently calling lords, nor bad treatment that they do not perform on them, giving them an infinite number of blows, fists, and even opening their backs with sticks and repeated blows. This is how they repay the Christians for the rowing they did to give them life and liberty.

In addition, some wealthy Algerians are prideful and pretentious, because their only glory is in having money, and he who has it (even though a Jew by birth) is venerated by all. They tend to be extremely boastful about anything they do that turns out well, especially at war or privateering, and even more so if it goes against the Christians, because they make an elephant out of an ant and never tell the truth about what happens without adding two or three falsehoods. And if the Christians do anything against them, or they have heard some new or prosperous happening in the Christian world, they will not repeat it; and if they say anything, it is to diminish and belittle the event.

Two Moors, Turks, or renegades will fight over nothing in the middle of the street and in strident voices, and there is no way to remind them to listen to reason, since they will yell as loud as they please. It is an amusing thing to see them, to hear how they debate and provoke each other with more rage than the hucksters and the female peddlers in the public plaza. And the same may be said about the obstinacy of their opinions on the Law and other things (that have been proved countless times). One can hardly find somebody who wishes to listen to reason, let alone obey.[5]

To the sin of Pride one must join, as her rightful daughter, the hypocrisy of the marabouts, which certainly exceeds that of other nations, both in the popular desire that holds them up as saints and in the gravity, continence, and posture with which they walk, gaze and look upon you, and more so if you are a Christian. Some marabouts even choose not to look at a Christian, to turn their faces away from them. They love it when the people rush up to kiss their hands and garments as they walk through the streets and squares of the city. During certain holidays, some marabouts—those living a solitary life in mountain retreats in order to enjoy applause, honor, and veneration—come to Algiers, some on foot and others on donkeys, and they walk all about the city, very broken down, dirty, emaciated, and disfigured, holding out their hands to be kissed as does a bishop in his diocese. And they go about continually chanting "Allah, Allah, Allah," which means "God, God, God." And after they enjoy this vanity for a few days and collect alms, they return to their mountain chapels.

Some marabouts who return from a pilgrimage to Mecca, having made known their arrival earlier in order to be seen, make a solemn entrance into Algiers and other chief cities of Barbary. Along with many people of the land, other marabouts then congregate and go out to receive the sainted pilgrim, who makes an entrance like a bishop when first received at his church, carrying a flag in front of him as is customary. Everybody runs forward to receive pardons and to kiss the marabout's hands and garments, and even the staff that he carries, and with this pomp he moves toward the main mosque.

To the same sin of Pride one must join, like daughter to mother, the disobedience that children here ordinarily show to their parents. This is quite a notable thing, because the moment a child is grown, he pays no more attention to his father than if he were a marble statue. And if the mother or father is a renegade, and they tell the child something disagreeable, he will loudly accuse them of being Christians and other undignified insults. But it is their just deserts that the parents hear these things because, as we said earlier, they practice no kinds of upbringing nor do they teach good customs to their children when they are little.

The second vice is Avarice, and although all the other sins are common to other peoples, this one seems to be particular to all Moors and Turks, because there is no man among them, no matter how powerful, rich, and grand, who would not perform all kinds of wickedness and the lowest and vilest deeds in the world for money.[6] He who does not give them something is not their friend, and their friendship with you will last as long as they expect some benefit. None of them will sacrifice anything for another unless he is first given a boon, or at least promised something that he can be sure of obtaining.

On the issue of money, they trust neither their wives nor even themselves: they are worse and more miserly than the ants of India (as described by Pliny), who hide grains of gold beneath the earth.[7] The moment one *real* arrives in the hands of these Turks and Moors, they hide it in some hole where no living soul knows anything about it; and not even on their deathbed do they wish to reveal the hiding place. It is a general custom that once something is buried, under no condition should it be touched, even if they are dying of hunger or perishing from poverty. And so their wives, as prominent as they might be, are no more to them than their slaves: the women do not spend a coin in the marketplace, and if they need some item or herb, they must first find their husbands, wherever they may be, and ask them for it.

And since to be avaricious is to perjure oneself and lie, one finds few Algerians who do not swear in vain, telling a thousand lies or inventing a thousand deceits, whether in doing business, buying and selling, or in ordinary talk and conversation, and all this with the aim of deceiving each other for benefit. And this occurs to such a degree that neither parents nor children trust that each generation would negotiate for the other, or that children would be allowed to travel with their parents' goods in order to contract business for them (as Christians do).

It is typical of the avaricious man to be enterprising. And if Algerians have to buy, sell, or do something for profit, they do not eat, drink, nor rest, day or night, until they finish it. It is also typical of the avaricious to practice no mercy, to be inhuman and hard of heart, something that is clearly seen in Moors and renegades, because they would not give a coin in alms to their brothers. The women, more tender by nature, dole out some pieces of bread to the poor and beggars in the streets, but the Moors and renegades push the poor people away from them with blows and punches.[8]

In the winter of 1579, the streets of Algiers were filled with impoverished Moors and their offspring, both sons and daughters (because an infinite number of people were dying of a great famine that reached all parts of Algiers, even to the mountains). Even while seeing so many mothers and fathers, boys and girls, perishing with hunger, and that it was raining heavily and nobody had coats and many were stuck in the mud, no man would take one of these souls into his house. Seeing a poor man at death's door during a heavy rainfall—a wretch crying out for bread with his soul in his mouth near the house of an Algerian neighbor—a very wealthy Turk, to make a show of his piety, put his hand under a roof gutter and, filling it with water, threw it into the mouth of the poor dying man, saying: "Be this for my soul; since you cannot eat bread, drink of this water." And with this he finished killing him—a death by drowning.

Among them there is no custom of marrying orphaned girls, nor redeeming captives, nor visiting the sick, nor feeding prisoners, nor caring for widows or orphaned children—works of piety that Christians so often practice. And all this is due to their immense avarice. And even though, as we said, their Law orders them to give two-and-a-half percent of what they own to the poor each year, they have interpreted this as meaning only a percentage of the money they earn; with all this, few are the men who give even these reduced alms, thanks to their greed.

They have no hospitals in Algiers, not even of the kind found in Turkey and Cairo for travelers, who are given there two or three days of lodging and food. There is only one house in Algiers that has the name of a hospital, the one constructed by Hasan Pasha,[9] son of Barbarossa, when he was king of Algiers in the year 1549. It has three rooms upstairs and two downstairs, but with no beds nor any equipment to cure the sick. But any Turk who wishes to cure himself in that house (which was made for them alone) is given a room, a Christian who guards the house all year to serve him, and water from a well located there. The sick man then finds his own doctor, medicines, bed, food, salt for his meals, and coal for his heat.

This same avarice causes all Algerians, large and small, generally to do business by themselves, or in the company of others to employ some mode of business practiced by Christians or Moors. Even the king himself (whoever he may be) tends always to deal in hides, wax, wool, wheat, lard, honey, and oil, which he buys wholesale and then sells as individual items in the shops of the city.

Similarly, this avarice makes the corsairs never stop working, all throughout summer and winter, in their careers of robbery, barely returning home before sailing off again. And as long as they are in Algiers, they have no other conversation, nor any other topic may be heard from them at home and in all the streets and the marina but that of their encounters with Christians: how they sacked this or that place, how they plan to make an attack on land, where Christians can be found unprotected. The Algerians then sail their vessels mostly in waters where the Christian galleys are trumpeting and banqueting, aiming to rob them.

And out to sea once again, if they do not find Christian vessels to rob, in order not to return home empty handed, they rob the ships of the French, with whom they have signed a peace treaty. And not content to rob these men, they drown them at sea (so as to hide their wickedness) and send their ships to the bottom; or at best, they are kind to them, taking all the biscuits, wine, oil, and vinegar that they wish, and even the merchandise the ships carry. And if some mast, or sail, or piece of rubber from a French ship is needed to repair their own galliots, they will ordinarily seize and carry them over to their vessels. In short, they do not encounter a French ship without forcing it to pay them something, pardoning neither friend nor enemy.

But the French deserve all this and much more, since without fear of God and with so much harm to Christianity, they continually provide the Algerians with all kinds of munitions and provisions, carrying them to Algiers in their ships. The French also warn the Algerians of what is happening in the Christian world; they give them notice of where at sea there are Christian vessels to rob, and which Christian galleys to guard against. For this the Turks call the French *karindas,* which means "brother" in Turkish.[10]

All the Algerians are very liberal in one thing only: their desire to burn alive a Christian to avenge the death of some Morisco renegade tried in Spain for justice or condemned by the Holy Office, as they have done and burned many for this reason (some of whose deaths we will describe in another part).[11] And because it is necessary to buy the Christian from his patron, they tend to walk the streets and stores begging for alms to pay him. And all the Algerians contribute something, a little or a lot, thinking to do great service and sacrifice to Allah in this, especially if the Christian is a priest or, in their language, a *papaz,* whom they infinitely despise and wish to harm.

The third vice and sin is Lust, which they profess so generally that there is no species of this sin that they do not practice and count on for their well-being in this world and the next. In keeping with the doctrine of their Muhammad, simple fornication is not considered a sin, and there are so many prostitutes (with not a single bordello legalized among them) that they themselves say that there is no woman in Algiers who is *not* one, sleeping not only with Turks and Moors but also with the Christians themselves, whom they importune and seek out in their houses, with no fear of death by being thrown into the sea, as is their custom.

In the same way, given that all the women (as we have said) are covered and walk about freely throughout the city, and that their husbands pay so little attention to them and dearly love their *garzones,*[12] rare is the woman who is chaste, especially since there are an infinite number of female go-betweens who make a living by pandering, and not one of them is punished for it.

Sodomy, as we said, is considered honorable, because he who can support the most garzones is the more honored for it. He is envied for this even more than for his own wives and daughters, when on Fridays and holidays he displays his boy-loves very richly dressed. And then all the young men of the city, and many who consider themselves serious men, vie with each other in offering the youths bouquets of flowers and expressing their passions and torments.

A man with a son should guard him Argos-eyed from taking up this vice (and few are those who do not take it up in time), because later they will have lovers who court them, send them gifts, and show them off in the street. No governor goes abroad, no Turk goes to war or on a cavalcade, no corsair goes privateering that he does not take his garzón to cook for him and service him in bed. Sinning with these boys, at midday and in the eyes of the whole world, does not seem strange. Many Turks and renegades, already grown and even old men, not only do not want to marry women other than these garzones, but they boast of never having known a woman in all their lives; rather they despise them and do not want to look at them.

One of these, a Greek by birth and chief among the ka'ids and richest renegades, swears to God that he is so affronted at having been born of a woman (he hated them so much), that if they should show him his mother, he would kill her with his own hands. This may explain why sodomy is so esteemed in Algiers, and in so public a manner, that barbers, in order to earn more and have a larger number of customers to trim and shave in their shops, staff them with boys who clip, wash, and shave Turks, renegades, and Moors. These boys are continually courted as if they were the loveliest and most prominent ladies in the world, and, in effect, these barber shops are public brothels. Bestiality is much used among them, imitating in this the Arabs, who are infamous in this vice, also much practiced by the marabouts, as we said earlier.

The fourth vice is Gluttony, although Muslims are not highly given to this, since most of them are more restrained. Drinking wine, however, is an ordinary thing among them, except for the marabouts who purposefully observe their law. But as far as Turks and renegades, they are generally very prone to gluttony and drunkenness, because all of them ordinarily drink wine and an alcoholic beverage they call *raki*. They tend to invite one another to great banquets, not for food and gifts but for much wine and brandy, and they remain in these banquets for two or three days and nights. And although the Germans have much infamy for this vice, the Turks and renegades exceed them, both in the time they spend in drinking and toasting each other as in the filth and tremendous shamelessness of their customs. They do not host a banquet (which they call a *sosfia*)[13] where they do not provide a bowl so that, when their stomachs are filled and they can drink no more, all of them (no matter how important and honorable they may be) will vomit across the table, into that bowl, and over the beards of everyone. This is the most revolting scene one can imagine.

Beyond this, upon drinking a toast they clap their right hands, each to the other with much laughter, and then they kiss each other most unchastely, and indulge in other very shameful ceremonies. Most infamous in this vice are the corsairs and *lewends,* who when in Algiers will spend as much or more than they have robbed. Nobody can walk along a street at any time without bumping into these drunkards, many of them leading citizens: *ka'ids,* governors, captains, and wealthy men. One will encounter such men more frequently in Algiers than German and Flemish drunks in Sevilla, Lisbon, Setúbal,[14] and Cádiz, so inebriated that it is necessary to take their arms and guide them along the road. Because of this, Algerians will generally not dine at someone's home without taking along a Christian slave who will guide them back home.[15]

The fifth vice is Ira, or Anger, to which they are very prone, becoming enraged of a sudden. One Algerian will easily fall upon another, on small occasions, yelling out a thousand insults and injuries in the middle of the street, even though they are leading figures, as we said. But they are particularly beastly to the poor Christians, and they take out their rabid anger on them with inhuman cruelties and modes of torment—deforming their arms and legs, cutting their ears, slicing off their noses, frightful and horrific deaths—something we shall discuss at length in another section, because an infinite number of things can be said about this.[16]

They are slow to pardon (even for minor infractions) their own children, their garzones, and their renegades, whom they love dearly.

Casting them down on the ground, they beat them with sticks so as to grind down their bones and organs. Nobody can be sure of these angry men, nor trust in their love, approving smiles, and flattery. And the same goes for their own wives, as prominent as they may be: when the men get angry with them, they give them a thousand blows and beatings.

They generally have no control when they dole out punishments, but rather blind themselves like beasts once they give into their rage, and until they leave a man as dead, they do not cease to give him blows and whippings. They are extremely keen to witness evil acts—hangings, burnings, hookings, or impalings—and there is not one of them (unless by miracle) who in such a case would intercede for another, or who seeing someone in torment, would show that it hurts and weighs on him. Rather (as if those suffering were not made of flesh and blood like themselves) they look upon them with laughter, even if they be Moors like themselves, and make fun of one another. The renegades do this much more: it seems that, upon leaving behind their faith and the name of Christian they also leave off being men and take on the bowels of tigers and wild beasts. And he who is more fierce, more inhuman, and cruel to everyone, Muslims and Christians, is taken for a greater man and stands chief among the renegades.

For a better understanding of the importance of anger and cruelty in Algiers, the following account should do: just as in the lands of Christians it is considered an honor to treat slaves and captives humanely, in Algiers it is an honor if they walk about like wrecks, their ears and noses cut off and their bodies showing signs of the rage of their masters. And when asked why this is so, the Algerians respond: "What, and are Christians not dogs?" Finally, if a Turk, Moor, or renegade beats to death one hundred Christians belonging to him, as they do many days, he not only goes unpunished but he is not even forbidden to do this. Rather he is reputed as virtuous and courageous, as we shall show in other writings.

The sixth vice is Envy, which is generally found in all Algerians and is notably directed toward everything, but especially toward the rich, because wealth is the only thing they want (as we said) for their happiness and supreme nobility. And envy is so great among them that not even father to son, nor son to father, can hide his feelings if he sees the other earns more or takes advantage of something more than he did. And no matter how close they may be as friends or kinsmen, if one gains an important political office, or buys or hires it, they will try to surpass him and push him out of it from pure envy, so that they each ruin the other.

In the same way, they are great gossips, which vice is born of envy, and they never say something good about another unless they have been given some present or get some benefit out of a person's house: in such a case, there is no more honorable man. Envy reigns especially among the privateering captains, so that no greater torment exists than to see someone arrive with more gains and booty, which they call *ghanima*. The same envy exists among the renegades and their garzones, about which young man is more valued, or more loved, by his patron. These jealousies are sometimes so intense that they kill each other with poison. And when they cannot kill each other, it often happens that they poison the master himself and with his death remove all competition.

For the same reason, they become overjoyed when one ka'id sees another ka'id, or a captain sees another captain, or a merchant sees another merchant diminished or fallen, or after some disaster of fortune, impoverished and laid low. And they lie who say that these men will aid, help, and succor each other, because it is all the reverse, since nobody consoles or encourages the downtrodden, seeing them beaten down and mistreated by fortune, and nobody visits them or shows sorrow at their fall, so inhuman are they all.

The seventh vice and sin is Acidia, or Sloth, which is very typical among them all, because if one takes the soldiers and ka'ids away from war, the corsairs from privateering, and the merchants from trading, the Turks, renegades and Moors of Algiers practice no virtuous, honest, and human occupation (as do other peoples).

They do not race horses or joust except during the three holy festivals of the year, as we said, and there is no military exercise, neither of fencing, nor playing ball, nor dancing, save for women, and then very disgracefully. The men neither fish nor hunt: the only occupation of those who do not hold mechanical jobs is to sit by the doors of the barbershops and pay amorous compliments to the garzones also seated there; the occupation of the merchants in their shops is to tell one another lies and news reports; and that of the corsairs is to walk down to the marina and the port to check out their vessels.

The other Algerians, wherever they get together, are all generally bigger producers of fiction and tellers of lies than were ever found in the grandstands of Seville or in the smelting furnaces of Málaga. They invent new arrivals from Turkey, disasters in the Christian world, seizures of ships and galleys, sacks of hamlets and landholdings, bonds of war of the Grand Turk, and other similar things with which they soon agitate the land and throw everything into confusion. There is no lack of topics to discuss, comment, and chew upon until, after a few days, they are exposed as lies. And they claim that captives owe much to them, because these news stories lighten the work of captivity, continually diverting the mind and imagination from their chains.

CHAPTER 37

Algerian Virtues

Along with human nature, God created nothing to which He did not grant some good quality and virtue, although often hidden from us. Because we see that even the viper, as poisonous as it is, has some good qualities, for excellent remedies can be made from its poisons. I say this because the Moors and Turks of Algiers are not without their virtues, some very human and natural. Although these are not enough to excuse or cover over their great vices, we still wish to list these virtues here.

First of all, the Algerian Moors and Turks have a very notable virtue and worthy custom that Christians could imitate. No matter how angry they become, nor what disaster befalls them, they never blaspheme nor renounce God. Moreover (as we said earlier when speaking of the janissaries), they have no words in either of their languages, Arabic or Turkish, with which to put down God.[1] Instead, when they are very angry, they tend to say: "Ijabi,"[2] which signifies "God bless," or "Bismala," which means "God make me worthy."[3] All their swearing never goes beyond calling upon God, saying "O Allah!" which means "by God." The renegades, especially Italians and Spaniards, must suppress the bad habit learned in their native lands of regularly swearing, blaspheming, and cursing in their Christian tongues, for which other Turks, if they understand the language, will scold them bitterly.

Second, these people never gamble, neither at card games nor dice, which they consider a great sin and the custom of rogues. They play only backgammon or chess to while away the time, never for money. The renegades, however, are the same card sharks in Algiers that they were in their native lands.

Third, the Algerians do not challenge, stab, or wound each other except for some great disaster. The reason for this may be that they possess no sense of honor and, as such, there are no points of honor among them to gain or lose. Along the same lines, they have a great facility for reconciliation: even after punching or wishing to kill each other, they will quickly become friends again and hug and kiss tenderly.

Fourth, they are extremely obedient to their kings, governors, and justices, because if the king orders something, they all tremble and lower their heads. This great obedience was reinforced by the rigor and punishment that their kings tend to use against those who do not obey them. All of them observe this obedience—whether janissaries or not—to all military officials: because a *ka'id* and an old *sipahi* is as obedient to an officer, or a Boluk-Bashi, or captain, as is the poorest Yoldash[4] and vile soldier.

Fifth, they can endure extreme hunger in war. They will often survive a cavalcade for many days on water and roots from the earth.

Sixth, the comrades treat each other in a brotherly way, and even those who are not comrades will favor and aid each other with great care in a military camp or at war. And when they divide their booty, they never quarrel or deceive each other.

Seventh, almost all Turks, no matter how poor, value cleanliness and proper dress, considering it a great vice (as it is) to go about filthy and disorderly, if they can help it. And to see a squadron of theirs, or a small cavalcade or *mahalla* of no more than five hundred or six hundred men, is to witness something marvelous, because they are exceedingly buff, and you never see a soldier with unclean weapons or a rusty harquebus but always very clean and polished.

Eighth, under no circumstances will they permit anybody (even a leading Turk or governor) to dare to speak evil of the Grand Turk, or sultan, in their presence, or to wish to censure or discredit what he has ordered or commanded, because at that moment they would punch in all his teeth or break his bones with sticks.

Ninth, in the same way they do not suffer any bad thing to be said about their marabouts, who are like Muslim churchmen, nor allow anyone to judge what they say or do, even if they live badly. The reason given is that nobody should question these men, who are ministers of God.

Tenth, negligent in the rearing of their children, they are most diligent in marrying off their grown daughters and accommodating them with the best possible husbands. They are most careful and solicitous about this practice, so much so that when their daughters are very young, they betroth and marry them off to the sons of friends in the same social class.

The eleventh virtue: he who finally determines to live like a good Muslim is indeed a devout one, and the elders are as observant of the Law and as devout in making the salat at the proper hours, attending the mosques when required, fasting, and abstaining from wine and liquor. Christians, God willing, should be as devout in their holy observances of the precepts of God.

CHAPTER 38

Death and Burial in Algiers

When the time of death approaches, a dying man will be accompanied by men only, a woman by women. All those gathered about the dying person insist that he or she call constantly upon Muhammad, right up until speech and senses are lost. For this they tend to place the head of the dying person toward the east, just as when they make the *salat*.[1]

Soon after death, they stretch the body on the ground and, having undressed it and placed it on some planks, they wash it with soap and hot water or with white earth. There is no secret part that is not thoroughly washed and scrubbed; they especially scrape the soles of the feet with a knife or blade, so vigorously that there is barely any skin left there. After this they dress the body, whether man or woman, with a laundered shirt and a very white pair of drawers. Then wrapping it in a sheet that covers everything—feet, hands, and head—they place the body again on the earth.

Muslims in charge of washing the dead do nothing else for a living—men for men, and women for women.[2] The washing done, relatives and friends of the deceased arrive and place the body on a bier rented from the marabouts. They then cover the body with a large cloth of colored silk and, if the dead person was a man, they put his turban atop the cloth, as he would have carried it when alive. The family must have received a license (there is no burying without a license) to bury the body from the Administrator of Goods of the Muslim State Treasury:[3] this functionary represents the king in finding out the identity of the dead in order to claim their goods, in the way we mentioned that the Grand Turk and, in his name, the kings of Algiers inherit from the dead. The family, then, take the deceased out into the street, where those invited to the funeral rites await, along with friends and relatives. These do not include women, who never accompany the dead—not even a mother, daughter, or very close relative.

The wealthiest and most leading citizens also invite some two, three, or four marabouts, who accompany the deceased and pray for him aloud, as if singing, and their song is nothing more than a constant repetition of "Allah, Allah," which means "God is, and God will be."[4]

They do not tend to carry candles or lit torches, as we Christians do. The deceased is accompanied by marabouts and other men, as we said, who walk alongside the bier in long strides. And opposite to the usage of other nations of the world—Christians, Jews, and gentiles—the deceased is always carried head first and feet last. The place of burial is always outside the city. In Algiers especially, everyone is generally buried in two different parts or fields: one outside the Gate of Bab ʿAzzun and the other outside of Bab al-Wad. Some bodies, although few, are buried in their farms, which become common grounds after serving as burial sites, and anyone can pick the fruit produced by the trees there. The janissaries also have a great enclosure, a very long and wide corral outside the Gate of Bab ʿAzzun and toward the east. They are buried there and in no other place.

If someone dies on Friday (their holy day), they do not take him out for burial until midday, the time of the salat, and then they pass through a mosque and take the body into it during the service, where everyone prays for the deceased.

Having exited the gates of the city, they tend to place the deceased over some tomb of their marabouts and saints, who are buried there in chapels, as we said. When I asked someone why they did this, he wittily responded that the deceased would receive from the marabout the power to enter Heaven, whereas I say that it must be to walk faster and more robustly toward Hell.

Having arrived at the place of the tomb, the first thing they do is to take the turban of the deceased, which they carry (as we said) over the bier, and toss it three times on the ground. And calling many times upon Muhammad, they place the body very quietly and carefully into the tomb, which is made in such a manner that the body does not fall or bump against the earth, because they claim that it is the gravest of sins to mistreat the deceased. Then the relatives give the poor (who tend to gather there on such occasions) some pieces of bread or dried figs as alms. The tendency is to give them mainly dried figs, because the Algerians claim that they gain as many pardons as there are seeds within the fig.

Extremely poor people who die are simply covered over with earth. The rest are placed in a hole made in the ground, which is covered with some stones, the gaps very carefully sealed with lime and plaster. But after these burials it often happens that, because the stones are small and slippery, jackals and dogs and other animals who are experienced gravediggers come by night and dig up and eat the bodies, so that in the morning nothing is found but bones.

Ordinarily they put over these graves some large and well-wrought stones, with another two small and rounded stones, one at the head and the other at the feet.[5] Almost all the deceased have their tombs raised a bit from the earth, two or three or four handspans high and with some steps made of glazed ceramic tiles or white stones, whatever the family wishes and can afford.

The great kings and governors are buried in large *kubbas*,[6] which resemble small chapels crowned with cupolas, very prettily decorated, and entered through a narrow door that is always closed with a lock and key. All around these chapels there are windows, where light can enter, although some have no more than a door to let the light shine through. In the middle of this little chapel is the tomb, raised from the ground with some stairs of stone, tiles, or bricks, as I said earlier, and very nicely worked in the same way, with two round stones, at the head and feet of the deceased, where they tend to inscribe an epitaph, or some words from the Qur'an, together with the name of the deceased and the quality of his personhood.

Wealthy people also tend to hire one or two marabouts, whom they place, armed, in a tent over the tomb of the deceased, if he or she is not buried in a chapel. These marabouts remain by the tomb for some four, five, six, and eight days, or however many they wish, night and day, locked in there praying for the deceased. And every afternoon, close to evening, the relatives of the deceased send them something to eat. And at the end of the mourning period, the marabouts are very well paid in cash.

The morning after the burial, friends and relatives visit the tomb. Weeping over it, they make the salat and pray for some time. When the men are done, the women come, along with their friends and relatives, to do the same. And afterward, while the women sit together in conversation, having brought up from the nearby seashore many small white bean-shaped stones, they take them in the right hand and pass them to the left (as if counting one, two, three, four). While counting, they repeat the phrase "Subjan Allah,"[7] meaning "God's morning," which is like saying "may God give the deceased clarity in the next world." And when it comes time to depart, they leave all the stones over the tomb, and those who do not use the stones pray with beads, like us Christians, repeating with each bead the same words of "Subjan Allah."

After three days, they return for the same ritual: to visit the tomb and pray for the deceased. And for the entire year afterward, it is the custom for the women to visit their dead on Monday mornings, Thursday afternoons, and Friday mornings. Some men may visit on the same days, usually during the mornings. Everyone, both men and women, stops to pray for the dead when passing a tomb or burial site, no matter what day it is. This is why the small stones remain there all the time. Their marabouts and learned men have persuaded them that when they visit the tombs like this, the spirits of the dead come out to be with them, and that the spirits of the men or women sit down on those stones placed at the head of the tomb, but the spirits of boys and girls sit down on the shawls of their mothers, grandmothers, or sisters, who tend to either sit or lie down over their tombs. And when they arise to return to their homes, they do so very slowly and quietly. Later they will shake their shawls out very softly, and with great care because, if they stand up noisily or shake their shawls robustly, they would do harm to the small, innocent souls of the children. Such are the doctrines, or persuasions, of the marabouts.

It is also general usage that no fire be lit in the house of the deceased for the first three days after the death. If the family must eat something at home, it cannot be roasted or stewed. Food can be sent to them from the outside, however, by friends and relatives. During these three days, their custom is to give alms for the love of God, as well as bread and figs to the poor for the soul of the deceased, as much as he or she tended to eat at a meal.

They wear no manner of mourning garments, although after the death of a husband, son, or father, the women tend to wear a saffron or black veil about the house for a few days. The chief sign of grief and loss among men is that they neither shave nor touch their beards for a month, although few actually do this and for not too many days.

As in other things, the Jews are very superstitious about their burials. They also wash and scrub their deceased with soap and hot water, dress them in freshly laundered garments, wrap them in new bed linen, and carry them to the gravesite with much company. But until they arrive outside of the city, they do not dare to recite their psalms or prayers, because the Turkish and Moorish boys would pelt them with a hail of stones. But once they have entered into the country, they begin to recite their Psalms in Hebrew until they arrive at the burial site, which is located outside the Gate of Bab al-Wad, to the left, entirely surrounded by a low wall to keep out animals. And this costs them no small amounts of money. With great wailing and much sighing, they bury their dead there, not stretched out on the ground, however, but rather squatting.[8]

The Jews also often place great stones on top of the tomb, and some others at the head and feet,[9] similar to the customs of Turks and Moors, and some with names and epitaphs of the deceased. Their women, not their men, also tend to cry over the sepulcher on Thursday afternoons, when you can see the gravesite all covered over with disheveled Jewish women, crying loudly and moaning over their dead ones.[10]

Apart from this, the Jews tend for a whole year after the death of a loved one to come together in the house of the deceased for one or two or more days a week. And to the sound of certain wooden clappers that they play, synchronized with each other and with their hand claps, they sing aloud and voice many praises of the dead person, expressing much pain and grief. They also mess up and tear out their hair in a circle, and give themselves blows, scratching and wounding their faces. The woman of the house who is most bereaved will, at the very least, bloody her entire face and that of her daughters and sisters, if she has them. The other women, who are not so affected, will only tear out their hair and slap themselves.

And if the bereaved woman cannot collect a large crowd of Jewish women to raise their voices in a common lament, she will place herself in a corner of her house and scratch herself to pieces, emitting so many "Ohs!" and such pained voices that no ear can bear to hear her.

Jewish men are not accustomed to put on mourning garb,[11] but their women do wear black headdresses and garments for many days. And what we said about Jewesses—that they make a loud group lament for their dead—Turkish, Moorish, and renegade women also do. Their mothers and daughters also tear out their hair and scratch their faces until they are much bloodied; but they do so only on the day of the death or, at most, for some two or three days in a row and no more.

CHAPTER 39

Algerian Buildings and Fountains

Apart from the forts and bastions of Algiers—located inside, outside, and around the city and already discussed—there are some buildings worth noting.

First of all, there are the mosques, of which there must be up to one hundred (large and small) in the whole of Algiers. All are governed by marabouts, who make their *salat* there, along with others, at the accustomed hours. These mosques have been built by Moors, Turks, and renegades and endowed with incomes, large and small, for the sustenance of the marabouts in charge of them, for furnishing the rugs continually used in them, and for the expense of oil for the lamps, few or many but all lit when they do the salat. Many of these mosques are finely worked in their vaults, arches, and columns, which if not made of marble—because little good marble is found in this land—are very elegantly constructed of bricks and plaster. The principal mosques in Algiers are seven.

The chief mosque, a very large and spacious structure, is close to the port, set midway between the arsenal of the vessels and the port.[1]

The second mosque is beside and to the west of this one. Finished in 1579, its construction was financed by a very rich Moor called El Cajes upon his death. It is very beautiful and finely worked and of reasonable grandeur.

The third mosque is near the house of the king and in the Souk of the Vegetables, where the kings tend to do their salat on Fridays.

The fourth is in the street of the Great Souk, further away from the house of the king but before the Gate of Bab al-Wad. The fifth is in the Souk of the Christians who sell herbs, behind the Bath of the King, where they make military capes.[2]

The sixth is in the street of the stables of the king, a bit farther on. The seventh mosque is even farther up and close to the citadel.[3]

These mosques (especially the first two) have very tall and ancient towers. They seem to date back to the Roman era because of their size and architecture.[4]

As notable as the mosques are the baths built by some kings, where men and women tend to bathe themselves daily. Leaving aside some fifty or sixty particular baths that are quite ordinary, there are two large and principal ones that have been excellently constructed. One of them is called the Bath of Hasan Pasha, because it was made by the son of Barbarossa, who was thus called. It has a great vault, and is very sturdy and beautiful, all worked of highly polished marble.

This bath is divided into two square rooms or areas, wide, long, and spacious. In the first room, the people disrobe, and their clothes are kept there very carefully. The bathers enter naked into the second room, where there are many chambers all around, each of which can fit some ten or twelve persons. And in each one there is a fountain that emerges from the very wall of the baths. Through bronze pipes that pass through all the walls of that second room comes much hot water, continuously heated in another chamber at the rear.[5]

The hot water for these baths does not come naturally, from a hot spring, but is artificially heated, through technology and ingenuity. This water falls into a basin of marble that, in each one of the rooms, is placed at the foot of a pipe. The bathers take as much water as they want in copper jars available there, and they either pour or have it poured over themselves.

Close to this basin and fountains of hot water is yet another supply of warm water, which also arrives through bronze pipes that run between the walls and falls into a separate basin. And all these rooms are usually so hot that they make the bathers sweat heavily.

There are always men available who make a living by bathing, scrubbing, and wiping the bodies of male bathers, and they provide this service until midday.[6] Many Black women take on this job because, from midday until night, the Algerian women come to bathe. And each one of the bathers pays two *aspers* to the man who rents the bath from the king, and they tip the Moorish man or woman who bathes them another asper, or whatever they want.

Those who go to the baths ordinarily carry their own clean towels to dry themselves, although the workers there are obliged to provide them to bathers who do not bring them. Not only are Moors and Turks admitted to the baths but also Christians who pay. Jews are not permitted in the baths, nor would they want anybody to touch them according to their superstitions.

The bath described above is almost in the middle of the city, and is heavily frequented day and night.[7] A second bath is called the Bath of Muhammad Pasha, after the builder,[8] and it lies more to the east, some distance from the first. It is made in the same form and manner, although it is smaller and less frequented that the first bath. These two are the principal baths and most worthy of note.

There are also some very remarkable houses, such as the Royal House and Chamber where all the kings live.[9] Although not as sumptuous and rich as the palaces of some Christian kings and princes, nor with marble columns since there is little marble around Algiers, at least it is very spacious, with two enormous patios, each some thirty-six feet in diameter and paved with bricks. This house has corridors atop white brick columns, beautifully worked with limestone and plaster, and with many chambers, known as *ghurfat*,[10] large and small, high and low and subterranean. All of these are very well constructed, and many are paneled in fine woods, pine and oak, and painted with Moorish and Turkish pictures. This is done with no human figure but with many flowers, leaves, and grasses, very charming and lifelike work all done by Christians, because I am aware of no Moor or Turk in Algiers who is a painter. This house alone, and no other in the entire city, has a very lovely, although small, garden.

There are other special houses of private citizens throughout the city, certainly as fine as many superior Christian houses, and they are of the design noted above, all with elegant and very open patios, such as the houses of the following: Ramadan Pasha, the Sardinian renegade;[11] Hadjdji Murad, the renegade Slav; Ka'id Dawud, a native Turk; Ka'id Mami, a renegade Spaniard; Ka'id Hamida Cajes, a Moor; Ka'id Mudhaffar, a Turk; Ka'id Hasan, a Greek renegade; and of others, including that of Ka'id Muhammad, the Jew.[12]

We already mentioned that the Algerians do not have hospitals, nor do they use public taverns as in other parts, even of Barbary and

Turkey. Only outside the walls and the Gate of Bab 'Azzun are there some very wretched inns, which offer neither bed nor board but only the ground to sleep on and a place to keep any beasts of burden. This is enough for the Moors, since they are all poor and desolate, although they can put up in the houses of friends, if they have any.

Also worthy of mention are the five public buildings set aside for the janissaries: three large and two smaller, all divided into higher and lower rooms, with spacious corridors and patios, and all with a water fountain in the middle. And (as I said) the large buildings each hold some 400, 500, and 600 men dwelling as comrades, and in the smaller two, between 200 and 300.

Worth noting, too, are the buildings called the Bagnios of the King, which are the houses—or, more accurately, the corrals—where they keep their Christian captives and slaves. One is called the Great Bagnio, which is constructed as a square, although not exactly, since it is longer than it is wide: seventy feet long and forty feet wide.

This Great Bagnio has upper and lower quarters, with many small rooms, and in the middle a cistern of lovely water. And to one side, on the lower level, is a church or chapel for the Christians, where (God be praised) Masses are celebrated all year. And often on holy days, these are solemnized and sung, with their vespers and with lovely harmony, because there is no lack of captive priests. There are more than forty priests, of every nation and quality, and even some very educated ones, doctors of law and of theology, religious and secular. Here also some sacraments are administered and sometimes the Word of the Lord is preached. And since never, by the grace of God, is there a lack of Christian worshippers, a great crowd of them, those who can, tend to come hear Mass on Sundays and feast days. And on Easter there are so many that they do not fit, and it is sometimes necessary to celebrate Mass on the outside patio. On such days the guards of the Bagnio, Turks and Moors, allow no one to enter who does not first pay them an asper, from which they make a great profit.

This Great Bagnio is located on the street of the Great Souk, which extends from the Gate of Bab 'Azzun to the Gate of Bab al-Wad, at some four hundred paces west of the Gate of Bab 'Azzun.

The other bagnio, called the Bagnio de la Bastarda, is not as large but is also divided into many habitations. This building in particular houses the Christians of the *makhzen*,[13] as they call the garrison placed in a stronghold, because the makhzen—essentially the city—is their patron and master, and the *agha* and janissaries order them about and use them as common laborers for public works. The king is obliged to give these captives their daily bread.

This bagnio has a chapel where Mass is celebrated on Sundays and feast days, there being no lack of priests. The Great Bagnio, the main and preferred site because it has a larger number of captive Christians, also never lacks someone to say Mass. There are kings (such as Hasan the Venetian, deputy of ʿUludj ʿAli),[14] who keep sometimes fifteen hundred or two thousand Christians in that bagnio, whereas the captives in the Bagnio de la Bastarda ordinarily number no more than four hundred or five hundred.

The captives in the Bagnio de la Bastarda enjoy more liberty because they can come and go as they please, as long as the agha and janissaries do not employ them. All the captives of the Great Bagnio, however, are always locked up and under close watch, with porters ever at their doors and guards who take quarterly turns watching them day and night.

This second bagnio is called Bagnio de la Bastarda, because when Hasan Pasha, the son of Barbarossa, destroyed the Count of Alcaudete, captain general of Orán, in the battle of Mostaganem, in August of the Year of Our Lord 1558, the Turks captured over eleven thousand Spaniards there.[15] And for those men in particular who corresponded to the king as his part of the booty (and they were many), they armed a *bastarda* (galley),[16] choosing men who were the most robust, well-disposed, and valiant for its rowers. So that they would not mix with the elite captives he had in the Great Bagnio, the pasha ordered them to be placed in this bagnio. And because these men were all the mariners of the bastarda, for these reasons they named this prison house the Bagnio de la Bastarda.

Given that we mentioned Christian chapels, there is another one heavily frequented every day, Sundays and feast days (since Mass is celebrated there continuously—or rather Masses, since there are so many priests). This chapel is in the home of a Christian who has been many years a captive and a master of the galleys of Algiers, a Catalonian called Master Pedro. He is a man who has worked an infinite number of good deeds for captives, using his home for many years to celebrate

Masses in order to console the poor and wretched Christians. Christian women ordinarily attend only this chapel to hear Mass, rarely going to the other chapels in order to avoid confronting the Moors and Turks who are generally there as guards or porters. This Master Pedro fled Algiers with up to seven other masters of galleys in a vessel sent from Valencia for their rescue in August of 1582.

We should also note the lovely water fountains within or close to the city walls of Algiers, which add considerably to its luster and ornamentation. First, in the house of the king there is a fountain whose water, which supplies the household and many people in the neighborhood, falls into a basin of marble. There is another fountain in the small plaza in front of the same king's palace, which Dja'far Pasha[17] constructed in the year 1580, completing it on April twentieth of that year. It has a very pretty receptacle for water, which comes into a well-wrought marble basin.

Another fountain flows outside the gate of the marina, close to the sea, which provides water for all the galleys, galliots, and sea vessels. The fourth fountain is located within the house of Ramadan Pasha, who was king of Algiers and Tunis. And in the three large dwellings of the janissaries, there are another three fountains, each within its own patio, which supplies the janissaries and other people. The copious supply of water flowing from these seven fountains is enough to give drink to an infinite number of people.

All this water emerges from a huge fountain located half a league to the south of Algiers (among certain mountains there). Running through pipes at intervals and sometimes in the open air, the water passes through the foot of the small mountain where the Fort of the Emperor, also known as the Fort of Hasan Pasha, is built, and it enters the city under the New Gate, which faces directly south. From there it is distributed among the seven fountains mentioned above. This water also supplies the cistern in the Great Bagnio of the king. So that if some war took place, it would be easy to seize and cut off the water supply of Algiers, and in such a case the whole city would die of thirst, because the water would not be enough for one-third of the population, since the cisterns of the city are few and all small, and the wells all contain salt water, as we said.

To remedy such a thing, ʿArab Ahmad, who was king of Algiers in 1573,[18] constructed two other fountains, one very beautiful and copious at a hundred paces from the Gate of Bab al-Wad (whose water runs through four pipes and is very soft, fresh, and clear). This first fountain has its origin in some small fountains that emerge slightly less than a mile and a half from the city towards the west, in those small mountains and charming hills where there are many farms, and notably close to the place where the king of Fès has his country house. These small fountains, all collecting into one, produce a great quantity of water. The other fountain constructed by ʿArab Ahmad is one hundred paces away, outside the Gate of Bab ʿAzzun toward the south. At the right hand of the gate a goodly flood of water emerges. Although it shares the same source and beginnings, it is very dense and salty, and few people use it.

One, two, or three miles away from Algiers there are many other very fresh and clear fountains and wells of water, more than anyone could wish, so many that there is hardly any country house (among the great number of them) that does not have its fountain or well of great quantities of excellent water.

Among the remarkable public buildings must be counted the sepulchers of the kings, and of some governors and marabouts, situated a few steps outside the city. And they are of the form we described above, with beautifully wrought chapels.

Outside the Gate of Bab al-Wad there are six *kubbas,* or sepulchers: the first one encountered there was built by Hasan Pasha, the Venetian renegade, in 1579. Buried in it are his one-year-old son and a nephew, the son of one of his sisters. When this youth came from Venice to visit him in Algiers, Hasan Pasha forced him to become a Muslim and renegade. He died within a year and went to Hell.

The second tomb belongs to Salah Raʾis Pasha.[19] The third one farther ahead belongs to Hasan the Corsican,[20] who succeeded Salah Raʾis, and to his renegade Yusuf, the man who killed Takali[21] and avenged the murder of Salah Raʾis, as we have written in our *Epítome de los Reyes de Alger* [History of the Kings of Algiers].[22] The fourth tomb belongs to the governor Safa, who was caliph, or lieutenant, of the king and governor of Algiers.

Of the other two tombs lower down toward the marina, the first and most important is that of Hasan Agha, the Sardinian renegade, also known as "the Castrated," who was king when Emperor Charles V was defeated in his attempt to take Algiers.[23] The second and smaller tomb is that of Takali, who was also a king of Algiers.

Outside the Gate of Bab ʿAzzun there are three tombs. The first belongs to the marabout Sidi Batqa and the second to Sidi Ali Ezzouaoui, also a marabout and a madman;[24] the third tomb, which is farther forward beyond the bridge, is that of a brother of the king of the Bani ʿAbbas, who, bringing a great present to Hasan Pasha, the son of Barbarrosa, died of the heat in Algiers. To honor his memory, King Hasan ordered a fine tomb to be built for him. And in truth, the architecture of this tomb makes it the most beautiful and elegant of them all. It was constructed by an Italian Christian captive, a notable master of the art.

CHAPTER 40

The Natural Beauty of Algiers

Located at a latitude, as we said, of 37¾ degrees, and, as such, in so temperate a climate, the city of Algiers is also very temperate and accommodating to human life. No matter how great a heat the summers may bring, the city, with its walls touching the sea, remains comfortable. In summer (particularly in the afternoons) everyone enjoys smooth and healthful gusts of fresh winds from the sea. And in winter the cold is never so great that it is necessary to approach a fire, save as a special treat. Snow is regarded as a miracle; hail is a great rarity.

The land is also very healthy, save when the occasional Evil Eye,[1] in early summer or autumn, molests Algerians, largely children. A plague also blows through the city every ten, twelve, or fifteen years, coming mainly from outside: because Moors and Turks do not care for their health (saying that it is hopeless to flee what God has ordained), and because ships with merchandise and clothing continuously arrive in the port of Algiers from all parts of the world, the plague would predictably come too. Without deaths from the plague, I cannot image where such a large population, which multiplies daily in Algiers, would fit. Another reason for this is that all the houses have many latrines, but the city does not have a system of public pipes to carry and discharge the waste, either at sea or elsewhere.

Traveling out to the countryside, one is struck by the great natural beauty that surrounds the city: the infinite number of farms, orchards, and vineyards; orange, lime, lemon, and citron groves; flowers, rosebushes, and trees of every stripe; and every kind of herb and vegetable produced across the entire year. All this bounty is sprinkled with countless fountains of clear waters, resplendent as crystal, that run throughout the land in abundance. One cannot imagine more fertile conditions in Thessaly nor in the land of Alcinous[2] than in the gardens of Algiers. And what is most notable is that most of these gardens are cultivated on and around the small mountains surrounding Algiers virtually outside its gates.

The goodness and fertility of the land is such—Nature having liberally shared its gifts and graces with it—that in the middle of summer and in times of intense heat, the plants and trees do not lose their green color but sustain themselves beautifully without drying up.

Because the fountains of water are so many and so reliable, the valleys of these hills and small mountains are everywhere dotted with streams that run to many areas before ending up as a small river that they call the Fiumara,[3] located a thousand paces west of the city. Thanks to the excess of water in those valleys, they are all filled with a thousand trees whose shades, together with the great freshness of the streams and the birdsong, contribute in the heat of summer to such an excellent freshness and recreation that nobody could desire more. During that time (chiefly in the afternoons) many men and women generally come out to enjoy themselves. Adding a grace note to these gardens and to the small mountains and valleys where they are planted are the very white houses that everyone, no matter how poor, maintains. Seen from afar, then, the landscape resembles the seacoast of Genoa.

These estates have yet another advantage in their good caretakers. Although there are over ten thousand estates, there is not one that is not tended by one or two Christian slaves, at the least, and many of them by four, five, six, and more. Day and night across entire years, these captives do nothing else save for the work of digging, scraping, watering, cutting, planting, cleaning, hoeing, and improving these grounds as much as possible. The Moors and Turks are very proud of these gardens, not only for their own recreation and that of their wives and children but also for the great profit they attain from all the fruit to be picked from them.

Beyond these small mountains are the larger ones, and the very beautiful and fertile plains of Mitidja,[4] as they are called, divided almost in half by a huge and beautiful river emerging from other mountains farther south, where a great quantity of windmills serve the whole of Algiers all year long.

A great number of Turks, renegades, and some citified Moors keep fine arable lands in these great plains, in which they grow much wheat, barley, beans, chickpeas, lentils, melons, cucumbers, and every kind of vegetable. They raise many hens, doves, cows, oxen, camels, sheep, and rams; they extract much honey and make lots of lard; and they rear many silkworms every other year. They even hunt and kill partridges, turtledoves, pigeons, and rabbits. All are in great abundance except for rabbits and deer.[5]

Beyond these plains, which measure some thirty leagues in length and three in width, are other low mountains, which are extremely graceful, fruitful, and abundant in every kind of tree and fruit, especially almonds and figs. The game here is also plentiful. These plains are all watered by numberless fountains of lovely icy cold waters, which arise there and run throughout the year, watering no end of charming groves where many wild pigs abound.

Half a league ahead (because the height of these mountains is no wider) there are other larger and longer fields and plains, twice the size of the Mitidja ones we mentioned earlier, and similarly all dotted by many farms and granges of Turks, renegades, and Moors. Many Berbers also live there in tents, and from these plains, in the same way, they pick up everything humanly necessary and useful for human life, including an incredible infinity of game, which the Moors and Turks, out of laziness, neither want nor know how to hunt.

It is well known (and something the Moors and Turks themselves say) that if such a land were worked and cultivated by the hands of Christians, no place on earth would equal it in riches and abundance. But because Moors and Turks are all enemies of hard work and not very diligent, the earth is for them not as liberal as it could be.

What we say about these lands surrounding the city of Algiers may also be understood about the greater part of the kingdom, and even about all of Barbary, from the Atlas Mountains[6] to the sea. This territory is extremely abundant, rich, and gracious, as many authors of antiquity note and to whose abundant testimony I now refer (for the many things I could say here about the bounty and fertility of this land, of all it produces for human life).[7]

The bounty of Algiers is not confined to the earth but also shows up in the sea, because if Moors and Turks knew how to fish like Christians, or at least left this work to the Christians, there would be no room on earth for the fish they would catch. Because even eight or ten boats of poor fisherman fishing at odd hours, without daring to sail more than half a league from the coast for fear of Christian frigates (which sometimes come from Mallorca and seize both these boats and their Moorish fishermen) would catch such a large and excellent haul that Algiers would be well supplied with fish.

These fish include many sardines, bream, dogfish, red snapper, dolphin, red mullet, sting rays, mackerel shark, and many other kinds of fish also found in Spain and Italy. There are also along the marina many limpets, sea urchins, some large and delicious snails, and much edible seaweed that they pick and sell, the sustenance of many poor Christian captives.

CHAPTER 41

The Government of Algiers

The government of this city and of the whole kingdom depends chiefly on one governor, whom the Ottoman sultan normally provides every three years, sometimes more and sometimes less, as he wishes. This governor is not always a Turk. He can be a renegade or Moor reared among Turks in their culture and customs, as may be seen in the treatise we wrote of the lives of all the kings and governors of Algiers.[1]

In the Turkish tongue, they call this governor a pasha,[2] a title that among the Turks is used for governors of great kingdoms, because those who govern other states and small provinces are called *sandjak-bey*.[3] And since among the Turks there is no king other than the Grand Turk, the term *pasha,* if we must speak correctly, does not mean king but rather governor, as one would call the man who governs Algiers and all the lands subject to him. The usage already among Christians, however, is to call the governor of Algiers—as well as that of Tunis and Tripoli [present-day Tarabulus] and other places—a king. The Moors call each of these governors *sultan,* which in their language signifies a king and supreme lord. The Grand Turk does not dole out this position for worthiness or for any services rendered, but rather as a favor to his pashas or supreme counselors and other intercessors, who are very self-serving and well paid. And it so happens that he who gives most, gets most, obtaining this and other major positions.

Regarding military matters, this king (for so we shall call him) communicates everything to the janissaries and his *agha,* and no war can begin without his permission. And when he does not appear in person, the enterprise not being important, he sends in a captain general whom they call *beylerbey*. In the absence of the king, this person represents him in war wherever he goes: he is like his lieutenant and general of all the cavalry and infantry, be they Moors or Turks. And after him, as we said earlier, the Boluk-Bashis are the captains and the men in charge of the janissaries, because their agha, if the person of the king is absent, never leaves Algiers.

This post of beylerbey is generally selected by the Grand Turk, along with that of the king, and both men come together from Constantinople. Given to a person expert and canny in the ways of war, the post commands much honor and respect.

During peacetime, the king has many who help him govern, primarily a Turk or renegade known as a *khalifa*. This person acts as the lieutenant of the king, taking his place whenever he leaves Algiers. He generally also serves as the counselor and aide to the king in all causes and businesses: when these are criminal, the king alone determines and concludes the issue, although as we said, the accused may appeal to the agha of the janissaries, who will often, at his wish or whim, revoke or moderate the king's sentence.

As for civil causes, these are handled by two judges: one *kadi* is a Turk by birth, and the other kadi, for the Moors, is himself a Moor. These men tend to be learned in their way, in their Law and the Qur'an. But no matter how greatly educated they are, they are all very ignorant and pronounce sentences in lawsuits according to their whim, because they are governed by no written laws, nor ordinances, nor statutes, nor decisions of doctors. The most learned of them, however, extract and pull together (as best they can) their judgment of particular cases from the Qur'an, and those who know less (the majority of them) follow whatever their lights tell them to be most just. And sometimes they pronounce the most laughable sentences, as happened in past years, when a windmill situated in the Fort of the Emperor, also called the Fort of Hasan Pasha, turned askew and killed a mule. The windmill was sentenced by the kadi to be stripped and thrown to earth for having killed the mule in this way.

Among these two kadis, there is this order or preeminence: that the kadi of the Moors can appeal to that of the Turks, but not the other way around; either of them, however, can appeal to the agha. This means that the agha is, in a certain way, the supreme legislator, not only over the judges and governors of justice but also over the very king of Algiers.

For good administration of their jobs, these kadis keep some scriveners, as many as they wish, who write down the contracts, determinations, and sentences that occur in front of both parties for whenever written proof may be needed.[4] The kadi of the Turks writes them in Turkish, and the kadi of the Moors, in Arabic.

They also have a porter whom they call a *ca'ush*[5] who serves as executor of the judgments and sentences, as a porter to call the parties to justice, and even as an executioner.

The judges' sentence is ordinarily beatings and more beatings for the condemned, who is stretched face down across the ground, and after his back is virtually flayed, they turn him on the other side and give him more blows on the stomach and chest, and even on the soles of the feet, for as long as the judge, king, or agha has ordered. For this punishment the ca'ush of the king, and of the agha, always carry some thick sticks or canes in their hands, with which they perform the job of executioners.

The Algerians seldom hang anyone, unless he is a public thief or criminal or killer. But if he is a Turk, everything is concealed and made to look good. And whoever gives money to the presiding judge, agha, or king can commit all the cursed deeds he wishes without any penalty or punishment.

All processes of civil or criminal causes are done only verbally, with no writing whatsoever, nor anything other than bringing forward witnesses, from which the judge moves summarily to sentencing.

The writings and contracts are signed by the hand of the kadi—not that he signs with his name, as we Christians do, but rather he imprints on the paper his seal. This is made of gold or silver in the mode of a ring (although not worn on a finger) and with certain designs, which (after wetting the seal in ink) remain as figures on the paper. In this same way the king, as well as all Turks in general, signs all writings and letters.

There are no aldermen to look out for the public good of the city, nor juries, nor trustees, nor public attorneys, not any other manner of civil government or police. There are only two officials: one, called the *mizwar*,[6] the other the *muhtasib*.[7] The mizwar is something like a bailiff, and he is in charge of apprehending evildoers, thieves, and adulterers and taking them to jail. He circles the city at night, accompanied by some hefty guards. Around two or three hours after night falls, they play some flutes and drums in the house of the king, which is, more or less, like the curfew in Spain and a sign to retreat from the streets. At a later time (two and a half or even three hours before daybreak), they play these instruments a second time. In between the time of these flutes and drums no Christian can walk the streets, under pain of being taken to jail and his master being fined ten *doblas,* which amount to four *escudos* of gold. And according to what the mizwar and his assistants say about the Christian, at jail they beat him up somewhat.

This job of mizwar tends to be sold at auction to the highest bidder, because he benefits greatly from these arrests. From the infinite number of arrangements he makes and the continuous briberies he exacts, he earns a great quantity of money.

The second position, the muhtasib, serves as a faithful overseer of the things in public stores. He is subject to the mizwar, and both divide the spoils that the muhtasib can scrape off the poor.

There are three jails in the city for all delinquents: one that the king has in his palace, where those brought before him are taken; another held by the agha in one of the houses of the janissaries; and another called the jail of the mizwar, where both law breakers and those condemned by the kadis are taken. And in all these jails the prisoners are mixed and scrambled together—Turks, Moors, Jews, and Christians—without any difference, and all stretched out on the ground. And almost all of them have their feet either bound together in stocks or fettered with shackles and chains, as the mizwar would have it.

The king and the agha also tend to send some janissaries and Turks, accompanied by bailiffs, as prisoners to the Great Bagnio, where they will be better accommodated and kept in a safe place. After paying a heavy bail, prisoners who are *ka'ids* are commonly put under house arrest as long as they have not committed very grave crimes, because in such a case they are sent to public jails like all the other criminals and without any more respect.

As for the business of the king's worldly goods and rents, he is served by diverse ministers, depending on how and where he exacts his tributes, rents, and profits. To begin with the tributes, the biggest slice is taken from the *dawars*[8] or encampments of the Arab Bedouins, who live in the fields in tents—in groups of 100, 200, 300, and up to 600 and more tents per encampment. Sometimes many dawars together will obey one chief among them, the most prominent whom they call a sheik. And each sheik pays a given sum to the king of Algiers every year, either all in cash or partly in cash and partly in wheat, rams, cows, camels, lard, and honey. Sometimes the Berbers pay all their tribute in these and other victuals. The sheik is in charge of extracting from the Berbers of his settlement or settlements the distribution they owe, according to the wealth and wherewithal of each.

Because the Berbers are all untamable, without any faith or truth among them, it is necessary for the king to send out, across the year, teams of Turks, janissaries, and soldiers to extract the tributes by force. And with these soldiers he also sends out the most trusted Turk or renegade from his house, who carries with him a list or memorial of all those settlements and of how much each one pays. This man receives the tribute as treasurer of the king.

The king of Algiers also receives those tributes of the pensions that all the ka'ids and governors of the lands are obliged to give him each year, because (as we said earlier) the governorships of the lands are sold to the highest bidder, and these men are obliged to hand over these moneys to the king of Algiers.

The third part of the king's rents come from that which the same ka'ids offer and promise the king when he gives them some *mahalla,* or squad of janissaries, so that they can make invasions and cavalcades against those Berbers who do not obey the Turks. These Berbers very often come, with all their tents and livestock, to the sierras near the kingdom of Algiers and its district, both to graze their livestock and to rob other Moors and Berbers who are vassals of the king of Algiers. And many times the ka'ids, along with the janissaries, hit on these Berbers and take an infinite number of camels, horses, cows, and other livestock and riches, and of all this they give to the king—a portion or more of it in money. And in the same way they give everything within Algiers to the king or to the person he sends as his emissary.

The fourth part of the king's rents consist in a portion of what the corsairs rob, because it is customary to give him one-seventh of their booty, whether of Christian captives or of money, clothing, and merchandise. Some kings demand the "king's fifth" and are not happier with any less. All the hulls of the Christian vessels that the corsairs seize go to the king, and as chief treasurer, his *el-amin*[9] is in charge of collecting these.

The fifth source of the king's rents comes from what he inherits from the dead, whether Turks, moors, or renegades, from whom he, in the name of the Grand Turk, enlarges his stock of worldly goods, as we have noted earlier, and this makes for a very large endowment. The responsibility for seeing to these inheritances falls to an official that the king chooses, called the Ka'id of the Dead, and for his work he receives one-tenth of the profit.

The sixth part of the king's rent is the tribute from Customs, that is, from the merchandise that Moors, Christians, or Turks bring by sea from outside the city of Algiers, and they all tend to pay eleven percent of its worth, both in coinage and in other kinds of merchandise. This is collected by the king's treasurer.

The seventh part of his rent is from the gains the king makes by investing in corsair activities, because almost all the kings of Algiers are accustomed to join up with the corsairs for gain and profit. For this the kings give the corsairs their provisions of bread and biscuits, as well as oil, honey, lard, olives, and rice with which to furnish their galliots and ships. They also give them all or part of the crew of galley slaves to serve on the vessels. These crews, amassed from Christian captives kept in their bagnio, are also given to the treasurer.

The eighth part also consists in money given the king by those persons to whom he rents the industries of hides, wax, and tallow. Only these men can buy from the Moors all the hides of cows, oxen, and cordovans, as well as all the wax and grease in Algiers and in its district, or in Bône [present-day Annaba], Collo, Béjaïa, and its districts. They then sell it all (save for the wax) to Christians, from which they make a great profit, which is also turned over to the treasurer.

The ninth part of the king's rents is the tribute paid at the gates of Algiers, a duty placed on all that the Moors and Turks (as long as they are not janissaries, *sipahis,* or ka'ids) bring into Algiers to sell, which the king also tends to rent out to the highest bidder. The royal treasurer also picks up these tributes.

The tenth part is the rent paid to the king by the Genoese for letting them fish the coral in Tabarka,[10] and by the French merchants of

Marseille so they can do the same in a trading post farther east of Bône. They call this the Bastion de France,[11] after a post the French have constructed there, and where they congregate with their ships.

The eleventh part of the king's rents come from what the kings of Labbès (Banu 'Abbas) and Kuko[12] tend to send him, at least every two years. Being at peace with the Turks, these kings send fine gifts to the kings of Algiers by way of friendship, tributes in their own mode, because if they do not send them they would be forced to do so. And there is nothing fixed here, nor any determined quantity, but every gift is always worth more than four or five thousand ducats, partly in coin and partly in camels, cows, and rams. In exchange, the king of Algiers tends to send each of them the odd Turkish garment along with a richly adorned sword.

If one adds up the sum of all these rents that the king of Algiers gets from so many sources—which I have discovered from those who particularly knew about these rents and through whose hands they passed (although it is impossible to know the exact yearly sum because it is almost always uncertain)—it goes beyond a total of between four thousand and five thousand ducats. From this the king is obliged to pay the janissaries and sipahis, as well as all the military and other officials and ministers. He spends on these people every year up to two thousand ducats or slightly more, because the salary of these people is not great. Moreover, almost half of the Berber tribes of the Zwawa,[13] as well as half of the janissaries, are distributed among places in the kingdom funded not by the king but rather by the ka'ids of those lands, who rent them out under the condition that they would pay these salaries from their revenues.

Along with these rents, the kings are obliged to send a gift to the Grand Turk at least once every three years, and another of similar value to the pashas of the Supreme Council of the Turk. And he who wants or tries always to have a job must not only please the Grand Turk but also, and even more, must lobby the pashas of his Council, because everything passes through their hands.

In order to keep the Ottoman sultan and the pashas of his Supreme Council happy, and to remain in their grace, the king of Algiers and the governors of other parts must rob the kingdoms and provinces they govern in order to send the sultan and his counselors hefty gifts of Christian slaves and great quantities of coins. Some kings tend to send the Grand Turk less than they send these pashas. The amounts given to the one or the other are neither fixed nor determined, but each king sends off as much as he wants, and the more he sends, the more praised, well received, and esteemed he is. And so thinking of nothing except how to rob and flay all their subjects in whatever way possible, these kings or governors accumulate great wealth, which (at the end of their reigns) they can carry or send to Constantinople.

ABBREVIATIONS

A Arabic
B Berber
Eng English
Fr French
Gk Greek
Heb Hebrew
It Italian
L Latin
N Afr North African
P Persian
Por Portuguese
Sp Spanish
SpA Spanish Arabic
T Turkish

GLOSSARY

AGHA (T): "chief," "master," or "commander," a term given to a high-ranking official in Ottoman times. In North African countries under Ottoman rule, the term referred most often to the commander of the janissary corps—that is, *agha* of the JANISSARIES—who had the responsibility of imposing the law and maintaining order in each city or province.

AGHA BOLUKLERI: squads of the AGHA of the JANISSARIES.

AKCE or *akche* (T): a small Ottoman silver coin used in the Balkans and Anatolia that Europeans called ASPER or *aspre*. It was the basic monetary unit in the Ottoman Empire until the end of the seventeenth century.

AL-KASR AL-KABIR or al-Qasr al-Kabir (A) (Alcazarquivir, Sp): a town in Northern Morocco, about fifty miles south of Tangier on the right bank of the Wadi Lukkus; best known among Western sources because in this area took place the Battle of the Three Kings, on 3 August 1578.

AL-AMIN (EL-AMIN) (A): title applied to treasurers, customs officers, stewards of estates, etc. *See also* AMIN

ALBANEGA (Sp), from *albaniqa* (SpA), from *albaniqah* (A). *See also* BANIKA

AL-DJAZA'IR (A): lit. "the islands"; referring to several islands off the port of Algiers.

AL-ʿID AL-KABIR (A): equivalent to ʿId al-adha or ʿId al-Qurban: the major sacrificial festival during the yearly pilgrimage, as opposed to the minor festival, or AL-ʿID AL SAGHIR.

AL-ʿID AL SAGHIR (A): lit. "the minor festival," also called ʿid al-Fitr, or "festival of the breaking of the fast" of Ramadan that marks the end of the fasting period. The Turkish term for this celebration is Seker Bayram.

AL-KSA or *ksa* (A): a large outer wrap, usually white, used by both sexes across the entire MAGHREB.

AMIN (A): a technical term used for the holders of various positions "of trust," such as treasurers, customs officers, and stewards of estates. In the law, the word denotes legal representatives. The most important technical meaning of the word *amin* is "head of a trade guild" (EoI). *See also* AL-AMIN

ʿARRAKIYYA or ʿarraqiyah (A): a skullcap, sometimes embroidered, worn by both sexes in the Arab East, either on its own or under a headdress.

ARNAUT (T): An inhabitant of Albania and neighboring mountainous regions, specifically one serving as a soldier in the Turkish army.

ʿASABA (A): the common word for a folded scarf in the MAGHREB.

ʿASBA (A): a folded scarf worn as a headband by women in Egypt, Syria, and Palestine.

ASHDJI (T): chief cook of an Ottoman regiment, who was also chief of the regimental prison.

ASHOR. *See* USHUR

ASPER (E): Turkish monetary unit. *See also* AKCE

BAB AL-DJADID, or Bab Djadid (A), the "New Gate": one of the main gates of Algiers, located in the southwest part of the city.

BAB AL-WAD (A), the "River Gate": one of the main gates of Algiers.

BAB ʿAZZUN (A), "Gate of Azzun": one of the main gates of Algiers, located in the south of the city.

BAGARINO (Sp, pl. bagarinos): a rower, who received a salary, as opposed to a galley slave. According to Sosa, this was the name given to the KABYLES who rowed in galleys and brigantines, hired and paid by the job.

BAGNIO (It), *baño* (Sp), from *banyol* (T): prison of the galley slaves; name given to the prison or slave house in Algiers. Captives held for ransom were kept in these prisons.

BALDI (A): an original inhabitant of Algiers. Also *beldi* (A): city dweller versus *arbi* (a Bedouin or peasant). Both terms *baldi* and *beldi* currently designate a particular social category of Tunisian society, a holdover from the sixteenth century.

BANIKA (A): term frequently applied in the Arab West to a hairnet or an element of women's hair covering.

BARBARY (Eng), Berbería (Sp): a geographical term stemming from the word "Berber" and used by sixteenth- and seventeenth-century Europeans to designate the North African region extending from Morocco to the west of Egypt; the Barbary States included the four countries of Morocco, Algeria, Tunisia, and Libya.

BARRAKAN (N. Afr): large enveloping outer wrap for both sexes (Libya).

BASHI (T): chief guardian of a BAGNIO; also chief of all the slaves of a BEY.

BASH-ODA (T): head of a garrison.

BASTARDA (It, Sp), *bastarde* or *bastardelle* (F): a galley larger than the *fallea sensile*, but smaller than the *galeassa* or *galliass*. The Ottoman Turks adopted the name *bashtarda, basharda* (T) from the Italian.

BASTION DE FRANCE (Fr): a trading post founded by a Corsican family of renegades for coral fishing in a bay close to Annaba. The fishing rights were established through a treaty undersigned by the governor of Algiers in 1550.

BEY (T): honorific title meaning "master" or "chief"; prince, ruler of an independent principality or governor of a district.

BEYLERBEY (also *beylerbeyi* or *beglerbegi*) (T): lit. "bey of beys," or "commander of commanders"; the Ottoman title for the provincial governor of a BEYLERBEYILIK; the highest rank in the provincial government of the Ottoman Empire.

BEYLERBEYILIK (T): a province, the largest administrative unit in the Ottoman Empire; the office of or government by the BEYLERBEY.

BISMILLAH (A): "In the name of Allah."

BLANCA (Sp): a small copper coin worth half a MARAVEDÍ during the sixteenth century.

BOLUK (T): term that designated infantry units under the command of a captain, or YAYABASHI.

BOLUK-BASHI (T): a degree of rank among the JANISSARIES, literally "captain of a division"; title given to the commanders of the BOLUKS of the AGHA, or AGHA BOLUKLERI.

BONEVOGLIE (It): lit. "men of good will"; voluntary rowers, either ex–galley slaves who had completed their sentences or vagabonds who had sold their freedom.

BOURBE (Eng, Fr): a European term for copper coinage still circulating in Morocco and Tunis during the eighteenth century.

BULGUR (T, also *bulghur*): a cereal food made from several different wheat species, most often from *durum* wheat. It is commonly used in North African and Greek cuisine.

BURDJ (A): a square or round tower, either adjacent to a rampart or isolated and serving as a bastion or dungeon.

BURNUS or *burnous* (A): a loose woolen hooded cloak woven in one piece; also a type of high cap or bonnet worn in the Prophet's time.

CACIZ or *casis, caxis* (Sp, Por): the standard term for MARABOUTS in sixteenth-century Spain and Portugal. It is also spelled *qasis* (A). The term comes from *qass* (A), a preacher of sermons.

CASTRA PRAETORIA (L): barracks of the Praetorian Guard of imperial Rome that were constructed in 23 CE by Lucius Aeolius Sejanus, the Praetorian prefect who served under Tiberius Caesar (14–37 CE).

CA'USH (T, modern *çavuş*): officials staffing the various departments of the Ottoman Palace. Their services were also used as ambassadors or envoys by the sultan. In North Africa, the term is still seen in its Arabic form (*shawish* or *shawush*), where it means a court usher or mace bearer.

CAFTAN. *See* KHAFTAN

ÇELEBI (T): a sixteenth-century title of respect given in Turkey to illustrious members of the military corps, and, by extension, to judges and scholars.

CETIL (Sp), *ceitil* (Por): a Portuguese coin minted in memory of the conquest of Ceuta, North Africa (1415), and commonly used in Castile in the sixteenth century. Its value was one third of a BLANCA.

CIANÍ (pl. *cianis*) (Sp from A dialectical ZYAN, and this from Abu Zayan, ruler of Tlemcen): low-karat gold coin, used among the Moors of Africa, that was worth one hundred aspers.

COMPLINE (Eng): the last part of the divine office with which the canonical hours of the day end.

CONTRAY (Sp), from Kortrijk, the Flemish name for Courtrai (Fr): a type of fine wool made in Flanders. Courtrai, or Kortrijk, is a Flemish city in Belgium, situated in western Flanders, on the frontier with France. The city has been historically connected with the textile industry since early modern times.

CONVERSO (Sp): a term applied to a Jew or Muslim who converted to Christianity. After the 1492 expulsion of the Jews and the Conquest of Granada, converted Hispano-Muslims were more commonly called Moriscos [little Moors].

CUZACA. See HAZUQAH

DAWAR (A) (Sp *aduar*): an encampment of the Arab Bedouin in which the tents are arranged in a circle around an open space where the cattle pass the night. In North Africa, this arrangement is called *duwar* or *dawwar*.

DELI (T): mad, heedless, fiery, daring, brave, exalted; a type of cavalry in the Ottoman Empire, formed in the Balkans toward the end of the fifteenth century.

DEVSIRME (T): the levy or human tax of Christian children to be trained for posts in the palace and in the administration of the *kapikulu* military corps, the elite JANISSARY corps of the Ottoman army; a youth so levied.

DIVAN (T, Diwan-i humayun): Imperial Council of the Ottomans, founded by Mehmed II after the conquest of Constantinople. The Divan remained the central organ of their government until the seventeenth century. The name was also applied to government bureaus that kept tax, military, and other records.

DJABAN or *jaban* (A): the original literal meaning of the term in Arabic was "cowardly."

DJINN (A): a Qur'anic term applied to bodies composed of vapor and flame, which came to play a large role in folklore.

DJUM'A OR YAWM AL-DJUM'A, "the day when people come together" (A): the Friday service, celebrated at noon in one mosque in each city, obligatory for all adult Muslim males.

DOBLA (Sp): an antique copper coin that wavered in value according to the times. This term should not be confused with *doblón* (Sp), doubloon (E), an antique gold coin, thus called by the common people during the reign of the Catholic Monarchs because it weighed two castellanos or *doblas*.

DUCADO (Sp): a gold coin worth 375 MARAVEDÍS in sixteenth-century Spain.

DURRA'A (also *der'a, dirra*) (A): a long robe with sleeves used by both sexes in the entire Maghreb. The sleeveless version is called a GANDURA (A).

ESCUDO (Sp): standard gold coin with the royal coat of arms inscribed on one of its faces. In the Spain of Philip II, a gold *escudo* was worth four hundred MARAVEDÍS.

FERDJA or *fradja* (A): a garment used by men only in Algiers and Tunisia similar to the *faradjiyya* (A), a long and slim article of clothing, with or without sleeves and with a deep opening in the chest, worn by both men and women under the caftan.

GALLIOT (Eng), *kalite* (T): small and swift Algerian vessel with fourteen to twenty-five benches, which was light and rounded in front and in the back. The galliot surpassed the Christian galleons in performance.

GANDURA (A): long sleeveless tunic worn by both sexes in Algiers.

GARZÓN (pl. *garzones*) (Sp): a term used in sixteenth-century Spain to refer to sodomites, especially to the *bardash,* or passive agent, in the sexual relation between men.

GHANIMA or *ghunm* (A): booty, in particular, moveable booty, which was distributed immediately.

GHLILA (A): long vest or jacket used by both sexes in Algiers.

GHURFAT (also *ghurfa* or *ghurfah*) (A): rooms on upstairs floors; among the Berbers in North Africa, a *ghurfat* signifies a fortified enclosure.

GONELA (A, from the It *gonnella*): a tunic of leather or silk, generally sleeveless, worn by both sexes.

GREGAL (Sp), *graegalis* (L, "of Greece"): a wind that blows from the east and the north, according to the division of the mariner's compass card used in the Mediterranean.

HADJDJ (A): the pilgrimage to Mecca, 'Arafat, and Mina, also known as the Great Pilgrimage, is one of the five pillars of Islam.

HADJDJI or *hadjdj* (A): honorific title given to someone who has performed the HADJDJ.

HA'IK or *hayk* (A): outer cape, usually white, worn in North Africa by both sexes.

HAMMAM (A): steam bath, often still referred to as "Turkish bath." A typical building of the Islamic world, the *hamman* is one of the essential amenities of the Muslim city, used for relaxation as well as to fulfill the laws of hygiene or religious regulation.

HANDSPAN. *See* PALMO

HARAM (A): a prohibition; something forbidden to the profane.

HAZUQAH or *hazuqa* (A): from the verb "to tighten," waistband worn over the *caftan* to fasten it.

HOLLAND [cloth] (Eng): very fine cloth used to make shirts and sheets.

HYDROMANCY (Eng): the superstitious art of divining by observations of water.

ICOSIUM (L): the Roman settlement on the mainland of Algiers.

IJABI or *ijaba* (A): seeking God's "response" by saying a prayer such as *istighfar:* "Astaghfiru Allah," meaning "seek forgiveness" or "seek divine protection."

INFORMACIÓN (Sp): legal inquiry or investigation that usually gave rise to a notarized affidavit or report.

JANISSARIES (Eng), *yeniçeri* (T): elite Turkish infantry; the Sultan's standing infantry corps, recruited from the DEVSIRME and paid from the public treasury. These youth were subjected to virtually monastic conditions, an iron discipline, hard physical training, and an education in the use of arms and military tactics.

KABYLES (Fr): a tribe of islamicized Berbers who inhabited the mountainous KABYLIA; descendants of inhabitants of the region before the arrival of the Arabs. The term Kabyle seems to have been introduced into geographic nomenclature by European writers from the sixteenth century onwards.

KABYLIA (Fr): a mountainous region in the Algerian Tell, inhabited by the KABYLES. The area was divided in the sixteenth century among three powers, which Europeans called, respectively, the kingdom of Kuko, the kingdom of Labbès (Banu ʿAbbas), and the principality of the Banu Djubar.

KADI (T), *qadi* (A): the judge who administered both the religious laws of Islam and the secular laws promulgated by sultans. Within the Ottoman Empire, a *kadi* was the judge and chief administrator of a judicial district.

KAFILA or *karwan* (A): a caravan composed of mules, donkeys, and, especially, camels.

KAHYA (T): an administrator or deputy who took care of the business affairs of an important government official or influential person.

KA'ID (T), *qaʾid* (A): a term generally used to designate a military leader ranging from captain to general, although it also meant a tribal chieftain. In Algiers, the title was given to the governors of districts or towns subject to the Turkish government. Their obligations were fiscal, judicial, and military.

KAPUDAN PASHA (also *kapudan pa*a or *kapudan-i derya*) (T): title given to the grand admiral of the Ottoman fleet.

KARINDAS or *kardes* (T): brother or sister; fraternal.

KASBA, *al-kasaba*, or *kasaba* (A): a fortified castle, residence of an authority in the center of a country or a town; principal town, chief town. In North Africa, the term occurs in the sense of fortress or citadel (dialect: *kasba*).

KHAFTAN (P), *caftan* (Eng): an ample full-length robe with sleeves and buttons down the front, very popular across the Arab world.

KHALIFA (A), caliph (Eng): title given to Saracen princes who, as successors of Muhammad, exercised supreme religious and civil power in some Muslim territories; also a deputy or a lieutenant of the PASHA.

KHAMIS (A): the vigil of DJUMʿA, or Thursday; in the *Encyclopaedia of Islam*, *khamis* is a term in military science: "the five elements into which the army is divided."

KHAWAJAH (A): a title used in many senses in Islamic countries, it was earlier applied to scholars, teachers, merchants, and ministers. In the Ottoman Empire, it designated a certain class of civil officials.

KUBBA or *qubba* (A), *kubbe* (T): a tomb surmounted by a dome; the general name for the sanctuary of a saint.

KURSIYYA (A): belt used by both sexes in Morroco.

LAA ILAAHA ILLA ALLAH WA-MUHAMMAD RASUUL ALLAH . . . (A): "There is no God but God and Muhammad is his prophet."

LAYLAT AL-KADR (A), also called Laylat Sabʿ wa-ʿIshrin (lit. "the night of 27 of Ramadan"): night when the angels descend to earth (Qurʾan 97). The Islamic tradition teaches that the Qurʾan was brought down from Heaven during this night, and that the angel Gabriel bound it into one volume, dictating it to Muhammad over the space of twenty-three years.

LEWEND (Eng), *levend* (T), *levante* or *levente* (Sp), *levantino* (It): name given to two kinds of Ottoman daily-wage irregular militia, either seagoing or land based. During the Ottoman maritime expansion, these *lewends* acted as guardsmen, rowers, and marines for shore invasions, but mainly as seagoing musket bearers.

LINGUA FRANCA (L): the cross-bred language spoken in Algiers, composed for the most part of Italian and Spanish.

MAGHREB or al-Maghrib (A): lit. the west, "the setting sun"; that part of Africa—including Tripoli, Tunisia, Algeria, and Morocco—which Europeans called Barbary or Africa Minor and, later, North Africa.

MAGHRIB (A): prayer at sunset.

MAHALLA (A), *mahalle* (T): name given in the Maghreb to a military camp on the move and, by extension, to Turkish expeditionary units on campaign to levy taxes within the territory.

MAKHZEN, *makhzan,* or *makhzin* (A): a storehouse; in North African usage it stands for "the State"; also indicates the political system based on the oath of allegiance of the tribal chiefs to the sultan.

MARABOUT (Eng, F), *murabit* (A, T): a saintly or venerated Muslim leader, often charismatic; descendant or leader of a sufi (mystic) order. The marabouts had enormous political power in sixteenth-century MAGHREB.

MARAVEDÍS (Sp): the smallest coin or unit in the Spanish monetary system; a gold ESCUDO was worth four hundred *maravedís.*

MAWLID or *malud* (A): the day, place, or celebration of a birth, especially of the prophet Muhammad; a festival celebrated on the twelfth day of Rabiʿ al-Awwal, or third month of the Islamic calendar. The term also designates a panegyric poem in honor of the Prophet.

MEDASA or *madasa* (A): North African usage for a type of footwear.

MEMORIAL (Sp): a written request or brief presented to a judge, regarding a legal or civil question.

MILHAFA, *mlahfa,* or *tamelhaft* (A): large outer wrap worn by both sexes in the entire MAGHREB.

MIR (T): commander; a military and political term used in eighteenth-century Ottoman Turkish administrative practice and virtually synonymous with BEYLERBEY.

MISTRAL (Sp), *magistral* (Lat): lit. "master-wind"; a violently cold northwest wind in the Mediterranean.

MITHKAL, *mitqal,* or *mithqal* (A): the oldest Arab unit of Troy weight; in Sosa's day it was also a Moroccan coin valued at half a PIASTER (Eng) or *kurush* (T).

MIZWAR or MAZWAR (A): lit. "he who precedes or is placed at the head." In North Africa, the chief of a religious brotherhood or a body of troops.

MORISCOS (Sp): Hispano-Muslims residing in Spain who were forced to convert to Christianity after the fall of Granada in 1492.

MUDÉJAR (Sp): Hispano-Arabic name given to a Muslim who remained, without changing religion, as a vassal of the Christians in a newly conquered territory.

MUHTASIB (A): inspector of markets and public morals who enforces regulations and levies dues and taxes on traders, artisans, and also on certain imports.

NKAB (also *nikab* or *niqab*) (A, N Afr): veil that covers the face of a married woman (Algiers, Morocco).

NUMIDIANS (Eng): a nomad Berber people who inhabited Numidia, the region of North Africa extending from the territory of Carthage up to the Muluya in Morocco.

ODABASHI (T): the name given to the commanders of the AGHA BOLUK-LERI, or squads of the AGHA of the JANISSARIES.

ODALI or Odaci (T): soldier, from squad (*oda*).

ODJAK or Ocak (T): lit. "fireplace, chimney, hearth"; under the Ottomans, an army unit; military corps of JANISSARIES.

ODJAK-ERI (modern spelling: Ocak-eri) (T, from *odjak* or *ocak:* "fireplace, chimney, hearth"). JANISSARIES were called "hearth-mates" (*odjak-eri, ocak-eri,* or *ocakli*).

OLDACI. *See* ODALI

OTRAK or Oturak (T): retired elders of the military corps.

OTTOMAN PORTE. *See* SUBLIME PORTE

PALMO (Sp): a span or unit of length based on the width of the expanded human hand, usually estimated as nine inches.

PAPAZ (Algerian *lingua franca*): name given in Algiers to Christian priests or ecclesiastics.

PARE or *para* (T): money; currency.

PASHA (T): the highest official title of honor under the Ottomans, a man who obtained a superior command, either at sea or as viceroy or governor of a province; title also given to certain high civil officials.

PESETA (Sp): Spanish unit of currency, coin that had a different weight and value across the times.

PIASTER, PIASTRE (E, F), from *piastra* (It): "thin metal plate." The name was applied to Spanish pieces of eight by Venetian traders in the Levant in the sixteenth century. *Piastre* was also a former coin of Turkey, one one-hundredth of a Turkish lira, replaced by the *kurush* in 1933.

PORTE (T). *See* SUBLIME PORTE

QUR'AN or al-Kuran (A): lit. "The Recitation"; Islam's sacred scripture, containing the revelations received by Muhammad over a period of twenty-two years (610–632 CE) and preserved in a fixed, written form.

RA'IS (pl. *ru'asa*) (A), *re'is* (T): head, chief, leader of a political, religious, juridical, tribal, or other group. In the Ottoman navy, the term was used to designate a commander. In sixteenth-century Algiers, *ra'is* was the name given to the captain of a GALLIOT, especially to a corsair who owned various ships.

RAKI (T): name given to several kinds of alcoholic beverages; also a non-sweet, usually anise-flavored aperitif.

RAMADAN (A): the ninth month of the Islamic calendar, when Muslims observe a rigorous, month-long fast from dawn to sunset.

REAL (pl. *reales*) (Sp): a silver coin worth thirty-four MARAVEDÍS at the end of the sixteenth century.

RIBAT (A): originally used to denote a fortified edifice, such as a small fort or a fortress, and also a *caravanserai*, or roadside inn. These diverse establishments would be situated on the frontiers, on coasts, or on difficult internal routes; a *ribat* is also a building usually reserved for Muslim mystics; the terms *ribat* and ZAWIYA refer to establishments with similar aims.

RUBIA (Sp): an Arabic gold coin equivalent to one fourth of a CIANÍ.

SALAT (A): the ritual prayer, one of the five pillars of Islam.

SALAT AL-ʿASR (A): afternoon prayer performed between midday and sunset.

SALAT AL-DJUMʿA (A): the prayer of Fridays, which takes place at midday in a mosque.

SALAT AL-ʿISHA (A): prayer at nightfall.

SALAT AL-MAGHRIB (A): sunset prayer.

SALAT AL-SUBH (A): dawn prayer.

SALAT AL-ZHUR (A): mid-afternoon prayer.

SANDJAK (T): flag, standard, banner; in Ottoman administration, also a Turkish administrative and territorial division.

SANDJAK-BEY, OR SANDJAK-BEYI (T): governor of a district or political region.

SANDJAKDAR (T): royal standard-bearer.

SANDUK (A): coffer or chest, but also open wooden coffin; meaning cenotaph, as well.

SENDAL (E), *cendal* (Sp): fine, transparent silk or linen fabric.

SFENDJ (A): the general name for Algerian fritters or doughnuts, prepared for wedding celebrations or for the first tooth of a baby.

SHAHADAH (A): profession of the Muslim faith; *Ashadu an la ilaha illa-llah, wa ashadu anna Muhammadan rasulu-llah* (I bear witness that there is no god but the one God, and I bear witness that Muhammad is the prophet of God).

SHARIF (A): honorable, noble, highborn, a term associated with honor and nobility. Claiming descent from distinguished ancestors, usually from Muhammad through his grandson Hasan, a *sharif* generally wears a green or white turban to distinguish himself from others.

SHASHIYYA or *shash* (A): hat without a brim of soft cloth, worn by both sexes in the MAGHREB.

SHERBIL or *serbil* (A): flat sandals, worn by both sexes in the MAGHREB.

SIDI or *sayyid* (A): honorific title before a name, usually a MARABOUT.

SIKKA (A); *cequí* (Sp) from *zicchi* (SpA); *sequin* (Fr); *zecchino* (Ital): an ancient coin of gold minted in various states of Europe, especially in Venice, and used in the Ottoman Empire and Africa.

SIPAHI (P), *sepoy* (Eng), *spahi* (Fr): in the Ottoman Empire, a *timar* holder; cavalryman. Created by Murad I (1360–1389), *sipahis* constituted the Muslim cavalry based in the territorial lands of the sultanate known as the TIMAR.

SOLAK (T): lit. "left-handed"; in the Ottoman military organization, the name of part of the sultan's bodyguard, which comprised four infantry companies of the janissaries, originally archers. The Solak soldiers used their left hands instead of their right hands as archers.

SOFRA (A, T): a round tray or platter on which food is placed in Turkey and may have been used, by extension, to refer to a banquet or dining table.

SOSFIA. *See* SOFRA

SOUALEF (B): tufts of hair over the temples.

SOUK (Eng), *suk* (A): market, both in the sense of the commercial exchange of goods and the market place in which this trade is normally conducted. Also the name of the streets or portion of the streets dedicated to the sale of merchandise or natural products (e.g., Souk of the Spices).

SOUSSE, also Souss, Sous, Sus, or Bilad al-Sus (A); Tamazirt n Sus (B): a region in southern Morocco, surrounding the Oued Sous, separated from the Sahara by the Anti-Atlas mountains.

SPAN. *See* PALMO

SUBH. *See* SALAT AL-SUBH

SUBLIME PORTE (T): Turkish official title of the central office of the Ottoman government; the Ottoman court at Constantinople.

SULTANI (T): in numismatics, the first Ottoman gold coin. Introduced in 1477–1478 CE by the Ottoman Empire, the *sultani* adopted the weight standard of the Venetian ducat.

TAGARINO (Sp), from *tagari* (SpA), and this from *tagri* (A): border; a term applied to MORISCOS born and raised among Christians and speaking both Spanish and Arabic so well that they could barely be distinguished from the Old Christians.

TARTURA, *tartur,* or *tantur* (A): a hat without a crown that was part of the uniform of the military Turkish elite in Algiers.

TAPIA (Sp): a superficial measurement of forty-nine to fifty square feet.

TIMAR (T): a fief or land grant in the Ottoman Empire under the care of a *timariot.*

TMAK (A): riding boots used across the MAGHREB.

ʿUSHR, *ʿushur,* or *ashor* (A), *ksher* (T): the tithe, or tenth, a form of ZAKAT (A), or obligatory alms. In the Ottoman Empire, it was the land tax levied on the produce of agricultural land owned by Muslims in the premodern era.

WEKIL-I KGHARDJ (T): paymaster general of a JANISSARY regiment; each regiment had this kind of officer, who oversaw the distribution of funds as well as the contributions for each regiment's independent campaign provisions.

YAYABASHI (T): chief infantryman, commander of the infantry or cavalry unit, BOLUK in the ODJAKS, or JANISSARY regiments.

YELEK (T): a sleeveless vest worn over other clothing in Algiers.

YOL-DASH (T): "comrades at arms," or soldiers. Janissaries were also called Odjak-eri (T, modern spelling: Ocak-eri), or "hearth-mates," from *odjak* or *ocak* (T): "fireplace, chimney, hearth."

ZAKAT (A): obligatory annual alms or tithe levied on wealth for distribution to the poor.

ZAWIYA (A): a building for religious study; a type of monastery; hostelry.

ZECCHINO (It); *zequín* or *cequí* (Sp); *sikka* (A); *sequin* (Fr): an ancient coin of gold minted in various states of Europe, especially in Venice, and admitted into Africa. It was also a monetary unit in Turkey, beginning in the era of Sultan Bayezid II (1481).

ZWAWA (A), Zouaoua (B): a confederation of KABYLE tribes living in the most remote gorges of the Djurjura mountain region and throughout the central and most western MAGHREB.

ZYAN (N Afr dialectical A): a gold coin of low assay value, used among the Moors of Africa and worth one hundred ASPERS.

NOTES

Introduction

1. During the first days of November 1519, Khayr al-Din and the Algerian people sent an embassy with four ships and forty slaves to Sultan Selim I, with an equal number of captives for the pashas of the Diwan. The text of this petition has survived in a Turkish translation housed at the Topkapi Palace in Istanbul. See Temimi, "Lettre de la population algéroise au Sultan Selim 1er en 1519."

2. For this denomination, see Currey, *Sea-Wolves of the Mediterranean,* 127; see also Playfair, *Scourge of Christendom.* Much later, Samuel Purchas would describe Algiers as "The Throne of Pyracie, the Sinke of Trade, and the Stinke of Slavery; . . . the Habitation of Sea-Devils, the Receptacle of Renegadoes and Traytors to their Country" (quoted in Chew, *The Crescent and the Rose,* 344).

3. From a political perspective, Sosa's *Topographia* covers the period of the *beylerbey* (governors) in the Turkish-Agerian Regency, which extended from the arrival of Ottoman forces in the early sixteenth century to 1587. However, the *Topography* centers in particular on the time of his captivity in Algiers from 1577 to 1581. His *Epítome de los reyes de Argel* [History of the Kings of Algiers], the second book of the *Topographia,* covers the history of Algiers from the first years of the century to the time of his death in 1587.

4. Dakhlia, "Une ethnographie du mélange," 7; my translation. Since its publication in 1612, Sosa's posthumous work was ascribed to the archbishop of Palermo (Sicily), Diego de Haedo. The reasons for this fraud are explained below.

5. Comparing various Western sources on North Africa in the sixteenth century, French historian Henri-Delmas de Grammont praised the *Epítome de los reyes de Argel* as "the most complete and exact of the documents" on the first seventy years of Algiers under Turkish rule (see De Grammont, preface to *Histoire des rois d'Alger,* 15). Our English translation of this work is forthcoming.

6. Sosa represents here the attitude of sixteenth-century Christians, who generally showed this kind of antipathy and disdain toward Islam. See among others, Chew's magisterial study on Islam and England during the Renaissance, *The Crescent and the Rose,* esp. 387–451; Bunes Ibarra, *La imagen de los musulmanes*; Matar, *Islam in Britain,* 153–67; Merle, *Le mirroir ottoman*; Turbet-Delof, *L'Afrique barbaresque*; and Wheatcroft, *Infidels.*

7. Dakhlia, "Une éthnographie," 7. Dakhlia attributes Sosa's work to Diego de Haedo, believing the latter was a captive in Algiers.

8. On Sosa's capture and captivity in Algiers, see Garcés, *Cervantes in Algiers,* esp. 32–38, 42–46, 70–73, 81–84.

9. Wheatcroft, *Infidels,* 49–51. The author distinguishes Islam and Christianity, which are the faiths that their adherents observe, from "Islam" and "Christianity," which are images constructed by their enemies (ibid., 36).

10. Chejne, *Islam and the West,* 125–27.

11. Wheatcroft, *Infidels,* 81.

12. See the Princeton Dante Project online, which includes the full text of the *Divine Comedy* in Italian, ed. G. Petrocchi, English trans. Hollander and Hollander, http://etcweb.princeton.edu/dante/pdp/.

13. Sosa offers diatribes against the lust and sexual customs of Algerians, especially against the renegades, who forsake Christ, "attracted by pleasure, by the good life of fleshly vice in which the Turks live. . . . addicted since childhood to the wickedness of sodomy imposed on them by their masters" (chapter 13).

14. Bunes Ibarra, *La imagen de los musulmanes,* 118–19.

15. Sosa, *Diálogo tercero. De los morabutos,* in Haedo, *Topografía,* 3:246, 253; hereafter cited as *Diálogo de los morabutos,* in *Topografía,* including volume and page number. Unless otherwise noted, all translations from the Spanish in the introduction are mine.

16. Braudel, *The Mediterranean,* 2:870.

17. See, for example, chapter 24, "On Algerian Merchants." Such passages recall Braudel's explanation of the primacy of Italian cities in the sixteenth century in terms of an economic domination characterized by their opening to the Levant and their conquest of the Mediterranean. See Braudel, *The Mediterranean,* vol. 1.

18. Braudel, *The Wheels of Commerce,* vol. 2 of *Civilization and Capitalism.*

19. See Dakhlia's excellent analysis of the lingua franca of the Mediterranean, which disappeared in the nineteenth century, *Lingua Franca.*

20. In the sixteenth century, the most important center for this traffic in Spain was Valencia, in whose port arrived a minimum of 217 ships com-

ing from Barbary between 1503 and 1600, a data that demonstrates the vitality of the Hispano-Muslim commerce. Cádiz, around 1591, sent some twenty to thirty ships to the Atlantic coast of Morocco. See Corrales, *Comercio de Cataluña,* 51–55.

21. See the fine studies by Mérouche, *Recherches sur l'Algérie à l'époque ottomane I* and *Recherches sur l'Algérie à l'époque ottomane II.* On the economic role of privateering in the Mediterranean, see Fontenay, "La place de la course dans l'économie portuaire."

22. Sosa, *Diálogo primero. De la captividad en Argel,* in Haedo, *Topografía,* 2:88. Hereafter cited as *Diálogo de la captividad,* in *Topografía,* including volume and page number.

23. Braudel, *Civilization,* 3:22.

24. Ibid.; and Corrales, *Comercio de Cataluña,* 51–58.

25. Kagan, "Philip II and the Geographers." I am indebted to Kagan's work for my descriptions of Renaissance cartography and city landscapes in my next paragraphs.

26. Marcus Vitrubius Pollio is the author of *De architectura,* a treatise on architecture, composed in Latin and Greek, which was rediscovered in 1414 by the Florentine humanist Poggio Bracciolini (1380–1459), a collector of classical texts. Known today as *The Ten Books of Architecture,* Vitrubius's work is the only surviving major book on architecture from classical antiquity.

27. See Kagan, *Urban Images of the Hispanic World, 1493–1793,* 1–18.

28. De Certeau, "Walking in the City," 82.

29. Braun and Hogenber, *Civitates orbis terrarum,* ed. Füssel. See also Braun and Hogenberg, *Ciudades de Europa y España,* ed. Goss. The collection has 363 plates, with 564 cities, maps, and coats of arms.

30. Kagan, preface to *Spanish Cities,* 1–13. Van den Wyngaerde produced a series of paintings of Zeeland and the kingdom of England for El Pardo, the hunting lodge constructed by Philip II near Madrid, which included vistas of London, Naples, Madrid, and Valladolid. The artist also painted panoramic views of other European and Spanish cities for the royal palace in Madrid (ibid., 1–2).

31. Iberian preoccupation with city maps and topographic views is also represented by Pedro Texeira (1595–1662), celebrated for his *Topografía de la Villa de Madrid* (1656). Texeira was the author of the major cartographic work begun in seventeenth-century Spain, *La descripción de España y de las costas y puertos de sus reinos* [Description of Spain and of the coasts and seaports of its kingdoms] (1634), an atlas with 116 full color images of Spain and the world.

32. See, for instance, the city maps of the Urbino Codex, in Miller, *Mapping the City*, 27 ff.

33. Miller, *Mapping the City*, 5.

34. Febvre and Martin, *L'Apparition du livre*, trans. Girard, *The Coming of the Book: The Impact of Printing, 1450–1800*; and Anderson, *Imagined Communities*.

35. García Martín, "Revolución en el 'arte' de los mapas," 97.

36. I am paraphrasing Miller's introduction to her fine study, *Mapping the City*, 1.

37. García Martín, "Revolución en el 'arte' de los mapas," 97.

38. Harley and Woodward, *The History of Cartography*, 1:506, 285.

39. Brotton, *Trading Territories*, 91.

40. See Hills, "Mapping the Early Modern City"; and Wood, *The Power of Maps*.

41. Harley and Woodward, *The History of Cartography*, 1:57.

42. Padrón, *The Spacious World*, 8.

43. Recall the surge of humanistic interest in the Renaissance for Roman topography, especially through the precise identification of ruins and historical sites of ancient Rome. Bernardo Rucellai's *De urbe Roma* and Francesco Albertini's *Opusculum de mirabilibus Novae et veteris urbis Romae* (1506–1509), as well as the drawings of the ancient city by Andrea Palladio (1508–1580) and Étienne Du Pérac (ca. 1525–1604), among others, are examples of the concern for the recuperation of the physical features of classical Rome. See Richardson, *A New Topographical Dictionary of Ancient Rome*.

44. Kagan, "Philip II and the Geographers," 42.

45. Apianus (Apian), *Cosmographia*, chap. 4, cited by Kagan, "Philip II and the Geographers," 42.

46. See Merle, *Le miroir ottoman*, 98–100; see also José Vives Gatell's analysis of Pero Tafur's narrative, in "Andanças e viajes de un hidalgo español (Pero Tafur, 1436–1439)," 123–215.

47. Merle, *Le miroir ottoman*, 98. Octavio Sapiencia, who depicted Constantinople in his *Nuevo tratado de Turquía* (1622), follows the model of urban description considered above, although in later chapters he expands his views of the Ottoman metropolis. See Sapiencia, *Nuevo tratado de Turquía*, chap. 2, "De la ciudad de Constantinopla, de todas las naciones que contratan en ella, de su canal, fortalezas, islas y ciudades que tienen escaleras en él, y de otras circunstancias."

48. De Certeau, "Walking in the City," 97.

49. Ibid., 151.

50. Ibid., 92.

51. Sosa, *Diálogo de los mártires de Argel,* 190; also included in Haedo, *Topografía,* 3:176.

52. Cervantes, *Don Quijote,* trans. Raffel, ed. de Armas Wilson, 271–72.

53. Lochman, *Contending Visions of the Middle East,* 2. See also Tolan, *Saracens.*

54. Lochman, *Contending Visions of the Middle East,* 2.

55. See among other events, the October and November 2005 civil unrest in France (Les émeutes de banlieues de 2005), a series of riots involving the burning of cars and public buildings, which started in Clichy-sous-Bois and spread to poor housing projects in various parts of the country. Increased civil unrest reappeared in the banlieues in 2007; see Daniel Strieff's article on these last riots, "Forging a Voice in 'France's High-Rise Hell.'"

56. García-Arenal, "Últimos estudios sobre los moriscos." See also the classic study by Cardaillac, *Moriscos et chrétiens,* as well as his edited volume, *Les Morisques et leur temps.*

57. García-Arenal, *Los moriscos*; and *La diáspora de los andalusíes*; with G. Wiegers, *A Man of Three Worlds*; as well as her article, "El entorno de los plomos: historiografía y linaje."

58. For studies coming out of Tunisia, see, among others, the works of Temimi listed in the bibliography.

59. See Zhiri, *Les sillages de Jean Léon Africain*; and the recent study by Pouillon et al., eds., *Léon l'Africain.*

60. For an excellent study on these crossings and coexistence in the early modern Mediterranean, see Dursteller, *Venetians in Constantinople.*

61. Clifford and Marcus, *Writing Culture.*

62. See Bourdieu, *Algeria 1960*; Abu-Lughod, *Veiled Sentiments,* and, by the same author, *Writing Women's Worlds.*

63. I thank Vincent Barletta for his early comments and input on this paragraph.

64. Morgan's *Complete History of Algiers* was reprinted in 1731 and translated into Dutch in 1733. The author's debt to Haedo (*sic,* Sosa) is both constantly reiterated and disclaimed throughout his work: "Haedo, my Author (from whom I pick and chuse just what I like, rejecting much Cant, Rubbish, and tedious Tautology)" (*Complete History of Algiers,* 2:247).

65. The French translation of Sosa's first book, the *Topography* proper, first appeared as "Topographie et histoire générale d'Alger," in 1870 and 1871 in the serial *Revue Africaine* (see Haedo, "Topographie et histoire générale

d'Alger," trans. Monnereau and Berbrugger, *Revue Africaine* 14 [1870] and *Revue Africaine* 15 [1871]). The French translation of his second book, *Epítome de los Reyes de Argel*, appeared as *Histoire des rois d'Alger* in 1881 (see Haedo, *Histoire des rois d'Alger*, trans. De Grammont). Both books have been reprinted respectively as Haedo, *Topographie et histoire générale d'Alger* (1998), and Haedo, *Histoire des rois d'Alger* (1998).

66. Haedo, *Topographia, e historia general de Argel, repartida en cinco tratados do se verán casos extraños, muertes espantosas y tormentos exquisitos*... (Valladolid, por Diego Fernández de Córdova y Oviedo, a costa de Antonio Coello, 1612).

67. Haedo, *Topografía e historia general de Argel*, ed. Bauer y Landauer, 3 vols. (1927–1929); cited here as *Topografía* with volume and page numbers.

68. Barbary was the name given by Europeans to the North African region that extends from present-day Morocco to Libya, a region that now encompasses the four countries of Morocco, Algeria, Tunisia, and Libya.

69. Sosa, *Diálogo de los mártires de Argel*, ed. Sola and Parreño (1990). This fascinating dialogue on Christian martyrology still awaits a critical edition.

70. Eneas Silvius to Nicholas V, in Piccolomini [Pope Pius II], *Briefwechsel*, 3:200; Eneas Silvius to Nicolas of Cusa, in ibid., 3:209; the same words were repeated in a speech at the Diet of Regensburg, in ibid., 3:540 (cited by Meserve, *Empires of Islam*, 65, 96, 282). For the repetition of these stories by later Western authors, see Smith, "Pope Pius II's Use of Turkish Atrocities," 407–15.

71. Piccolomini, *Der Briefwechsel*, 3:542.

72. Meserve, *Empires of Islam*, 65.

73. Braudel, *En torno al mediterráneo*, 49.

74. On the Iberian campaigns in North Africa, see Braudel, *En torno al mediterráneo*; Hess, *The Forgotten Frontier*, 26–43; and Wolf, *The Barbary Coast*.

75. The text of the 1494 Latin papal bull, with its Spanish translation, appears in the appendix to Dousinague, *La política internacional*, 521–24.

76. Dousinague, *La política internacional*, 128–38, 154–67, 184–229, 344–71; see also Dousinague, *Testamentaria de Isabel la Católica*, 445–75. On Isabella's testament on Hispano-Moroccan relations, see Hakim, "El testamento de Isabella la Católica," 27–35.

77. Bernáldez, *Memorias del reinado de los Reyes Católicos*, 490–94.

78. Garcés, *Cervantes in Algiers*, 31.

79. Bunes Ibarra, "El orientalismo," 37–53, an essay to which I am indebted in the following pages. See also by Bunes Ibarra, *La imagen de los musulmanes*.

80. Bunes Ibarra, "El orientalismo," 37–38.

81. Dakhlia, *L'empire des passions,* 189.

82. See, among other works, Vitkus, *Turning Turk.* For the view of the North African peoples in French literature, see Turbet-Delof, *L'Afrique barbaresque dans la littérature française*; for Spain, see García-Arenal, "Spanish Literature." On the relations between Spain and North Africa, see the collection edited by García-Arenal and Aguilar, *Repertorio bibliográfico.*

83. Cervantes's Barbary plays include: *El trato de Argel* [Life in Algiers]; *Los baños de Argel* [*The Bagnios of Algiers*]; *El gallardo español* [The Gallant Spaniard]; and *La gran Sultana* [*The Great Sultana*], although this drama is actually set in Constantinople. For a didactic approach, see Garcés, "Staging Captivity." Two of the plays have been recently translated into English. See *The Bagnios of Algiers; and, The Great Sultana: Two Plays of Captivity,* trans. Fuchs and Ilika.

84. Fuchs, *Exotic Nation.*

85. Bunes Ibarra, "El orientalismo," 41–42.

86. Morales, *Diálogo de las guerras de Orán,* fols. 257–58.

87. See Valensi, *Birth of the Despot,* on images of oriental despotism. For the representation of the Islamic "other," especially in England, see Chew's classic work, *The Crescent and the Rose,* esp. 100–149; and Watt, *Muslim-Christian Encounters.* Vitkus provides a good synthesis of the Western demonization of the Turks in his introduction to *Three Turk Plays from Early Modern England,* 1–53. His recent study *Turning Turk* departs from these views.

88. Busbecq, "First Letter," Vienna, 1 September 1555, in *Turkish Letters,* 59–60.

89. The scope of this study does not permit me to discuss some of the important works produced by Portuguese travelers and captives. Worth noting, among others, is the treatise of the humanist Damião de Góis (1502–1574) on Prester John and Ethiopian religion and culture: *Fides, religio, moresque Aethiopum* (1540); as well as António de Saldanha's *Crónica de Almançor, Sultão de Marrocos (1578–1603),* a chronicle of Sultan Moulay Ahmed Al-Mansour, who acceded to the Moroccan throne in 1578 after the Battle of the Three Kings.

90. See Leo Africanus, *The History and Description of Africa.* On Leo Africanus, see Davis's biography, *Trickster Travels*; Zhiri, "Leo Africanus, Translated and Betrayed," and, by the same author, *Les sillages de Jean Léon l'Africain*; as well as the recent collection edited by Pouillon et al., *Léon l'Africain.*

91. Sosa, *Diálogo de los morabutos,* in *Topografía,* 3:201.

92. On the Morisco émigrés and their culture, see Luce López-Baralt's fundamental study, *La literatura secreta de los últimos musulmanes de España.* Like

Sosa's Morisco friend, who loaned him a copy of Leo Africanus, a Morisco exile in Tunis, a prolific writer who recited sonnets of Lope, Quevedo, and Góngora, is studied by López-Baralt; see *La literatura secreta,* 463–95.

93. Ibn Rashiq (d. 1064) practiced literary criticism and was well known for his work concerning poets and poetry.

94. On Mármol Carvajal's discourse, centered on the commercial interests of the Spanish colonizers, see Martínez-Góngora's recent study, "El discurso africanista del Renacimiento."

95. García-Arenal, "Spanish Literature," 65.

96. Torres, *Relación,* chaps. 49–53. For a summary of Mármol Carvajal and Diego de Torres, see García-Arenal, "Spanish Literature," 53–59.

97. García-Arenal, "Spanish Literature," 53–54.

98. Ibid., 55; and Guernier, *Le destin de l'Afrique du Nord.*

99. Torres, *Relación,* 36.

100. Possibly this was part of a spy's report, written by Sosa for the Spanish Crown. Upon his return to Spain, Sosa stated that he had sent various reports from Algiers. In Sosa's letter to Philip II, dated 26 August 1582, the former captive claims that, during his Algerian captivity, he sometimes wrote to the king, "notifying and describing events there because I understood this was in the service of your Majesty" (BL, Add 28342, fols. 8–11).

101. Morales, Approval, in Carvajal, *Descripción general de África.*

102. See Hess, *The Forgotten Frontier.*

103. García-Arenal, "Spanish Literature," 58. Several Moroccan travelers described their trips to Spain, such as Al-Gazzal, who recounted his embassy to Charles II in 1766, and Muhammad ibn Utman al Miknasi, among others. See Pérès, *L'Espagne vue par les voyageurs musulmans,* cited by García-Arenal, "Spanish Literature," 58–59; see also Matar, *Europe through Arab Eyes,* especially the letter written by Mulay Isma'il to Philip V, in 1717, complaining of the actions of the Cadiz Inquisition against a Jew, an envoy of Mulay Isma'il.

104. Garcés, *Cervantes in Algiers,* chap. 2.

105. Astrana Marín offers a detailed account of these eighteenth-century discoveries in *Vida ejemplar y heroica de Miguel de Cervantes Saavedra,* 1:217–23.

106. An Información was a legal document or notarized affidavit that was presented by a former captive who returned from captivity in Barbary. The term also referred to a legal or juridical inquiry regarding an event, crime or offense.

107. See Cervantes, *Información de Argel,* 47–170.

108. Ibid., 156.

109. Ibid., 162–63.

110. See Gonzalo Sánchez-Molero's article, "La '*Epístola a Mateo Vázquez*,' redescubierta y reivindicada," and his recent erudite study, *La epístola a Mateo Vazquez: historia de una polémica literaria en torno a Cervantes*.

111. See Sosa's testimony in Cervantes, *Información de Argel*, 157.

112. Ibid., 155.

113. Ibid., 166; and Garcés, *Cervantes in Algiers*, 68.

114. Cervantes, *Información de Argel*, 166.

115. Pilot Pedro Griego, and some of the sailors who escaped by jumping overboard, testified that the corsairs fell upon the ship with such speed that she was immediately conquered (AGS, Estado, Leg. 1073, doc. 82–83). Galley slave Domingo Sponto, who broke away from the Algerian galliots at the moment of the attack, provides additional information on this capture (AGS, Guerra Antigua, Leg. 83, doc. 84).

116. Among other Knights of Malta, Fra Antonio de Toledo and Fra Francisco de Valencia were imprisoned with Cervantes in Hasan's *bagnio* (slave prison). Cervantes mentions them in *El trato de Argel*. On the capture of the *San Pablo*, see Dal Pozzo, *Historia della sacra religione*, 1:130. The loss of the *San Pablo* is registered in the Liber conciliorum Magni Magistri Johannis Levesque de la Cassière, Annorum 1574–77, fols. 4r.–5v, Arch. 95–96, in Mizzi, ed., *Catalogue of the Order of St. John of Jerusalem in the Royal Malta Library*, 2:677–770.

117. Sosa, *Epítome de los reyes de Argel*, in *Topografía*, 1:370, 374.

118. Garcés, *Cervantes in Algiers*, 73–77.

119. *Ka'id* (T) or *qa'id* (A): a term generally used to designate a military leader ranging from captain to general, although it also meant a tribal chieftain. In Algiers, the title was given to the governors of districts or towns subject to the Turkish government. Their obligations were fiscal, judicial, and military.

120. Sosa, *Diálogo de la captividad*, in *Topografía*, 2:3–4; and Garcés, *Cervantes in Algiers*, 74.

121. Sosa, *Diálogo de la captividad*, in *Topografía*, 2:1–4, 85.

122. Ibid., 2:5.

123. Mármol Carvajal, *Descripción general de África*, vol. 2, fol. 91.

124. Leo Africanus, *History and Description of Africa*, pt. 3, "On Fez, the New." On the Jews in Morocco, see the collection edited by García-Arenal, *Entre el islam y occidente*; and García-Arenal and Wiegers, *A Man of Three Worlds*.

125. On these conversions, see the collective work edited by García-Arenal, *Conversions islamiques*; Rostaggno, *Mi faccio turco*; and Scaraffia, *Rinnegati*.

On the roles of the converts to Islam in Cervantes, see Garcés, "'Grande amigo mío': Cervantes y los renegados."

126. Sosa, *Epítome de los reyes de Argel*, in *Topografía*, 1:377.

127. Garcés, *Cervantes in Algiers*, 75.

128. Sosa, *Diálogo de la captividad*, in *Topografía*, 2: 3–4. The *span* was a unit of length based on the width of the expanded human hand, usually estimated as nine inches. Sosa's count, then, would give us a measure for the dungeon of about 15 feet deep, by 6 1/2 feet wide, by 8 feet long.

129. Sosa, *Diálogo de los morabutos*, in *Topografía*, 3:213.

130. Sosa, *Diálogo de la captividad*, in *Topografía*, 2:103, 176.

131. Ibid., 2:124.

132. Ibid., 2:140; see also Garcés, *Cervantes in Algiers*, 76.

133. Whitehead, introduction to *Hans Staden's True History*, lxxxix. See also Hulme and Youngs, *Cambridge Companion to Travel Writing*.

134. Whitehead, introduction to *Hans Staden's True History*, lxxxix.

135. Sosa, *Diálogo de los morabutos*, in *Topografía*, 3:260.

136. Ibid., 3:210.

137. *Kapi* (T): "gate" and, by extension, "Ottoman Porte," or the sultan's palace; a term also used for the grand vizier's palace and the seat of government. The word similarly designates military or civil functions directly subordinate to the Porte, e.g., *kapi kullari*, literally "slaves of the Porte," that is, the sultan's troops. *Bayt* (A): dwelling, whether the "tent" of the nomads or the "house" of sedentary peoples. In Arabic, the term refers to a dwelling of medium dimension, perhaps suitable for one family.

138. Shuval, "Remettre l'Algérie à l'heure ottomane," 5. On the kapi, see also Shuval, "Households in Ottoman Algeria"; and "The Ottoman Algerian Elite and its Ideology"; Kunt, *The Sultan's Servants,* 95; Findley, *Bureaucratic Reform in the Ottoman Empire*, 32; and Hathaway, *The Politics of Households in Ottoman Egypt*, 18. On the sultan's kapi, see Peirce, *The Imperial Harem*.

139. Shuval, "Remettre l'Algérie à l'heure ottomane," 5.

140. Ibid., 5.

141. Sosa, *Epítome de los reyes de Argel*, 361; see also Bennassar and Bennassar, *Los cristianos de Alá,* 418. Cervantes adds that 'Uludj 'Ali—"a good man, who treated his slaves most humanely"—had three thousand slaves, and when he died, his will provided that the slaves be divided between the Grand Turk and the renegades who had been in his service (*DQ* I, 40).

142. Sosa, *Diálogo de los morabutos,* in *Topografía*, 3:234, 243–49.

143. Garcés, *Cervantes in Algiers,* 81–82.

144. Ibid., 45–49.
145. Whitehead, introduction to *Staden's True History*, cxxxvi; Clifford and Marcus, *Writing Culture*; Clifford, *The Predicaments of Culture*; Geertz, *The Interpretation of Cultures*; and Marcus, *Rereading Cultural Anthropology*.
146. Whitehead, introduction to *Hans Staden's True History*, lxxxix.
147. On Paulinus of Nola, see Brown, *Augustine of Hippo*, 152–53, 160–63.
148. Sosa, *Diálogo de los mártires de Argel*, ed. Sola and Parreño, 65.
149. Ibid., 55.
150. Ibid., 59.
151. Ibid., 71.
152. On Haedo's participation as prosecutor in Fray Luis de León's trial, see Alcalá, *Proceso inquisitorial de Fray Luis de León*, esp. 72–74, 97–99. Haedo's accusations against Fray Luis de León include the following: a) that he had affirmed that the Sacred Scriptures in the Vulgate edition had many errors; b) that the Gospel could be interpreted according to the exegesis of the Jews and rabbis; c) that Fray Luis had claimed that the Songs of Solomon were *carmen amatorium ad suam uxorem* [love songs for the proper spouse], and that he had translated them into Castilian.
153. Diego de Haedo's appointment as Inquisitor in Valencia and, later, Zaragoza, appear in AHN, Inq., Lib. 356, fol. 170r; and AHN, Inq., Lib. 357, fols. 32v–33r.
154. The bibliography on the Spanish Inquisition in Sicily is staggering. See Lea, *The Inquisition in the Spanish Dependencies*, esp. 1–44; Koenisberger, *The Government of Sicily under Philip II of Spain*; Garufi, *Fatti e personaggi dell' Inquisizione in Sicilia*; Monter, *Frontiers of Heresy*; Rivero Rodríguez, "La Inquisición española en Sicilia," and by the same author, "Corte y 'Poderes Provinciales'"; Sciuti Russi, "Inquisición, política y justicia en la Sicilia de Felipe II," as well as "La Inquisición española en Sicilia." On the political and administrative reforms advanced by Philip II in Sicily, see Sciuti Russi, *Astrea in Sicilia*.
155. Sciuti Russi, *Astrea in Sicilia*, 140.
156. Lea, *The Inquisition in the Spanish Dependencies*, 209.
157. Garufi, *Fatti e personaggi*, 228.
158. Sciuti Russi, *Astrea in Sicilia*, 142.
159. Ibid., 143.
160. Rivero Rodríguez, "Corte y 'Poderes Provinciales,'" 74–75. On Philip II and power elites, see Bouza Álvarez and Martínez Millán et al., *La corte de Felipe II*.

161. Elias, *La sociedad cortesana*, 9–10.

162. Rivero Rodríguez, "Corte y 'Poderes Provinciales,'" 74.

163. Di Castro, *Avvertimenti a Marco Antonio Colonna*, 7.

164. Rivero Rodríguez, "Corte y 'Poderes Provinciales,'" 98.

165. See "Encartamento de todo lo que ha pasado entre Marco Antonio Colonna y los Inquisidores Don Fco. de Rojas y licenciado Aedo sobre la executoria de sus provisiones desde el día que vinieron (21 de octubre 1577) hasta el 17 de noviembre de 1577." AGS, Estado, Leg. 1148, fol. 9.

166. On Colonna's life and times, see Bazzano's lucid biography, *Marco Antonio Colonna*.

167. Koenigsberger, *La práctica del imperio*, 188–89.

168. A detailed letter written by Cardinal Granvelle, president of the Council of Castile, in regard to Colonna's death as he was approaching the count of Medinacelli's estate in Andalusía, claims that this death was due to a fall from his carriage, which occurred as they climbed the very difficult terrain that led to the count's palace. According to Granvelle, Colonna was hit on the head and died a week later. Letter from Cardinal Granvelle to Judge Gregorio Bravo, Madrid, 9 August 1584, AGS, Estado Sicilia, Leg. 1155, fol. 265.

169. "The king to Olivares" and "The king to the Pope," October 20, 1584, requesting Haedo's appointment to the bishopric of Agrigento (AGS, SP, Lib. 639, fols. 77r–v and 78r.) Haedo took possession of the bishopric of Agrigento on 24 February 1585 and was consecrated bishop on 31 March 1585, in Palermo. See Pirri, *Sicilia Sacra*, Agrigentinae Ecclesie Notitia III, Lib. III, fol. 764. See also "Haedo to the Council of the Inquisition," 4 April 1585, AHN, Inq., Lib. 879, fol. 217r.

170. Denis, "Haedo," 50–51. De Grammont, *Histoire d'Alger sous las domination turque (1515–1830)* (1887), owes much to the *Epítome de los reyes de Argel*.

171. Pérez Pastor, *Documentos cervantinos*, 1:235, n. 1.

172. Astrana Marín, *Vida ejemplar y heroica de Miguel de Cervantes*, 2:468.

173. Camamis, *Estudios sobre el cautiverio en el Siglo de Oro*, esp. 132–34, 140–43.

174. On Antonio de Sosa, see Sola, "Antonio de Sosa: un clásico inédito amigo de Cervantes"; and by the same author, "Miguel de Cervantes, Antonio de Sosa y África"; see also the editors' forewords in Sosa, *Diálogo de los mártires de Argel*, by Parreño and Sola (9–23, 26–52); as well as Sola and de la Peña, *Cervantes y la Berbería*, 277–91; and Garcés, *Cervantes in Algiers*, 32–37, 43–49, 70–89, 97–99, 148–51 and passim.

175. Garcés, *Cervantes in Algiers,* 71–72.

176. For instance, an Augustinian friar, named Antonio de Sosa, was one of the accusers of Fray Luis de León in his Inquisition trial. On the Portuguese front, see, among others: Fra Antonio de Sousa (?—d. 1597), a Dominican friar and bishop of Bizeu, who was the son of the famous governor of India, Martin Affonso de Sousa; Fra Antonio de Sousa, a nephew of the former Dominican and a writer, who was ambassador to Spain (d. 1652); Don António de Sousa (d. 1631), son of Luís de Sousa and grandson of Don Francisco de Sousa, first Marquis of Minas. This Antonio de Sousa served in the Portuguese armadas and later in Brazil; António de Sousa Coutinho (sixteenth century to 1668), a military and Colonial Portuguese administrator, who was the last governor of Ceilão (actual Sri Lanka); António de Sousa de Macedo, third Baron of Mullingar (1606–1682), a Portuguese writer and journalist, who studied law at Coimbra and had a brilliant political career. He was the author of *Flores de España, Excelências de Portugal* (1631) and other works in Latin, Spanish, and Portuguese. See Pereira and Rodrigues, *Portugal; diccionario historico,* vol. 6, as well as Sousa, *História genealógica da casa real portuguesa.*

177. "Papal Bull by Gregory XIII for Doctor Antonio de Sosa," AMAE, Embajada de España ante la Santa Sede, Leg. 35, fols. 133–35.

178. Sciuti Russi, *Astrea in Sicilia,* 104.

179. Cervantes, *Información de Argel,* 166.

180. See his nomination as bishop of Siracusa by Philip II in AGS, SP, Lib. 842, fol. 77r–v.

181. In September 1562, Orozco de Arce wrote the Grand Inquisitor, Fernando de Valdés, thanking him for his nomination as bishop of Siracusa, yet complaining that the Church was old and had poor revenues ("The Licenciado Juan Horozco de Arze to Don Fernando de Valdés," Palermo, 23 September 1562, AHN, Inq., Lib. 274C, fol. 279r). Orozco de Arce took possession of the bishopric of Siracusa on 24 December 1562. He appointed as vicar, among others, "Dr. Antonio Sosa, lusitano" (Pirri, *Sicilia Sacra,* Syracusanae Ecclesie Notitia II, Lib. III, XC, fol. 641). The Abbot Rocco Pirri (1577–1651) is considered the father of ecclesiastical history in Sicily. His monumental work, *Sicilia Sacra,* is the most complete source of information for the history of the Sicilian churches since medieval times.

182. Sosa claims in various letters to the king that he was vicar general of the bishoprics of Siracusa and Catania for many years; this is corroborated by Pope Gregory XIII in the papal bull addressed to Sosa on 11 November 1583. Pirri confirms that Bishop Orozco de Arce appointed Doctor

Sosa as vicar in Siracusa (1563) (Pirri, *Sicilia Sacra,* Syracusanae Ecclesie Notitia II, Lib. III, XC, fol. 641); see note 169 above.

183. Orozco de Arce was forty-seven years old when he died; he was interred in the cathedral of Catania. See Pirri, *Sicilia Sacra,* Cataniensis Ecclesie Notitia I, Lib. III, LXI, fol. 514.

184. "De la persona y letras de A. de Sosa se tiene muy buena relación y pues el decanato se puede dar esta vez al extranjero o por alternativa, parece que estará bien proveído en él," Consultation of the Council of Italy, AGS, SP, Leg. 2, fol. 69. Italics mine.

185. In a memo addressed to the court, the Sicilian Duke of Terranova, president of Sicily, insists that the law should include vacancies that occurred by death of the incumbent, as well as by promotions or resignations. The Council of Italy cagily responds that his Majesty will do what is in the best interest of the kingdom. 11 August 1572, AHN, Estado, Leg. 2267.

186. "El Dr. Sosa Teólogo," AGS, Cámara de Castilla, Leg. 404–90, año 1571.

187. AGS, Cámara de Castilla, Leg. 404–90, without a specific date (ca. 1571).

188. Memo of the Council of Italy, dated 28 October 1576, regarding Philip II's nomination of Doctor Sosa to the deanship of the cathedral of Agrigento and specifying that this nomination had been sent to the pope. AGS, SP, Lib. 639, fol. 81v.

189. "El rey al Duque de Terranova acerca del pago de dineros del decanato de Agrigento" [The king to the Duke of Terranova, regarding the payment of moneys from the deanship of Agrigento], 24 December 1576, AGS, SP, Lib. 845, fol. 1.

190. Consultation of the Council of Italy, "El Doctor A. de Sosa, cautivo," AGS, SP, Leg. 3.

191. "The king to Colonna," 8 September 1577, AGS, SP, Lib. 845, fols. 73v–74r.

192. "The king to Colonna," 2 November 1577, AGS, SP, Lib. 845, fols. 91v–94r.

193. "The king to Colonna," 20 December 1577, AGS, SP, Lib. 845, fols. 101v–103r.

194. ADA, Reg. 1578/79, fol. 392v; Reg. 1578/79, fols. 396r–396v, 399r.

195. Consultation of the Council of Italy, 12 March 1580, AGS, SP, Leg. 982.

196. "The king to Colonna," 29 November 1580, AGS, SP, Lib. 846, fol. 83r.

197. "Zuñiga to the king," Naples, 9 June 1581, AGS, Estado, Leg. 1084.

198. "Relatione delle cose seguite in Algieri dalli nueve juglio sino a questo giorno [25 de agosto]." This is a thirteen-page spy's report on Algerian news. Both Sosa and Captain Juan de Bolaños, a former captive in Algiers and a friend of Cervantes, sent the report to Mateo Vázquez, together with a handwritten noted jointly signed by them. IVDJ, Envío 62, Caja 2, fols. 25 and 26.

199. 11 September 1581, AGS, Cámara de Castilla, Leg. 510, fol. 26.

200. "The king to Olivares," AMAE, Embajada de España ante la Santa Sede, Leg. 35, paq. 4, fol. 125.

201. Pérez Pastor, *Documentos cervantinos,* 1:235–37.

202. Ibid.

203. BL, Add 28342, fols. 8–11.

204. It has been impossible to determine the exact place of Sosa's studies in Castile. From various documents we know that he was a Doctor in Theology as well as in Canon and Civil law. The references to a certain Antonio de Sosa (or Sousa) who obtained his law degree from the University of Salamanca in 1535 seems to refer to another person, since Sosa was described in 1583 by a secretary to the viceroy of Naples as being around forty-five years of age. AMAE, Embajada de España ante la Santa Sede, Leg. 35.

205. See Ezquerra Revilla, "El ascenso de los letrados eclesiásticos"; and "La visita de Antonio de Pazos al Tribunal de la Inquisición de Sicilia (1574–1577)."

206. AMAE, Madrid, Embajada de España ante la Santa Sede, Leg. 35, paq. 4, fol. 125.

207. "Pleito criminal ante la audiencia arzobispal de Madrid, contra el Doctor Sosa" [Criminal trial before the archi-episcopal audience in Madrid against Doctor Sosa], AMAE, Embajada de España ante la Santa Sede, Leg. 35, paq. 4, fol. 143.

208. "Don Sylvestro Mauroli," 13 August 1593, AGS, SP, Lib. 1043, fols. 128v–130r.

209. Various hysterical letters from Mauroli, written from Genoa in 1583 and 1584, inform ambassador Olivares that Sosa lives with a concubine; that the pope does not want to appoint Mauroli to the deanship; and that he has not been received at the Vatican, while Sosa meets with cardinals and dignitaries. He also states that he is buying books for Philip II's library

at the Escorial. AMAE, Embajada de España ante la Santa Sede, Leg. 35, fols. 126–126A, 129–129A, 130–130A, 131–131A.

210. "Antonii de Sousa supplicato sup modo iudauci religiones catholica et cap infideles . . . ," ASV, Misc. Arm. V, Cap. 4, n. 68. I have translated this important document, which, unfortunately, I cannot include in this introduction due to its length.

211. Various declarations in Portuguese, from several witnesses, refer to the request for this safe conduct (8 November 1583). AMAE, Embajada de España ante la Santa Sede, Leg. 35, paq. 4, fol. 144.

212. AMAE, Embajada de España ante la Santa Sede, Leg. 35, paq. 4, fols. 133–35.

213. "Papal Brief from Gregory XIII," AMAE, Embajada de España ante la Santa Sede, Leg. 35, paq. 4, fols. 133–35.

214. On these confrontations regarding ecclesiastical jurisdictions and Spain and its territories, see Hinojosa, *Los despachos de la diplomacia pontificia*; and Bouza Alvarez and Martínez Millán et al., *La corte de Felipe II*. Sosa's case represented a tiny victory for the pope.

215. Rivero Rodríguez, "De todo di aviso a vuestra señoria," 284.

216. "The king to Olivares," AMAE, Embajada de España ante la Santa Sede, Leg. 35, paq. 4, fol. 125.

217. Cabrera de Córdoba, *Historia de Felipe II, rey de España*, 2:831.

218. Ibid., 2:831.

219. Ibid., 2:830–31.

220. Philip II to the Marquis of Briático, President of the Kingdom of Sicily, 25 April 1585, AGS, SP, Lib. 850, fols. 93v. and 94r.

221. ADA, Reg. 1578/79, fol. 399r.

222. AGS, SP, Lib. 850, fols. 93v–94 r.

223. A letter from Haedo to the Grand Inquisitor, dated 4 April 1585, confirms that he took possession of his bishopric in Agrigento on 24 February and that he was consecrated on the last Sunday of March of that year. He affirms he plans to leave for Agrigento on 8 April, where he will strive with all his forces to do his job right. AHN, Inq., Lib. 879, año 1582–87, fol. 217.

224. ADA, Reg. 1584/1585, fols. 424v–425r. The *Atti Capitolari* [Minutes of the Chapter], at the Archivio Capitolari of the cathedral of Agrigento begin with volume 1 (1580–1619), but the first ten pages are blank; the documents for the years 1580 to 1587 are sparse. Volume 1 seems to have been put together in 1590, according to its opening words: "In nomine Domine. Amen. Die decimo aprile 1590." See Gregorio, *La chiesa agrigentina*.

225. ADA, Reg. 1584/85, fols. 319r–320r.

226. We presume that the archbishop's palace in Agrigento had a good library, with classical authors, one that Sosa could consult at his leisure. The Biblioteca Lucchesiana, donated to Agrigento in 1765 by Bishop Andrea Lucchese Palli, probably absorbed many of the books originally housed at the archbishop's palace in Agrigento. Today it is one of the richest libraries in Italy, which holds precious manuscripts in Greek and Latin, as well as many incunabula with miniatures and Arabic codices in parchment.

227. On the dialogue form in Quattrocento Italy, especially in the work of Lorenzo Valla, see Kelly, *Modern Historical Scholarship,* 40–46. For Spain, see Murillo, "Diálogo y dialéctica en el siglo XVI español." Myers offers a fine discussion on Fernández de Oviedo's use of dialogue, in *Fernández de Oviedo's Chronicle of America,* 99–101.

228. Grafton, *New World, Ancient Texts,* 18–19.

229. I have counted around one hundred Greco-Roman and Church authors and humanists across Sosa's multivolume work, many of whom are cited in his *Diálogo de la captividad.*

230. Pinto Crespo, *Inquisisión y control ideológico,* 29.

231. Ibid., 89.

232. La Mantia, "Origine e vicende dell'Inquizitione in Sicilia," 538.

233. For Antonio de Sosa's death, see Pirri, *Sicilia Sacra,* Agrigentinae Ecclesie Notitia III, Lib. III, fol. 772. Pirri states that Sosa left as mortal remains eight *onzas* (ounces). Unfortunately, I have not been able to obtain any other data on Doctor Sosa's death. The obituary list of bishops and dignitaries at the cathedral of Agrigento only starts in the 1600s.

234. Pirri, *Sicilia Sacra,* Agrigentinae Ecclesie Notitia III, Lib. III, fol. 764.

235. Another of Haedo's nephews, Fernando de Matienzo y Haedo, also accompanied his uncle during his tenure as bishop of Agrigento. Matienzo was later named Inquisitor in Palermo. He was nominated to the deanship of the cathedral by Philip III, while his uncle Haedo was archbishop of Palermo, and appointed dean by Pope Clement III on 5 August 1605. According to Pirri, Matienzo died in Palermo, "full of riches," in 1613 (*Sicilia Sacra,* fol. 771). Yet Bishop Haedo seems to have brought with him other members of his family, such as his niece Portia de Haedo, whose nuptial capitulations are housed at Archivio di Stato di Agrigento, among the countless business documents signed by Haedo.

236. Diego Galán affirms that he traveled with Fra Diego de Haedo from Trapani to Valencia in June 1600, arriving in the midst of the festivities

for Philip III's marriage. This date is erroneous, since the marriage of Phillip III with Margaret of Austria took place in 1599, so they must have sailed to Spain in that year; see Galán, *Relación*, 157–66. On the "recreational courts" and theatrical pageants staged for the king and his retinue, see Ferrer Valls, *La práctica escénica cortesana*, 1991.

237. Fra Diego de Haedo took the habit in the Monastery of San Benito el Real of Valladolid on 25 July 1577. See Pérez de Urbel, *Varones Insignes de la Congregación de Valladolid*, 137–38; and Zaragoza Pascual, "Abadologio del Monasterio de Nuestra Señora de la Misericordia de Frómista (1437–1835)," 135–58.

238. Cervantes, *Viaje del Parnaso*, chap. 1, p. 69.

239. García Santo-Tomás, *Espacio urbano*, 85; and Calderón, *Antes que todo es mi dama*, cited by García Santo-Tomás, *Espacio urbano*, 85.

240. Garcés, *Cervantes en Argel*, 400–402.

241. See Canavaggio, *Cervantes*, 191–220.

242. The *Topographia* was published by Diego Fernández de Córdova (active 1611–1614), a printer and brother of Francisco Fernández de Córdova (active in Valladolid, 1600–1621), who published a posthumous edition of Cervantes's *Galatea*. See Delgado Casado, *Diccionario de impresores españoles*, 1:219–31.

243. Cervantes, *La Galatea*, Valladolid: por Francisco Fernández de Cordoua, a costa de Geronymo Martinez . . . , 1617. I thank my student Pablo García-Piñar for pointing this out to me.

244. On Haedo, see Koenigsberger, *The Government of Sicily under Philip II of Spain*, esp. 167–69; reedited as *The Practice of Empire*; Spanish edition, *La práctica del imperio*. See also Garufi, *Fatti e personaggi*; and Sciuti Russi, *Astrea in Siclia*.

245. See Pirri, *Sicilia Sacra*, fols. 763–64; and Veneziano, "Arco per l'entrata dell' Illmo, e Revmo Monsignor D. Diego Aedo, Arcivescovo di Palermo," 191–97.

246. Lo Piccolo, *Diari Palermitani inediti (1557–1760)*, 41.

Preliminary Materials

1. *Maravedís* (Sp): the smallest coin or monetary unit in the Spanish monetary system; a gold *escudo* was worth four hundred *maravedís*.

2. *Tasa,* a cognate of English "tax," was the statement of price fixed by the Royal Council for an unbound book. This official notice, which had

to be affixed to the beginnings of all published books, exemplifies the Spanish Crown's control of printing.

3. This phrase suggests that the author of the book was Fra Diego de Haedo, abbot of Frómista, whereas he clearly states in his Dedication to his uncle, the late archbishop Diego de Haedo of Palermo, Sicily, that he was only the editor (and corrector) of the "papers" presumably written by Archbishop Diego de Haedo—both uncle and nephew had the same name. The censors, then, did not read this Dedication with care.

4. The copyright privilege was obtained by the author, printer, or editor for a book to circulate for a given amount of time in the realms of the Spanish Crown.

5. The clerk of the Chamber was the royal secretary who assisted at court hearings or at a supreme tribunal for expediting business and extending decrees. These interventions (in the editorial arena) were determined by the Pragmatic of 7 September 1558, which reinforced the measures to avoid the printing of dangerous books. Miguel de Ondarza Zavala signed the evaluation for Miguel de Cervantes's *La Galatea* in 1585.

6. This so-called Law of Censorship was systematized on 7 September 1558, when Princess Juana, sister of Philip II and regent of the king, signed a decree prohibiting the import of foreign books, and ordered that all published books should in the future carry the permit of the Council of Castile. Some dozen years earlier, in 1545, the Inquisition had elaborated what was the first Spanish Index, followed by another in 1551. In 1559, the Inquisitor General Valdés published a new Index, considerably enlarging that of 1551 and dealing a hard blow to Spanish intellectual life.

7. Jorge de Tovar, from Toledo, secretary to and favorite of Philip III, also signed the copyright privilege of the *Exemplary Novels* of Cervantes on November of 1612.

8. Approval for a book to be published had to be granted by the king and, in the case of religious authors, by a prelate. Although the *Topographia* was already written in 1604, four more years passed between this date and Antonio de Herrera's approval in 1608, and again, four additional years, before the book's publication in 1612. See Astrana Marín, *Vida ejemplar y heróica de Miguel de Cervantes Saavedra*, 7:53; and Camamis, *Estudios sobre el cautiverio en el Siglo de Oro*, 147–48.

9. Antonio de Herrera y Tordesillas (1549–1625) was royal chronicler of Castile (1598) and of the Indies. The first official historian of America, he wrote the *Historia general de los hechos de los castellanos en las islas y Tierra Firme del mar*

Océano [General History of the deeds of the castilians on the Islands and mainlands of the ocean sea] (1610–1615), also known as the *Décadas* [Decades].

10. Fra Antonio Cornejo was Abbot of this Benedictine monastery from 1604 to 1607.

11. Fra Gregorio Lazcano governed the Monastery of Saint Benedict of Valladolid between 1613 and 1614, when he died.

12. Master Fra Diego de Haedo was the nephew of the archbishop of Palermo of the same name. Fra Haedo entered the Benedictine order in 15 July 1577. His title "Maestro" [Master] referred to a doctorate in Theology. After serving as prior of his monastery, he moved to Sicily in 1593, where for six years he served his uncle the archbishop as secretary. Upon returning to Spain, Fra Haedo was named abbot of Our Lady of Frómista. He carried out of Sicily the "papers" of Antonio de Sosa's manuscript, which he edited and printed in Valladolid in 1612. Fra Haedo died on 19 March 1613.

13. According to Fra Diego de Haedo, the information contained in the work to follow came principally from the *Diálogos* (*De la captividad*; *De los mártires de Argel*; *De los morabutos*) composed by Christian captives "who were many years in Algiers." This is an indirect reference to Doctor Antonio de Sosa, the true author of the Dialogues, who died in 1587, leaving his manuscripts in the hands of Bishop Haedo. The younger Diego de Haedo—a doctor of theology—had the role of editor of the "foul papers" given to him by his uncle, the Archbishop Diego de Haedo, when he was in his service at Agrigento and Palermo between 1593 and 1599.

14. In 1577, Brother Miguel de Alonsotegui, a Mercedarian monk, wrote a *Crónica de Viscaya* that remains unpublished. Alonsotegui was a consultant to the Inquisition and commander of the monastery of the Shod Mercedarians of Burceña.

15. The surname originated in the aristocratic ancestral home or fort that ruled over a *latifundium,* or great extension of land where the lord resided. Such ancestral homes bestowed surnames on their owners through a sobriquet bequeathed to their descendants. We see here the efforts of the younger Haedo to establish the antiquity of the family surname.

16. The elder Diego de Haedo held the position of Inquisitor in Valencia and Zaragoza, and, finally, between 1577 and 1584, in the kingdom of Sicily. He was nominated to the bishopric of Agrigento, Sicily, by King Philip II, and confirmed by Pope Sixtus V. He took charge of his office in Agrigento on 2 April 1585 and was promoted to archbishop of Palermo, the first seat of Sicily, in 1589. He died in Palermo in 1608.

17. Diego Enríquez de Guzmán, fifth count of Alba de Liste (ca. 1530–1604) was viceroy of Sicily from 1585 to 1591. He was a Knight of the Order of the Golden Fleece since 1600 and a nephew of the famous third duke of Alba, Fernando Álvarez de Toledo, known in history as the "butcher of Flanders."

18. Although Archbishop Haedo was effectively named president of the kingdom of Sicily in 1591, he never assumed office because of a promise made to the viceroy, Don Enrique de Guzmán, count of Alba de Listes, not to do so until a day after he left Sicily. Because of bad weather in Messina, the viceroy had to disembark and return to Palermo until the arrival of the new viceroy in 1592.

19. Frómista was a major communications hub and a staging post on the Pilgrims' Road to Santiago de Compostela. In 1835, the Spanish state proceeded with the dissolution of the monasteries, which resulted in the eventual disappearance of the monastery of Frómista.

20. The Fe de erratas was a list of corrections missing from a text, detected during a side-by-side comparison of the printed text with the original manuscript. The laws of censure and printing in sixteenth-century Spain gave a book its final shape, which included: the title page, license for printing, appraisal of the book, the approval, the fixed price, the list of errata, the text, and the colophon. See Díaz, *El libro español antiguo,* 19–54.

21. Agustín de Vergara was a professor of Latin at the University of Valladolid, active between 1591 and 1622. He probably died in 1622, as suggested by an announcement in the Archives of the Royal Chancery of Valladolid: "Vacancy in the Highest Chair of Latin (morning classes) at the University of Valladolid. Chair left vacant due to the death of Agustín de Vergara, its last holder" (ARCV, "Provisiones de Cátedras," signatura Caja 337, 23).

Chapter 1. The Founding of Algiers

1. Leo Africanus, also called al-Hassan b. Muhammad al-Wazzan al-Zayyati (or al-Fasi, alternately, al-Gharnati), was born in Granada between 1489 and 1495. After the 1492 conquest of Granada by King Ferdinand II of Aragon and Queen Isabella I of Castile, his family emigrated to Fès, where Leo studied Arabic letters, grammar, and rhetoric, as well as Islamic jurisprudence, philosophy, history, and the classics. Around 1510, Leo was captured

on the island of Djerba by Sicilian corsairs and given as a gift to Pope Leo X (Giovanni di Medici), who had him catechized and baptized. Leo Africanus's geographic and ethnographic descriptions of lands visited at the beginning of the sixteenth century made him one of the most cited geographers of the early modern period. Sosa here follows Leo Africanus, *Della descrittione dell'Africa,* vol. 1, pt. 4. See Leo Africanus, *History and Description of Africa,* pt. 4.

2. Strabo (64 BCE–ca. 19 CE) was a Greek geographer, historian and philosopher, born in Pontus (modern Turkey). Large parts of his *Geography,* spanning seventeen volumes and regarded as an encyclopedia of the geographical knowledge of his day, have come down to us complete.

3. Pliny the Elder, or Gaius Plinius Secundus (23–79 CE), naturalist and author, was admiral of the Roman navy at Misenum during the eruption of Mount Vesuvius, from which he died. He was author of *Natural History* [*Naturalis Historia*], a vast scientific encyclopedia in thirty-seven volumes. Sosa could have used the very popular fifteenth-century edition by Filippo Beroaldo, titled *Libros naturalis historiae,* published in Parma in 1476 and reprinted many times in Italy (Treviso, 1479; Parma, 1480, 1481; Venice, 1483, 1487, 1491).

4. Polybius (ca. 203–120 BCE), remembered as a "pragmatic" historian, wrote *Histories,* a forty-book account of the Mediterranean world that spans the fifty-three years (220–167 BCE) during which Rome subjugated Carthage to become the dominant Mediterranean power.

5. In addition to his astronomical tables (included in *Almagest*), the Greek geographer, astronomer, and mathematician Ptolemy, or Claudius Ptolemaeus (ca. 100–170 CE), wrote the *Geographia Claudij Ptoloma Alexandrini, philosophi ac mathematici prestantissimi,* a text that became a point of reference until the Renaissance. The cartographer Sebastian Münster (1488–1552) translated, edited, and published Ptolemy's *Geographia* in book 6 of his *Cosmographia* (Basel, 1550).

6. The Roman emperor Antoninus Augustus Pius was born Titus Aurelius Fulvius (86–161 CE) and adopted by the emperor Hadrian as his successor in 138 CE. The *Itinerarium,* composed under the order of Emperor Antoninus, is a compilation of all imperial military roads, cities, and way stations, as well as the distances between these in miles.

7. Sosa commits an error shared by various ancient and modern authors when he invokes Strabo to confirm that Algiers is situated over the site of Iol Caesarea. The identity of Algiers with Icosium and that of Cherchell

[Sharshal] with Iol Caesarea have been confirmed by archeological investigations. The latitudes cited here by Sosa are also noted in the coordinates of Ptolemy.

8. There were actually various small islands in front of the port of Algiers. The main island housed a fortress called El Peñón de Argel constructed by the Spaniards, who occupied it until 1529. The capital of Mauritania under King Juba II, called Caesarea, is actually present-day Cherchell, or Sharshal, in Algeria, and not Algiers, as Sosa and Leo Africanus, among others, suggest.

9. In a marginal note here, Sosa again cites Münster, *Cosmographia*, bk. 6, as well as Onofrius Panvinius, *De republica romana* (1558). Panvinius (1529–1568) was a church historian and Augustinian theologian involved in the revision of the Vatican Library. Sosa may have known him in Rome or Sicily.

10. Juba I was defeated by Julius Caesar at Thapsus in 46 BCE.

11. The Roman historian Gaius Sallustius Crispus (86–34 BCE), better known as Sallust, accompanied Caesar on this African campaign and was named by him governor of the province of Africa Nova. See Sallust, *Jugurthine War*. In a marginal note here, Sosa also cites "Marius and Sulla," whose stories appear in Plutarch's *Parallel Lives* (see n. 15 below).

12. Juba II (ca. 50 BCE–24 CE), king of Numidia and of Caesarean Mauritania, was a prolific writer in Greek of works of history, geography, and theater. Here, Sosa cites Pliny, *Natural History*, bk. 5, chap. 1.

13. Cleopatra Selene II (40 BCE–6 CE), also known as Cleopatra VIII of Egypt, was the only daughter of Antony and Cleopatra. After the double suicide of her parents, she and her siblings were taken to Rome by Octavian, the future emperor Caesar Augustus. Between 26 and 20 BCE, Caesar Augustus arranged a marriage of Selene with King Juba II of Numidia, and he named the bride, Queen of Numidia. The married couple settled in Mauritania, renaming its capital Caesarea (the modern Cherchell [Sharshal] in Algiers).

14. Suetonius, or Gaius Suetonius Tranquilus (ca. 69–140 CE), the Roman historian, is known for his *Lives of the Twelve Caesars* [*De vita Caesarum*], a series of biographies about the earlier emperors, from Augustus to Domitian. Sosa's materials on Augustus, Mark Antony, and Cleopatra were taken from book 2.

15. Plutarch (ca. 46–120 CE) was a Greek historian, biographer, essayist, and Middle Platonist. His best known work *Parallel Lives* [*Vidas Paralelas*]—a

series of biographies of famous Greeks and Romans arranged in pairs to illuminate their common virtues or vices—explores the influence of character on the lives of such figures as Pericles, Alcibiades, Alexander the Great, Marius, Sulla, Pompey, Mark Antony, Brutus, Julius Caesar, and Cicero. Plutarch's *Lives* has had an enormous influence on English and French literature. His *Moralia*, a series of discursive inquiries into customs, manners, and beliefs, influenced writers as different as Montaigne and Emerson.

16. Sosa cites in the margin Josephus (Titus Flavius Josephus, 37–100 CE), a Jewish historian who described the destruction of Jerusalem in *De bello judaico* [*War of the Jews*] (Paris, 1511). The story of Archelaus, king of Capadoccia, appears in *War of the Jews*, bks. 1, 4–5.

17. The reconstruction of the port city called Tower of Stratton, renamed Caesarea by Herod, appears in Josephus, *Antiquitates Judaicae*, bk. 15, chap. 9, as well as in *De bello judaico*, bk. 1, chap. 21. Sosa also gives a marginal citation here to St. Jerome's *Commentary on Matthew*, bk. 4, chap. 16.

18. Sosa cites in the margin Pliny, *Natural History*, bk. 5, chap. 2.

19. Sosa cites in the margin Suetonius, *Lives of the Twelve Caesars*, bk. 4; Pliny, *Natural History*, bk. 5, chap. 5; and Münster, *Cosmographia*, bk 6.

20. Sosa cites in the margin Pliny, *Natural History*, bk. 5, chap. 2, as well as Cicero's *Pro Archia*.

21. Sosa cites in the margin a trio of authors who wrote Latin treatises on the Roman Empire: Sextus Pompeius Festus (second or third century CE), a grammarian who composed an epitome of the work of the philologist Marcus Verrius Flaccus; "Asconius on Verre," which alludes to the commentaries of the Roman grammarian and historian Quintus Asconius Pedianus (ca. 9 BCE–76 CE) on the seven unpublished speeches of Cicero (106–146 BCE) against Caius Verre (ca. 119–43 BCE), the Roman politician accused of extortion against the Sicilians; and Onofrius Panvinio, author of *De republica Romana* (1558).

22. Aulus Gellius (ca. 125–180 CE), Latin lawyer and writer, possibly of African origin, wrote the *Noctes Atticae*, twenty books that serve as a source of information into the culture of his age.

23. Hadrian (Publius Aelius Traianus Hadrianus) (76–138 CE) was a Stoic philosopher, an Epicurean, a patron of the arts, and a Roman emperor (117–138 CE). Apart from the second Roman-Jewish war (132–135 CE), in which 580,000 Jews died and fifty cities were destroyed, Hadrian's government was relatively peaceful. The fortifications he constructed at the limits of his empire are famous, such as the massive Hadrian's Wall in Great Britain.

24. Valentinian III (419–455 CE) was crowned Emperor of the West in Rome in 425 CE and was assassinated in 455 CE. His reign was marked by the dismemberment of the Roman Empire: the conquest of the province of Africa by the Vandals in 439 CE; the loss of Britain in 446 CE; the loss of a great part of Hispania and of Gaul to the barbarians; and the sack of Sicily and the coasts of the western Mediterranean by the armadas of the Vandal Genseric. Sosa cites Pliny, *Natural History,* bk. 5, chap. 2.

25. Genseric, half-brother and successor to Gunderic (d. 428 CE) was the first Vandal king of Africa (428–77 CE). With a tribe of 80,000 warriors, Genseric crossed over from Iberia to Africa in 429 CE, pillaging and looting and, a year later, besieging Saint Augustine's city of Hippo Regius (near present-day Annaba). Building the kingdom of the Vandals and Alans into a powerful state, Genseric went on to conquer Sicily, Corsica, Sardinia, and the Balearic Islands. In 455 CE, the Vandals sacked Rome.

26. Leontius (Greek, Λεόντιος, formally "Leo") had an unpopular reign as Byzantine emperor from 695–698 CE. Prior to his reign, Leontius, a military leader, was imprisoned by the Byzantine emperor Justinian II after losing the Battle of Sebastopolis to the Arabs in 693 CE. Upon being freed in 695 CE, Leontius organized a revolt against Justinian, whom he soon deposed and exiled to the Crimea (after having the emperor's nose and tongue slit). During Leontius's own reign as emperor, in 697 CE, Carthage fell to the Arabs. A year later, after his soldiers launched a rebellion against him, Leontius was deposed, mutilated, and imprisoned in Constantinople. He was executed in 705 CE, when Justinian II returned to power.

27. Sosa here paraphrases a passage about Temendfust by Leo Africanus in *History and Description of Africa,* pt. 4, which situates the Roman city of Rusgunia, in accordance with the *Itinerarium* of Antoninus, twelve miles from Icosium.

28. Sosa cites in the margin Flavius Blondus (1388–1463 CE), author of the *Historiarum ab inclinatione Romanorum imperii, Decades III* [Decades of the History of the Decline of the Roman Empire] (Venice, 1483), a work that covers the period from the fall of the Roman Empire until 1440 CE. Flavius Blondus was a humanist, historian, and archeologist of the Italian Renaissance. Here, Sosa also cites Carrionis, also known as Ludovico Carrione Brugensi (1547–1598 CE), a scholar born in Bruge of Spanish parents, who published various commentaries on Latin authors such as Sallust and Gaius Valerius Flacus.

29. In 1529, after taking over the Spanish fortress El Peñón de Argel, Khayr al-Din Barbarossa had it demolished, using its materials to build a wharf connecting the small islands off the port to the mainland.

Chapter 2. Why the City Is Called Algiers

1. Given the context here, it seems that Sosa is speaking of the whole Iberian Peninsula and not just the part east of Badajoz. But because he was also a naturalized citizen of Castile who identified strongly with that region, he may mean "España" in the more politically charged sense of "Spain" (with Castile out front).

2. Alarbes, or Arabs: term originally used to refer to the Muslims who conquered the North of Africa and invaded the Iberian Peninsula. According to Sebastián de Covarrubias, who distinguishes three Arabias ("Felix, Petrea, Deserta"), these peoples "come from a region between Judea and Egypt, so called from Arabo, son of Apollo." See Covarrubias, *Diccionario de la Lengua Castellana o Española,* 194, our translation. During the sixteenth and seventeenth centuries, the concept "Arab" changed in meaning. The term denominated the groups who lived in the desert zones of Africa and Arabia, while the term "Moors" (Sp *moros*) was exclusively applied to the inhabitants of the cities in Barbary; this last group was differentiated from the nomad shepherds (Arabs or Bedouins) and the inhabitants of the mountainous regions of North of Africa (Berbers). In the text, Sosa refers to the Arabs who, with the aid of Berber forces, invaded the Maghreb and the Iberian Peninsula in 711 CE.

3. Sosa's marginal note here refers to Lucian of Samosata (ca. 125–180 CE), the Assyrian rhetorician and satirist who wrote in Greek. The reference to Lucian's "Specudomante" may be a corruption of his Latin dialogues titled *Alexander seu Pseudomantis* [Alexander the Oracle-Monger]. The citation of *Suidam,* also in the margin, may refer to *Suda* (Greek *Souidas* or *Souda*), a Byzantine lexicographic compendium attributed to Eustace of Thessalonica (ca. 125–181 CE), which includes commentaries on Homer and Pindar, as well as on early Christian writings.

4. Sosa refers here to Augeas, a mythological king whose stables housed the single greatest number of cattle in the country and had never been cleaned until Heracles came along and, for his fifth labor, cleaned them in a single day and killed Augeas for refusing to honor his agreement to give him one-tenth of his cattle.

5. Throughout the medieval period, the Ibero-Romance vernaculars (esp. Castilian, Catalan, and Portuguese) incorporated a large number of Arabic words into their lexicons, a process inspired in large part by the economic, technological, and intellectual prestige of Arabo-Muslim culture during this time. In line with dominant Ibero-Christian ideologies during the late sixteenth century, Sosa refers to this phenomenon as a "plague."

6. As Leo Africanus points out, al-Djaza'ir (A) means "the islands" (see *History and Description of Africa*, pt. 4). The Latin form of the name, Icosium, was given to the Roman settlement on the mainland.

7. Sosa errs on the French term for Algiers in the sixteenth century, which oscillated between Alges, Alget, Algiere (1542), and Algier (1587).

Chapter 3. Algiers as a Muslim Kingdom

1. Sosa's marginal note here—"Vide Joan Leonem descript Afri., pt. 4"—refers to Leo Africanus, *History and Description of Africa*, pt. 4.

2. Between 1508 and 1510, the Spanish conquered various coastal sites in North Africa, such as El Peñón de Vélez (1508), Orán (1509), and Béjaïa and Tripoli (1510), where they constructed walled cities. The legendary sailor Pedro Navarro sacked all these cities, distributing the booty among his men and selling the inhabitants into slavery.

3. Salim al-Tumi was the chief of an Arab tribe called the Taleba, then lords of Mitidja, where he had established himself with the permission of the Kabila tribe of the Bani Nelikeuch.

Chapter 4. How Algiers Came under the Turks

1. Sosa refers here to Ferdinand II, king of Aragón and Navarre, who married Isabella I of Castile in 1469.

2. To seal this treaty, Count Pedro Navarro constructed a fortress over the islet of Algiers called, after the great rocks that sustained it, El Peñón de Argel.

3. The corsairs 'Arudj and Khayr al-Din Barbarossa were the founders of the state of Algiers. 'Arudj Barbarossa acquired his political stature in the context of the Iberian conquest of the North African coastal cities. Under the banner of Islam against the Spaniards, he obtained the support of the

Turks and Berber tribes, as well as that of numerous colonies of Valencian and Aragonese Moriscos that had been established in those regions.

4. This statement suggests that Sosa wrote his *Epítome de los Reyes de Argel* first, although it follows the *Topography* proper as book 2.

Chapter 5. The Ramparts of Algiers

1. The crossbow (Sp *ballesta*) was an old portable weapon composed of a wooden casing like that of the modern rifle, with a channel through which emerged arrows and pellets impelled by the elastic force of a spring.

2. The Gregal (from *graegalis* [L]: of Greece) is a wind that blows from between the east and the north, according to the division of the mariner's compass card used in the Mediterranean.

3. A span (Sp *palmo*) is a unit of length based on the width of the expanded human hand (usually taken as nine inches).

4. The mistral (from *magistral* [L]: lit. "master-wind") is a violently cold northwest wind experienced in the Mediterranean.

5. Fabricated in Algiers, the galliot was smaller than a galleon and swift, with fourteen to twenty-five benches. Light and rounded in front and back, it surpassed the galleons in performance. While the Christian galleons had six to eight rowers per bench, who were often recruited from prisons, the Algerian galliots had ten oarsmen per bench, all of them experienced seamen.

6. Born in Alexandria, Egypt, and of Arabic origin, 'Arab Ahmad Pasha was installed as governor-general of Algiers in 1572. Although Ahmad was his proper name, the Turks and Berbers commonly referred to him as the Arab Ahmad. Sosa describes his governorship in chapter 20 of *Epítome de los Reyes de Argel* [History of the Kings of Algiers].

Chapter 6. The Gates of Algiers

1. According to *Encyclopaedia of Islam,* five main gates gave access to Algiers: to the north, Bab al-Wad (the River Gate); to the south, Bab 'Azzun (Gate of 'Azzun); to the southwest, Bab al-Djadid (the New Gate); and on the harbor side, the Fishery Gate and the Fleet Gate. Sosa also mentions other small gates existing around 1580–1581. See the "al-Djaza'ir" entry in *Encyclopaedia of Islam,* 2nd ed. (ed. Bearman et al.).

2. *Kasba, al-kasaba, kasaba* (A): fortified castle, residence of an authority in the center of a country or a town; principal town, chief town. In North Africa, the term occurs in the sense of a fortress or citadel (dialect: *kasba*). The term has survived in the Iberian Peninsula, until our own day, in the form *alcazaba* (Sp), the term used by Sosa.

3. "Barbary" was the term that sixteenth- and seventeenth-century Europeans used to designate the North African region extending from Morocco to the west of Egypt, a region that today includes the four countries of Morocco, Algeria, Tunisia, and Libya.

4. A *tapia* was a superficial measurement of forty-nine to fifty square feet.

Chapter 7. The Fortifications of Algiers

1. Sosa uses the term *caballeros,* which in Spanish military parlance means a defensive fortification, elevated over others in the same space in order to protect them with its fire or dominate them in the case of enemy occupation.

2. As seen in the previous chapter, Sosa's intent is to present a detailed descriptive plan of the city of Algiers, with all its strengths and weaknesses, in order to bring about a Spanish invasion of the corsair city.

3. The term *ka'id* (A) was the title used by the governors of lands and cities in Algiers colonized by the Turks. The title was also granted to anyone who held a public post in the municipality or house of the pasha.

4. *Khalifa* (A): *caliph;* title given to Saracen princes who, as successors of Muhammad, exercised supreme religious and civil power in some Muslim territories. In this case, however, *khalifa* is used in the sense of a deputy or a lieutenant of the pasha.

5. Hasan Pasha, son of Khayr al-Din, was three times governor of Algiers: 1544–1551, 1557–1561, and 1562–1567. His first command (as deputy to his father, who was both *beylerbey* of Algiers [provincial governor] and *kapudan pasha* [grand admiral] of the Ottoman armada) was to strengthen the fortifications of Algiers. Sosa refers to this administrator in chapter 6 of his *Epítome de los Reyes de Alger* [History of the Kings of Algiers].

6. Sosa alludes here to Juan Cañete, a Valencian corsair who operated out of Mallorca. Cañete tried to burn the port of Algiers in 1550 and was executed nine years later. Another Valencian corsair, Juan Gasco, succeeded in burning the port in 1560 only to be captured on the high seas and impaled

by the Algerians. Sosa narrates their stories in his *Diálogo de los mártires de Alger* [Dialogue of the Martyrs of Algiers].

Chapter 9. The Castles and Forts outside Algiers

1. *Burdj* (A): square or round tower, either adjacent to a rampart or isolated and serving as a dungeon.

2. 'Uludj 'Ali (Euchalí, or Ochalí, as the Spaniards called him) was a renegade from Calabria who rose to become the nineteenth pasha of Algiers. He was also known as Uchalí Fartax or "el Tiñoso" [scabby-headed], as Cervantes calls him in the inset story of "The Captive's Tale" in *Don Quijote* I, 40.

3. The casemate is a highly resistant vault where one or more pieces of artillery can be installed.

4. As is clear, this and earlier chapters were designed as a detailed plan of the internal and external fortifications of Algiers, advertising their weak points, with the intention of sending it to the Spanish crown to bring about an attack on the city.

5. In one of these very caves, the slave Miguel de Cervantes hid some fourteen captives in 1577. The cave was located some three miles east of Algiers, on a farm that belonged to the Greek renegade Ka'id Hasan. In 1580, Sosa testified that he had been involved in the plot: "I was one of those who communicated with the said Miguel de Cervantes many times and in great secrecy about the said business." Sosa added that, while the fugitives were in hiding, Cervantes visited him, "pleading with me many times that I also hide myself with the rest in the said cave; and the day that he went to hide himself there he came to bid me farewell." See Cervantes, *Información de Argel,* 157; our translation.

Chapter 10. The Houses and Streets of Algiers

1. Calculating eight to ten inhabitants per household, Algiers would have a population of approximately 120,000 toward the end of the 1570s.

2. The *souk* is the name given in Algeria and Morocco to the marketplace. The natives also give this name to the streets or portion of the streets dedicated to the sale of merchandise or of natural products (e.g., Souk of the Spices).

3. This refers to the conquest of Tunis by Don Juan of Austria in October 1573, in which the soldier Miguel de Cervantes participated. In July of 1574, an impressive Ottoman armada made up of some three hundred ships with 70,000 men on board, aided by 100,000 land troops, attacked the citadel of Tunis and the fort of La Goleta, capturing these military posts, where thousands of Spanish and Italian soldiers died after a heroic resistance.

Chapter 11. The Inhabitants and Neighbors of Algiers

1. According to Sosa, the Christian slave population of Algiers was close to 25,000 circa 1580. Later chronicles mention between 30,000 and 40,000 slaves. See the quantitative tables included in Davis, *Christian Slaves, Muslim Masters,* xiv–xxiii.

2. *Baldi* (A): the original inhabitants of Algiers. See also *beldi* (A): people of the city or capital versus *arbi* (Bedouin or peasant).

3. The generic term "Moors," which generally designated a Muslim in contrast to a Christian, is used in this case to refer to the Maghrebis of the cities, the so-called *baldi.*

4. Sosa uses *zaragüelles* as the Spanish equivalent of *sarawil* (SpA) or *serwal* (A): wide pleated trousers used for both sexes in the entire Maghreb.

5. The *gonela* (A, from the Italian *gonnella*) is a tunic of leather or silk, generally sleeveless, worn by both sexes. Sosa also uses *goneila,* which may be a faulty transliteration of gonela.

6. Sosa uses *adorra* for *gandura* (A), a long tunic with short sleeves, used by men in Morocco and by both sexes in Algiers.

7. *Burnus* or *burnous* (A): a loose woolen hooded cloak woven in one piece; also a type of high cap or bonnet worn in the Prophet's time.

8. Sosa refers to *borceguíes* (Sp), boots of yellow, orange, or red leather, with or without soles; probably *tmak* (A): riding boots used across the entire Maghreb.

9. Sosa uses *mendexa* for *medasa* or *madasa* (A): North African usage for a type of footwear.

10. The Kabyles, a tribe of islamicized Berbers who inhabited the mountainous area of Kabylia east of Algiers, were descendants of inhabitants of the region before the arrival of the Arabs. The term Kabyle seems to have been introduced into geographic nomenclature by European writers

from the sixteenth century onward. See the "Kabylia" entry in *Encyclopaedia of Islam,* 2nd ed. (ed. Bearman et al.).

11. During the sixteenth century, the Kabylia region was divided among three powers, which European writers called, respectively, the kingdom of Kuko, the kingdom of Labbès (Banu 'Abbas), and the principality of the Banu Djubar. The first two kingdoms were located in the chain of Atlas Mountains that crosses through Morocco and Algiers.

12. Salaried rowers, possibly from the verb *bogar* (Sp): to row.

13. Zwawa (also Zouaoua): tribes belonging to one of three Berber groups scattered throughout the central and the farthest Maghreb.

14. Sosa cites in the margin Leo Africanus, *History and Description of Africa,* pt. 4.

15. *Mahalla* (A): in North Africa, the annual campaign led by emissaries of the Turkish government of Algiers to collect taxes from among the Bedouin and Berber tribes.

16. *Agha* (T): in Ottoman times, the term meant "chief," "master," or "commander." In North African countries under Ottoman rule, it referred to the commander of the corps of janissaries.

17. Ornamental tattooing among women continues to be a prominent feature of Berber cultural practice in rural Morocco and Algeria. For an insightful analysis of this practice, see Becker, *Amazigh Arts in Morocco.*

18. Sosa uses the term *alquicel* for *alkisá* (SpA) or *al-ksa,* or *ksa* (A): a large outer wrap, usually white, used by both sexes across the entire Maghreb.

19. *Barrakan* (N Afr): a heavy wrap worn by men in Medieval Tunisia; also a large enveloping outer wrap for both sexes in present-day Libya.

20. Sosa's irony in this paragraph does not distinguish between the Bedouins he belittles and the Berber armies who invaded Spain in 711 CE.

21. These were Moriscos or Hispano-Muslims who were obliged to convert to Christianity after the conquest of Granada in 1492. Thousands of Moriscos from Granada and other regions of Spain opted then, and again in the sixteenth century, for exile in North Africa.

22. Mudéjar (Sp): Hispano-Arabic name given to a Muslim who remained, without changing religion, as a vassal of the Christians in a newly conquered territory. The term Tagarino—from the Hispano-Arabic *tagari* (SpA), and this from *tagri* (A), lit. "border"—was applied to Moriscos born and raised among Christians and speaking both Spanish and Arabic so well that they could barely be distinguished from Old Christians. Sosa uses the term to refer to Moriscos who were natives of Valencia and of the Spanish Levant.

23. From the number of houses that Sosa calculates for the Moriscos of Algiers, we may deduce their population at some 8,000 to 10,000 toward the end of the 1570s. During his captivity in Algiers, Sosa noted the continuous arrival of exiled Moriscos: "From the first day that I entered Algiers, I have written down . . . the number of those who came and even in which month, week, day, and hour they came, and how they came" (*Diálogo de los morabutos* [Dialogue of the Marabouts], in *Topografía*, 3:253, our translation).

Chapter 12. Turks

1. *Çakal* (T argot): an astute, crafty, wily, cunning man—a mean wretch. In his first letter on his trip to Istanbul (1555), the imperial ambassador Busbecq says that the name derives from the jackal, which obtains its food through shrewdness and robbery instead of violent methods. See Busbecq, *Turkish Letters,* 44.

2. "The Turk" was the name given in Christian Europe to the Ottoman sultan.

3. After the sack of Constantinople in 1453, the Turkish Empire incorporated Bosnia, Serbia, and Albania, which in time became Ottoman provinces. Under Selim I (1512–1520) and Süleyman the Magnificent (1520–1566), the Ottoman Empire extended itself toward the Balkans (Romania, Wallachia, Greece, Cyprus, Crete, Moldavia, and Transylvania), including the main part of Hungary; toward the Near East, including parts of Persia, Palestine, Syria, and Egypt; and toward the Adriatic Sea and the central and western Mediterranean, including Algiers and Tripoli.

4. Although ethnic differences existed between the inhabitants of Anatolia and Romania, this passage reveals Sosa's preference for the Ottoman subjects of the Balkan Peninsula, considered descendants of the ancient Greeks, over the Turks of Asia Minor and the Middle East.

Chapter 13. Renegades

1. In sixteenth-century Europe, the term *renegade* applied to a Christian who converted to Islam, that is, an apostate. Many of these converts were Christian captives incarcerated in Barbary who, because they could not be ransomed, embraced Islam in order to obtain their freedom. Between

1500 and 1650, thousands of Christian renegades from the western Mediterranean, both as captives and free men, flocked en masse to Islamic countries, prompting a great interchange of men, ideas, and technologies. Recent historical studies calculate that over 300,000 inhabitants of the Mediterranean world became "Turks by profession" in the early modern period.

2. Prester John was the legendary Christian king living more or less in Ethiopia and sought out by the Portuguese in their voyages to India.

3. Whereas fornication in Counter-Reformation Europe constituted a mortal sin, sexual freedom in Barbary was ample and included, among other accessible pleasures, those offered by young men. This was the infamy that public opinion in Europe attributed to Turks and inhabitants of Barbary. Many young men, captives or renegades, accepted the sexual practices that offered them advantageous compensations. Cervantes himself described and condemned these practices in his literary production, especially in *El trato de Argel* [*Life in Algiers*].

4. As a Doctor of Jurisprudence, Sosa here exhibits his legal knowledge, confirmed by his degree *in utroque iure*, that is, in both civil and canon law.

5. There were clear economic advantages to be gained by apostasy and integration into the new Turkish-Algerian society. Incorporation into the social nuclei of the Ottoman centers via matrimony usually represented a smart move for the renegade, who obtained not only his liberty but also, and very often, additional financial compensations through business dealings with his father-in-law and his associates.

6. Sosa's term *sosfia* may be a variation or distortion of *sofra* (T), the round platter or dining table on which food is placed in Turkey and, by extension, a banquet. Another possibility is that "sosfia" is derived from *sefa* (A) or the diminutive *sfifa*: a plate of *kuskusu* (couscous) with sugar, eggs, and cinnamon. This definition is courtesy of Hadjira Bennour from Orán, Algeria.

7. We assume that this phrase, incorrectly cited by Sosa, is the *shahadah*, or profession of the Muslim faith: *Ashadu an la ilaha illa-llah, wa ashadu anna Muhammadan rasulu-llah* [I bear witness that there is no God but the one God, and I bear witness that Muhammad is the prophet of God].

8. Sosa's use of *cuzaca* may refer to *hazuqah* or *hazuqa* (A), from the verb "to tighten"; it could also be a variation of *hizam* (*hizamah* or *h'zamah* in North African dialect): waistband worn over the caftan to fasten it. See Wehr, *A Dictionary of Modern Written Arabic*, 203.

9. The 1609 circumcision of the son of the Marquis of Villena, viceroy of Sicily, was marked by a great celebration in Istanbul. Captured by

Turkish-Algerian corsairs, the youth was sent to the sultan as a trophy of war and forced to convert to Islam. The ceremony was described by the Venetian ambassador Simon Contarini, who observed the event, together with other guests, from behind latticework windows. Contarini cited by Lucchetta, "Il medico del Bailaggio di Constantinopoli," 44.

10. As Sosa suggests, the apostasy of captives who were artillerymen, captains, pilots, shipbuilders, and skilled workmen—as well as deserters from the Spanish citadel in Orán—were especially welcomed by the Algerians. These renegades were frequently incorporated into Maghrebi armies, corsair fleets, and urban administration. See Garcés, *Cervantes in Algiers,* 58–59, 141.

11. *Dobla* (Sp): an antique copper coin that wavered in value according to the times. This term should not be confused with *doblón* (Sp), doubloon (E), an antique gold coin, thus called by the common people during the reign of the Catholic Monarchs because it weighed two castellanos or *doblas.*

12. By these calculations, using a multiplier of eight to ten to allow for extended families, we may conjecture that at the time when Sosa studied this society, Algiers had 50,000 or 60,000 Christian renegades, including men, women, and children.

Chapter 14. Ka'ids

1. *Ka'id* (T), *qa'id* (A): an imprecise term, generally used to designate a military leader, whose rank may vary from captain to general, although it also meant a tribal chieftain. In Algiers, the title was given to the governors of districts or towns subject to the Turkish government. Their obligations were fiscal, judicial, and military. This position included the lucrative activity of collecting taxes ascribed to a district or a territorial division. Any functionary who had governed a district for some time could keep the title.

2. *Sipahi* (T): cavalry soldier and special cavalry corps in the army.

3. Boluk-Bashi (T): a degree of rank among the janissaries, literally "captain of a division"; title given to the head of various groups of functionaries in the administrative organization of the Ottoman Empire, especially the commander of the units of infantry and cavalry (*boluk*).

4. Hadjdji Murad, a renegade Slav from Ragusa (present-day Herzegovina), was the chief ka'id of Algiers and one of the richest men in Barbary. Hadjdji Murad's daughter, immortalized by Cervantes in "The Captive's Tale" (*Don Quijote* I, 39–41), married the future sultan of Morocco, 'Abd al-Malik, who died in 1578 in the famous battle of al-Kasr al-Kabir fighting against

King Sebastian of Portugal. For more on Hadjdji Murad, see Garcés, *Cervantes in Algiers,* 50–54, 206–11.

5. In the sixteenth century, *çelebi* was a title of respect give in Turkey to illustrious members of the military corps, and, by extension, to judges and scholars. The fact that two renegades—Ka'id Muhammad Çelebi and Ka'id Murad Çelebi—had added the title to their Muslim name suggests that they belonged to the highest rank of civil servants in Algiers.

6. This list clearly evidences the preponderance of Christian renegades among the functionaries of the Turkish-Algerian government: of the twenty-three ka'ids listed by Sosa, twelve were Christian renegades from Mediterranean countries (Spain, Italy, etc.), one was an Englishman and another, a Jewish renegade.

Chapter 15. Sipahi

1. Between the fourteenth and sixteenth centuries in the Ottoman Empire, this land grant or *timar* (T) had an annual value of less than 20,000 acres. A *timariot* would live on his land for part of the year in order to collect taxes permitting him to subsist as well as to equip his military subordinates.

2. *Escudo* (Sp): standard gold coin with the royal coat of arms inscribed on one of its faces. In the Spain of Philip II, a gold escudo was worth four hundred *maravedís*.

3. *Para* or *pare* (T): money; currency.

4. Possibly the Venetian ducat. The Ottoman Empire also used the ducat for trade as well as local coins called the *akche* (*asper*), the *para*, and the *kurush*.

Chapter 16. Janissaries

1. Sultan Murad I (1360–1389) presumably founded the janissary corps, an elite military corps of the Ottoman Empire (ca. 1365). Murad III (1574–1595)—who governed during the time when Sosa was a captive in Algiers—was the son of Selim II (1566–1574), and grandson of Süleyman the Magnificent (1520–1566).

2. The janissaries were originally formed of Christian youth obtained by means of a human tax called the *devshirme*. Within schools for cadets (*acemi oglam*), these youth were subjected to virtually monastic conditions, an iron discipline, hard physical training, and an education in the use of arms and military tactics.

3. There are various books titled *De rebus Turcicis*. A likeness to the name Gesnerius suggests a reference to Honigerus Koningshoff, *De rebus Turcicis* (1577). Sosa could also be alluding to Girolamo Balbi (Balbus), *De rebus Turcici libers* (1526), among other works of the period on the Turks.

4. Sosa may be referring to the Augustinian Andrea Biglia, *I comentarii Historici de defectu fidei et Orientis,* also known as *De origine Turcarum* (1435); or to Sagundino, *De origine et rebus gestis Turcarum* (1456), which inspired in part the work of Giovio, *Commentario de le cose de' Turchi* (1532), translated into Latin and other vernacular tongues. There were other works with the title *De origine Turcarum,* such as the small treatise by the Greek humanist Gaza (1400–1475). The Croatian humanist Djurdjević, or Georgijević, known as Georgieuiz (1510–1566), was also the author of various treatises on the Turks, including *De Turcarum moribus epitome* (1533), *De Turcarum ritu et ceremoniis* (1544), and *De origine imperii Turcorum* (1553).

5. Salah Ra'is, a famous corsair and companion of Khayr al-Din Barbarossa, was the *beylerbey* (provincial governor) of Algiers between 1552 and 1556; his son Muhammad Pasha governed Algiers from January 1567 to March 1568. Sosa relates his history in chapter 27 of *Epítome de los Reyes de Alger* [History of the Kings of Algiers].

6. Dja'far Pasha, of Hungarian origin, governed Algiers between 1580 and 1582.

Chapter 17. Agha of the Janissaries

1. The *agha* of the janissaries was the official of highest rank of the palace guard for the Sublime Porte, and was part of the privy council of the Grand Turk. Together with the Grand Vizier, the agha of the janissaries had the responsibility of imposing the law and maintaining order in the capital. In Algiers and the other Ottoman provinces, the agha of the janissaries had a similar position.

2. From the standpoint of fiscal autonomy and responsibility for the discipline of its own members, each janissary regiment was run as a separate entity with strong objection to outside interference in its members' welfare. This structure fostered a sense of regimental pride and loyalty, a source of janissary strength that neither the sultan nor the agha of the janissaries himself was disposed to tamper with.

3. *Kadi* (T), *qadi* (A): a judge who administered both the holy law of Islam and the secular laws promulgated by the sultans. Within the Ottoman Empire, a *kadi* was the judge and chief administrator of a judicial district.

Chapter 18. Ranks of the Janissaries

1. Sosa uses Oldaxi, probably his term for Yol-dash (T): "comrades at arms," or soldiers. Janissaries were also called Odjak-eri (T, modern spelling: Ocak-eri), or "hearth-mates," from *odjak* or *ocak* (T): "fireplace, chimney, hearth."
2. Odabashi (T): the name given to the commanders of the *agha bolukleri*, or squads of the agha of the janissaries.
3. Otrak (or Oturak) (T): retired elders of the military corps.
4. Bash-oda (T): head of a garrison.
5. Divan (Eng); Divan-i Humayun (T); Diwan-i Humayun (P): imperial Council of the Ottomans, founded by Mehmed II after the conquest of Constantinople and remaining the central organ of their government until the seventeenth century.
6. Solak (T): lit. "left-handed"; guardsmen in attendance of the sultans. Comprising four infantry companies of the janissaries, these Solak soldiers used their left instead of their right hands as archers in order to avoid any disrespectfulness.
7. Boluk (T): term that designated infantry units under the command of a captain, or Yayabashi. Boluk-Bashi was the title given to various leading functionaries in the Ottoman state: these commanders were mounted and had an iron mace and a shield tied to their saddles.
8. Sosa uses Murbaluco Basha for Mir Boluk-Bashi. *Mir* (T): commander; Sosa's reference is probably to a commander of the Boluk-Bashi. See also *mir-i miram* (T): "supreme commander," a military and political term used in eighteenth-century Ottoman Turkish administrative practice, virtually synonymous with king or "provincial governor" and used to denote the honorary rank of king.
9. Yayabashi (T): commanders of the *boluk*, or janissary regiments.
10. Djum'a or Yawm al-Djum'a (A): the Friday service, celebrated at noon in one mosque in each city, obligatory for all adult Muslim males.
11. Kahya (T): an administrator or deputy who took care of the business affairs of an important government official or influential person.
12. In 1886, Henri-Delmas de Grammont gave a similar list of ranks for the Ottoman regency, perhaps borrowed from Haedo [Sosa]: *ioldach* (soldier), *solachis* (guards of the Janissary corps), *oukilhadjis* (officer), *odabachis* (lieutenant), *boulouk-bachis* (captain), *agha-bachis* (commander), and, finally, *agha* (captain general of the militia). See De Grammont, *Histoire d'Alger sous la domination turque*, 60.

Chapter 19. Customs of the Janissaries at War

1. The Numidians, a nomad Berber people, inhabited Numidia, the region of North Africa extending from the territory of Carthage up to the Muluya in Morocco. In the third century BCE, Numidia was comprised of two kingdoms united under the authority of Masinissa (ca. 238–ca. 148 BCE), an ally of the Romans. Ultimately, Numidia was converted into a Roman province. The invasion of the Vandals (429 CE) and the Arab conquest (seventh and eighth centuries CE) brought economic ruin to the territory.

2. For the activities of the *mahalla,* Sosa uses the colloquial Spanish verb *garramar,* which means to steal, to grab at something with astuteness and deceit.

3. *Beylerbey* (T): lit. "bey of beys," meaning "commander of commanders" or "lord of lords," this is the Ottoman title used for provincial governors. In the above lines, however, Sosa means a military officer.

4. *Bulgur* (T, also *bulghur*) is a cereal food made from several different wheat species, most often from *durum* wheat. It is commonly used in North African and Greek cuisine.

5. From *kuskusu* (A): a typical Maghrebi culinary preparation made with semolina.

6. Each regiment had a paymaster general, who oversaw the distribution of funds held in trust for use by those in special need as well as the collection of contributions for each regiment's independent fund for campaign provisions.

7. *Ashdji* (T): lit. "cook"; chief cook of the regiment, who was also the chief of the regimental prison.

8. *Sanjakdar, sancakdar,* or *sandjak dar* (T). See *sandjak* (T): flag, standard, banner; also a Turkish administrative and territorial division.

Chapter 20. Customs of the Janissaries in Peacetime

1. The barracks of the Praetorian Guard of imperial Rome, known as Castra Praetoria, were constructed in 23 CE by Lucius Aeolius Sejanus, the Praetorian prefect who served under Tiberius Caesar (14–37 CE). In 312 CE, Constantine defeated Maxentius at the Battle of the Milvian Bridge north of Rome: after Maxentius drowned, his body was fished out of the Tiber, decapitated, and his head paraded through Rome.

2. In chapter 21 of his *Epítome de los Reyes de Argel* [History of the Kings of Algiers], Sosa describes the famine that gripped the city in 1579 and 1580,

when thousands of poor Moors and Berbers died. According to his account, between January 17 and February 17 of 1580, over five thousand citizens starved to death within the city itself.

3. This is surely the *rabab* or *rebab* (A), a string instrument of the viola family used in North Africa and the Middle East. One of the key instruments of Arabic-Andalusian music, the rabab was the favorite instrument of the Ottoman Empire, heard in all parts, from the palace to the teahouse.

4. Sosa reveals here his ethnocentric European vision of the music of the Maghreb.

5. This claim is an error on Sosa's part.

6. *Asper* (E), *akce* or *akche* (T): a small Ottoman silver coin used in the Balkans and Anatolia. It was the basic monetary unit in the Ottoman Empire until the end of the seventeenth century.

7. *Piaster, piastre* (E, F), from *piastra* (It): "thin metal plate." The name was applied to Spanish pieces of eight by Venetian traders in the Levant in the sixteenth century. The *piaster* was also a former coin of Turkey, replaced by the *kurush* in 1933.

Chapter 21. Customs of the Algerian Corsairs

1. The galliot, made in Algiers, was a small and very fast galley, with fourteen to twenty-five benches. The brigantine was a smaller vessel, with long and narrow oars, easy to manage. Whereas the heavy Christian galleys carried six to ten rowers per bench, often recruited from the prison population, the speedy Algerian galliots had ten rowers per bench, all experienced. See Belhamisi, *Histoire de la marine algérienne (1516–1830).*

2. Sosa uses the term *magacén,* from *makhzen, makhzan,* or *makhzin* (A): a storehouse. In North African usage the term stands for "the State"; *makhzen* also indicates the political system based on the oath of allegiance of the tribal chiefs to the sultan. Sosa refers here to the slaves confined in the Bagnio de la Bastarda and assigned to the public works of Algiers. See chapter 39 of this volume. Cervantes also describes these slaves in "The Captive's Tale," an inset story in *Don Quijote* (I, 40), where he notes both their services to the city and the extreme difficulty of securing their freedom.

3. Most European authors called the *beylerbey,* or *beylerbeyi,* "kings," including Sosa himself. In reality, these figures had the status of viceroys, named by the sultan, as Sosa explains in the closing chapter of this volume. The title of beylerbey of Africa, given to Khayr al-Din and other admirals of

the Ottoman navy, granted them the power of issuing orders (through a delegation) in a sovereign manner over Algiers, the small pashas of Tunis, and the area of Tripoli. In 1544, while beylerbey of Africa, Khayr al-Din appointed his son Hasan as governor of Algiers. The governor was a caliph who exercised power through a delegation.

4. We have used the term *captain* where Sosa uses the Spanish *arráez*, from *ra'is* (A), *re'is* (T): head, chief, leader of a political, religious, juridical, tribal, or other group. In sixteenth-century Algiers, *ra'is* was the name given to the captain of a galliot, especially to a corsair who owned various ships. In the Ottoman navy, the term was used to designate a commander.

5. In his play *Los baños de Argel* [*The Bagnios of Algiers*], Cervantes notes that for those Christian captives who were artisans, carpenters, and shipbuilders it was almost impossible to be liberated (1.5.714–19).

6. Sharshal has replaced the conventional French form Cherchell. We are using Cherchell, however, the name used by Sosa and sixteenth-century Europeans.

7. We have used the familiar English term *marabout*, from *murabit*, the common form in both Turkish and Arabic. A marabout is a Muslim who professes a certain religious state similar in exterior form to that of the Christian anchorites or hermits.

8. *Bonevoglie* (It): In the sixteenth century, these were paid voluntary rowers, either ex–galley slaves who had completed their sentences or vagabonds who had sold their freedom.

9. The Christian corsairs known as the Knights of Saint John of Jerusalem of Malta also invested in a similar manner in corsair activities directed against Ottoman ships and territories. These activities included a complex system of distribution with eleven percent of the booty for the victorious captain, ten percent for the Grand Master of the Order of Malta, and even a small portion for the nuns of Saint Ursula in La Valetta. See Garcés, *Cervantes in Algiers*, 80, 82.

10. In the Ottoman Empire, the term Hodja (modern orthography *hoca*) designated a certain class of civilian officials.

11. *Lewend* (E) from *levend* (T): name given to two kinds of Ottoman daily-wage irregular militia either sea going or land based. Sosa uses the Spanish terms *levante* and *levente* interchangeably. During the hey-day of Ottoman maritime expansion, these lewends, either Muslim or Christian, were hired for a period of the campaign. They acted as guardsmen, rowers, and marines for shore invasion, but mainly as seagoing musket bearers.

12. This marabout, a contemporary of the expedition to Algiers of Charles V in 1541, was called Sidi Batqa according to Ben Mansour, *Alger XVIe–XVIIe siècle,* 262. In honor of the services given Algerians by this holy man (also known as Sidi Abou'tteka or Sidi Betka), all of their ships upon leaving harbor saluted his *kubba,* or tomb, located up on a cliff outside the Gate of Bab 'Azzun, by shouting "Bismillah" [In the name of Allah]. See Devoulx, *Les Édifices réligieux de l'ancien Alger,* 205.

13. Sosa's faulty transliteration is "a la hora, a la hora," whose original is "Bismillah," or "In the name of Allah."

14. Porto Farina (or Ghar al-Milh), twenty miles from Bizerte, was the naval arsenal of the rulers of Tunisia.

15. This was called "doing the book," or *kitab al-tanbih.* The Book of Omens [Libro de presagios] was a horoscope that enjoyed great success across the Maghreb. See Ben Mansour, *Alger XVIe–XVIIe siècle,* 521, n. 5.

16. Various European authors offered a wealth of details on the sorcery and "diabolic sacrifices" practiced in Barbary; see Turbet-Delof, *L'Afrique barbaresque,* 75, 166 n. 20.

17. Sosa contrasts the dexterity of the Algerian corsairs with the backwardness of the Christian sailors, who remained behind because of their heavy galleons. Cervantes underlines this in the remarks of Ginés de Pasamonte about the peace and quiet aboard the galleys of Spain (*Don Quijote* I, 22).

18. Sosa's transliteration here refers to the period called *hasum* (A) (also *al-husum, al-hasum, h'esoum,* or *es sab'a*), which, according to various Hispano-Arabic calendars, began on the twenty-fourth of February and lasted until the fourth of March. The Qur'an has allusions to this period (Sura 69:7), which is characterized by a violent wind that brings sterility to the land. See Dozy, *Supplément aux dictionnaires arabes,* 1:287.

19. Sosa refers here to his *Diálogo de los mártires de Alger* [Dialogue of the Martyrs of Algiers], which relates various martyrdoms of Christian captives, especially of galley slaves.

20. *Ghanima* or *ghunm* (A): booty, in particular moveable booty, which was distributed immediately.

21. As Sosa mentions in the next chapter, the captain of the Algerian corsairs in 1581 was Mami Arnaut, an Albanian renegade.

22. Probably a distortion of *sofra* (T): a term that designates the round tray or platter on which food is placed in Turkey. By extension, *sofra* is generally used for dining: one is invited to dine by saying "*sofra'ya*" [to the table].

23. *Raki* (T): name given to several kinds of alcoholic beverages; also an unsweetened, usually anise-flavored, aperitif.

24. *Garzón* (pl. *garzones*) (Sp): a term used in sixteenth-century Spain to refer to sodomites, especially to the *bardash,* or passive agent, in the sexual relation between men.

Chapter 22. Catalogue of Corsairs

1. Arnaut: An inhabitant of Albania and neighboring mountainous regions, specifically one serving as a soldier in the Turkish army.

2. Dali Mami was the master of the enslaved Miguel de Cervantes, a captive in Algiers for over five years. See Garcés, *Cervantes in Algiers.*

3. Muhammad the Jew was Sosa's slave owner.

4. As this list makes clear, the largest faction of Algerian corsairs in 1581 were Christian renegades from Italy, Corsica, Sicily, Spain, Greece, and Albania. The impressive number of Italian renegades bears noting.

Chapter 23. Corsairs with Frigates

1. A terrifying and vivid representation of one of these raids appears in Cervantes's play, *Los baños de Argel* [*The Dungeons of Algiers*].

2. These are the *bonevoglie* (It), or voluntary rowers, mentioned in chapter 21.

Chapter 24. Algerian Merchants

1. Sosa refers here, among others, to his master, the Jewish renegade Muhammad, who had the treasury of Algiers under his charge.

2. *Peseta* (Sp): Spanish unit of currency, coin that had a different weight and value across the times.

3. In 1536, Francis I of France (1494–1547) signed contracts with the Ottoman Empire that permitted the establishment of French merchants in Turkey, with individual religious liberty. The Franco-Turkish union caused a scandal in Europe, especially when Barbarossa captured Nice and, with the connivance of the French, wintered with all his fleet in Toulon in 1543

and 1544. France continued her alliance with Turkey to the end of the sixteenth century.

4. Bastion de France: a trading post founded by a Corsican family of renegades for coral fishing in a bay close to Bône (Annaba), through a treaty undersigned by the governor of Algiers in 1550. This site also served for the exchange of French merchandise from Marseilles for wheat, wax, hides, gold, spices, and other exotic goods from Africa.

5. Sosa's transliteration may refer to *liyya* or *liayyah* (A): animal fat in North African usage; or to *aliyan* or *aliyanah* (A): lit. "fat in the tail."

6. Possibly *tafl* or *tfal* (A): a kind of mud used like soap for washing; the term also refers to a tender, soft, potter's clay.

Chapter 25. Algerian Laborers and Artisans

1. Sosa uses the term *puntos,* or "points" of honor, from the Spanish *pundonor,* meaning professional or military honor or pride. He also reflects here the disparagement, inherited from the Middle Ages, of the Spaniards of his day for manual labor, considered degrading to nobles as well as professional soldiers. The rupture of these rigid social hierarchies on the part of Ottoman and Algerian society scandalized Europeans. Sosa likens military careers among Christians, especially those of the working class, with nobility and honor.

Chapter 26. Algerian Fashions

1. *Yelek* (T): a sleeveless vest, worn over other clothing in Algiers.
2. Sosa uses *tafetán* (Sp) for the term *khaftan* (P): Originally from Persia, this long garment with sleeves became very popular across the Arab world.
3. *Sendal* (E), *cendal* (Sp): fine, transparent silk or linen fabric.
4. Sosa uses the word *cuzacas,* probably a faulty transliteration. The Arabic name is presumably *hazuqah* or *hazuqa* (not a modern usage) from the verb *hazaqa:* to tighten. This could be a variation of *hizam* (or *hizamah/h'zamah* in North African dialect): waistband worn over the caftan to fasten it. See Wehr, *A Dictionary of Modern Written Arabic.*
5. *Tmak* (A): riding boots, a term used across the Maghreb. Sosa uses the term *borceguíes* (Sp): Moorish half-boots of smooth leather, with or with-

out soles; slippers or shoes were worn over the boots without soles. Covarrubias states that the boots from Morocco were famous. See Covarrubias, *Diccionario de la Lengua Castellana o Española* (1611).

6. *Ra'is* (pl. *ru'asa*) (A), *re'is* (T): head, chief, leader of a political, religious, juridical, tribal, or other group. In the Ottoman navy, the term was used to designate a commander. In sixteenth-century Algiers, *ra'is* was the name given to the captain of a galliot, especially to a corsair who owned various ships.

7. These popular shoes, called *terlik* in Turkish, are used by both men and women. Made of leather or another material and frequently decorated, these shoes have slightly pointed toes but no heels.

8. *Contray* (Sp), from Kortrijk, the Flemish name for Courtrai (Fr): a type of fine wool made in Courtrai or Kortrijk, a Flemish city in Belgium, situated in western Flanders, on the frontier with France. The city has been historically connected with the textile industry since early modern times.

9. *Ferdja*, or *fradja* (A): garment worn by men in Algeria and Tunisia and similar to the *faradjiyya* (A), a long and slim article of clothing, with or without sleeves and with a deep opening in the chest, worn by both men and women under the caftan.

10. *'Arrakiyya* or *'arraqiyah* (A): skullcap for men (Mor, Alg, Tun).

11. Sosa uses *tortora* as his transliteration of *tartura, tartur, tantur* (A): in Algiers, a hat without a crown that was part of the uniform of the military Turkish elite. The usual headgear of the janissaries was called *uskuf* (T).

12. *Deli* (T): lit. "mad, heedless, brave, fiery." A class of cavalry in the Ottoman Empire, formed in the Balkans at the end of the fifteenth or beginning of the sixteenth century. They were called *deli* on account of their extraordinary valor and recklessness.

Chapter 27. The Marabouts of Algiers

1. Marabout (Eng, Fr) (*murabit*, A, T): a religious leader and teacher of Islamic religion in western Africa and, historically, in the Maghreb; generally a scholar of the Qur'an who professes a certain religious state resembling in outward appearance that of Christian anchorites or hermits. The term *murabit* originally designated a species of warrior-monk who lived in a *ribat*, or fortified monastery, on the frontiers of Islam. It is also the epithet that Muslims give to religious men who, having died in a state of sanctity,

rest in tombs or chapels (*zawiya*) visited by the faithful. The term is also applied to the living descendants of these saintly figures.

2. *Caciz, casis, caxis* (Sp, Por): the standard term for marabouts in sixteenth-century Spain and Portugal. It is also spelled *qasis* (A). The term comes from *qass* (A), a preacher of sermons.

3. *Salat:* the ritual prayer, one of the five pillars of Islam.

4. Sosa uses a faulty transliteration and translation of the *shahada:* "le yla, Alá Mahamet era cur Alá" [God is, and God will be, and Muhammad is his prophet]. We have corrected this phrase in the text.

5. *Subh* or *salat al-subh,* also *fajr* (A): morning prayer. Sosa uses *caban,* which is probably a distortion of *fajr.* On the five times of prayer for Muslims, see Rippin, *Muslims,* 101.

6. Sosa uses *dohor* for *zhur* (A) or *salat al-zhur:* (A): prayer at midday.

7. *'Asr* (A) or *salat al-'asr* (A): prayer offered between midday and sunset. Compline is the last part of the Christian divine office, with which the canonical hours of the day end.

8. *Salat al-maghrib* (A): prayer at sunset. Sosa calls this *magarepe,* a deformation of *maghrib.*

9. *'Isha'* or *salat al-'isha'*(A): prayer at nightfall. Sosa calls it *latumat,* again a distortion of the Arabic terms.

10. We have not found the Arabic word corresponding to Sosa's *picos.* For a related term, see *qabdah/cabda/kabzeh* (A): palm, one-fourth of a foot or 12.5 cm.

11. In Spain, since the fifteenth century, on the day of Saint Nicholas, cathedral choirboys chose one among themselves to be the "Little Bishop of Saint Nicholas." This boy would ride along the streets of the city, mounted on a white mule and doling out benedictions to the delight of the public.

12. Sosa's error: the Qur'an is written in Arabic.

13. Sosa represents here the current attitude of sixteenth-century Christians, who generally showed this kind of antipathy and disdain toward Islam.

14. Also Sidi Bou Tayeb.

15. Sosa uses the term *garañón* (Sp), which means a stud horse or camel.

16. The tomb of Sidi Bournous (also Sidi Barnous or Sidi Bennour) is found at the top of the foothills of the mountain of Bouzaréa, which faces the Gate of Bab al-Wad.

17. The complete phrase *Astaghfiru lillah* (A), also *Astaghfiru Allah* and *Astaghfir Allah,* means "I seek forgiveness from God."

18. Most likely *berrada* (*al-barrada*) (A): water jug.

19. Leo Africanus relates a similar story that occurred in Cairo, in the chapter titled "Other Diverse Rules and Sects of the Superstitious Credulity of Many." See his *History and Description of Africa,* pt. 3, p. 153.

20. This is the mosque of the sheik Sidi Ali Ezzouaoui (also Sidi Ali Zouaoui), located outside the Gate of Bab 'Azzun. This religious center included the chapel of the saint, a small mosque, a cemetery, and a fountain whose waters were said to have particular virtues, such as healing sporadic fevers and inducing fertility in sterile women.

21. The chapel of this marabout was located one hundred meters from the Gate of Bab 'Azzun, together with a small mosque.

22. See chapter 21 n. 12. The date of the death of Sidi Batqa (or Sidi Betqa) is an error, since this marabout was alive in 1541, during the expedition of Charles V to Algiers. See Devoulx, "Les édifices religieux de l'ancien Alger," 445.

23. The ancient fort of 'Uludj 'Ali, mentioned in chapter 9.

24. An error, as Sidi 'Abd al-Rahman Tha'alibi died in the year 873 of the Hegira, or 1468–1469 CE, as noted in an inscription over his tomb that was translated by Gorguos, "Bou Ras, historien inédit de l'Afrique septentrionale," 121.

25. Sidi Ahmed Tidjani. This Islamic religious center was converted into a barracks for gendarmes during the first years of the French occupation. It was no longer in existence in 1870–1871, when Dr. Monnereau and A. Berbrugger published their French translation of the *Topographia.*

26. Sidi Yacoub el-Andalusi (Sidi Yacoub El-Andaloussi), also Sidi Ya'qub al-Andalusi. Some one thousand meters northeast of Algiers was found the *kubba,* or saint's tomb, of Sidi Yacoub, a marabout whose history has been forgotten.

27. Hydromancy is the superstitious art of divining by observations of water.

28. *Djinn* (A): a Qur'anic term applied to bodies composed of vapor and flame, which came to play a large role in folklore.

Chapter 28. The Jews of Algiers

1. After their expulsion in 1492, many Spanish Jews immigrated to the Maghreb, settling in Fès, Marrakech, Orán, and Tétouan, among other North African cities. Two communities coexisted in these cities, and each

maintained its own language (Arabic or Spanish), religious and legal traditions, and synagogues. See Zafrani, *Juifs d'Andalousie et du Maghreb*.

2. This phrase contains a veiled allusion to Sosa's master Muhammad, a renegade Jew in charge of the public treasury in Algiers during the period when Sosa was a captive (1577–1581).

3. Sosa was the interlocutor of these Jews in Algiers, who were perhaps friends of his master Muhammad.

4. The mistreatment of the Jews in Morocco and in the Mahgreb during the sixteenth century is described by a traveler from Granada, Luis de Mármol Carvajal: "the Jews in Africa experience great vituperation by the Moors, who wherever they go spit on their faces and beat them up." See Mármol Carvajal, *Descripción general de África*, vol. 2, f. 91. Leo Africanus also refers to the contempt expressed for the Jews in Fès, during the early sixteenth century, and to the dress restrictions imposed on them. See Leo Africanus, *History and Description of Africa*, pt. 3, "On Fès, the New."

5. Probably Soria, Spain.

6. Sosa alludes anew to his master Muhammad, who openly challenged Hasan Pasha, the Venetian, when the latter asked him to give up his Christian captives in 1577. Among these captives were Sosa himself and a Knight of the Order of Malta. Because Muhammad had converted to Islam, Hasan Pasha could not confiscate his slaves. See Garcés, *Cervantes in Algiers*, 75.

Chapter 29. Languages and Currencies

1. The Sousse, or Sous (A): a region in southern Morocco, surrounding the Oued Sous, separated from the Sahara by the Anti-Atlas Mountains. The center for foreign trade of the Sous during the seventeenth century was Agadir, a city situated ten kilometers north of the Sous River.

2. The Kabylia region is much farther away from Algiers than four leagues. On the Kabyle, see chapter 11 n. 10. Sosa does not appear to know the Kabyle language and its various dialects.

3. The term "Franks," originally used by Muslims as "Ifrandj" or "Frandj" (A) for the inhabitants of Charlemagne's empire, was later extended to Europeans in general. In early modern times it was used fairly broadly for the inhabitants of continental Europe and the British Isles.

4. The battle of al-Kasr al-Kabir, or the Battle of the Three Kings, took place on 3 August 1578.

5. The analogy between the *lingua franca* of Barbary and the "guinea speech" used by Spanish and Portuguese writers to represent the dialect of African slaves is significant. Rather than being a sign of culture, this speech was a mark of inferiority for Europeans. See Garcés, *Cervantes in Algiers,* 145–46.

6. Sosa's use of "here" suggests that he either wrote or revised this chapter when he returned to Spain or Sicily.

7. Sosa uses *motical* for *mithkal, mitqal,* or *mithqal* (A), the oldest Arab unit of Troy weight. In Sosa's day it was also a Moroccan coin valued at half a *piaster* (Eng) or *kurush* (T).

8. Sosa uses *zequín* (also *cequí*) (Sp) from *zikki* (Hispano-Arabic); *sikka* (A); *sequin* (Fr); *zecchino* (It): an ancient coin of gold minted in various states of Europe, especially in Venice, and admitted into Africa. It was also a monetary unit in Turkey, beginning in the era of Sultan Bayezid II (1481).

9. *Real* (Sp): a silver coin worth thirty-four *maravedís* at the end of the sixteenth century.

10. Sosa uses *burba* for *bourbe,* a European term for copper coinage still circulating in Morocco and Tunis during the eighteenth century. See Pamuk, *Monetary History of the Ottoman Empire,* 109–10.

11. *Blanca* (Sp): a small copper coin worth half a *maravedí* during the sixteenth century.

12. *Cetil* (Sp), *ceitil* (Por): a Portuguese coin minted in memory of the Conquest of Ceuta, North Africa (1415), commonly used in Castile in the sixteenth century. Its value was one third of a *blanca*.

13. *Akce* or *akche* (T); *asper* in Western sources: a small silver coin used in the Balkans and Anatolia. It was the basic monetary unit in the Ottoman Empire until the end of the seventeenth century.

14. A *rubia* was an Arabic gold coin equivalent to one fourth of a *ciani.* *Ciani* (Sp from A dialectical *zyan,* and this from Abu Zayan, ruler of Tlemcen): low-karat gold coin, used among the Moors of Africa, that was worth one hundred aspers.

15. A *dobla* (from Latin *dupla*) was an antique Castilian gold coin that wavered in value according to the times.

16. Sosa uses *ziana* for *zyan* (N Afr dialectical Arabic, from Abu Zayan, ruler of Tlemcen): a gold coin of low assay value, used among the Moors of Africa, worth one hundred aspers. Sosa uses both the Spanish cianí and the transliteration ziana for zyan.

17. *Sultani* (T): in numismatics, the first Ottoman gold coin. When introduced in 1477–1478 CE, it adopted the weight standard of the Venetian ducat.

18. Djaʿfar Pasha was *beylerbey* of Algiers (1580–1582).

Chapter 30. Marriage Ceremonies

1. *Sfendj or sfenj* (A): general name for North African fritters or doughnuts, very popular in Morocco and Algiers.

2. A similar description of a wedding in Algiers appears in act 2 of Cervantes's play *Los baños de Argel* [*The Bagnios of Algiers*].

3. Yawm al-Khamis: Thursday. Instead of the old names for the days of the week, Islam uses cardinal numbers in altered form, so that Friday becomes "the day of the assembly" and Saturday, the "Sabbath," as follows: Yawm al-Ahad (Sunday), Yawm al-Ithnain (Monday), Yawm al-Thalatha' (Tuesday), Yawm al-Arbʿa' (Wednesday), Yawm al-Khamis (Thursday), Yawm al-Djumʿa (Friday), Yawm al-Sabt (Saturday). See *Encyclopaedia of Islam* (ed. Houtsma et al.).

4. *Sharif* (A): noble, exalted, eminent; in North Africa, a person who traces his origin to the Prophet's family through ʿAli and Fatima.

Chapter 31. Childbirth and Child Rearing

1. Sosa presents here the stereotyped vision of Europeans of the time concerning the Muslim religion and its beliefs, often compared to demonizing cults.

2. This refers to the *khamsa* (A, also *mkhammsa, khumsa*): a piece of jewelry known as the "hand of Fatma." Named after the Prophet's favorite daughter and very popular in the Middle East and in India, this is the only amulet tolerated by Islamic authorities.

3. See chapter 20, "Renegades."

4. Here, Sosa cites in the margin Leo Africanus, *History and Description of Africa*, pt. 5. The cutting of the clitoris done in Syria and Egypt is mentioned by Leo Africanus in his chapter on Cairo, *History and Description of Africa*, pt. 8.

5. *Haram* (A): a term representing everything that is forbidden to the profane and separated from the rest of the world. The cause of this prohibition could be either temporary or intrinsic impurity or a permanent and sublime state of purity.

Chapter 32. Algerian Women's Fashions

1. This refers to the *faraziyya* (A), a long and narrow article of clothing, with a deep opening in the chest, with or without sleeves and worn by both men and women under the *caftan*.

2. *Durra'a* (A, also *der'a, dirra*): long robe with sleeves for both sexes, used in the entire Maghreb. The short-sleeved version used by both sexes in Algiers is called a *gandura* (A).

3. Sosa uses *malaha*, probably referring to *milhafa* (or *mlahfa*) or *tamelhaft* (A): large outer wrap worn by both sexes, entire Maghreb. He could also be alluding to *melia, melya, or m'aya* (A): a large rectangular wrap traditionally in wool but often lighter fabric for performance. Fastened at shoulders with two *hilal* (large pins) and woollen yarn belt wrapped around the hips.

4. *Gonela* (A, from the It *gonnella*): a tunic of leather or silk, generally sleeveless, worn by both sexes. We have not been able to find *goneyla,* probably a transliteration of dialectical Arabic. Sosa could also mean *ghlila* (A): vest for both sexes in Algeria. See "Glossary of Maghribi Clothing" under the *libas* (A) entry in *Encyclopaedia of Islam,* 2nd ed. (ed. Bearman et al.).

5. Probably a *ha'ik* (or *hayk*) or *tahaykt* (A): a cape, usually white, used in North Africa by both sexes.

6. *Banika* (A): term frequently applied in the Arab West to an element of women's hair covering. We have not been able to find *lartia:* a possibility is *lasa* (A): a woman's head scarf of white silk or cotton net into which flat metal strips have been decoratively hammered (Syr.-Pal.). In the Maghreb, a woman's hat was also called a *bikha* (A).

7. Marçais, in *Le costume musulman d'Alger* (1930), calls the Turkish plait garnished with gold fringes an *açaba* or *qaffali,* stating that *açaba* was still used then, while *kefali* or *qaffali* had fallen into disuse. In Egypt, Syria, and Palestine, *'asba* (A) is currently used for a folded scarf worn by women. *'Asaba* (A) is the common word in the Maghreb.

8. *Nkab* (A, N Afr, also *nikab* or *niqab*): a veil that covers the face of married women in Algeria and Morocco; virtually synonymous with *litham.*

9. *Shashiyya, shash* (A): hat with no brim, of soft cloth, worn by both sexes in the Maghreb.

10. *Babushat* (A): a word used in all the Maghreb for slippers used by both sexes.

11. *Sherbil* or *serbil* (A): sandals used by both sexes in the Maghreb.

12. Here Sosa uses *albanega* (Sp), from *albaníqa* (SpA): a hairnet for gathering and covering the hair, and the Arabic of Tetuan still uses the word with a very similar meaning; this Spanish term would be interchangeable with the Arabic *banika*. See note 6 above.

13. *Soualef* (B): tufts of hair over the temples.

14. *Ciani* (Sp from A dialectical *zyan*, and this from Abu Zayan, ruler of Tlemcen): low-karat gold coin, used among the Moors of Africa, that was worth one hundred aspers.

15. Sosa calls them *alhuyque*, which is probably his transliteration for *ha'ik* or *tahaykt* (A): a white cape, used in North Africa by both sexes. See note 5 above.

Chapter 33. Women's Pastimes, Home Decorating, and Cooking

1. Possibly *tafl* or *tfal* (A): a kind of mud used like soap for washing; tender, soft, potter's clay.

2. Sidi Yacoub el Andalusi (also Sidi Yaqub). His *kubba*, or tomb, is found approximately one thousand meters northeast of Algiers. In chapter 27 on the marabouts, Sosa notes that the women of Algiers visited this tomb on Wednesdays.

3. A name probably taken from the district of Fiumara, a municipality in the Province of Reggio Calabria, in the Italian region of Calabria.

4. Sidi Bournous (or Sidi Burnus), whose tomb is found at the top of the mountain called Bouzaréah (A), in front of the Gate of Bab al-Wad.

5. Devoulx calls him Sidi Abou 'tteka, or Sidi Betka (according to usual pronunciation). See Devoulx, *Les Édifices religieux de l'ancien Alger,* 205. Sosa mentions Cid Butica [Sidi Batqa/Sidi Betka] also in chapters 21, 35, and 39.

6. Sidi ʿAbd al-ʿAziz or Sidi ʿAbd el-ʿAziz: the chapel of this marabout was located some one hundred meters from the Gate of Bab ʿAzzun, along with a small mosque.

7. The tomb of Sidi ʿAli Zouaoui (or Sidi ʿAli Ezzouaoui) was located outside the Gate of Bab ʿAzzun, in an area that included the chapel of the

saint, a small mosque, a cemetery, and a fountain of miraculous waters. See Devoulx, "Les édifices religieux de l'ancien Alger," *Revue africaine,* 4:174.

8. Sidi Bou-Tayeb (also Boutayeb), the chief marabout of the main mosque in Algiers; Sosa mentions him in chapter 27.

9. Perhaps Sidi Bel-Abbes.

10. Sidi ʿAbd al-Rahman or Sidi ʿAbd el-Rahman.

11. Sidi Joumʿa or Sidi Joumʿah or Sidi Jumʿah.

12. Probably a distortion of *sofra* (T): a term that designates the round tray or platter on which food is placed in Turkey. By extension, *sofra* is generally used for dining: one is invited to dine by saying *"sofra'ya"* [to the table].

13. This is a clear indication that Sosa also conversed with the women of Algiers about their customs.

14. This kind of woman is called an *ʿarif* (A): lit. "one who knows"; a gnostic.

15. *Sanduk* (A): coffer, chest, but also an open wooden coffin; the term also means a cenotaph.

16. *Maʾida* (A): a solid, low tray-table; also *khuwan* (A).

Chapter 34. Islamic Feast Days and Festivals in Algiers

1. Sosa is writing during the period when the Julian calendar (denoted as old style) ruled in the West: it had months of thirty or thirty-one days, apart from a February of normally twenty-eight days, except for twenty-nine days every four years (i.e., leap years). The Gregorian calendar (new style), which was first introduced into Catholic countries in 1582, is now used across the whole world. The Julian calendar differed from the Gregorian by the omission of only three leap years for every four hundred years.

2. In effect, the Muslim calendar is based on a lunar year, as opposed to the Gregorian calendar, which is based on the solar calendar. Twelve lunar months add up to some 354 days on average; as such, the Muslim year is shorter, by eleven days more or less, than the solar (tropical) calendar. The Muslim calendars ignore this difference so that the months move across the solar system, with each year beginning eleven days before the Gregorian year.

3. Ramadan is the only month of the year mentioned in the Qurʾan, in the passage related to the fasting during this period (2:161–65).

4. Each month begins with the appearance of the new moon; as such, the duration of a month cannot be predicted beforehand. There is a norm,

however, related to Ramadan: if the moon has still not appeared in the thirtieth night after the start of Ramadan, due to adverse conditions of climate, then the fasting is considered to be over. This means that Ramadan cannot last more than thirty days.

5. They can obtain a dispensation, but they do not take advantage of it because they are obliged to exchange the days in which they eat for others in which they fast, and it seems especially hard for them to fast when everybody else is eating.

6. Laylat al-Kadr (A, also called Laylat Sabʿ waʾIshrin), the night of the twenty-seventh of Ramadan, described in the Qurʾan as a night "more precious than a thousand months" (97:3), is when the angels descend to earth. Such a night brings with it benedictions until the arrival of dawn. The Islamic tradition teaches that the Qurʾan was brought down from Heaven during this night, and that the Angel Gabriel bound it into one volume, dictating it to Muhammad in the space of twenty-three years. Sosa's term *axerim* is probably a contraction or faulty transliteration of Laylat Sabʿ waʾIshrin.

7. Al-ʿId al-Saghir, lit. "minor festival" (also called ʿId al-Fitr, lit. "festival of the breaking of the fast"), was the fiesta celebrated on the first of Shawwal and in the days that followed. Because this festival, although "minor," marks the end of the fasting period, it is celebrated with more joy and delight than the major festival, or al-ʿId al-Kabir. Sosa alludes to the Turkish term for this celebration, Seker Bayram.

8. Sosa uses the term *pasapasa* for a game of prestidigitation or sleight-of-hand.

9. Clearly here Sosa's terms *caba* and *axerim* mean "Sabʿ waʾIshrin," that is, one word confused as two.

10. ʿUludj ʿAli (1520–1587) was a Calabrian corsair and renegade who came to be governor of Algiers (1568–1571) and grand admiral (*kapudan pasha*) of the Turkish armada, rebuilding this armada after the battle of Lepanto. His name in Western literature has been Italianized as Occhiali or Ochali and Hispanicized as Uchalí. Sosa dedicates to him chapter 18 of his *Epítome de los reyes de Argel* [History of the Kings of Algiers] while Cervantes praises him in *Don Quijote* (I, 40).

11. Al-ʿId al-Kabir, lit. "major festival," as opposed to the "minor festival" (al-ʿId al-Saghir); the major festival is also known as ʿId al Adha or ʿId al-Kurban.

12. *Mawlid* or *malud*: the day, place, or celebration of the birth of a person, especially of the prophet Muhammad, a festival celebrated on the twelfth

day of Rabi' al-Awwal, or the third month of the Islamic calendar. The term *mawlid* also designates a panegyric poem in honor of the Prophet.

13. The allusion to the prophets of Baal refers to the false gods mentioned in the Bible. Sosa's prejudices against Islam are manifest here.

14. A holy day celebrated by the Catholic Church on the second of February in honor of the feast of the Purification of the Virgin Mary. A procession is made and a Mass is heard with the candles lit.

15. The women can participate in the prayer on Fridays, but they are not obliged to do so. See Rasdi, *The Mosque as a Community Development Centre,* esp. 171.

Chapter 35. A Miscellany of Muslim Customs in Algiers

1. 'Abd al-Malik of Morocco (1541–1578) fled with his brothers Ahmad and 'Abd al-Mu'min to Tlemcen and later to Algiers, when his brother 'Abdallah assumed the throne (1577). 'Abd al-Malik moved to Constantinople but 'Abd al-Mu'min remained in Tlemcen, where he was later assassinated by henchmen sent by 'Abdallah. See García-Arenal, *Ahmad al-Mansur,* 22–23.

2. Sosa uses *ceba* for *subh,* or *salat al-subh* (A): morning prayer. The five salats that must be performed by all Muslims are the *salat al-subh;* the *salat al-zhur,* or the mid-afternoon prayer; the *salat al-Asr,* or the late afternoon prayer; the *salat al-maghrib,* or the sunset prayer, and the *salat al-isha,* or the night prayer. See Rasdi, *The Mosque as a Community Development Centre,* 171.

3. Al-Abbasi: El-Abbès. Possibly a tribal gang (related to the Bani Abbas, or Ouled Abbas), who were known by the name.

4. Hadjdj (A): the pilgrimage to Mecca, Arafat, or Mina, one of the five pillars of Islam, is also called the Great Pilgrimage. He who does this is called a *hadjdj* or *hadjdji.*

5. Hadjdji Murad, or Agi Morato (his Italianized name as used by Sosa and Spaniards), was an important Ottoman functionary, a representative of the Grand Turk and one of the most important ka'ids of Algiers during the decade of the 1570s. From 1572 on, he was involved in secret negotiations with the Spanish, aiming to establish a peace with the Ottoman Empire, a treaty finally signed in 1589.

6. This is a credible description. While not done very often today, the Hadjdj until recent decades was considered something quite extraordinary and the pilgrim used to be treated with great deference, especially in popular

and rural milieus. The hardship of the trip is legendary; in the past, it took months, years, or decades to complete.

7. It is doubtful that this act occurred regularly.

8. Sosa has a marginal citation here to Leo Africanus, *History and Description of Africa,* pt. 4.

9. Sosa transliterates the name as Rábita. This mosque's name was either Mesdjed Errabta (after the ascetic or holy woman) or Mesdjed el-Merabta (after their Saint Ezzerzoua). It was demolished in 1832 by the French for reasons of public utility. See Devoulx, "Les Edifices réligieux de l'ancien Alger," *Revue africaine* 11:447.

10. *Sharif* (A): honorable, noble, highborn, or high-bred, a term associated with honor and nobility. A sharif claims descent from distinguished ancestors, usually from Muhammad through his grandson Hasan. The title is particularly important in, but not limited to, Shii Islam, where veneration for Muhammad and his family has led to the particular eminence of his descendants. A sharif usually wears a green or white turban to distinguish himself from others. The Sunni rulers of Jordan and Morocco claim sharif status.

11. ʿ*Ushr,* ʿ*ushur* or *ashor* (A): the tithe or tenth, a form of *zakat* (A): obligatory alms. In the Ottoman Empire, it was the land tax levied on the produce of agricultural land owned by Muslims in the pre-modern era.

12. Site of the oracle at Delphi, within a temple dedicated to the god Apollo. Delphi was revered throughout the entire Greek world as the site of the Omphalos or conical block of stone regarded as the central point of the earth.

13. Sosa's "Dodo Naxos" is doubtless a reference to Dodona, a major oracular site in ancient Greece, similar to Delphi and associated with an oak tree. Naxos did have temples, but was not an oracular site. It was common for urns to be situated at oracular sites.

14. This marabout was called Sidi Batqa, according to Ben Mansour, *Alger XVIe–XVIIe siècle,* 262. In honor of his services, Algerian sailors upon leaving port always saluted his tomb outside the Gate of Bab ʿAzzun, saying aloud "bismillah" [In the name of Allah]; Devoulx calls him Sidi Betka in *Les Edifices religieux de l'ancien Alger,* 205; Sosa also mentions him in chapters 21 and 34.

15. Sosa uses Jaban (A) as his transliteration: lit. "cowardly."

16. Having set sail from Barcelona for Valetta, Malta, Sosa and his family were among the 290 passengers captured from the galley *San Pablo* of the

Order of Malta, which had taken refuge after a tempest in the island of Saint Peter, close to Sardinia.

17. The Sicilian Carlo d'Aragona e Tagliava, Duke of Terranova and Prince of Castelvetrano, was president of the kingdom of Sicily between 1571 and 1577. The incident described above is recounted by Sosa in chapter 21 of his *Epítome de los Reyes de Alger* [History of the Kings of Algiers], where he describes how the Duke of Terranova escaped from this attack of the Algerian corsairs by crashing his ship against the island of Capri and jumping out of the ship.

18. Luis Brevez Fresco, Genoese merchant and spy, is the author of a secret report about Algiers that Doctor Sosa sent to Mateo Vázquez in 1582. See the introduction to this volume.

19. The last master of Montesa was Pedro Luis Garcerán de Borja, son of the Duke of Gandía, brother of Saint Francisco de Borja. In 1566, he was named captain general of the kingdoms of Tlemcen and Ténès, and governor of the cities and plazas of Orán and Mers-el-Kebir. In 1572, the Inquisition of Valencia arrested him for sodomy and condemned him to ten years imprisonment in the monastery of Montesa and a fine of six thousand ducats. He soon ingratiated himself with Philip II and obtained as a prize the major land grant of Calatrava and, in 1591, the viceroyship of Catalonia.

20. *Karwan* or *kafila* (A, also *al-qafila*): caravan; these caravans were composed of mules, donkeys, and, especially, camels. From the seventeenth century on, the term *kafila* was also used to designate merchant reunions or their equivalent.

21. Between 1563 and 1583, Tangier or Tangiers (present-day Tanger) was occupied by the Portuguese.

22. Probably a slang word used in North Africa from the root of the verb *katama* (A): to hide, but also to suppress, repress, restrain, check, curb, subdue.

23. Dja'far Pasha, Hungarian renegade, was *beylerbey* of Algiers from September 1580 until May 1582. Sosa describes him as a just and honest ruler, who treated Christian captives well; see his *Epítome de los Reyes de Alger* [History of the Kings of Algiers], chapter 22.

24. There is great controversy about the permissibility of manumitting a non-Muslim slave in Islam; yet Muslim religious scholars are of the opinion that freeing the slave after seven years is highly recommended (compare Exodus 21:2, Deuteronomy 15:12). Manumission is permitted when the slave is mutilated by the master, or if he is smitten with leprosy or blindness.

According to Imam Ja'far al-Sadiq, if a slave is Muslim and has worked for seven years then he should be set free. Forcing him to work after seven years is not permissible. In the Ottoman Empire, the manumission contract (*kitaba*, based on Qur'an 24:33) was used by the state as a device to end slavery by giving slaves the means to buy their freedom from their masters.

25. This is the first of the three dialogues that culminate Sosa's work: *Diálogo primero. De la captividad en Argel* [Dialogue of Captivity in Algiers], *Diálogo Segundo. De los mártires de Argel* [Dialogue of the Martyrs of Algiers], and *Diálogo Tercero. De los morabutos de Argel* [Dialogue of the Marabouts].

26. *Mizwar* (A, also *mazwar*): he who precedes, he who is placed at the head. In North Africa, chief of a religious brotherhood, the superintendent of a *zawiya*, or the chief of a body of troops, equivalent to the Arabic *mukaddam* (chief, captain).

27. Sosa reveals here the Iberian concept of honor, based on rigid social hierarchies. From the point of view of the European aristocracy, Algerian society seemed constituted by low status beings, without honor or virtue.

28. Ramadan Pasha was beylerbey of Algiers between 1574 and 1577, and, once again, in 1583.

Chapter 36. Algerian Vices

1. Sosa cites in the margin chapter 13 of St. John's Apocalypse. The comparison of Algiers to the seven-headed beast of the Apocalypse was very common in the age. Pierre Dan, a French Trinitarian and ransomer of captives, picks up the same thread in his *Histoire de Barbarie, et de ses corsaires* (1647).

2. The Battle of Lepanto, in which the Christian armadas of Spain, Venice, and the Holy See clashed with that of the Ottoman Empire, took place on 7 October 1571.

3. In 1573, Don Juan of Austria captured Tunis, setting up a puppet government with Muley Muhammad to head the Moorish and Berber populations. Tunis, along with Muley Muhammad, would be recaptured by the Turks in 1574. Cervantes has his Captive discuss these events in *Don Quijote* (I, 39).

4. Sosa refers here to the conquest of Portugal in 1580 by Philip II. The great amassment of troops and soldiers in 1579 and 1580 throughout all of Andalucía and Cádiz, as well as the passage of galleys with infantry, made the Algerians think that the Spanish king was about to attack Algiers. In his

Epítome de los Reyes de Argel [History of the Kings of Algiers], Sosa stresses the "tremendous fright experienced by every Algerian that all these preparations were aimed against their city" (*Topografía* 2:383–84, our translation).

5. Words such as these call attention to the hot certainty shown by Sosa and the majority of Christians of the age about their religious beliefs, which they considered in accord with reason.

6. Many Western travelers mentioned greed among the most cited vices of the Turks. Imperial ambassador Busbecq states that it was necessary to advance in Ottoman territories with a purse in hand: "those who want to live among the Turks must resolve to open their purses as soon as they enter their territory, and not ever close them until they have actually left the country" (Busbecq, *Ambassade en Turquie et Amasie de Mr. Busbequis,* f. 58, our translation).

7. Pliny recounts the myth of the existence of some giant ants in India, who extract grains of gold from the gold-bearing alluvium (*Naturalis Historia,* bk. 11, chap. 31). The oldest source for this fable is found in Herodotus, *Historiae,* bk. 3, chaps. 102–5.

8. Sosa's claim is strange, including the case mentioned below, because giving charity is common among Muslims. Other Western authors, however, praise both the liberality of the Turks and their charity. As proof of their openhandedness, Juan Sagredo mentions the alms they give and the many hospitals they have constructed for the poor; see his *Memorias históricas de los monarcas othomanos,* 1:5. Sosa cites in the margins B. Greg., *Moralia,* bk. 31. The reference is probably to Pope Gregory I, also known as Gregory the Great (ca. 530–604), a prolific author who wrote a *Moralia*; see Gregory I, *Morals on the Book of Job.* Another possibility is the *Moralia* by Plutarch (ca. 46–120 CE), Greek biographer and moral philosopher, whose treatises on various ethical, religious, and cosmic questions influenced later authors such as Montaigne and Francis Bacon. For translations of Plutarch's *Moralia* in early modern Spain, see Morales Ortiz, *Plutarco en España.*

9. Hasan Pasha, was the son of Barbarossa. Hasan governed Algiers as his father's lieutenant between 1544 and 1551, and again, after Barbarossa's death, between 1557 and 1561. Like his father, Hasan Barbarossa spent most of his life in the Levant, although he is said to have been present at Lepanto in 1581.

10. Sosa uses the term *kardaxi* [*kardaji*] for *karindas* or *kardes* (T): brother or sister; fraternal.

11. In his *Diálogo de los mártires de Alger* [Dialogue of the Martyrs of Algiers], Sosa refers to the case of Alicax, a Morisco processed and burned by

the Inquisition of Valencia in 1576. By way of retaliation for this burning, the Algerians executed a captive priest, Father Miguel de Aranda, in 1577.

12. In sixteenth-century Spain, the term *garzón* (pl. *garzones*) referred to sodomites, especially to the *bardash,* or passive agent in the sexual relation between men.

13. Probably a distortion of *sofra* (T): a term that designates the round tray or platter on which food is placed in Turkey. By extension, *sofra* is generally used for dining: one is invited to dine by saying *"sofra'ya"* [to the table].

14. Setúbal is a Portuguese city situated in the estuary of the Sado River, some forty kilometers south of Lisbon.

15. While some Western authors affirmed that the Turks were abstinent, others stated that they were inveterate drunkards. Anecdotes abound on both sides. Fajardo y Acevedo alludes to their fondness for the tavern, while Busbecq speaks of their abstinence, which was one of the characteristics of their combatants. See Fajardo and Acevedo, *Relación universal de todo el imperio ottomano,* MS 2793, f. 194; Busbecq, *Ambassade en Turquie et Amasie,* 187.

16. Sosa describes these tortures in both his *Dialogo de la captividad* [Dialogue of Captivity] and his *Diálogo de los mártires de Argel* [Dialogue of the Martyrs of Algiers].

Chapter 37. Algerian Virtues

1. As earlier noted in chapter 20, "Customs of the Janissaries," Sosa's affirmation is incorrect.

2. Sosa uses the term *exabi* for *ijabi* or *ijaba* (A): seeking God's "response" by saying a prayer such as *istighfar:* "Astaghfiru Allah" ["I seek forgiveness from Allah," or "I seek Divine protection"] or "Aʿudhu bi-Allahi mina ash-shaytaani ar-rajeem" [I seek refuge with Allah from Satan, the accursed].

3. Probably "Bismillah" (A) (Bism Allah): "In the name of Allah" or "In the name of God" rather than Basmala (Basmalah) (A): the noun that is used as the collective name of the whole of the recurring phrase "bism Allah al-rahman al-rahim" ["In the name of God, the Clement, the Merciful"]. Our guess is that Sosa likely means the more common "Bismillah," since the second is the rather learned usage requiring sophisticated knowledge of grammar or theological terminology.

4. Yol-dash (T): "comrades at arms," or soldiers. Janissaries were also called Odjak-eri (T, modern spelling: Ocak-eri), or "hearth-mates," from *odjak* or *ocak* (T): "fireplace, chimney, hearth"; also an army unit.

Chapter 38. Death and Burial in Algiers

1. Normally the *shahada* (A), or Islamic confession of faith, was recited in the ear of the moribund, whose face was turned toward Mecca. See *djanaza* (A): corpse, coffin, and then, funeral.

2. A person whose job was to wash the dead was called a *gassal* or *gassil* (A). The social position of a gassal was higher than that of a person who did laundry.

3. This functionary was called *sahib bayt al-mal,* or administrator of the goods of the Bayt al-mal—the treasury of the Muslim state. He was responsible for picking up vacant inheritances in the name of the Turkish government. On the laws of inheritance in Islam, see "Mirath" in the *Encyclopaedia of Islam* (ed. Bearman et al.). See also Akram Khan, *Islamic Economics and Finance,* 33.

4. This appears to be a bad translation of the shahada—"I testify that there is no god but God and I testify that Muhammad is the messenger of God."

5. *Mashhad* (A): generally a tomb, usually with an inscription saying that the deceased was a Muslim. Here it refers to tombstones; *mashhad* also means shrine or commemorative mosque.

6. *Kubba* or *qubba* (A): dome or domed building.

7. Sosa's transliteration is "Cebam Allah" for "Subhan Allah" or "Subhanallah" (A).

8. This is an error on Sosa's part. According to Jewish religious laws, the deceased is buried in the earth in a horizontal manner with no coffin. Transverse stones are immediately located atop the body, forming a vault to isolate it from contact with the earth that is supposed to cover it. Sosa may be confusing this ceremony with another procedure: during medieval times, Jews in Muslim countries used to bury their damaged sacred books in the *geniza* or *genizah* (Heb), a place in their cemeteries where Hebrew writings were deposited in order to prevent the desecration of the name of God. The buried sacred book would therefore not always appear entirely horizontal.

9. The Jews use only one gravestone for each of their dead.

10. The following paragraphs with detailed descriptions of the mortuary rites celebrated by Jews in Algiers can be explained by Sosa's incarceration in the house of the renegade Jew Muhammad, where the captive may have witnessed many Jewish ceremonies, especially on the part of Jewish women and other Jews who had not converted to Islam.

11. Obliged by the Ottoman government to wear black garments as distinctive of their culture, the Jews indicated their mourning by throwing over their heads the hood of the *burnus* generally used in Algiers.

Chapter 39. Algerian Buildings and Fountains

1. Sosa probably refers to the Grand Mosque (Jama Kebir, ca. 1097 CE), traditionally said to be the oldest mosque in Algiers. This mosque occupies some two thousand square meters.

2. Sosa may be alluding here to the *kaba* (A): a cape with sleeves used by soldiers, sometimes a luxury cape with sleeves and buttons, generally made of brocade.

3. Sosa refers to the mosque of Sidi 'Abd al-Rahman Tha'alibi, also known as the Mosque of the Old Kasba (A), situated near the site of the citadel of Algiers.

4. The Great Mosque, constructed in 1324 CE, has stones with Roman inscriptions, which may have been taken from the ruins of Icosium.

5. This is a *hipocaust*, or oven, situated beneath the pavement (or in another chamber) that in classical antiquity heated the rooms.

6. Sosa seems to allude to the original indigenes of the Oasis of Beni Mzab or Mzabites who until the nineteenth century practiced this profession in Algiers and other cities of North Africa. Hugh Chisolm notes that "the butchers, fruiterers, bath-house keepers, road-sweepers and carriers of the African littoral from Tangier to Tripoli are nearly all Mzabites." See Chisolm, *Encyclopaedia Britannica*, 19:145.

7. Monnereau and Berbrugger, the French translators of Haedo/Sosa's *Topographia* (1998), indicate that this bath still existed in 1870, known under the name of Hamman Sidna, or Bath of Our Lord [Hasan]. See Haedo, *Topographie et histoire générale d'Alger*, 210.

8. Muhammad Pasha, who governed Algiers from 1566 to 1568.

9. Dar al-Sultan (lit. "house or 'realm' of the sultan"; the residence of the *beylerbeys*), also known as the Djenina, or "small garden." A magnificent description of this house, made in 1854 by Berbrugger, has been reproduced in the French translation of Haedo [Sosa], *Topographie et histoire générale d'Alger*, 211–18.

10. *Ghurfat* (A, *ghurfa* or *ghurfah*): rooms on upstairs floors; *ghurfat al-juluws*: sitting room; in North Africa, among the Berbers, *ghurfat* signifies a fortified enclosure.

11. Ramadan Pasha governed Algiers from 1574 to 1577, and again in 1583.

12. Muhammad the Jew, Sosa's master, had one of the finest houses in Algiers.

13. *Makhzen, makhzan,* or *makhzin* (A): a storehouse; in North African usage it stands for "the State"; it also indicates the political system based on the oath of allegiance of the tribal chiefs to the sultan.

14. Hasan the Venetian was the slave and renegade of the Calabrian ʿUludj ʿAli, who became the grand admiral of the Ottoman fleet (1571–1587). Hasan was, therefore, *his* renegade, that is, his lieutenant. The Great Bagnio, or "Bagnio of the King," held all the elite captives of the government and of other prominent figures in Algiers. Cervantes was a captive there between 1575 and 1580.

15. In this battle, the Count of Alcaudete, governor of Orán, lost his life. Among the thousands of soldiers taken captive on this occasion was his son, Don Martín of Córdoba, whose rescue cost the enormous sum of 23,000 *escudos* of gold. Some of these captives, still imprisoned in Algiers between 1577 and 1581, provided information to Sosa for his *Epítome de los Reyes de Argel* [History of the Kings of Algiers].

16. In Turkish, as in Venetian usage, the *bastarda* was a galley larger than the *fallea sensile,* but smaller than the *galeassa,* or *galliass.* The bastarda had a rounded poop resembling a watermelon. The Ottoman Turks adopted the name *bashtarda, basharda* (T) from the Italian *bastarda* (Fr *bastarde* or *bastardelle,* Sp *bastarda*).

17. Djaʿfar Pasha was king of Algiers from 1580 to 1581.

18. ʿArab Ahmad governed Algiers from 1571 to 1573.

19. Salah Raʾis, who governed Algiers from 1552 to 1556, succeeded Hasan Pasha, the son of Barbarossa. In the semi-independent Regency, or *beylerbeyilik,* of Algiers, the term *raʾis* (pl. *ruaʾsa*) became associated with commanders of corsair ships.

20. Hasan the Corsican briefly governed Algiers (1556–1557) after the death of Salah Raʾis. When Istanbul dispatched Muhammad Takali as the new governor of Algiers, the janissaries who had supported Hasan blocked the newcomer's entrance into Algiers. Takali, however, conspired with the raʾis and with members of the Odjak and managed to enter the city. Hasan was captured and impaled on the Gate of Bab ʿAzzun.

21. Muhammad Takali: chosen as ruler of Algiers by the Grand Turk in 1556, an appointment refused by the janissaries and secured by the corsairs.

Takali was assassinated by Yusuf, a renegade of Hasan the Corsican, in 1557. In the archives of Algiers, Takali also appears written as Tekali, Tekerli, etc.

22. See chapter 8 of Haedo [Sosa], *Epítome de los Reyes de Argel* [History of the Kings of Algiers]. This passage suggests that Sosa wrote the *Epítome* before the *Topographia* (proper).

23. The Sardinian Hasan Agha governed Algiers as the caliph of Khayr al-Din when the latter was named *kapudan pasha* of the Ottoman armada in 1535. Hasan administered the Regency of Algiers until 1545.

24. This refers to the tomb of the sheik Sidi Ali Ezzouaoui, located outside the Gate of Bab 'Azzun, as mentioned in chapters 27 and 33. This mosque was destroyed by the French.

Chapter 40. The Natural Beauty of Algiers

1. This was probably a plague called "evil eye," most likely trachoma or ophthalmia, eye diseases prevalent in North Africa and other Mediterranean countries.

2. Sosa's use of the adjective *alcinoeos* probably refers to Alcinous, the king of the Phaeacians in Homer's *Odyssey*.

3. Fiumara is both a town and a region in the province of Reggio Calabria (Italy). As such, it was probably an Italian word used by Christian captives and renegades, in Algiers, to refer to the small river mentioned by Sosa. This stream of water that gives its name to the Gate of Bab al-Wad is simply called Wadi (river or dry riverbed).

4. Mitidja: a plain of fourteen hundred kilometers situated south of the city of Algiers. Part of these lands has been urbanized.

5. Sosa's claim is very odd because deer and rabbits abound in Algiers.

6. The European name for the Atlas Mountains, which cross North Africa, reflects the belief of the ancient Greeks that they were the home of the god Atlas. In Arabic these mountains are called Jazirat al-Maghrib (Island of the West) because they are like an "island" of relative fertility in a desert region west of Egypt.

7. Sosa cites in the margin Pliny, *Natural History*, bk. 5.

Chapter 41. The Government of Algiers

1. Sosa suggests at various points that he wrote his *Epítome de los Reyes de Argel* [History of the Kings of Algiers] before the *Topography* proper.

2. *Pasha* (T): In the Ottoman Empire, a man who obtained a superior command, either at sea or as viceroy or governor of some province.

3. *Sandjak-bey* (T): governor of a district or political region; from *sandjak* (T), a political region and an administrative unit in Ottoman administration, and *bey* (T), a title given to the highest civil functionaries and to military officers of the rank of colonel or lieutenant colonel. Algiers, under the Turks, was the first sandjak of the Barbary Coast.

4. *ʿAdl* (A): assessor of the *kadi;* lit. "a person of good morals." His testimony was necessary to validate the acts. The first of these, called *bash-ʿadl,* has the office of a forensic scribe.

5. *Caʾush* (T): officials staffing the various Ottoman Palace departments. Their services were also used as ambassadors or envoys by the sultan or his grand vizier. In North Africa, the term is still seen in its Arabic form (*shawish* or *shawush*), where it means a court usher or mace-bearer.

6. *Mizwar* (A): lit. "he who precedes; he who is placed at the head." In North Africa, he is the chief of a religious brotherhood or chief of a body of troops.

7. *Muhtasib* (A): inspector of both merchandise and public morality who reinforces the payment of taxes and market regulations, levying dues and taxes on traders, artisans, and also on certain imports.

8. *Dawar* (A) (Sp *aduar*): an encampment of the Arab Bedouins in which the tents are arranged in a circle around an open space where the cattle pass the night. In North Africa, this arrangement is called *duwar* or *dawwar.*

9. *Al-amin* (*el-amin*) (A): title applied to treasurers, customs officers, stewards of estates, etc. *Amin:* used to denote the holders of various positions of trust, particularly those whose functions entail economic or financial responsibility. In works on the Law, the word denotes legal representatives. One technical meaning of *amin* is head of a trade guild.

10. Tabarka (A): a rocky islet off the coast of Tunisia, where the Genovese family of the Lomellini constructed a fort around 1535 by order of Charles V. The Lomellini purchased a grant of coral finishing from the Turkish-Algerian Regency and maintained a garrison on this island from 1540 to 1742.

11. Bastion de France: a trading post founded by a Corsican family of renegades for coral fishing in a bay close to Bône, through a treaty undersigned by the governor of Algiers in 1550. This site also served for the exchange of French merchandise from Marseilles for wheat, wax, hides, gold, spices, and other exotic goods from Africa.

12. In the sixteenth century, the Kabyle peoples were divided between three powers, according to Western writers: the kingdom of Kuko, the kingdom of Labbès (Banu 'Abbas), and the kingdom of the Banu Djubar. During the Turkish domination, the different Kabyle groups sometimes allied themselves with, sometimes rebelled against, and sometimes negotiated with the rulers of Algiers.

13. Zwawa (also Zouaoua): tribes belonging to one of three Berber groups scattered throughout the central and the farthest Maghreb.

ARCHIVAL SOURCES

Archivio Capitolari, Cattedrale di Agrigento (ACA)
Atti Capitolari, vol. 1, 1580–1619

Archivio Diocesano, Agrigento (ADA)
Reg. 1578/79
Reg. 1584/1585

Archivio di Stato di Venezia (ASVE)
Sen., Dis., Cost., filza 68

Archivo de la Real Chancillería de Valladolid (ARCV)
"Provisiones de Cátedras," signatura Caja 337

Archivo del Ministerio de Asuntos Exteriores, Madrid (AMAE)
Embajada de España ante la Santa Sede, Legajo 35–4

Archivo General de Simancas, Valladolid (AGS)
Cámara de Castilla, Legajos 404–90, 510
Estado, Legajos 1073, 1084, 1148, 1155
Guerra Antigua, Legajo 83
Secretarías Provinciales, Legajos 2, 3
Secretarías Provinciales, Libros 639, 842, 845, 846, 850, 982, 1043

Archivo Histórico Nacional, Madrid (AHN)
Estado, Legajo 2267
Inquisición, Libros 274, 356, 357, 879

Archivo Segreto Vaticano, Rome (ASV)
Misc. Arm. V., Cap. 4, n. 68

Biblioteca Apostolica Vaticana, Vatican City
    MSS Vat. Lat. 5298, fols. 83r–118v

Biblioteca Nacional, Madrid (BN)
    MS 2793
    MS 14630

British Library, London (BL)
    Add. 28342

Instituto de Valencia de Don Juan, Madrid (IVDJ)
    Envío 62, Caja 2

BIBLIOGRAPHY

Abu-Lughod, Lila. *Veiled Sentiments: Honor and Poetry in a Bedouin Society.* Berkeley: University of California Press, 1986.
———. *Writing Women's Worlds: Bedouin Stories.* Berkeley: University of California Press, 1992.
Albertini, Francesco. *Francisci Albertini opusculum de mirabilibus novae urbis Romae.* Heilbronn: Henninger, 1886.
Alcalá, Ángel, ed. *Proceso inquisitorial de Fray Luis de León. Edición paleográfica, anotada y crítica.* Salamanca: Junta de Castilla y León, Consejería de Cultura y Turismo, 1991.
al-Ghassni, Wazir Muhammad ibn 'Abd al Wahab. *Voyage en Espagne d'un ambassadeur marocain, 1690–1691.* Translated by Henry Sauvaire. Paris: E. Leroux, 1884.
Allende Salazar, Ángel. *Biblioteca del bascófilo. Ensayo de un catálogo general sistemático y crítico de las obras referentes á las Provincias de Viscaya, Guipúzcoa, Álava y Navarra.* Madrid: Imprenta de Manuel Tello, 1887.
Anderson, Benedict R. O'G. *Imagined Communities: Reflections on the Origin and Spread of Nationalism.* New York: Verso, 1991.
Antoninus Augustus Pius. *Itinerarium provinciarum omnium Antonini Augusti, cum Fragmento eiusdem necnon indice haud quaque aspernando.* Paris: Henriccus Stephanus Estienne, 1512.
Apian, Peter. *Cosmographia Petri Apiani, Per Gemmam Frisivm . . . iam demum ab omnibus vindicata mendis, ac nonnullis quoque locis aucta. Additis eiusdem argumenti libellis ipsius Gemmae Frisij.* Antuerpiae: Veneunt Gregorio Bontio, 1553.
Aranda, Emanuel d'. *Les captifs d'Alger.* Edited by Latifa Z'Rari. Paris: J.-P. Rocher, 1998.
Asconius Pedianus, Quintus. *Orationum Ciceronis quinque enarratio.* English and Latin. *Commentaries on Five Speeches of Cicero.* Edited and translated by Simon Squires. Bristol: Bristol Classical Press, 1990.
———. *Q. Asconii Pediani Orationum Ciceronis quinque enarratio: recognovit breviqve adnotatione critica instruxit Albertus Curtis Clark.* Oxonii: Typographeo Clarendoniano, 1907.

Astrana Marín, Luis. *Vida ejemplar y heroica de Miguel de Cervantes Saavedra.* 7 vols. Madrid: Instituto Editorial Reus, 1949–1952.

Atlas of the World. 15th ed. New York: Oxford University Press, 2008.

Balbi, Hieronymi (Girolamo). *De rebus Turcicis libers.* Roma: Minitivm Calvvm, 1526.

Barletta, Vincent. *Covert Gestures: Crypto-Islamic Literature as Cultural Practice in Early Modern Spain.* Minneapolis: University of Minnesota Press, 2005.

———, ed. and trans. *A Memorandum for the President of the Royal Audiencia and Chancery Court of the City of the Kingdom of Granada,* by Francisco Nuñez Muley. Chicago: University of Chicago Press, 2007.

Barrios Aguilera, Manuel. *Granada morisca. La convivencia negada.* Granada: Editorial COMARES, 2002.

Barrios Aguilera, Manuel, and Mercedes García-Arenal, eds. *¿La historia inventada? Los libros plúmbeos y el legado sacromontano.* Granada: Universidad y Legado Andalusí, 2008.

———, eds. *Los plomos del Sacromonte. invencion y tesoro.* Valencia: Universitat de València, 2006.

Bazzano, Nicoletta. *Marco Antonio Colonna.* Roma: Salerno Editrice, 2003.

Becker, Cynthia J. *Amazigh Arts in Morocco: Women Shaping Berber Identity.* Austin: University of Texas Press, 2006.

Belhamisi, Moulay. *Histoire de la marine algérienne (1516–1830).* Alger: Entreprise Nationale du Livre, 1983.

Ben Mansour, Abd El Hadi. *Alger XVIe–XVIIe siècle. Journal de Jean-Baptiste Gramaye "évêque d'Afrique."* Paris: Les Éditions du Cerf, 1998.

Bennassar, Bartolomé, and Lucile Bennassar. *Les chrétiens d'Allah. L'histoire extraordinaire des renégats. XVI et XVII siècles.* Paris: Perrin, 1989.

———. *Los cristianos de Alá. La fascinante aventura de los renegados.* Translated by José Luis Gil Aristu. Madrid: Nerea, 1989.

Bernáldez, Andrés. *Memorias del reinado de los Reyes Católicos.* Madrid: Real Academia de la Historia y Consejo Superior de Investigaciones Científicas, 1962.

Beroaldo, Filippo, ed. *Libros naturalis historiae,* by Plinius Secundus T. Vespasiano. Parma, 1476. Reprint Treviso, 1479; Parma, 1480, 1481; Venice, 1483, 1487, 1491.

Biglia, Andrea. *Comentarii Historici de defectu fidei in Oriente* [ca. 1433]. MSS Vatican City, Biblioteca Apostolica Vaticana. Vat. Lat. 5298, fols. 83r–118v.

Blondus, Flavius. *Historiarum ab inclinatione Romanorum imperii, Decades III.* Venice: Octavianus Scotus, 1483.

Bourdieu, Pierre. *Algeria 1960: The Disenchantment of the World: The Sense of Honour: The Kabyle House or the World Reversed: Essays.* Translated by Richard Nice. New York: Cambridge University Press, 1979.

Bouza Álvarez, Fernando J., and José Martínez Millán et al. *La corte de Felipe II.* Madrid: Alianza Editorial, 1994.

Braudel, Fernand. *Civilization and Capitalism, 15th–18th Century.* 3 vols. Translated by Siân Reynolds. Berkeley: University of California Press, 1992.

———. *En torno al mediterráneo.* Edited by Roselyne de Ayala and Paule Braudel. Translated by Agustín López and María Tabuyo. Barcelona: Paidós, 1997.

———. *The Mediterranean and the Mediterranean World in the Age of Philip II.* Translated by Siân Reynolds. 2 vols. New York: Harper and Row, 1972.

———. *The Wheels of Commerce.* Vol. 2 of *Civilization and Capitalism, 15th–18th Century.* Translated by Siân Reynolds. Berkeley: University of California Press, 1992.

Braun and Hogenberg. *Civitateso orbis terrarum.* Coloniae: Apud auctores, et . . . apud Philippum Gallaeu, 1575–1612. English trans., *Cities of the World: 363 Engravings Revolutionize the View of the World: Complete Edition of the Color Plates of 1572–1617.* Edited by Stephan Fussel. Directed and produced by Benedikt Taschen. Köln: Taschen GmbH, 2008.

Brotton, Jerry. *Trading Territories: Mapping the Early Modern World.* Ithaca, NY: Cornell University Press, 1998.

Brown, Peter. *Augustine of Hippo: A Biography.* London: Faber and Faber, 1967. Reprint, 1979.

Bunes Ibarra, Miguel Ángel de. "El orientalismo español de la edad moderna: la fijación de los mitos descriptivos." In *El orientalismo desde el sur,* edited by José Antonio González Alcantud. Barcelona: Anthropos, 2006. 37–53.

———. *La imagen de los musulmanes y del Norte de África en la España de los siglos XVI y XVII. Los caracteres de una hostilidad.* Madrid: Consejo Superior de Investigaciones Científicas-Instituto de Filología, 1989.

Busbecq, Ogier Ghiselin de. *The Turkish Letters of Ogier Ghiselin de Busbecq.* Translated by Edward Seymour Forster. Baton Rouge: Louisiana State University Press, 2005.

Busbecq, Ogier Gislain de. *Ambassade en Turquie et Amasie de Mr. Busbequis, nouvellement traduite en françois par S. G. Guadon.* Paris, 1646.

Cabrera de Córdoba, Luis. *Historia de Felipe II, rey de España.* Edited by José Martínez Millán and Carlos Javier de Carlos Morales. 4 vols. Salamanca: Junta de Castilla y León, 1998.

Camamis, George. *Estudios sobre el cautiverio en el Siglo de Oro*. Madrid: Gredos, 1977.
Canavaggio, Jean. *Cervantes*. Translated by J. R. Jones. New York: Norton, 1990.
Cardaillac, Louis. *Moriscos et chrétiens. Un affrontement polémique (1492–1640)*. Paris: Klincksiek, 1983.
———. ed. *Les Morisques et leur temps*. Paris: CNRS, 1983.
Cardallaic, Louis, Juan Aranda Doncel, and Bernard Vincent, eds. *Les Morisques et l'Inquisition*. Paris: Publisud, 1990.
Carrasco Urgoiti, María Soledad. *Estudios sobre la novela breve de tema morisco*. Barcelona: Edicions Bellaterra, S. L., 2005.
———. *The Moorish Novel: "El Abencerraje" and Pérez de Hita*. Boston: Twayne Publishers, 1976.
———. *Los moriscos y Pérez de Hita*. Barcelona: Edicions Bellaterra, S. L., 2006.
———. *El moro retador y el moro amigo. Estudios sobre fiestas y comedias de moros y cristianos*. Granada: Universidad de Granada, 1996.
———. *Vidas fronterizas en las letras españolas*. Barcelona: Ediciones Bellaterra, S. L., 2005.
Carrione Brugensi, Ludovico. *Conjuratio Catilinae; bellum Jugurtinum; historiarum libri a Lud. Carrione collecti et restituti: Portii Latronis declamatio in Catilinam; adversariae Sallustii et Ciceronis incerto auctore cum scholiis et emendationibus Aldi Manutii, Cyp. a Popma, et Lud. Carrionis*. Lugduni [Lyon]: Stoer, 1596.
Casas, Bartolomé de las. *Brevísima relación de la destrucción de las Indias*. Edited by Consuelo Varela. Madrid: Castalia, 1999.
———. *The Devastation of the Indies: A Brief Account*. Translated by Herma Briffault. Introduction by Bill M. Donovan. Baltimore: Johns Hopkins University Press, 1992.
Cervantes, Miguel de. *The Bagnios of Algiers; and, The Great Sultana: Two Plays of Captivity*. Translated by Barbara Fuchs and Aaron Ilika. Philadelphia: University of Pennsylvania Press, 2010.
———. *Comedia llamada trato de Argel hecha por Miguel de Cervantes questuuo cautiuo en el siete años*. Ms. 14630. Biblioteca Nacional, Madrid.
———. *Don Quijote*. Translated by Burton Raffel. Edited by Diana de Armas Wilson. New York: W. W. Norton, 1999.
———. *Don Quijote de la Mancha*. Edited by Luis Andrés Murillo. 2 vols. Madrid: Castalia, 1978.
———. *El trato de Argel*. Miguel de Cervantes. *Obra completa*. Vol. 2. Edited by Florencio Sevilla Arroyo and Antonio Rey Hazas. Madrid: Alianza, 1996.

---. *Novelas ejemplares.* Edited by Harry Sieber. 2 vols. Madrid: Cátedra, 2001.

---. *Información de Argel.* In *Información de Miguel de Cervantes de lo que ha servido á S. M. y de lo que ha hecho estando cautivo en Argel . . . (Documentos).* Edited by Pedro Torres Lanzas. Madrid: El Árbol, 1981. 45–166.

---. *La Galatea.* Valladolid: por Francisco Fernández de Cordoua, a costa de Geronymo Martínez, 1617.

---. *Los baños de Argel.* Miguel de Cervantes. *Obra completa.* Vol. 14. Edited by Florencio Sevilla Arroyo and Antonio Rey Hazas. Madrid: Alianza, 1998.

---. *Viaje del Parnaso. Poesías completas I.* Edited by Vicente Gaos. Madrid: Castalia, 1973.

Chejne, Anwar G. *Islam and the West: The Moriscos, a Cultural and Social History.* Albany: State University of New York Press, 1983.

Chew, Samuel C. *The Crescent and the Rose: Islam and England during the Renaissance.* New York: Oxford University Press, 1937.

Chisolm, Hugh. *The Encyclopaedia Britannica: A Dictionary of Arts, Sciences, Literature and Information.* New York: Encyclopaedia Britannica, 1910–1911.

Cicero, Marcus Tullius. *Pro Archia; Post reditum in Senatu; Post reditum ad quirites; De domo sua; De haruspicum responsis; Pro Plancio.* Edited and translated by Neville Watts. Cambridge, MA: Harvard University Press, 1999.

Clifford, James. *The Predicaments of Culture: Twentieth-Century Ethnography, Literature, Art.* Cambridge, MA: Harvard University Press, 1988.

Clifford, James, and George E. Marcus, eds. *Writing Culture: The Poetics and Politics of Ethnography: A School of American Research, Advanced Seminar.* Berkeley: University of California Press, 1986.

Colley, Linda. *Captives: Britain, Empire, and the World, 1600–1850.* London: Pimlico, 2002.

Corrales, Martín E. *Comercio de Cataluña con el Mediterráneo musulmán [siglos XVI–XVIII]: el comercio con los enemigos de la fe.* Barcelona: Ediciones Bellaterra, 2001.

Covarrubias, Sebastián de. *Diccionario de la Lengua Castellana o Española.* 1611. Madrid: Turner, 1984.

---. *Tesoro de la Lengua Castellana o Española.* Edited by Ignacio Arellano and Rafael Zafra. Universidad de Navarra-Iberoamericana Vervuert-Real Academia Española, 2006.

Currey, E. Hamilton. *Sea-Wolves of the Mediterranean: The Grand Period of the Moslem Corsairs.* New York: E. P. Dutton and Company, 1910.

Dadson, Trevor J. *Los moriscos de Villarrubia de los Ojos (Siglos XV–XVIII): historia de una minoría asimilada, expulsada y reintegrada.* Madrid: Iberoamericana, 2007.

Dakhlia, Jocélyne. Introduction to *Histoire des rois d'Alger,* by Diego de Haedo, translated into French by Henri-Delmas de Grammont. Saint-Denis: Editions Bouchène, 1998. 1–15.

———. "Une ethnographie du mélange." In *Topographie et histoire générale d'Alger,* by Diego de Haedo, translated into French by Dr. Monnereau and A. Berbrugger. Saint-Denis: Editions Bouchène, 1998. 7–16.

———. *L'empire des passions: L'arbitraire politique en Islam.* Paris: Aubier, 2005.

———. *Lingua Franca. Histoire d'une langue métisse en Méditerranée.* Arles: Actes Sud, 2008.

Dan, Pierre. *Histoire de Barbarie, et de ses corsaires. Des royavmes, et des villes d'Alger, de Tvnis, de Salé, & de Tripoly. Divisée en six livres. Ov il est traitté de levr govvernement, de leurs mœurs, de leurs cruautez, de leurs brigandages, de leurs sortileges, & de plusieurs autres particularitez remarquables. Ensemble des grandes miseres et des crvels tourmens qu'endurent les Chrestiens captifs parmy ces infideles.* 2nd ed. Paris: P. Rocolet, 1649.

Danismend, Ismail Hami. *Osmanli Devlet Erkân.* Istanbul: Türkiye Yayineyi, 1971.

Dante Alighieri. *Divina Comedia. Inferno.* Edited by G. Petrocchi. Milan: Mondadori, 1967. *The Divine Comedy, Inferno.* Translated by Robert Hollander and Jean Hollander. New York: Doubleday, 2000. Princeton Dante Project, http://etcweb.princeton.edu/dante/pdp/.

Dapper, Olfert. *Eigentliche beschreibung der insulen in Africa.* Amsterdam: J. von Meurs, 1671.

Davis, Natalie Zemon. *Trickster Travels: A Sixteenth-Century Muslim between Worlds.* New York: Hill and Wang, 2006.

Davis, Robert C. *Christian Slaves, Muslim Masters: White Slavery in the Mediterranean, the Barbary Coast, and Italy, 1555–1800.* Hampshire: Palgrave, 2004.

De Certeau, Michel. "Walking in the City." In *The Practice of Everyday Life.* Translated by Stephen Rendall. Berkeley: University of California Press, 1988. 91–110.

De Grammont, Henri-Delmas. *Histoire d'Alger sous la domination turque (1515–1830).* 1887. Paris: Editions Bouchène, 2002.

———. Préface to *Histoire des rois d'Alger,* by Diego de Haedo, translated into French by Henri-Delmas de Grammont. Adolphe Jourdan, 1881. Reprint Saint-Denis: Bouchène, 1998. 15–16.

Delgado Casado, Juan. *Diccionario de impresores espanoles, siglos XV–XVII.* 2 vols. Madrid: Arco Libros, 1996.
Denis, Ferdinand. "Haedo." *Nouvelle biographie générale.* Paris: Firmin Didot, 1853. 50–51.
Deny, J. "Les registres de solde des janissaires conservés à la Bibliothèque Nationale d'Alger. *Revue Africaine* 61 (1920): 18–46.
Devoulx, Albert. *Les Édifices religieux de l'ancien Alger.* Alger: Typographie Bastide, 1870.
———. "Les édifices religieux de l'ancien Alger." *Révue africaine* 9 (1865): 443–57.
Díaz, José Simón. *El libro español antiguo: análisis de su estructura.* Kassel: Reichenberger, 1983.
Di Biasi, Giovanni Evangelista. *Storia cronologica de Viceré, luogotenenti e presidenti del Regno di Sicilia.* 3 vols. Palermo: Solli, 1790–91. Reedited as *Edizioni della Regione Siciliana.* 5 vols., 1974–75.
Di Castro, Scipio. *Avvertimenti a Marco Antonio Colonna quando ando Viceré de Sicilia.* Palermo: Sellerio, 1992.
Dousinague, José M. *La política internacional de Fernando el Católico.* Madrid: Espasa-Calpe, 1944.
———. *Testamentaria de Isabel la Católica.* Edited by Antonio de la Torre y del Cerro. Valladolid: Instituto "Isabel la Católica" de Historia Eclesiástica, 1968.
Doutée, Edmond. *Magie et religion dans l'Afrique du Nord.* París: Maisonneuve, 1994.
Dozy, Reinhart Pieter Anne. *Supplement aux dictionnaires arabes.* 3e ed. 2 vols. Paris: G. P. Maisonneuve et Larose, 1967.
Dursteller, Eric F. *Venetians in Constantinople: Nation, Identity and Coexistence in the Early Modern Mediterranean.* Baltimore: The Johns Hopkins University Press, 2006.
Ehlers, Benjamin. *Between Christians and Moriscos: Juan de Ribera and Religious Reform in Valencia, 1568–1614.* Baltimore: The Johns Hopkins University Press, 2006.
Elias, Norbert. *La sociedad cortesana.* México: Fondo de Cultura Económica, 1993.
———. *The Court Society.* Translated by Edmund Jephcott. Oxford: Blackwell, 1983.
Encyclopaedia of Islam. 2nd ed. Edited by P. Bearman, Th. Bianquis, C. E. Bosworth, E. van Donzel, and W. P. Heinrichs. Leiden: Brill, 2009. Brill Online, http://www.brillonline.nl/subscriber/entry?entry=islam_SIM-2683.

Encyclopaedia of Islam. CD-ROM edition. Vol. 1. Leiden: Koninklijke Brill NV, 1999.

Encyclopaedia of Islam; a Dictionary of the Geography, Ethnography and Biography of the Muhammadan Peoples. 4 vols. Edited by Martijn Theodoor Houtsma, T. W. Arnold et al. Leiden: E. J. Brill; London: Luzac & Co. 1913–1936.

Epalza, Mikel de, and Juan Bautista Vilar, eds. *Planos y mapas hispánicos de Argelia.* Madrid, Insituto Hispano-Árabe de Cultura, 1988.

Esquer, Gabriel. *Iconographie historique de l'Algérie depuis le XVIe siècle jusqu'à 1871.* Paris: Plon, 1929.

Ezquerra Revilla, J. Ignacio. "El ascenso de los letrados eclesiásticos: el presidente del Consejo de Castilla Antonio Mauriño de Pazos." In *La Corte de Felipe II,* edited by José Martínez Millán. Madrid: Alianza Editorial, 2002. 271–303.

———. "La visita de Antonio de Pazos al Tribunal de la Inquisición de Sicilia." *Miscelánea Comillas: Revista de teología y ciencias humanas* 60, no. 117 (2002): 571–90.

Fajardo y Acevedo, Antonio. *Relación universal de todo el imperio otomano . . .* Madrid: Biblioteca Nacional, MS 2793.

Febvre, Lucien Paul Victor, and Henri-Jean Martin. *L'Apparition du livre.* Translated by David Girard as *The Coming of the Book: The Impact of Printing, 1450–1800.* New York: Verso, 1986.

Ferrer Valls, Teresa. *La práctica escénica cortesana: de la época del emperador a la de Felipe III.* London: Tamesis Books 1991.

Findley, Carter V. *Bureaucratic Reform in the Ottoman Empire: The Sublime Porte, 1789–1922.* Princeton, NJ: Princeton University Press, 1980.

Fletcher, Richard. *Moorish Spain.* Berkeley: University of California Press, 1992.

Fontenay, Michel de. "La place de la course dans l'économie portuaire: l'exemple de Malte et des ports Barbaresques." *Annales: Economies, Sociétés, Civilisations* 43, no. 6 (1988): 1321–47.

Fuchs, Barbara. *Exotic Nation: Maurophilia and the Construction of Early Modern Spain.* Philadelphia: University of Pennsylvania Press, 2009.

Galán, Diego. *Relación del cautiverio y libertad de Diego Galán, natural de la villa de Consuegra y vecino de la ciudad de Toledo.* Edited by Miguel Ángel de Bunes and Matías Barchino. Toledo: Diputación Provincial de Toledo, 2001.

Galmés de la Fuente, Álvaro. *Estudios sobre la literatura española aljamiado-morisca.* Madrid: Fundación Menéndez Pidal, 2004.

———. *Los manuscritos aljamiado-moriscos de la Biblioteca de la Real Academia de Historia (Legado Pascual de Gayangos).* Madrid: Real Academia de Historia, 1998.

———. *Los moriscos: desde su misma orilla.* Madrid: Instituto Egipcio, 1993.

Galmés de la Fuente, Álvaro, ed. *Tratado de los dos caminos por un morisco refugiado de Túnez.* Edited by J. C. Villaverde. Introduction by Luce López-Baralt. Madrid/Oviedo: Instituto Universitario Seminario Menéndez Pidal de la Universidad Complutense/Seminario de Estudios Árabo-Románicos de la Universidad de Oviedo, 2003.

Garcés, María Antonia. *Cervantes en Argel: Historia de un cautivo.* Madrid: Editorial Gredos, 2005.

———. *Cervantes in Algiers: A Captive's Tale.* 2nd rev. ed. Nashville: Vanderbilt University Press, 2005.

———. "'Grande amigo mío': Cervantes y los renegados." In *USA Cervantes. 29 Cervantistas en Estados Unidos,* edited by Georgina Dopico Black and Francisco Layna Ranz. Madrid: Consejo Superior de Investigaciones Científicas-Ediciones Polifemo, 2008. 545–95.

———. "Staging Captivity: Cervantes's Barbary Plays." In *Approaches to Teaching the Spanish Comedia,* edited by Margaret Greer and Laura Bass. New York: Modern Language Association, 2006. 166–73.

García-Arenal, Mercedes. *Ahmad al-Mansur: The Beginnings of Modern Morocco.* Oxford: Oneworld, 2009.

———. "El entorno de los plomos: historiografía y linaje." In *Los plomos del sacromonte: invención y tesoro,* edited by Manuel Barrios Aguilera and Mercedes García-Arenal. Valencia: Universitat de Valencia. 51–78.

———. *La diáspora de los andalusíes.* Barcelona: CIDOB Edicions; Icaria Editorial, 2003.

———. *Los moriscos.* Madrid: Editora Nacional, 1975; repr. facsimile ed., Granada: Universidad de Granada, 1996.

———. "Religious Dissent and Minorities: The Morisco Age." *Journal of Modern History* 81 (December 2009): 888–920.

———. "Spanish Literature on North Africa in the XVI Century: Diego de Torres." *Maghreb Review* 8 (1983): 53–59.

———. "Últimos estudios sobre los moriscos: estado de la cuestión." *Al-Qantara* IV (1983): 111–14.

———, ed. *Conversions islamiques: identités religieuses en Islam Méditerranéen–Islamic Conversions: Religious Identities in the Mediterranean.* Paris: Maisonneuve et Larose, 2001.

———, ed. *Entre el islam y occidente: los judíos magrebíes en la edad moderna. Seminario celebrado en la Casa de Velázquez, 16–17 noviembre, 1998. Actas reunidas y presentadas por Mercedes García Arenal.* Madrid: Casa Velázquez, 2003.

García-Arenal, Mercedes, and Gerard Weigers. *A Man of Three Worlds: Samuel Pallache, a Moroccan Jew in Catholic and Protestant Europe*. Translated by Martin Beagles. Foreword by David Niremberg and Richard Kagan. Baltimore: Johns Hopkins University Press, 2003.

García-Arenal, Mercedes, and Manuel Barrios Aguilera, eds. *¿La historia inventada? Los libros plúmbeos y el legado sacromontano*. Granada: Universidad y Legado Andalusí, 2008.

García-Arenal, Mercedes, and Miguel Ángel de Bunes. *Los españoles en el Norte de África: Siglos XV–XVIII*. Madrid: Mapfre, 1992.

García-Arenal, Mercedes, and Victoria Aguilar. *Repertorio bibliográfico de las relaciones entre la península ibérica y el Norte de África, siglo XV–XVI*. Madrid: Consejo de Investigaciones Científicas, Instituto de Filología, 1982.

García Martín, Pedro. "Revolución en el 'arte' de los mapas. A propósito de la edición completa del *Civitates Orbis Terrarum*." *La aventura de la Historia* 123 (2009): 94–97.

García Santo-Tomás, Enrique. *Espacio urbano y creación literaria en el Madrid de Felipe IV*. Madrid: Iberoamericana, 2004.

Garufi, Carlo Alberto. *Fatti e personaggi dell' Inquisizione in Sicilia*. Palermo: Sellerio, 1978.

Gaza, Theodorus. *De origine Turcarum* [ca. 1474]. In *Opusculorum, graecorum et latinorum, vetustiorum, libri duo*, by Leonis Allati Aymminta. Coloniae Agrippinae: I. Kalcovivm, 1653.

Geertz, Clifford. *The Interpretation of Cultures*. New York: Basic Books, 1973.

Gelio, Aulo. *Noches áticas. III, Libros XI–XVI*. Edited and translated by Amparo Gaos Schmidt. Mexico City: Universidad Nacional Autónoma de México, 2006.

Gellius, Aulus. [*Noctes Atticae*]. *The Attic Nights of Aulus Gellius*. Translated by John C. Rolfe. Cambridge, MA: Harvard University Press, 2007.

Geuffroy, Antoine, and Nikolaus Hoeniger Von Koeningshofen. *Pars i. Aulae turcicae, othommanicique imperii descriptio: qua turcarum palatina imperii descriptio . . . Pars ii. Solymanni xioi & Selymi xiii. Turcar. impp. contra christianos. uicissim & christianorum contra hos sub auspiciis trium potentis*. Basel: Sebastian Henricpetri, 1577.

Georgieuiz, Bartholomaeo. *Exhortatio contra Turcas*. Ad Illustrissimum Principem Maximilianum Archiducem Austriae . . . . Antwerp, 1545.

———. *De Turcarum moribus*. Lyon: Tomaesium, 1553.

———. *De Turcarum Moribus epitome. De origine Imperii Turcorum eorumque administratione & disciplina, . . .* Lyon: Ioan. Tomaesium, 1562.

———. *De turcarum ritu et ceremoniis.* Antwerp: Gregorium Bontium, 1544.
Giovio, Paolo. *Commentario delle cose de' Turchi.* Roma: Antonio Baldo, 1532. Translated by Peter Ashton. London: Edvvarde Whitechurche, 1546.
———. *La prima [seconda] parte dell' historie del suo tempo.* Translated by M. Lodovico Domenichi. Florence: Torrentino, 1553–1554.
Góis, Damião de. *Fides, religio, mores que aethiopum sub imperio Preciosi Joannis (quem vulgo Presbyterum Joannem vocant)* . . . . Louvain, 1540.
Gonzalo Sánchez-Molero, José Luis. *La Epístola a Mateo Vázquez. Historia de una polémica literaria en torno a Cervantes.* Alcalá de Henares: Centro de Estudios Cervantinos, 2010.
———. "La '*Epístola a Mateo Vázquez*' redescubierta y reivindicada." *Cervantes: Bulletin of the Cervantes Society of America* 27, no. 2 (2007): 181–211.
Goodwin, Godfrey. *The Janissaries.* London: Saqi Books, 1994.
Goodwin, Jason. *Lords of the Horizon: A History of the Ottoman Empire.* New York: Henry Holt, 1999.
Gorguos, A. "Bou Ras, historien inédit de l'Afrique septentrionale." *Revue africaine* 5 (1861): 114–24.
Goss, John, ed. *Ciudades de Europa y de España. Mapas antiguos del siglo XVI de Braun & Hogenberg.* Madrid: Ediciones LIBSA, 1992.
Grafton, Anthony. *New World, Ancient Texts.* Cambridge: Cambridge University Press, 1992.
Gregorio, Domenico de. *La chiesa agrigentina: notizie storiche.* Agrigento: Siculgrafica, 1996.
Gregory I, Pope. *Morals on the Book of Job.* Translated by J. Bliss. Oxford: J. H. Parker, 1844–1850.
Guadix, Diego de. *Recopilación de algunos nombres arábigos que los árabes pusieron a algunas ciudades y a otras muchas cosas.* Edited by Elena Bajo Pérez and Felipe Maíllo Salgado. Oviedo: Universidad de Oviedo, 2005.
Guernier, Eugène. *Le destin de l'Afrique du Nord: la Berbérie, l'Islam et la France.* Paris: Edition de l'Union Française, 1950.
Haedo, Diego de. *Diálogo primero. De la captividad en Argel.* In *Topografía e historia general de Argel,* vol 2.
———. *Diálogo segundo: De los mártires de Argel.* In *Topografía e historia general de Argel,* 3:1–192.
———. *Diálogo tercero. De los morabutos de turcos y moros.* In *Topografía e historia general de Argel,* 3:193–274.
———. *Epítome de los Reyes de Argel.* In *Topografía e historia general de Argel,* 1:213–426.

———. *Histoire des rois d'Alger.* Translated into French by Henri-Delmas de Grammont. Alger: Adolphe Jourdan, 1881. Reprint Saint-Denis: Bouchène, 1998.

———. *Topografía e historia general de Argel.* Edited by Ignacio Bauer y Landauer. 3 vols. Madrid: Sociedad de Bibliófilos Españoles, 1927–29.

———. *Topographia, e historia general de Argel, repartida en cinco tratados do se verán casos extraños, muertes espantosas y tormentos exquisitos que conviene se entiendan en la Cristiandad* . . . Valladolid: por Diego Fernández de Córdova y Oviedo, a costa de Antonio Coello, 1612.

———. *Topographie et histoire générale d'Alger.* Translated into French by Dr. Monnereau and A. Berbrugger. Saint-Denis: Editions Bouchène, 1998.

———. "Topographie et histoire générale d'Alger." Translated into French by Dr. Monnereau and A. Berbrugger. *Revue Africaine* 14 (1870): 364–75, 414–43, 490–519.

———. "Topographie et histoire générale d'Alger." Translated into French by Dr. Monnereau and A. Berbrugger. *Revue Africaine* 15 (1871): 41–69, 90–111, 202–37, 307–9, 375–95, 458–73.

Hakim, Mohamed Ibn Azzuz. "El testamento de Isabel la Católica y sus consecuencias funestas sobre las relaciones hispano-marroquíes." In *Huellas comunes y miradas cruzadas: Mundos árabe, ibérico e iberoamericano,* edited by Mohamed Salhi. Rabat: Facultad de Letras y de Ciencias Humanas, 1995. 27–35.

Harley, J. B., and David Woodward. *The History of Cartography.* 6 vols. Chicago: University of Chicago Press, 1987.

Harris, A. Katie. *From Muslim to Christian Granada: Inventing a City's Past in Early Modern Spain.* Baltimore: Johns Hopkins University Press, 2007.

Harvey, L. P. *Islamic Spain: 1250 to 1500.* Chicago: University of Chicago Press, 1992.

———. *Muslims in Spain: 1500 to 1614.* Chicago: University of Chicago Press, 2005.

Hathaway, Jane. *The Politics of Households in Ottoman Egypt: The Rise of the Qazdaglis.* Cambridge: Cambridge University Press, 1997.

Herodotus. *Historiae.* [*The History*]. Translated by David Grene. Chicago: University of Chicago Press, 1987.

Herrera y Tordesillas, Antonio. *Historia general de los hechos de los castellanos en las islas y Tierra Firme del mar Océano, o, "Décadas."* Edited by Mariano Cuesta Domingo. 4 vols. Madrid: Universidad Complutense de Madrid, 1991.

———. *The General History of the Vast Continent and Islands of America: Commonly Call'd the West-Indies, from the First Discovery Thereof: with the Best Ac-*

counts the People Could Give of Their Antiquities. New York: AMS Press, 1973.

Hess, Andrew C. *The Forgotten Frontier: A History of the Sixteenth-Century Ibero-African Frontier.* Chicago: University of Chicago Press, 1978.

Hills, Helen. "Mapping the Early Modern City." *Urban History* 23, no. 2 (August 1996): 147–70.

Hinojosa, Ricardo de. *Los despachos de la diplomacia pontificia en España. Memoria de una misión oficial en el Archivo secreto de la Santa Sede.* Vol. 1. Madrid, 1896.

Homer. *Odyssey.* Translated by Robert Fagles. New York: Penguin Books, 1996.

Hulme, Peter, and Tim Youngs, eds. *The Cambridge Companion to Travel Writing.* Cambridge: Cambridge University Press, 2002.

Itinerarium provinciarum Antonini Augusti; Vibius Sequester De fluminum, & aliarum rerum nominibus in ordinem elementorum digestis; P. Victor De regionibus urbis Romae; Dionysius Afer De situ orbis Prisciano interprete. Opuscula praescripta . . . ad exemplar Aldinum diligenter emendata fuere. Lugduni: Haeredes Simonis Vincentij, 1545.

Jerome. *Commentary on St. Matthew.* Translated by Thomas P. Scheck. Washington, DC: Catholic University of America Press, 2008.

Josefo, Flavio. *La guerra de los judíos.* Madrid: Gredos, 1997–1999.

Josephus, Flavius. *Antiquitates Judaicae.* Cambridge, MA: Harvard University Press, 1998.

———. *De bello judaico.* Book 1. Latin and Greek. Oxoniae: E. Theatro Sheldoniano, 1700.

———. *De bello judaico.* Book 2. Latin and Greek, Selections. Oxoniae: E. Theatro Sheldoniano, 1700.

———. *Guerra de los judíos y destrucción del Templo y Ciudad de Jerusalén.* Translated by Juan Martín Cordero. Barcelona: Iberia, 2002.

———. *The Wars of the Jews: In Two Books. With the most deplorable history of the siege and destruction of the city of Jerusalem, ... Epitomiz'd from the works of Flavius Josephus.* [Electronic Resource]. Translated by Sir Roger L'Estrange, Knight. 4th ed. London: Tho. Norris, 1724.

Kagan, Richard L. "Philip II and the Geographers." In *Spanish Cities of the Golden Age: The Views of Anthony van den Wyngaerde,* edited by Richard L. Kagan. Berkeley: University of California Press, 1989. 40–53.

———. Preface to *Spanish Cities of the Golden Age: The Views of Anthony van den Wyngaerde,* edited by Richard L. Kagan. Berkeley: University of California Press, 1989. 1–13.

———. *Urban Images of the Hispanic World, 1493–1793*. New Haven, CT: Yale University Press, 2000.

Kelly, Donald R. *Modern Historical Scholarship*. New York: Columbia University Press, 1970.

Khan, Muhammad Akram. *Islamic Economics and Finance: A Bibliography*. London: Mansell, 1995.

Koenigsberger, Helmut Georg. *The Government of Sicily under Philip II of Spain: A Study in the Practice of Empire*. London: Staples Press, 1951.

———. *La práctica del Imperio*. Prólogo de J. M. Batista i Roca. Epílogo de Pablo Fernández Abadejo. Translated by Graciela Soriano. Madrid: Alianza Editorial, 1989.

———. *The Practice of Empire*. Ithaca, NY: Cornell University Press, 1969.

Koningshoff, Honigerus. *De rebus Turcicis*. In *Aulae Turcica. Pars II, Solymanni XII et Selymi XIII Turcar. Impp. Contra Christianos . . . .*, by Anton. Geufraei. Basel: Sebastian Henricpetri, 1577.

Kunt, Ibrahim Metin. *The Sultan's Servants: The Transformation of Ottoman Provincial Government, 1550–1650*. New York: Columbia University Press, 1983.

La Mantia, Vito. "Origine e vicende dell'Inquizitione in Sicilia." *Rivista storica siciliana* 3 (1886): 481–598.

———. *Origine e vicenda dell'inquisizione in Sicilia*. Palermo: Sellerio, 1977.

Laguna, Andrés. *De origine regum Turcarum*. In Torquato, Antonio. *Prognosticon . . . de eversione Europae et alia quaedam*. Antwerp: M. Nutius, 1544.

Lea, Henry Charles. *The Inquisition in the Spanish Dependencies: Sicily, Naples, Sardinia, Milan, the Canaries, Mexico, Peru, New Granada*. New York: Macmillan, 1908.

Leo Africanus. *Della descrittione dell'Africa / et dell cose notabili / che quivi sono / per Giovanni Lioni Africano. Delle navigationi et viaggi nel qual si contiene la Descrittione dell'Africa*. Vol. 1. Edited by Giovanni Battista Ramusio. Venice: Heredi di Luca Antonio Giunti, 1550.

———. *The History and Description of Africa and of the Notable Things therein Contained. Written by Al-Hassan Ibn-Mohammed Al-Wezaz Al-Fasi, a Moor, Baptised as Giovanni Leone, But Better Known as Leo Africanus*. 3 vols. Translated by John Pory, 1600. Edited by Robert Brown. London: Hakluyt Society, 1896.

León Africano, Juan. *Descripción general del África, y de las cosas peregrinas que allí hay*. Translated and edited by Serafín Fanjul. Granada: Fundación El Legado Andalusí, 2004.

Lochman, Zachary. *Contending Visions of the Middle East: The History and Politics of Orientalism*. West Nyack, NY: Cambridge University Press, 2004.

López-Baralt, Luce. "El cálamo supremo (Al-Qalam al-'Ala) de Cide Hamete Benengeli." In *Mélanges María Soledad Carrasco Urgoiti*, edited by Abdeljelil Temimi. Vol. 2. Zagouan: Foundation Temimi pour la Recherche Scientifique et l'Information, 1999. 343–61.

———. *Islam in Spanish Literature: From the Middle Ages to the Present*. Translated by Andrew Hurley. New York: Brill; San Juan: Editorial de la Universidad de Puerto Rico, 1992.

———. *La literatura secreta de los últimos musulmanes de España*. Madrid: Trotta, 2009.

———. *Un Kāma Sūtra español*. Madrid: Siruela, 992.

Lo Piccolo, Francesco. *Diari Palermitani inediti (1557–1760): cronache da un archivio parrocchiale*. Palermo: Flaccovio, 1999.

Lucchetta, Francesca. "Il medico del Bailaggio di Constantinopoli. Fra terapie e politica (sec. XV–XVI)." In *Veneziani in Levante: Musulmani a Venezia*. Quaderni di Studi Arabi, Supplemento al n. 15. Rome: Herder, 1997. 5–50.

Lucian of Samosata. *Alexander seu Pseudomantis*. In *The Works of Lucian of Samosata*. 4 vols. Translated by H. W. Fowler and F. G. Fowler. Oxford: Clarendon Press, 1905. 2:237.

Marçais, George. *Le costume musulman d'Alger*. Paris: Plon, 1930.

Marcus, George, ed. *Rereading Cultural Anthropology*. Durham, NC: Duke University Press, 1992.

Mármol Carvajal, Luis del. *Descripción general de África (1573–1599)*. Facsimile ed. Madrid: Consejo Superior de Investigaciones Científicas, 1953.

———. *L'Afrique de Marmol / de la traduction de Nicolas Perrot, sieur d'Ablancourt; divisée en trois volumes, et enrichie des cartes géographiques de M. Sanson; avec l'Histoire des chérifs, traduite de l'espagnol de Diego Torres, par le duc d'Angoulesme le père*. 3 vols. Paris: Billaine, 1667.

———. *Primera parte de la Descripción general de Affrica con todos los sucessos de guerras que a auido entre los infieles, y el pueblo Christiano, y entre ellos mesmos desde que Mahoma inuento su secta, hasta el año del señor mil y quinientos y setenta y vno*. Vol. 1. Granada: Rene Rabut, 1573.

———. *Segvnda parte y libro septimo de la Descripcion general de Affrica, donde se contiene las prouincias de Numidia, Libia, la tierra de los negros, la baxa y alta Etiopia, y Egipto, cõ todas las cosas memorables della*. Málaga: I. Rene, 1599.

Márquez Villanueva, Francisco. *El problema morisco (desde la otra ladera)*. Madrid: Libertarias, 1991.

Martínez-Góngora, Mar. "El discurso africanista del Renacimiento en *La primera parte de la Descripción general de África* de Luis del Mármol Carvajal." *Hispanic Review* 77, no. 2 (Spring 2009): 171–95.

Martínez Torres, José Antonio. *Prisioneros de los infieles. Vida y rescate de los cautivos cristianos en el Mediterráneo musulmán [siglos XVI y XVII]*. Barcelona: Bellaterra, 2004.
Matar, Nabil. *Britain and Barbary, 1589–1689*. Gainesville: University Press of Florida, 2005.
———. *Islam in Britain, 1558–1685*. Cambridge: Cambridge University Press, 1998.
———. *Turks, Moors, and Englishmen in the Age of Discovery*. New York: Columbia University Press, 1999.
———, ed. *Europe through Arab Eyes, 1578–1727*. New York: Columbia University Press, 2009.
Menocal, María Rosa. *La joya del mundo. Musulmanes, judíos y cristianos, y la cultura de la tolerancia en al-Andalus*. Barcelona: Plaza Janés, 2003.
———. *The Ornament of the World: How Muslims, Jews, and Christians Created a Culture of Tolerance in Medieval Spain*. Boston: Little, Brown and Co., 2002.
Merle, Alexandra. *Le miroir ottoman: une image politique des hommes dans la littérature geographique espagnole et francaise (XVIe-XVIIe siècles)*. Paris: Presses de l'Université de Paris-Sorbonne, 2003.
Merouche, Lemnouar. *Recherches sur l'Algérie à l'époque ottomane I. Monnaies, prix et revenues 1520–1830*. Saint Dennis: Bouchène, 2006.
———. *Recherches su l'Algérie à l'époque ottomane II. La course: mythe et réalité*. Saint Dennis: Bouchène, 2007.
Meserve, Margaret. *Empires of Islam in Renaissance Historical Thought*. Cambridge, MA: Harvard University Press, 2008.
Miller, Naomi. *Mapping the City: The Language and Culture of Cartography in the Renaissance*. New York: Continuum, 2003.
Mizzi, Joseph, ed. *Catalogue of the Records of the Order of St. John of Jerusalem in the National Library of Malta*. 2 vols. Valetta: Malta University Press, 1979.
Monter, E. William. *Frontiers of Heresy: The Spanish Inquisition from the Basque Lands to Sicily*. New York: Cambridge University Press, 1990.
Morales, Ambrosio de. Approval. In *Descripción general de África,* by Luis del Mármol Carvajal. Facsimile ed. Madrid: Consejo Superior de Investigaciones Científicas, 1953.
Morales, Baltasar de. *Diálogo de las guerras de Orán*. (Córdoba, 1539); rev. ed. *Guerras de los españoles en África, 1542, 1543 y 1632*. Madrid, 1889.
Morales Ortíz, Alicia. *Plutarco en España: Traducciones de Moralia en el siglo XVI*. Murcia: Universidad de Murcia, 2000.
Morgan, Joseph. *A Complete History of Algiers: To Which Is Prefixed, an Epitome of the General History of Barbary, from the Earliest Times: Interspersed with Many*

Curious Remarks and Passages, Not Touched on by Any Writer Whatever. 2 vols. London: J. Bettenham, 1728–1729.

Münster, Sebastian, ed., *Cosmographiae universalis Lib. 6 in quibus, iuxta certioris fidei scriptorum traditionem describuntur, Omnium habitabilis orbis partium situs, propriaeque dotes.* . . . Basileae, 1550.

———, ed. *Geographia universalis: vetus et nova / complectens Claudii Ptolemai Alexandrini.* . . . Basileae: Henricum Petrum, 1540.

Murillo, Luis Andrés. "Diálogo y dialéctica en el siglo XVI español." *Revista de la Universidad de Buenos Aires* 4 (1959): 55–66.

Myers, Kathleen Ann. *Fernández de Oviedo's Chronicle of America: A New History for a New World.* Austin: University of Texas Press, 2007.

Narváez, María Teresa. *Tratado (Tafsira) del Mancebo de Arévalo.* Madrid: Trotta, 2003.

Núñez Cabeza de Vaca, Alvar. *Castaways: The Narrative of Alvar Núñez Cabeza de Vaca.* Edited by Enrique Pupo-Walker. Translated by Frances M. López-Morillas. Berkeley: University of California Press, 1993.

Ortelius, Abraham. *Theatrum orbis terrarum.* Antwerp, 1570.

Oxford Atlas of the World, 15th ed. New York: Oxford University Press, 2008.

Padrón, Ricardo. *The Spacious World: Cartography, Literature, and Empire in Early Modern Spain.* Chicago: University of Chicago Press, 2004.

Pamuk, Şevket. *A Monetary History of the Ottoman Empire.* Cambridge: Cambridge University Press, 2000.

Panvinio, Onofrio. *De republica Romana.* Venice: Antonium de Castro, 1558.

Panvinius, Onofrius. *Republicae Romanae commentariorvm libri. tres.* . . . Paris: Egidium & Nicolaum Gillios, 1588.

Parreño, José M. Foreword to *Diálogo de los mártires de Argel,* by Antonio de Sosa, edited by Emilio Sola and José M. Parreño. Madrid: Hiperión, 1990. 9–23.

Peirce, Leslie P. *The Imperial Harem: Women and Sovereignty in the Ottoman Empire.* New York: Oxford University Press, 1993.

Pereira Esteves, João Manuel, and Guilherme Rodrigues. *Portugal; diccionario historico, chorographico, heraldico, biographico, bibliographico, numismatico e artistico.* 7 vols. Lisboa: J. Romano Torres, 1904–1915.

Pérès, Henri. *L'Espagne vue par les voyageurs musulmans de 1610 à 1930.* Paris: Librairie d'Amérique et d'Orient, A. Maisonneuve, 1937.

Pérez de Urbel, Justo. *Varones Insignes de la Congregación de Valladolid, según un manuscrito del Siglo XVIII.* Pontevedra: Museo Provincial de Pontevedra, 1967.

Pérez Pastor, Cristóbal. *Documentos cervantinos hasta ahora inéditos.* 2 vols. Madrid: Establecimiento Tipográfico de Fortanet, 1897–1902.

Pérez Villanueva, Joaquín, and Bartolomé Escandell Bonet, eds. *Historia de la Inquisición en España y América*. 3 vols. Madrid: Biblioteca de Autores Cristianos, Centro de Estudios Inquisitoriales, 1984–2000.

Perry, Mary Elizabeth. *The Handless Maiden: Moriscos and the Politics of Religion in Early Modern Spain*. Princeton: Princeton University Press, 2005.

Pinto Crespo, Virgilio. *Inquisición y control ideológico en la España del siglo XVI*. Madrid: Taurus, 1983.

Piccolomini, Eneas Silvius [Pope Pius II]. *Der Briefwechsel des Eneas Silvius Piccolomini*. Edited by Rudolph Wolkan. 4 vols. Vienna: A. Holder, 1909–1918.

Pirri, Rocco. *Sicilia Sacra disquisitionibis et notitiis illustrata*. Vol. 2 of *Thesaurus antiquitatum et historiarum Siciliae quo continentur rarissimi & optimi quique scriptores qui nobilissimarum insularum Siciliae, Sardiniae, Corsicae et adjacentium situm*... cura & studio Joannis Georgii Graevii. Lugduni: Batavorum, 1723.

Playfair, R. Lambert. *The Scourge of Christendom: Annals of British Relations with Algiers Prior to the French Conquest*. London: Smith, Elder & Co., 1884.

Plinio Segundo, Cayo. *Historia natural. Obra completa*. Vol. 1, Libros I–II. Madrid: Gredos, 1995.

Plinius Secundus T. Vespasiano, *Libros naturalis historiae*. Edited by Filippo Beroaldo. Parma, 1476. Reprint Treviso, 1479; Parma, 1480, 1481; Venice, 1483, 1487, 1491.

Pliny the Elder. *Natural History* [*Naturalis Historia*]. Translated by H. Rackham et al. Loeb Classical Library. 10 vols. Cambridge, MA: Harvard University Press, 1938–1963.

Plutarch. *Lives*. 8 vols. Translated by John Langhorne and William Langhorne. New York: David Huntington, 1816.

———. *Plutarch's Morals*. Translated from the Greek by Several Hands. Corrected and Revised by William W. Goodwin, with an Introduction by Ralph Waldo Emerson. 5 vols. Boston: Little, Brown and Co., 1878. Available online at http://oll.libertyfund.org/title/1753 (accessed September 2010).

Plutarco. *Vidas Paralelas*. Vol. 4, *Arístides & Catón; Filopemen & Flaminino; Pirro & Mario*. Madrid: Gredos, 2007.

———. *Vidas Paralelas*. Vol. 5, *Lisandro & Sila; Cimón & Lúculo; Nicias & Craso*. Madrid: Gredos, 2007.

Polybius. *The General History of Polybius*. Translated by Mr. Hampton. 5 vols. 3rd ed. in 2 vols. London: H. S. Woodfall for J. Dodsley, 1772.

Pouillon, François, Alain Messaoudi, Dietrich Rauchenberger, and Oumelbanine Zhiri, eds. *Léon l'Africain*. Paris: Karthala, 2009.

Pozzo, Fra Bartolomeo dal, Conte. *Historia della sacra religione militare di S. Giovanni Gerosolimitano detta di Malta.* 2 vols. Verona: G. Berno, 1703–1715.

Ptolemy, Claudius. *Geographia.* Edited by Sebastian Münster. Basel, 1540. Amsterdam: Theatrum Orbis Terrarum, 1966.

———. *Geography of Claudius Ptolemy.* Translated by Edward Luther Stevenson. New York: New York Public Library, 1932.

———. *Ptolemy's Almagest.* Translated by G. J. Toomer. Princeton, NJ: Princeton University Press, 1998.

Ptolemaeus, Claudius. *Geographia Claudij Ptolemai Alexandrini, philosophi ac mathematici praestantissimi . . . , libri VIII.* Basilae: Henrichi Petri, 1552.

Ramusio, Giovanni Battista. *Terzo volvme delle navigationi et viaggi: nel qvale si contengono le nauigationi al mondo nuouo, alli antichi incognito, fatte da don Christoforo Colombo Genouese.* In Venetia: Nella stamperia de Givnti, 1556.

———. *Navigationi et viaggi* [1563–1606]. Introduction by R. A. Skelton. Edited by George Bruner Parks. Amsterdam: Theatrum Orbis Terrarum, 1967–1970.

Rasdi, Mohamad Tajuddin Haji Mohamad. *The Mosque as a Community Development Centre: Programme and Architectural Design Guidelines for Contemporary Muslim Societies.* Skudai, Johor Darul Ta'zim: Penerbit Universiti Teknolog Malaysia, 1998.

Richardson, Lawrence. *A New Topographical Dictionary of Ancient Rome.* Baltimore: Johns Hopkins University Press, 1992.

Ríos, Ángel de los. *Ensayo histórico, etimológico y filológico sobre los apellidos castellanos desde el siglo X hasta nuestra edad.* Madrid: M. Tello, 1871.

Rippin, Andrew. *Muslims: Their Religious Beliefs and Practices.* London and New York: Routledge, 2001.

Rivero Rodríguez, Manuel. "Corte y 'Poderes Provinciales': el virrey Colonna y el conflicto con los Inquisidores de Sicilia." *Cuadernos de Historia Moderna* 14 (1993): 73–101.

———. "'De todo di aviso a vuestra señoría por cartas': Centro, periferia y poder en la corte de Felipe II." In *Espacios de poder: cortes, ciudades y villas (S XVI–XVIII),* edited by Jesús Bravo. 2 vols. Madrid: Universidad Autónoma, 2002. 1:267–290.

———. "La Inquisición española en Sicilia (siglos XVI a XVIII)." In *Historia de la Inquisición en España y América,* edited by Joaquín Pérez Villanueva and Bartolomé Escandell Bonet. 3 vols. Madrid: Biblioteca de Autores Cristianos, 1984–2000. 3:1031–1222.

Rostaggno, Lucia. *Mi faccio turco. Esperienze ed immagini dell'Islam nell'Italia moderna*. Rome: Insituto per L'Oriente C. A. Nallino, 1983.

Rucellai, Bernardo. *De urbe Roma, seu Latinus Commentarius eiusdem in Pub. Victorem ac Sext. Rufum De regionibus urbis: Accedit ipsius Pub. Victoris ac Sax. Rufi textus Ex fide complurium MScriptorum Vaticana Bibliothecae*. Florentia: Allegrini, 1770.

Sagredo, Juan. *Memorias históricas de los monarcas othomanos, que escrivio en lengua toscana . . . traduzidas en castellano por Don Francisco de Olivares Morillo*. Madrid, 1684.

Sagundino, Niccolo. *N. Secundini (Segundini) Otthomannorum familia, seu de Turcarum imperio historia, addita complemento Jo. Rami a capta Constantinopoli usque ad nostra tempora*. Vienna, 1551.

———. *De origine et rebus gestis Turcarum*. 1456.

Saldanha, António de. *Crónica de Almançor, Sultão de Marrocos (1578–1603). Chronique d'Al-Mansour, Sultan du Maroc (1578–1603)*. Edited by António Dias Farinha. Translated by Léon Bourdon. Lisbon: Instituto de Investigacão Científica Tropical, 1997.

Sallust [Gauis Sallustius Crispus]. *Bellum Jugurthinum and Crispi Conivratio. Catilinae et Bellum Ivgvrtinvm: fragmenta eiusdem historiarum . . . .* Venecia: Aldus Manutius, 1567.

———. *The Jugurthine War / The Conspiracy of Catiline*. Translated by S. A. Handford. Baltimore: Penguin Books, 1963.

Sansovino, Francesco. *Historia vniuersale dell'origine et imperio dé Turchi*. Venezia: Altobello Salicato, 1582.

Sapiencia, Octavio. *Nuevo tratado de Turquía*. Madrid, 1622.

Scaraffia, Lucetta. *Rinnegati. Per una storia dell'identità occidentale*. Roma: Laterza, 1993.

Sciuti Russi, Vittorio. *Astrea in Sicilia. Il ministerio togato nella societa siciliana dei secoli XVI e XVII*. Naples: Casa Editrice Jovene, 1983.

———. "Inquisición, política y justicia en la Sicilia de Felipe II." In *Felipe II (1527–1598): Europa y la monarquía católica*, edited by José Martínez Millán. 4 vols. Madrid: Editorial Parteluz, 1998. 3:387–412.

———. "La Inquisición española en Sicilia." *Studia historica. Historia moderna* 26 (2004): 75–99.

Shuval, Tal. "Households in Ottoman Algeria." *Turkish Studies Association Bulletin* 24:1 (Spring 2000): 41–64.

———. "The Ottoman Algerian Elite and its Ideology." *International Journal of Middle East Studies* 32 (2000): 323–44.

———. "Remettre l'Algérie à l'heure ottomane." *Revue du Monde Musulman et de la Méditerranèe,* 95–96–97–98 (2002): 423–48.

Smith, Leslie F. "Pope Pius II's Use of Turkish Atrocities." *Southwestern Social Science Quarterly* 46, no. 4 (1966): 407–15.

Sola, Emilio. "Antonio de Sosa: un clásico inédito amigo de Cervantes (Historia y Literatura)." In *Actas del Primer Coloquio Internacional de la Asociación de Cervantistas, Alcalá de Henares 29/30 nov.–1/2 dic.1988.* Barcelona: Anthropos, 1990. 409–12.

———. "Miguel de Cervantes, Antonio de Sosa y África." In *Actas del Primer Encuentro de Historiadores del Valle de Henares.* Guadalajara-Alcalá de Henares, 1988. 617–23.

———. Foreword to *Diálogo de los mártires de Argel,* by Antonio de Sosa. Edited by Emilio Sola and José M. Parreño. Madrid: Hiperión, 1990. 26–52.

Sola, Emilio, and José F. de la Peña. *Cervantes y la Berbería: Cervantes, mundo turco-berberisco y servicios secretos en la época de Felipe II.* México: Fondo de Cultura Económica, 1995.

Sosa, Antonio de. "Ad Papam Gregorium XIII." In *Chronica Sacri/et Militaris Ordinis/B. Mariae de Mercede,/Redemptionis Captivorum,* edited by Fray Bernardo de Vargas. Vol. 2. Panormi: Apud Ioannem Baptistam Maringum, 1622. 107–9.

———. "Carta a Nuestro Santissimo Papa Gregorio XIII, el Colegio de los Ilustrissimos, y Reverendissimos Señores Cardenales . . . ." In *Gloriosa / Fecundidad / de Maria / en el Campo de la / Catolica Iglesia,* edited by Fray Francisco de Neyla. Barcelona: Rafael Figueró, 1698. 190–95.

———. *Diálogo de los mártires de Argel.* Edited by Emilio Sola and José M. Parreño. Madrid: Hiperión, 1990.

———. *Diálogo primero. De la captividad en Argel.* In Haedo, *Topografía e historia general de Argel,* vol. 2.

———. *Diálogo segundo. De los mártires de Argel.* In Haedo, *Topografía e historia general de Argel,* 3:1–192.

———. *Diálogo tercero. De los morabutos de turcos y moros.* In Haedo, *Topografía e historia general de Argel,* 3:193–274.

———. *Epítome de los Reyes de Argel.* In Haedo, *Topografía e historia general de Argel,* 1:213–426.

———. *Topografía de Argel.* In Haedo, *Topografía e historia general de Argel,* 1:1–212.

Souidas. *Suidæ lexicon, Græce & Latine. Textum Græcum cum manuscriptis codicibus collatum a quamplurimis mendis purgavit, notisque perpetuis illustravit:* versionem Latinam Æmilii Porti . . . correxit; indicesque auctorum & rerum adjecit Ludolphus Kusterus . . . . Cantabrigiæ: typis academicis, 1705.

Sousa, António Caetano de. *História genealógica da casa real portuguesa.* Edited by M. Lopes de Almeida and César Pegado. 12 vols. Coimbra; Atlántida, 1946–54.

Staden, Hans. *Hans Staden's True History: An Account of Cannibal Captivity in Brazil.* Edited and translated by Neil L. Whitehead and Michael Harbsmeier. Durham, NC: Duke University Press, 2008.

Strabo. *Geography* [*Geographia*]. Translated by Horace Leonard Jones. 8 vols. Loeb Classical Library: Cambridge, MA, 1917–1932.

Strieff, Daniel. "Forging a Voice in 'France's High-Rise Hell': As Fears of Radicalism Grow, Muslims Take a Pragmatic Approach to Politics." MSNBC.com, May 9, 2007. http://www.msnbc.msn.com/id/12812186/. Accessed 10/10/2010.

Suetonio. *Vida de los doce Césares.* Libros 4–8. Madrid: Gredos, 1992.

Suetonius [Gaius Suetonius Tranquilus]. *The Lives of the Twelve Caesars (De vita Caesarum): An Unexpurgated English Version.* Edited by Joseph Galore. New York: Modern Library, 1931.

Temimi, Abdeljelil. *Études d'histoire maghreébine à l'époque moderne.* Zaghouan: Fondation Temimi pour la Recherche Scientifique et l'Information, 1997.

———. *Études sur les relations Islamo-Chrétiennes.* Zaghouan: Fondation Temimi pour la Recherche Scientifique et l'Information, 1996.

———."Lettre de la population algéroise au Sultan Selim 1er en 1519." *Revue d'Histoire Maghrébine/al-majalla al-tārīkhīya al-maghrībiya* 5 (1976): 95–101.

———. *Problématiques et développement de la recherche historique dans le monde arabe: études ottomans et moriscologie.* Tokyo, Japan: Islamic Area Studies Project, 1998.

———, ed. *Actas del XIe Congreso de Estudios Moriscos sobre huellas literarias e impactos de los moriscos en Túnez y en América Latina.* Tunis: Fondation Temimi pour la recherche scientifique et l'information, 2005.

———, ed. *Actes du Ve Symposium international d'Études morisques sur le Ve centenaire de la chute de Grenade 1492–1992.* Zaghouan: Ceromdi, 1993.

———, ed. *Coût du non Maghreb et les nouvelles approches pour l'avenir.* Tunis: Fondation Temimi pour la recherche scientifique 2009.

———, ed. *Etudes sur l'histoire du Maghreb ottoman au XVIe siècle.* Tunis: Fondation Temimi pour la recherche scientifique, 2009.

———, ed. *Le IIe Congrès du dialogue arabo-turc sur modernisation et modernisme dans les pays arabes et en Turquie au XXe siècle.* Zaghouan: Fondation Temimi pour la recherche scientifique et l'information, 2001.

———, ed. *Mélanges de reconnaissance à l'historien Abdurrahim A. Abdurrahim.* Tunis: Fondation Temimi pour la recherche scientifique, 2007–2009.

———, ed. *Mélanges Luce López-Baralt.* Zaghouan: Fondation Temimi pour la recherche scientifique et l'information, 2001.

———, ed. *Mélanges María Soledad Carrasco Urgoiti.* Zaghouan: Fondation Temimi pour la recherche scientifique et l'information, 1999.

———, ed. *Morisques, Méditerranée, & manuscrits Aljamiado / actes du Xe Congrès international d'études morisques tenu durant 9–12 mai 2001.* Zaghouan: Fondation Temimi pour la recherche scientifique et l'information, 2003.

Temimi, Abdeljelil, and Güner Öztek, eds. *Relations Arabo-Turques et role des elites dans la modernisation: actes du IIIe Congrès international Arabo-Turc Istanbul, 22–26 Mai 2002.* Zaghouan: Fondation Temimi pour la recherche scientifique et l'information, 2003.

Temimi, Abdeljelil, and Mohamed Salah Omri, eds. *The Movement of People and Ideas between Britain and the Maghreb: actes du IIème congrès du dialogue britano-maghrébin tenu à l'Université d'Exeter, 14–17 septembre 2002.* Zaghouan: Fondation Temimi pour la recherche scientifique et l'information, 2003.

Temimi, Abdeljelil, Mohamed Salah Omri; and Mu'assasat al-Tamimii lil-Bahth al-'Ilmi wa-al-Ma'lumat, eds. *Actes du Ier congres international sur la Grande Bretagne et le Maghreb: etat de recherches et contacts culturels.* Zaghouan: Fondation Temimi pour la recherche scientifique et l'information, 2002.

Texeira, Pedro. [*La descripción de España*]. *El atlas del rey planeta: la "Descripción de España y de las costas y puertos de sus reinos" de Pedro Texeira (1634).* Edited by Felipe Pereda and Fernando Marías. Madrid: Nerea, 2002.

———. *Topographía de la Villa de Madrid.* 1656. Madrid: Imprenta Artesanal del Ayuntamiento, 2000.

Tolan, John Victor. *Saracens: Islam in the Medieval European Imagination.* New York: Columbia University Press, 2002.

Tolomeo. *Geographia Claudij Ptoloma Alexandrini, philosophi ac mathematici prestantissimi....* Edited and translated by Sebastián Münster. Basilea, 1552.

Torres, Diego de. *Relación del origen y suceso de los xarifes y del estado de los reinos de Marruecos, Fez y Tarudante.* Sevilla, 1586. Edited by Mercedes García-Arenal. Madrid: Siglo XXI, 1980.

———. *Relation de l'origine et svccez des cherifs, et de l'estat des royavmes de Marroc, Fez, et Tarvdant, et autres prouinces qu'ils vsurperent*. Faicte & escrite en espagnol par Diego de Torres. Mise en François par M.C.D.V.D.D.A. Paris: Iean Camvsat, 1636.

Turbet-Delof, Guy. *L'Afrique barbaresque dans la littérature française aux XVIe et XVIIe siècles*. Genève: Droz, 1973.

Valensi, Lucette. *The Birth of the Despot: Venice and the Sublime Porte*. Translated by Arthur Denner. Ithaca, NY: Cornell University Press, 1993.

Veneziano, Antonio. "Arco per l'entrata dell' Illmo, e Revmo Monsignor D. Diego Aedo, Arcivescovo di Palermo." *Opere di Antonio Veneziano, poeta siciliano*. Palermo, 1861. 191–97.

Verrius Flaccus, Marcus, Sextus Pompeius Festus. *M. Verrii Flacci quae extant et Sexti Pompeii Festi de verborum significatione, libre XX*. Edited by Andre Dacier. London: A. J. Valpy, 1826.

Viaje de Turquía. Edited by Marie-Sol Ortola. Madrid: Castalia, 2000.

Villegaignon, Nicolas Durand de. *Carlo V Emperatoris Expeditio in Africam Ad Algeriam*: Per Nicolaum Villagagnomem equitem rhodium gallum. Argentorati: Vuendelinum Rihelium, 1542.

———. "A Lamentableand Piteous Treatise, Verye Necessarye for Everie Christen Manne to Reade: Wherin Is Contayned, Not Onely the High Entreprise and Valeauntnes of Charles V. And His Army (in His Voyage Mde to the Town of Argier in Affrique, against the Turckes, the Enemyes of the Christen Fayth, Th'inhabitoures of the Same), but Also De Myserable Chaunces of Wynde and Wether; with Dyverse Other Adversities, Ahble to Move a Stonye Hearte...." Translated by Ricardus Grafton. In *Harleian Miscellany: A Collection of Scarce, Curious, and Entertaining Pamphlets and Tracts as Well as Manuscript and in Print. Selected from the Library of Edward Harley, Second Earl of Oxford. 1542*, edited by William Oldys and Thomas Park. Vol. 4. Harleian Miscellany. London: White and Co., 1809. 532–43.

Vincent, Bernard. *Minorías y marginados en la España del siglo XVI*. Granada: Diputación Provincial, 1987.

Vincent, Bernard, and Antonio Domíguez Ortíz. *El río morisco*. Biblioteca de Estudios Moriscos: Universidad de Valencia / Universidad de Granada / Universidad de Zaragoza, 2006.

———. *Historia de los moriscos: vida y tragedia de una minoría*. Madrid: Revista de Occidente, 1978.

———. "Las mujeres moriscas." In *Historia de las mujeres en Occidente*, edited by G. Duby and M. Perrot. Vol. 3. Madrid: Taurus, 1991–1993. 323–33.

———. "Les morisque et les pronoms chrétiens." In *Les morisques et leur temps,* edited by Louis Cardaillac. Paris: CNRS, 1983. 55–69.

Vitkus, Daniel J. Introduction to *Three Turk Plays from Early Modern England: Selimus, a Christian Turned Turk, and The Renegado,* edited by Daniel J. Vitkus. New York: Columbia University Press, 2000. 1–53.

———. *Turning Turk: English Theater and the Multicultural Mediterranean, 1570–1630.* New York: Palgrave Macmillan, 2003.

Vitrubius. [Marcus Vitrubius Pollio]. *The Ten Books on Architecture: The Corsini incunabulum.* [*De architectura*]. Annotations and autograph drawings by Giovanni Battista da Sangallo. Edited with an Introduction by Ingrid D. Rowland. Rome: Edizione dell'Elefante, 2003.

Vives Gatell, José. "Andanças e viajes de un hidalgo español (Pero Tafur, 1436–1439), con una descripción de Roma." *Analecta Sacra Tarraconensia* 19 (1949): 123–15.

Watt, William Montgomery. *Muslim-Christian Encounters: Perceptions and Misperceptions.* London: Routledge, 1991.

Watt, William Montgomery, and Pierre Cachia. *A History of Islamic Spain.* Edinburgh: Edinburgh University Press, 1992.

Wehr, Hans. *A Dictionary of Modern Written Arabic.* 3rd ed. Edited by J. Milton Cowan. New York: Spoken Language Services, 1976.

Wheatcroft, Andrew. *Infidels: A History of the Conflict between Christendom and Islam.* New York: Random House, 2004.

Whitehead, Neil L. Introduction to *Hans Staden's True History: An Account of Cannibal Captivity in Brazil.* Edited and translated by Neil L. Whitehead and Michael Harbsmeier. Durham, NC: Duke University Press, 2008. i–civ.

Wiegers, Gerard. *Islamic Literature in Spanish and Aljamiado.* Leiden: Brill, 1991.

———. "La diáspora morisca en el Magreb: la obra de polémica anti-cristiana de Muhammad Alguazir (c. 1610)." In *La expulsión de los moriscos (14 de octubre de 1997–9 de junio de 1998),* edited by J. M. Perceval et al. Valencia: Bancaja 1998, 90–121.

Wiegers, Gerard, and Mercedes García-Arenal. *A Man of Three Worlds: Samuel Pallache, a Moroccan Jew in Catholic and Protestant Europe.* Translated by Martin Beagles. Foreword by David Niremberg and Richard Kagan. Baltimore: Johns Hopkins University Press, 2003.

Wolf, John B. *The Barbary Coast: Algiers under the Turks, 1500 to 1830.* New York: Norton, 1979.

Wood, Denis. *The Power of Maps.* New York: Guilford Press, 1992.

Yule, Sir Henry, and Arthur Coke Burnell. *Hobson-Jobson: A Glossary of Colloquial Anglo-Indian Words and Phrases, and of Kindred Terms, Etymological, Historical, Geographical and Discursive.* Edited by William Crooke. London: J. Murray, 1903.

Zafrani, Haïm. *Juifs d'Andalousie et du Maghreb.* Paris: Maisonneuve et Larose, 1996.

Zaragoza Pascual, Ernesto. "Abadologio del Monasterio de Nuestra Señora de la Misericordia de Frómista (1437–1835)." *Publicaciones de la Institución Tello Téllez de Meneses* 71 (2000): 135–58.

———. *Los abades trienales (1499–1568).* Vol. 2 of *Los generales de la Congregación de San Benito de Valladolid.* Silos: Imprenta de Aldecoa, 1976.

Zhiri, Oumelbanine. "Leo Africanus, Translated and Betrayed." In *The Politics of Translation in the Middle Ages and the Renaissance,* edited by Renate Blumenfeld-Kosinski, Luise von Flotow, and Daniel Russell. Ottawa: University of Ottawa Press, 2001. 161–74.

———. *Les sillages de Jean Léon l'Africain, du XVIe au XX siècle.* Casablanca: Wallada, 1995.

Zósimo. *Nueva historia.* Translated by José María Candau Morón. Madrid: Gredos, 1992.

INDEX

ʿAbd al-ʿAziz, 100
ʿAbd al-Malik (Muley Maluch), 111, 216, 341n1
ʿAbd al-Muʾmin, Muley, 216–17, 341n1
Abu al-Fehri, 100
Abu-Lughod, Lila, 25
adultery, 230, 267
Africanus, Leo, 43, 93, 97–98, 309n8
  about, 34, 307n1
  on name of Algiers, 99, 313n6
  as source for Sosa, 34–35, 50, 73
  studies about, 23
agha, 121, 265, 266
  definition, 318n16
  of janissaries, 135–36, 137, 323n1
Albertini, Francesco, 290n43
Alcalá, Ángel, 52
alcohol, 196, 197, 219, 239–40, 344n15, 346n15
Alexander VI (pope), 28, 31
Algiers
  climate, 199
  as commercial center, 8–9
  as corsair city, 1–2, 8, 9, 27, 28–29, 102
  cosmopolitan nature of, 2, 7
  government, 265–72
  immigration into, 1, 7, 21, 27, 102, 291n55
  languages spoken, 9
  as Muslim kingdom, 100–101
  name, 99, 313n6
  natural beauty of, 261–62
  population, 316n1
Algiers history
  Charles V attack on, 16, 114, 116, 222
  destroyed by Vandals, 97
  rise in sixteenth century, 27
  Roman Empire and, 93–98
  Spanish conquest, 28, 100, 313n2
  Turkish conquest, 103
Algiers topography
  buildings, 253–58, 349n16
  cartographic view of, 13, 14–15, 16, 17
  castles and forts, 113–15
  caves, 116, 316n5
  gates, 106–8, 113, 314n1
  geographic location, 93, 261
  marketplace, 42, 117, 316n2
  military fortifications, 109–11, 113, 115–16
  moat, 112
  mountains surrounding, 113, 114, 116, 263
  port, 104–5, 107–8
  ramparts of, 104–5, 109
  streets, 117
  surrounding countryside, 98, 261–62, 263
Ali Pichinino, Kaʾid, 130

381

alms-giving, 205, 236
  as Muslim obligation, 211, 214, 220, 345n8
Alonsotegui, Miguel de, 90, 306n14
Ambrose, Saint, 73
el-amin, 270, 351n9
Amiza Ra'is, 160
Amud (renegade), 47, 49
Anatolia, 124
animals, 263, 350n5
animal sacrifice, 153, 213, 220
Annaba, 95, 121, 128, 155, 166, 270
Antonius Augustus Pius (Roman emperor), 93, 94, 97, 308n6
Apianus, Petrus, 17
Apparition du livre, L' (Febvre and Martin), 12
Arab
  origin of term, 312n2
'Arab Ahmad, 105, 110, 111, 112, 118, 259
  about, 314n6, 349n18
Arabic, 99, 181, 184, 244, 313n5
  as language of Qur'an, 176
  writing taught, 175, 196, 197
A'raj, Ahmad al-, 35
Arapsa Ra'is, 160
Archelaus, 95
architecture, 11, 30, 117, 147, 254, 260
Aristotle, 72
Arnaut (Genoese renegade), 63
Arrianus, 72
Asconius Pedianus, Quintus, 310n21
ashor, 220, 342n11
Atlas Mountains, 263, 318n11, 350n6
Augustine, Saint, 73
Augustus Caesar, 94–95, 147

Bab al-Djadid gate, 106, 112, 314n1
Bab al-Djazira gate, 107, 110
Bab al-Wad gate, 106, 109, 113, 117, 148, 211, 251, 256, 259, 314n1
Bab 'Azzun gate, 106, 117, 118, 122, 148, 154, 179, 248, 256, 314n1
Bagarinos, 120, 153, 163
Baldis, 119–20, 185, 317n2
Bali, Hadjdji, 160, 218
Banu Djubar principality, 318n11, 352n12
Barbarossa, 'Arudj, 102–3, 119, 133, 313n3
Barbary, 292n68
  See also Maghreb
Barletta, Vincent, 22
Barrios Aguilera, Manuel, 22
Bastion de France, 166, 271, 330n4, 351n11
baths, 191, 254–55, 348nn5–7
  Jews not permitted in, 255
  women and, 191, 203–4, 254
  See also washing
Battista Alberti, Leon, 10–11
beards, 170–71, 219
Bedouins, 122, 212, 268–69, 312n2
begging, 122, 177–78, 236
Béjaïa, 28, 100, 313n2
  corsairs in, 28, 155
Belgrade, 27
Bendeli 'Ali, Ka'id, 129
Benedictine Order, 51, 75, 87, 88
Bennassar, Bartolomé, 22
Bennassar, Lucile, 22
Berbers, 37, 129, 141, 312n2
  tribute collected from, 141–42, 269
  as "untamable," 269
  villages of, 131, 269
Bernabé Pons, Louis F., 22

Bernard, Saint, 73
beylerbey, 142, 265–66, 325n3, 326n3
Bizerte, 155, 156
Boccaccio, 72
Boccho (Mauritanian king), 94
Bolaños, Juan de, 64, 301n198
Bône. *See* Annaba
bonevoglie, 153, 327n8
Book of Omens, 155, 328n15
book printing, 12
    See also censorship
Bourdieu, Pierre, 25
Bracciolini, Poggio, 289n26
Braudel, Fernand, 8, 9, 288n17
Braun, Georg, 11–12, 13, 17
bravery, 33, 172–73, 219–20, 331n12
breast feeding, 195
Brevez Fresco, Luis, 63–64, 224, 343n18
Brevísima relación de la destrucción de las Indias (Las Casas), 24–25
Briático, Marquis of, 71
Britain and Barbary, 1589–1678 (Matar), 23
buildings, 253–58
    architecture, 11, 30, 117, 147, 254, 260
    Bagnio de la Bastarda, 256–57
    Bagnio of the King, 256, 349n14
    bastardas, 349n16
    Great Bagnio, 256, 258, 349n14
    See also mosques; tombs
Bunes Ibarra, Miguel Ángel de, 22
burial, 247–49, 347n3
    by Jews, 251, 347nn8–10
Burtughali, Muhammad al-, 34
Busbecq, Ogier Ghiselin de, 33, 319n1

Cabrera de Córdoba, Luis, 70
Cádiz, 33, 289n20
Calderón de la Barca, Pedro, 76
calendars
    Islamic, 209–10, 328n18, 336n3, 339n2, 340n12
    Julian and Gregorian, 339n1
Caligula, 95–96
Camamis, George, 57
Canary Islands, 60
Cañete, Juan, 315n6
Captives (Colley), 22
caravans, 225, 343n20
Carrasco Urgoiti, Soledad, 23
Carrionis (Ludovico Carrione Brugensi), 311n28
cartography, 10–13, 289n31
    military purposes of, 16
censorship, 73–74
    and approval of *Topographia,* 74, 84–86
    index of banned books, 73, 305n6
    law of, 73, 305n6, 307n20
Cervantes, Miguel de, 30, 33, 74, 296n141, 316n5
    on Algerian corsairs, 328n17
    arrival in Algiers, 2, 29
    on Christian captives, 20, 327n5
    liberation of, 63
    poetry of, 39–40
    second escape attempt by, 49
    slave master of, 329n2
    as soldier, 317n3
    and Sosa, 38–41, 49, 65, 75–76, 77
    works
    —"The Captive's Tale," 20
    —"Epístola a Mateo Vázquez," 40
    —*La Galatea,* 77

Cervantes, Miguel de (*cont.*)
—*Información de Argel,* 39, 40–41, 58
—*Persiles,* 77
—*El trato de Argel,* 42
Cervantes en Argel (Garcés), 304n240
Cervantes in Algiers (Garcés), 22, 38–39, 42, 48, 57, 66
Cervantes y la Berbería (Sola and de la Peña), 22
Charles V, 17, 27, 41, 53
   attack on Algiers by, 16, 114, 116, 222
chastity, 191, 226–27, 238
Cherchell, 152, 162, 166, 309n8, 327n6
childbirth, 194–95
child rearing, 195–97
children
   beating of, 240–41
   disobedience toward parents, 235
   dress, 172
   punishment in school, 176–77
   separation by race, 211–12
Chisholm, Hugh, 348n6
chorography, 17
chrétiens d'Allah, Les (Bennassar and Bennassar), 22
Christianity
   Algiers as "scourge of," 2, 287n2
   conflicts with Islam, 9–10, 27–28, 29, 31, 232
   Jews' hatred of, 183
   Muslim hatred for, 45, 133, 229–30, 238
   religious images in, 223–24
Christians in Algiers
   chapels of, 229, 257–58, 259
   hypocrisy toward, 224–26, 234
   during Islamic ceremonies, 212
   legal restrictions on, 268
   as merchants, 166
   population of, 119
   See also renegades; slaves
Christian Slaves, Muslim Masters (Davis), 22
Cicero, 72, 310n21
circumcision
   female, 196, 336n4
   male, 126–27, 196, 320n9
Civitates orbis terrarum (Braun and Hogenberg), 11–12, 13
   map of Algiers in, 14–15
Claudius (Nero Claudius Drusus), 96
cleanliness, 118, 245
Cleopatra, 94, 309n13
Clifford, James, 24
Colley, Linda, 22
Colonna, Marco Antonio, 53–54, 55, 56, 71, 298n168
Complete History of Algiers (Morgan), 25, 291n64
Constantine (city in Algeria), 121, 141, 166
Constantine (emperor), 147, 325n1
Constantinople, 13, 18, 26, 165, 166, 172
conversion, 43–44
   ceremony, 126–27, 320nn6–8
   of Jews, 43, 164, 182
   motivations for, 43–44, 149, 228, 320n5
   See also renegades
Cornejo, Fra Antonio, 87, 88, 306n10
corsairs
   avarice of, 237–38
   booty of, 156, 157–58
   captain of, 158, 159

Christian galley slaves of, 153, 154, 157, 158, 233, 270
cleanliness and order of, 156–57
dexterity of, 155, 328n17
drunkenness of, 240
with frigates, 162–63
funding of, 153–54, 270
as janissaries, 133–34
of Knights of Saint John, 327n9
lewends of, 154, 240, 327n11
personal slaves of, 152
provisioning of, 154
raids on Spain by, 162–63
renegades as, 151, 329n4
See also privateering
Cosa, Juan de la, 10
cosmetics, 4–5, 197, 200
Cosmographia (Ptolemy), 10
currency, 185–87, 335nn8–16
Customs House, 107, 146
Cuzco, 12
Cyprus, 27

Dadson, Trevor J., 22
Dakhlia, Jocélyne, 23, 29–30
Dali Mami, 42, 160, 329n2
Dan, Pierre, 32, 344n1
dancing, 194, 211–12
 at marriages, 189–90, 191
 women and, 5, 47, 205–6
Dante Alighieri, 6
Daut, Ka'id, 129
Davis, Natalie Zemon, 23
Davis, Robert C., 22
Dawud, Ka'id, 160, 255
death, 247, 347n1
de Certeau, Michel, 11, 18–19
de Grammont, Henri-Delmas, 56, 287n5, 324n12
de la Peña, José F., 22

Delle navigationi e viaggi (Ramusio), 34
Denis, Ferdinand, 56
De origine Turcarum, 133, 323n4
De rebus Turcicis, 133, 323n3
De Rei Aedificatoria (Battista), 10–11
Descripción general de África (Mármol Carvajal), 35, 37–38
di Castro, Scipio, 55
disease, 261
Divan, 138, 146, 324n5
Dja'far (Genoese renegade corsair), 161
Dja'far (Genoese renegade surgeon), 223
Dja'far (Mallorcan renegade), 23
Dja'far, Beylerbey, 160
Dja'far, Ka'id (English renegade), 129
Dja'far, Ka'id (Hungarian renegade), 130
Dja'far, Ka'id (Neapolitan renegade), 130
Dja'far Agha, Ka'id, 129
Dja'far Montez, 161
Dja'far Pasha, 134, 187, 227–28, 258, 323n6, 343n23, 349n17
Djerba, 27, 155, 156, 165
Djidjelli, 103, 128, 217
Djum'a, 139, 147, 215, 324n10
Donardi (Greek renegade), 161
Don Juan of Austria, 118, 233, 317n3, 344n3
dreams, 176, 219
dress, 169–73, 245
 of Baldi Moors, 120, 317nn4–9
 of Bedouin, 122
 caftans, 169, 330n2
 of children and youths, 172
 coats and wraps, 121–22, 170, 198, 199, 318nn18–19, 331n9, 336n3

dress (*cont.*)
  footwear, 120, 122, 170, 200, 317nn8–9, 330n5, 331n7, 338nn10–11
  headwear, 120, 122, 171, 172–73, 199, 331n11, 337nn6–8
  of janissaries, 171–72
  of Jews, 182–83, 202
  of Kabyle and Zwawa, 121–22, 318nn18–19
  of marabouts, 176
  of Moriscos, 123
  trousers, 120, 170, 182, 317n4
  tunics, 120, 198, 317nn5–6, 336n4
  women's, 198–200, 337nn6–8
Du Pérac, Étienne, 290n43

Ehlers, Benjamin, 22
Elias, Norbert, 54
England, 165
Enríquez de Guzmán, Diego (count of Alba de Liste), 91, 307nn17–18
envy, 241–42
Europe through Arab Eyes (Matar), 23–24

Fajardo y Acevedo, Antonio, 346n15
famine, 148, 325n2
Farat, Boluk-Bashi (Greek renegade), 48
farmers and farming, 119, 131–32, 263
fashions, 169–73, 198–202
  See also dress
fasting, 210–11, 340n5
feast days, 5, 175, 206, 209–15
Febvre, Lucien, 12

Ferdinand the Catholic, 27, 28, 73, 102, 313n1
  and Sicily, 53, 59
Fernández de Córdova, Diego, 304n242
Fernández de Córdova, Francisco, 304n242
Feru Ra'is, 160
Fès, 34, 43, 95, 141, 156, 185
  trade with, 166, 181
Festus, Sextus Pompeius, 310n21
fighting, 149, 234, 240
fishing, 263–64, 270–71
Fiumara, 262, 350n3
Flavius Blondus, 311n28
foods, 208
  bulgur, 142, 147, 208, 325n4
  couscous, 142, 208, 214, 325n5
Formentera, 156
forts, 16, 37, 102, 109, 111, 113–14
  of Hasan Pasha, 116, 258, 266
  of Muhammad Pasha, 114
  of 'Uludj 'Ali, 114
fountains, 258–59
France, 165, 291n55, 329n3
  privateer attacks on ships from, 237–38
Francis I of France, 329n3
Friday
  as holy day, 139, 147, 215, 324n10, 341n15
Frómista, 307n19
Fuchs, Barbara, 22, 30–31

Galán, Diego, 75, 303n236
Galen, 72
Galmés de la Fuente, Álvaro, 22
gambling, 149, 197
Garcerán de Borja, Pedro Luis, 225, 343n19

García-Arenal, Mercedes, 21–22, 23, 36, 37
García Martín, Pedro, 12
García Santo-Tomás, Enrique, 76
gardens, 51, 98, 120, 262
Gasco, Juan, 20, 315n6
Gellius, Aulus, 97, 310n22
Genoa, 8, 9, 165
Genseric (Vandal king), 97, 311n25
Ghassani, Wazir Muhammad abn 'Abd al Wahab al-, 38
gift-giving, 152, 211, 224–25
Giger, Ka'id, 161
Gil, Fra Juan, 40–41, 49, 58
Giovio, Paulo, 73
Girón (El Dorador), 49
gluttony, 196, 239–40
Góis, Damião de, 35, 293n89
Goths, 98, 121
government
  expenses, 271–72
  income, 129, 131, 158, 247, 268–71
  justice system, 135, 189, 227, 230, 266–68, 323n3
  and Ottoman Empire, 1, 265, 271–72, 287n3
  role of pashas, 265–66, 351n2
Grafton, Anthony, 72
Granada, 60
  Christian conquest of, 27, 28, 30–31, 102
  emigration of Moors from, 27, 28, 102, 122, 123, 318n21
Granvelle, Cardinal, 298n168
greed, 235–36, 237, 345n6
Gregory XIII (pope), 58, 68, 69, 299n182
Griego, Pedro, 295n115
Gunderic (Vandal king), 97, 311n25

Hader, Ka'id, 130
Hadjdj, 234, 341n5
Hadjdji Murad, Ka'id, 129, 321n4
Hadrian, 97, 310n23
Haedo, Diego de (elder)
  as bishop, 56, 72, 74, 77–78, 90, 298n169, 302n223, 303n235, 306n16
  death, 75, 78
  as Inquisitor, 52–53, 55, 56, 297n152, 306n16
  named president of Sicily, 91, 307n18
  relations with Sosa, 72, 74–75
  Topography of Algiers ascribed to, 25, 36, 51, 74–77, 78, 83, 84, 287n4
Haedo, Diego de (younger), 303n236, 306n12
  dedication of *Topographia* by, 89–91
  edits and publishes *Topographia*, 51–52, 75, 305n3, 306n13
hair
  braids, 199, 218
  facial, 170–71, 219
  shaved heads, 170
  women's, 4, 127, 199, 200
Hamida Cajes, Ka'id, 130
hangings, 267
Haran, Muhammad al-, 36
Harris, A. Katie, 22
Harvey, L. P., 22
Hasan, Ka'id, 116, 130, 255, 316n5
Hasan Agha, 260, 348n23, 350n23
Hasan Pasha (son of Barbarossa), 111, 114, 237, 257, 260, 315n5, 345n9
Hasan Pasha (the Venetian), 44, 114–15, 148, 223, 257, 334n6, 349n14

Hasan the Corsican, 259, 349n20
Hasan the Genoese Fornaro, 161
Hasan the Genoese, 160
Heraclius, 37
Herod, 95
Herodotus, 72
Herrera y Tordesillas, Antonio de, 86, 305n9
Hesiod, 72
Hess, Andrew, 38
Heygi, Ottmar, 22
Hills, Helen, 13
Histoire de la Barbarie et de ses corsaires (Dan), 32
History and Description of Africa (Leo Africanus), 34–35, 50, 93, 97–98
Hogenberg, Franz, 11–12, 13, 17
home furnishings, 207–8
homosexuality, 125, 148, 238, 239, 320n3, 329n24
  by corsairs, 159
  by marabouts, 178, 180
honor, 168, 230–31, 245, 330n1, 344n27
hospitals, 237, 255
housing
  architecture of, 117
  density, 117
  encampments, 268–69, 351n8
  of janissaries, 146–47, 256
  of Moriscos, 123
  of Turks in Algiers, 124
  of Zwawa, 122
hypocrisy, 224–26, 234

Ibn Rashiq, 35, 294n93
image veneration, 223–24
immigrants, 1, 7, 21, 27, 102, 291n55
inheritance, 227–28
  emancipated slaves and, 126
  percentage going to king, 247, 270
Innocent VIII (pope), 60
Inquisition, 52–53, 73–74
  index of banned books, 73, 305n6
  Muslim retaliation for actions of, 45, 46, 238, 345n11
  in Sicily, 53–54, 55, 56, 74
Iol Caesarea, 93–94, 95, 96, 99, 308n7
Isabella (queen of Castille), 27, 28, 73, 313n1
'Isa Ra'is, 160
Islam
  conflicts with Christianity, 9–10, 27–28, 29, 31, 232
  European stereotypes and hostility toward, 29–30, 31–32, 37, 38
  Friday as holy day in, 139, 147, 215, 324n10, 341n15
  in modern times, 21
  pilgrimage to Mecca in, 218, 234, 341n6
  portrayed as beast of the Apocalypse, 232, 344n1
  religious festivals of, 211–14
  saints in, 217–18
  Sosa's antipathy toward, 3, 6, 214, 221, 223, 232, 288n6, 341n13
  See also mosques; prayer; Qur'an
Islam in Britain, 1558–1685 (Matar), 23
Islam in Spanish Literature (López-Baralt), 23
Italy, 27–28, 55, 288n17
Itinerarium (Antoninus, emperor), 93, 94, 308n6

Jaffer (Roman renegade), 48
jails, 268
janissaries, 127, 144, 145, 148, 215
　agha of, 135–36, 137, 141, 323n1
　in battle, 143–44
　burial of, 248
　cavalry of, 143
　composed of Christian youth, 133, 322n2
　cooking for, 143, 147, 149–50, 171
　and corsairs, 133–34
　discipline of, 135, 323n2
　dress, 171–72
　fear and respect for, 149
　food of, 142–43, 147–48
　founding of, 133
　housing, 146–47, 256
　Jews prohibited from becoming, 134
　number of, 141
　plundering raids by, 129, 141–42, 269
　as prisoners, 268
　punishment for insulting, 149, 231
　salaries, 127, 137, 138, 139, 140, 150
　schools for, 322n2
　untouchability of, 231
janissary ranks, 137–40, 265–66
　Bash-Boluk-Bashi, 140
　Bash-oda, 138
　Boluk-Bashi, 129, 139, 142, 143, 145, 266, 321n3, 324n7
　Kahya, 140, 324n11
　Mir Boluk-Bashi, 139, 324n8
　Odabashi, 137–38, 143, 324n2
　Otrak, 138
　Solak, 138, 324n6
　Yayabashi, 139
　Yol-dash, 137, 324n1

Jefferson, Thomas, 25
Jerome, Saint, 73
jewelry, 5, 200–201
Jews, 181–83, 333n1
　burials and mourning by, 251–52, 347nn8–11
　child rearing by, 197
　dress, 182–83, 202
　economic status of, 183
　hatred toward Christianity by, 183
　ill treatment of, 43, 182, 324n4
　language of, 181, 185, 333n1
　marriage of, 196–97
　neighborhoods of, 182, 333n1
　occupations of, 181
　religious conversion by, 43, 164, 182
　restrictions against, 43, 134, 255
　tribute paid by, 182
　women, 196–97, 202, 207
João III, 35
Josephus, Titus Flavius, 310n16
Juba I, 94, 309n10
Juba II, 94, 95, 309n12
Jugurta (Numidian king), 94
Julius Caesar, 94
justice system, 135, 189, 227, 230, 266–68, 323n3
Justinian, 72

Kabyles, 120–22, 185, 212, 317n10, 334n2
Kadi Ra'is, 161
kadis, 135, 189, 192, 227, 230, 266–67
ka'ids, 128–30, 142, 269, 322n6
　definition, 315n3, 321n1
Kāma Sūtra español, Un (López-Baralt), 23

Kari Ra'is, 161
Kasba, 106, 109, 112, 114, 315n2
Kasr al-Kabir, al-, battle of, 185, 334n4
Kaur 'Ali, 161
Kelibia, 155
Khader, Ka'id, 161
khalifa, 266, 315n4
Khayr al-Din Barbarossa, 133, 287n1, 326n3
  builds port of Algiers, 98, 105, 312n29
  as founder of state of Algiers, 1, 313n3
Knights of St. John (of Malta), 27, 41, 42, 295n116, 327n9
Kollo, 166
Kuko, 120, 186, 271, 318n11, 352n12

Labbès, 120, 186, 271, 318n11, 352n12
laborers and artisans, 119, 168
land grants, 131, 322n1
languages, 9, 184–85
  Arabic, 99, 175, 176, 181, 184, 196–97, 244, 313n5
  lingua franca, 9, 185, 335n5
  Turkish, 149, 175, 176, 184, 195, 265
Larache, 156
Las Casas, Bartolomé de, 24–25
Lazcano, Fra Gregorio de, 88, 306n11
laziness and sloth, 207, 242–43, 263
Leghorn (Livorno), 2
León, Fra Luis de, 52, 297n152
Leontius, 97, 311n26
Leo X (pope), 34

Lepanto, Battle of (1571), 27, 233, 344n2
Liali, Ka'id, 130
lingua franca, 9, 185, 335n5
Lipari, 156
literatura secreta de los últimos musulmanes de España, La (López-Baralt), 23
López-Baralt, Luce, 23
Lucan, 72
Lucian of Samosata, 312n3
lust, 238–39
lying, 220, 235–36, 243

Macrobius, 72
Maghreb
  and European colonization, 25, 37
  European study of, 22, 29–30, 31–32, 35
  lingua franca of, 9, 185, 335n5
  "lost land" leitmotif of, 31
  Moors' immigration to, 27, 28, 102, 122, 123, 318n21
  Ottoman conquest of, 26–27, 319n3
  as privateering center, 1–2, 27–29, 154–55
  Spanish conquest of, 28, 100, 118, 233, 313n2, 317n3
  trade with, 165–66, 181
Mahamut Bey, Ka'id, 130
Malta, 27
Mami, Ka'id, 161, 255
Mami Arnaut, 160, 328n21
Mami Gancho, 161
Mamija (Genoese renegade), 161
Mami the Calabrian, 161
Mami the Corsican, 161
Manes, Ka'id, 130

mansions and palaces, 255, 348n9
maps. *See* cartography
marabouts, 153, 174–80, 210–11, 234, 250
  begging by, 177–78
  as crazy and witless, 178–79
  defined, 327n7, 331n1
  dress of, 176
  duties of, 174–75
  as hermits, 177
  and mosques, 174, 179, 215, 216, 333n20
  name of, 174, 331n1, 332n2
  pilgrimage to Mecca by, 234–35
  and prayer, 174–76, 177
  reverence and respect for, 217, 221, 245
  as schoolmasters, 175–76
  sexual practices of, 177, 178, 179, 180, 217, 221
  and sorcery, 179–80
  view of salvation by, 220
Marcus, George, 24
Marín, Luis Astrana, 57
Marja Mami, 161
Mark Antony, 94, 309n13
Mármol Carvajal, Luis del, 35, 37–38, 334n4
Márquez Villanueva, Francisco, 22
marriage, 188–93, 246
  arranged, 189
  ceremony, 189–91
  dissolution, 226–27
  dowry, 189, 191–92, 197
  of Jews, 196–97
  polygamy, 188, 192–93
  of renegades, 188–89
  sexual consummation of, 191
Martin, Henri-Jean, 12
Martínez Torres, José Antonio, 22

Masinissa, 325n1
Matar, Nabil, 23–24
Matienzo y Haedo, Fernando de, 303n235
Mauritania, Caesarean, 94–97, 309n8
Mauroli, Don Silvestre, 68, 70, 301n209
Maxentius, 147, 325n1
meat
  pork not eaten, 219
  religious rites preparing, 217
Mecca pilgrimage, 218, 234, 341n6
Mehmed II, 324n5
Mercator, Gerardus, 10
merchants, 8, 12, 119, 164–67
Mers-el-Kebir, 28, 343n19
Mexía, Pero, 73
Mexico City (Tenochtitlan), 12
Mitidja, 262, 351n4
mizwar, 267, 268, 351n6
Mohács, 27
Montiano y Luyardo, Agustín, 39
Moors
  Baldi, 119–20, 317n2
  Bedouins, 122, 212, 268–69, 312n2
  Kabyles, 120–21, 212, 317n10
  Moriscos, 21–22, 27, 28, 102, 122–23, 318n21
  Mudéjares, 123, 318n22
  Tagarinos, 123, 318n22
Morales, Ambrosio de, 38
Morgan, Joseph, 25, 291n64
Moriscos, 28, 46, 122–23, 318n21
  deportation of, 27
  historical study of, 21–22
  population of in Algiers, 318n23
  raids on Spain by, 162

mosques, 253–54
  Djum'a services, 139, 147, 215, 324n10
  during fasting, 210
  furnishings in, 216
  Grand Mosque, 253, 348n1
  Great Mosque, 348n4
  marabouts and, 174, 179, 215, 216, 333n20
  el-Merabta, 220, 342n9
  number of, 253
  women not permitted in, 196, 213, 216
Mostaganem, 121, 128, 141
  battle of (1558), 257, 349n15
Motafer, Ka'id, 129
mourning, 250–51
  by Jews, 251–52, 348n11
Mudéjares, 123, 318n22
Mudhaffar, Ka'id, 255
Muhammad (prophet), 6, 214
  Law of, 220
  Sosa antipathy toward, 176, 232, 332n13
  See also Qur'an
Muhammad, Ka'id (from Biskra), 130
Muhammad, Ka'id (Sosa slaveowner), 130, 161, 334n6
  as government official, 42–43, 334n2
  house of, 47, 48, 255, 349n12
  as Jewish renegade, 43, 44
  and Sosa's escape, 64
Muhammad Çelebi, Ka'id, 129, 322n5
Muhammad Pasha, 114, 134, 255, 323n5, 348n8
muhtasib, 267, 351n7
Münster, Sebastian, 73, 133, 308n5

Murabit Sain, Ka'id, 130
Murad, Hadjdji (Agi Morato), 218, 255, 341n5
Murad, Ka'id (renegade from Ibiza), 130
Murad Çelebi, Ka'id, 130, 322n5
Murad I, 322n1
Murad III, 133, 322n1
Murad Ra'is (the Great), 160
Murad Ra'is (the Small), 160
Murad the Frenchman, 160
music, 149, 189, 326n3
Mustafa (French renegade), 48
Mustafa, Hadjdji, 218

Naples, 58, 155, 165
Narváez, María Teresa, 22
Naufragios (Núñez Cabeza de Vaca), 24–25
Navarro, Pedro, 100, 102, 313n2
Numidians, 141, 325n1
Núñez Cabeza de Vaca, Alvar, 24–25

obedience and disobedience, 235, 245
occupations
  of Baldi Moors, 119
  farmers, 119, 131–32, 263
  of Jews, 181
  of Kabyle Moors, 120
  laborers and artisans, 119, 168
  merchants, 8, 119, 164–67
  of Moriscos, 123
Ondarza Zavala, Miguel de, 83, 84, 305n5
Orán, 95, 141
  Spanish conquest, 28, 100, 313n2
  trade with, 166, 181
Order of Malta, 41, 57

Orozco de Arce, Juan, 58–59, 299nn181–82, 300n183
Ortelius, Abraham, 11, 12
Ottoman Empire
   expansion of, 26–27, 319n3
   Grand Turk of, 133, 158, 227–28, 245, 265, 271–72
   meritocracy under, 33
   patronage in, 47–48
   Turkish-Algerian Regency of, 1, 271–72, 287n3
Ovid, 72

Padrón, Ricardo, 16
Paduan Ra'is, 161
Palladio, Andrea, 290n43
Panvinius, Onofrius (Onofrio Panvinio), 309n9, 310n21
Parreño, José María, 57
Paulinus, Saint, 50
Pazos, Antonio Mauriño de, 67
Peñón de Argel, 102, 309n8, 312n29, 313n2
Peñón de Vélez, 313n2
Pere Jordán (Spanish slave), 48
Pérez, Antonio, 67
Pérez Pastor, Cristóbal, 56–57, 65
Perry, Mary Elizabeth, 22
Philip II, 11, 60–61, 233, 289n30, 344n4
   concern over Sosa captivity, 61–62, 63
   death, 75
   and Inquisition, 53, 55, 74
   patronage system under, 54
   persecution of Sosa by, 70–71
   and Sosa ransom efforts, 61, 62–63, 64
Philip III, 75, 84–85, 303n235, 304n236

Piccolomini, Aeneas Sylvius (Pius II), 26
piety, 3, 4, 236, 246
Pirri, Rocco, 58–59, 75, 299nn181–82
Pius V (pope), 27
plague, 261
Plato, 72
Pliny, 72, 93, 94, 95, 96, 235, 345n7
   about, 308n3
Plutarch, 95, 96, 309n15
Polybius, 93, 308n4
polygamy, 188, 192–93
Pompey (Roman general), 94
poor, 120, 122, 183, 196, 208
   alms for, 205, 211, 214, 220, 236, 250
   burial of, 249
   dress of, 166, 200
   inns with corrals for, 118, 256
population
   of Algiers, 316n1
   of Christians, 119
   of Moriscos, 319n23
   of renegades, 8, 127, 319n1, 321n12
   of sipahi, 132
   of slaves, 119, 317n1
   of Turks, 124
pork, 219
Porto Farina, 155, 328n14
Portulano (Cosa), 10
Praetorian Guard, 147, 325n1
prayer, 214, 332nn3–9
   marabouts and, 174–76, 177
   morning, 216–17, 341n2
   uninterrupted nature of, 216–17
   washing prior to, 210, 217
   See also mosques

Prester John, 125, 320n2
pride, 232–34
Prisioneros de los infieles (Martínez Torres), 22
privateering, 154–55
  Algiers as haven for, 1–2, 8, 28–29, 102
  expenses of, 153–54, 270
  of French ships, 237–38
  government sponsorship of, 158, 269–70
  of Iberian ships, 27–28
  raids on Spain, 162–63
  religious defense of, 153
  ships for, 151, 162–63
  See also corsairs
prostitution, 238
Ptolemy (Claudius Ptolemaeus), 17, 72, 93, 94, 97
  about, 308n5
  Cosmographia, 10
Ptolemy (son of Juba and Selene), 95
punishment, 45, 135, 138, 144, 231, 245, 267
  for adultery, 230
  beatings as, 267
  of children, 176–77, 195–96, 197
  and pardoning, 240–41
  and rage, 240, 241
  self-, 120–21, 178
  under Spanish Inquisition, 52, 54, 74
Purchas, Samuel, 287n2

Qur'an, 155, 195, 199, 266, 340n6
  marabouts and, 175–76
  Sosa disdain for, 3, 153, 176
  See also Islam

racial characteristics
  of Baldi Moors, 119
  of Bedouin, 122
  of Kabyles and Zwawa, 121
  of Kabyle Moors, 120
racial separation, 211–12
Ramadan, 210, 211, 339nn3–4
Ramadan Pasha, 42, 109, 111, 231, 255, 344n28
Ramírez, Jerónimo, 50, 65
Ramírez, María and Mariana, 65
Ramusio, Giovanni, 34
Reconquista, 28, 30
Relación del origen y suceso de los Xarifes (Torres), 35–36, 37
religious festivals, 211–14
  al-ʿId al-Kabir (Great Festival), 213–14, 395n11
  al-ʿId Saghir (Seker), 211, 340n7
  Laylat al-Kadr, 211, 340n6
  mawlid (malud), 214, 340n12
  Sabʿ wa-ʿIshrin, 212–13, 340n6
renegades, 319n1
  Jewish, 43, 164, 182
  as laborers and artisans, 168
  language of, 185
  marrying of, 188–89
  in military, 127, 133–34, 321n11
  motivations for converting by, 43–44, 149, 228, 320n5
  Muhammad, Kaʾid as, 43–44
  native countries of, 125
  population of in Algiers, 8, 127, 319n1, 321n12
  Sosa view of, 8, 228, 288n13
  women as, 229
  See also conversion
Resuan, Kaʾid, 130
Rhodes, 27, 41
Rinegatti (Scaraffia), 22

Rivero Rodríguez, Manuel, 54
robbery, 118, 217
  See also privateering
Rojas, Juan de, 53, 56
Romania, 124, 133, 172
Roman-Jewish War (132–135 CE), 310n23
Rome
  Empire of, 93–98, 147, 325n1
  topography of, 290n43
Rucellai, Bernardo, 290n43

Saffa, Ka'id, 111
Sagredo, Juan, 345n8
Salah Ra'is, 134, 259, 323n5, 349n19
Salazar, Juan Vázquez de, 66, 67
Saldanha, António de, 293n89
Salé, 28, 156
Salim al-Tumi, 101, 103, 313n3
Sallustius Crispus, Gaius, 309n11
salvation, 220–21
sandjak-beys, 265, 351n3
San Pablo (galley) of Malta, 41–42, 65, 224, 295nn115–16, 342n16
San Pietro, 156
Sapiencia, Octavio, 290n47
Scaraffia, Lucetta, 22
schools, 196, 223
  for janissaries, 322n2
  marabouts as schoolmasters, 175–76
  punishment of children in, 176–77
  religious festivals in, 214–15
  women and, 203
science, 99, 223
Sciuti Russi, Vittorio, 53, 58
Sebastian, Don (king of Portugal), 185

Sejanus, Lucius Aeolius, 325n1
Selene II, 94–95, 309n13
Selim I, 1, 287n1, 319n3
Seville, 12, 211
sexual practices, 6, 148, 288n13, 320n3
  anal intercourse, 227
  bestiality, 239
  children and, 196, 197
  of corsairs, 159
  homosexuality, 125, 148, 159, 178, 180, 238, 239, 320n31, 329n24, 346n12
  by marabouts toward men, 178, 180
  by marabouts toward women, 177, 179, 221
  pandering, 238
  in polygamous marriages, 192
  prostitution, 238
  of renegades, 125
  See also marriage
al-Shaikh, Muhammad, 35
Sharif dynasty, 35
sharifs, 192, 220, 342n10
ships
  construction of, 151, 152
  frigates, 162–63
  galliots, 105, 155, 314n5, 326n1
  used in privateering, 151, 162–63
Shuval, Tal, 47
Sicilia Sacra (Pirri), 58, 299n181
Sicily, 55, 59, 73, 165
  Spanish inquisition in, 53–54, 55, 56, 74
Sidi 'Abd al-'Azuz, 179
Sidi 'Abd al-Rahman Tha'alibi, 179, 333n24
  tomb of, 204, 339n10
Sidi Ahmed Tidjani, 179, 333n25

Sidi 'Ali Ezzouaoui, 179
  tomb of, 204, 260, 338n7, 350n24
Sidi Batqa, 154, 179, 328n12, 333n22
  tomb of, 204, 260, 338n5
  veneration of, 21, 342n14
Sidi Bou Noua, 179
Sidi Bournous, 177
  tomb of, 177, 204, 338n4
Sidi Boutayeb, 176
  tomb of, 204, 339n8
Sidi Yacoub el Andalusi, 179, 333n26
  tomb of, 204, 338n2
Silla, Lucius, 94
Sinan Ra'is, 160
sipahi, 131–32, 135–36
slaves, 49, 201–2
  as booty, 157–58
  buying and selling of, 2, 164–65
  elite captives as, 20, 46, 49, 257, 349n14
  galley slaves, 153, 154, 157, 158, 233, 270
  manumission of, 229, 343n24
  number of in Algiers, 119, 317n1
  ransoming of, 8, 20, 32, 44, 46, 166
  sexual advantage taken of, 189
  in shipbuilding, 151, 152
  treatment of, 45, 46, 47–48, 157, 233, 240, 241
  women as, 189, 202
Sola, Emilio, 22, 57
Sosa, Antonio de
  and Agrigento cathedral, 60, 62, 69, 71
  antipathy toward Islam of, 3, 6, 214, 221, 223, 232, 288n6, 341n13
  arrival in Algiers, 2, 29
  authorship of *Topographia*, 51, 56–58, 306n13
  captivity of, 6–7, 19–20, 42, 44–45, 46
  capture of, 6, 41–42, 61
  in Castile, 66, 301n204
  and Cervantes, 38–41, 49, 65, 75–76, 77
  as common Portuguese name, 57, 299n176
  death of, 71, 75
  escape by, 63–65, 301n198
  as ethnographic observer, 2, 3, 7, 34, 46, 49–50
  granted Castilian citizenship, 60, 66
  as high-ranking Church member, 5, 6, 20, 45, 57–58, 59
  legal knowledge by, 51, 320n4
  literary citations by, 72–73
  nephew of, 65, 78
  papal absolution of, 68–69
  and Philip II, 45, 61–62, 67, 70–71
  political agenda of, 6, 33, 36, 37
  preparation of *Topographia* by, 72, 73, 303n226
  ransom efforts for, 61, 62–63, 64, 65
  reading habits, 50–51
  relations with Diego de Haedo, 72, 74–75
  relations with other Christian captives, 48–49, 51, 58
  religious dialogues by, 7, 46–47, 217–18, 221, 222
  scandal around, 67–68, 73, 74, 76–77
  as shrewd businessman, 62

as spy, 37, 67–68, 294n100, 315n2, 316n4
writes down observations as captive, 20
Sosa, Fra Diego de, 62, 63
Souk street, 117, 145, 164, 256
Sousse, 95, 155, 166, 184, 334n1
Spain
  armada against Algiers, 115, 222, 233, 344n4
  conflicts with Islam, 26, 27–28
  conquests in Maghreb, 28, 100, 118, 233, 313n2, 317n3
  emigration from, 21, 27, 28, 102, 122, 123, 318n21
  history of Moriscos in, 21–22
  Inquisition in, 52–53, 73–74
  military superiority of, 29
  relations with papacy of, 70
  webs of patronage in, 54–55
Spiritu Sancto, Giacomo di, 62, 71
Sponto, Domingo, 295n115
Staden, Hans, 49
storks and snails, 218
Strabo, 72, 93, 94, 308n2
Stromboli, 156
Suda (Eustace of Thessalonica), 312n3
Suetonius Tranquilus, Gaius, 72, 94, 95, 96, 309n14
Süleyman the Magnificent, 27, 319n3

Tabarka, 166, 270, 351n10
Tacitus, 72
Tagarinos, 123, 318n22
Takali, Muhammad, 260, 349nn20–21
Tangiers (Tanger), 28, 96, 225, 343n21
tattoos, 121, 318n17
taverns, 255–56

taxes
  ashor tithe, 220, 342n11
  collection of, 121, 141, 318n15
  exemption from, 119, 132
  income from, 268–71
Temendfust (Cape Matafuz), 97–98
Ten Books of Architecture (Vitrubius), 10, 289n26
Terranova, Duke of (Carlo d'Aragona e Tagliava), 59, 224, 300n185, 343n17
Tétouan, 156, 166, 185, 209, 333n1
Texeira, Pedro, 289n31
Theatrum orbis terrarum (Ortelius), 11, 12
Three Turk Plays from Modern England (Vitkus), 24
Thucydides, 72
Tiberius Caesar, 147
Tlemcen, 121, 141, 166, 181, 186
  kingdom of, 95, 100
Toledo, Fra Antonio de, 295n116
tombs, 204–5, 259–60, 347n5
  of Bani 'Abbas brother, 260
  of Hasan Agha, 260
  of Hasan Pasha, 259
  of Jews, 251
  of marabouts, 177, 204, 260, 338n2, 338nn4–7, 339nn8–11, 350n24
  of Salah Ra'is Pasha, 259
  of Takali, 260
  types of, 249
  visiting of, 195, 204–5, 250
Topographia, e Historia general de Argel (Sosa), 1, 2–3, 36
  attributed to Haedo, 25, 36, 51, 74–77, 78, 83, 84, 287n4
  Benedictine Order approval of, 87, 88

Topographia, e Historia general de Argel (Sosa) (*cont.*)
  censor's approval of, 74, 84–86
  contradictory perspectives in, 3–4
  edited by Fra Diego de Haedo, 51–52, 75, 305n3, 306n13
  ethnographic nature of, 2, 3, 7, 25, 34, 36, 46, 49–50
  extant Spanish version of, 25
  French translation of, 25, 291n65
  historical and literary nature of, 3, 36, 72
  king's approval of, 83, 84–85, 305n8
  as little-known work, 25
  political agenda of, 6, 33, 36, 37
  preparation by Sosa of, 72, 73, 303n226
  publication of, 25, 75, 304n242, 305n8
  Sosa authorship established, 51, 56–58, 306n13
  as source for studies by Morgan, 25
  as spy report, 37, 67–68, 294n100, 315n2, 316n4
  subtitle of, 6–7, 78
  topographical concerns of, 10, 17–19
  volumes
  —*Diálogo de la captividad en Argel*, 2, 7, 9, 43, 72, 73, 78
  —*Diálogo de los mártires de Argel*, 2, 7, 25–26, 39, 65, 78
  —*Diálogo de los morabutos*, 2, 7, 47
  —*Epítome de los reyes de Argel*, 2, 25, 34, 103, 287n3, 287n5
  —*Topography of Algiers*, 2, 36
Torres, Antonio González de, 9, 44, 49
Torres, Diego de, 35–36, 37
torture, 52, 65, 240
Tovar, Jorge de, 85, 305n7
Tower of Stratton, 95, 310n17
trade, 165–66, 237
  marketplace, 42, 117, 316n2
  Mediterranean as center of, 9
  merchants, 8, 12, 119, 164–67
  Renaissance expansion of, 29
  in slaves, 2, 164–65
travel books, 12
Trickster Travels (Davis), 23
Tripoli, 9, 25, 156, 158, 265
  Ottoman conquest, 27
  Spanish conquest, 28, 313n2
Tunis, 9, 28, 156, 158
  Spanish conquest of, 118, 233, 317n3
  trade with, 166, 181
Turkish, 149, 175, 176, 184, 195, 265
Turkish Letters (Busbecq), 33
Turks. *See* Ottoman Empire
Turks, Moors and Englishmen in the Age of Discovery (Matar), 23
Turning Turk: English Theater and the Multicultural Mediterranean (Vitkus), 24

'Uludj 'Ali (Euchalí, Ochalí), 66, 113, 213, 224, 316n2
  about, 340n10
  slaves of, 48, 296n141
urination, 217
usury, 43, 167

Valdés y Salas, Fernando de, 305n6
Valdivia, Fra Francisco de, 84
Valencia, 8, 9, 27, 28, 288n20
  trade with, 165, 166
Valencia, Fra Francisco de, 295n116

Valentinian III, 97, 311n24
Valetta (Malta), 2, 41
Valla, Lorenzo, 73
Valle, Fra Juan de, 87
Vandals, 97, 121, 311n26
van den Wyngaerde, Anton
 (Antonio de las Viñas),
 11, 289n30
Vázquez, Mateo, 64
Vega, Hernando de, 66, 67
veiling of women, 190, 199, 201,
 337n8
Veneziano, Antonio, 78
Venice, 9, 12, 27, 165
Vergara, Agustín de, 92, 307n21
Verre, Caius, 310n21
Verrus Flaccus, Marcus, 310n21
Viaje de Turquía, 33
vices, Algerian, 196, 232–42
 anger and cruelty, 240–41
 disobedience, 235
 envy, 241–42
 gluttony and drunkenness, 196,
  239–40, 346n15
 greed, 235–36, 237, 345n6
 hypocrisy, 224–26, 234
 lust, 238–39
 lying, 220, 235–36, 243
 pride and presumption, 232–34
 sloth, 207, 242–43, 263
Vienna, 27
Vincent, Bernard, 22
Virgil, 72
virtues, Algerian, 244–46
 cleanliness and proper dress, 245
 diligence in marrying off
  daughters, 246
 endurance, 245
 fraternalism, 245
 no blasphemizing, 149, 244

no gambling, 149, 244
 obedience, 245
 piety, 3, 4, 236, 246
 rarely fight, 149
 sense of reconciliation, 245
Vitkus, Daniel, 23, 24
Vitrubius Pollio, Marcus, 10,
 289n26
Voyage en Espagne (al-Ghassani), 38

washing, 199, 203, 254
 of dead, 245n2, 247
 before prayer, 210, 217
 after sexual activity, 191, 217
 by women, 191, 203
 See also baths
water, 118, 258–59
wealthy, 213, 233
 burial of, 248, 249
 home furnishings of, 207, 208
 Jews among, 182, 183
Whitehead, Neil, 46, 49
Wiegers, Gerard, 22
wine, 199–200, 219
 See also alcohol
witchcraft and sorcery, 179–80,
 195, 205–6
witness-giving, 230
women
 adultery by, 230
 and afterlife, 221
 alms-giving by, 236
 among Baldi Moors, 119
 at baths, 203–4, 254
 Black, 202, 206, 212, 254
 and chastity, 191, 226–27, 238
 cosmetics, 4–5, 197, 200
 dress, 5, 122, 198–200, 337nn6–8
 education, 203
 familiar spirit, 47, 204, 205

women (*cont.*)
  female circumcision, 196, 336n4
  and Friday prayer, 341n15
  guarding and accompanying of, 193, 201–2
  hair, 4, 127, 199, 200
  household activities, 5, 203, 207
  jewelry and ornaments, 5, 200–201
  Jewish, 196–97, 202, 207
  among Kabyle and Zwawa Moors, 121
  kept unseen, 118, 189, 201
  laziness of, 207
  not permitted in mosques, 196, 213, 216
  partying and dancing by, 5, 47, 205–6
  as renegades, 229
  as slaves, 189, 202
  veiling, 190, 199, 201, 337n8
  witchcraft and sorcery by, 205–6
  work by, 121, 203, 207
  wrestling, 212

Yusuf, Ka'id, 231
Yusuf Ra'is, 160
Yusuf Remolar, 161

Zúñiga, Juan de, 63
Zwawa, 120–22, 271, 318n13, 352n13

MARÍA ANTONIA GARCÉS
is professor of Hispanic Studies at Cornell University.

DIANA DE ARMAS WILSON
is professor emerita of English at the University of Denver.

www.ingramcontent.com/pod-product-compliance
Lightning Source LLC
Chambersburg PA
CBHW071436300426
44114CB00013B/1455